T0305163

Job Insecurity, Precarious Employment and
Burnout

NEW HORIZONS IN MANAGEMENT

Series Editor: Professor Sir Cary Cooper, *50th Anniversary Professor of Organizational Psychology and Health at Alliance Manchester Business School, University of Manchester, UK, and President of the Chartered Institute of Personnel and Development and British Academy of Management*

This important series makes a significant contribution to the development of management thought. This field has expanded dramatically in recent years and the series provides an invaluable forum for the publication of high-quality work in management science, human resource management, organizational behaviour, marketing, management information systems, operations management, business ethics, strategic management and international management.

The main emphasis of the series is on the development and application of new original ideas. International in its approach, it will include some of the best theoretical and empirical work from both well-established researchers and the new generation of scholars.

For a full list of Edward Elgar published titles, including the titles in this series, visit our website at www.e-elgar.com

Job Insecurity, Precarious Employment and Burnout

Facts and Fables in Work Psychology Research

Edited by

Nele De Cuyper

Professor in Personnel Psychology, Faculty of Psychology and Educational Sciences, KU Leuven, Belgium

Eva Selenko

Professor of Work Psychology, Loughborough Business School, Loughborough University, UK

Martin Euwema

Professor of Organizational Psychology, Faculty of Psychology and Educational Sciences, KU Leuven, Belgium

Wilmar Schaufeli

Professor Emeritus of Work and Organizational Psychology, Utrecht University, the Netherlands, and at KU Leuven, Belgium

NEW HORIZONS IN MANAGEMENT

Edward Elgar
PUBLISHING

Cheltenham, UK • Northampton, MA, USA

Published by
Edward Elgar Publishing Limited
The Lypiatts
15 Lansdown Road
Cheltenham
Glos GL50 2JA
UK

Edward Elgar Publishing, Inc.
William Pratt House
9 Dewey Court
Northampton
Massachusetts 01060
USA

A catalogue record for this book
is available from the British Library

Library of Congress Control Number: 2023939821

This book is available electronically in the **Elgar**online
Business subject collection
http://dx.doi.org/10.4337/9781035315888

ISBN 978 1 0353 1587 1 (cased)
ISBN 978 1 0353 1588 8 (eBook)

Printed and bound in Great Britain by
TJ Books Limited, Padstow, Cornwall

This liber amicorum is dedicated to Professor Hans De Witte

Contents

Figures

Tables

Contributors

Dirk Antonissen has an academic background in Psychology and Finance. Under his leadership (first as CEO, then as Managing Partner), ISW, the small spin-off venture of the Leuven University, grew into Pulso Group, a European company of reference for psychosocial well-being, with ventures in Paris, Lisbon, Athens, Frankfurt and Hamburg.

Elfi Baillien (PhD) is Professor of Psychosocial Risks and Digital Wellbeing at the Faculty of Economics and Business, KU Leuven, Belgium. Her research interests include antecedents, developmental processes and organizational interventions as related to negative employee behaviour (e.g., workplace (cyber)bullying), and employee well-being (e.g., work stress, technostress). She has published her work in a range of impact factor journals such as *Work & Stress*, *Journal of Occupational and Organizational Psychology*, *Group and Organization Management*, *Journal of Business Ethics*, *Computers in Human Behavior* and *New Media & Society*.

Jaak Billiet (*1942) (PhD in the Social Sciences) is Emeritus Professor at the Centre for Sociological Research (KU Leuven). He combines methodological research on the quality of cross-national over-time surveys with substantial research on religious change, ethnocentrism and social identity. He received at the 2015 conference of the European Survey Research Association the Award for Outstanding Services to Survey Research.

Paula Brough is Professor of Organizational Psychology and Director of the Centre for Work, Organization and Wellbeing at Griffith University in Brisbane, Australia. Paula's primary research areas are occupational stress and coping, employee mental health and well-being, work engagement, work–life balance, workplace conflict and the psychosocial work environment.

Andreea Corbeanu is affiliated with the Department of Cognitive Science, Faculty of Psychology and Educational Sciences, University of Bucharest. Her research interests are currently centred around individual differences and job attitudes in the context of employee performance. As a practitioner, Andreea has worked on numerous consulting projects. She is currently the administrative secretary of the European Association of Work and Organizational

Psychology, and an active member of several research-focused endeavours, such as the Assessment and Individual Differences Lab and Research Central.

Nele De Cuyper is Professor at the Research Group Work, Organization and Personnel Psychology, KU Leuven, Belgium. At the core of her research is employability in relation to individual's health and well-being, attitudes, behaviour and career and with a specific focus upon more precarious or vulnerable groups.

Audrey Eertmans holds a PhD in Psychology (KU Leuven, 2006). After a career as a researcher in the field of Health Psychology at KU Leuven, she joined the Pulso Group in 2006. Today, she is Director, responsible for operations, research and development, aiming at the implementation of well-being tools.

Martin Euwema is Professor of Organizational Psychology, and chair of the research unit Occupational and Organization Psychology and Professional Learning at KU Leuven, Belgium. He has a special interest in conflict and mediation, leadership and team dynamics, both in organizations and in business families.

Isabelle Ferré Hernandez (MSc) is a doctoral student at the Division of Psychology, Department of Clinical Neuroscience at the Karolinska Institute, Sweden. Her research interests include job stress, working hours, recovery from work and occupational health, well-being and safety.

Gabriel Fischmann (PhD) is a technical manager and visiting lecturer. He combines his management background with research in Organizational Psychology, most recently focusing on the link between job insecurity and employee performance. His interests include scale development and validation, as well as improving the measurement of organizational variables.

Lode Godderis is CEO at IDEWE (idewe.be), a Belgian External Service for Prevention and Protection at Work and is Professor of Occupational Medicine at the Centre for Environment and Health of the University of Leuven. He investigates the impact of work on health by unravelling the underlying mechanism and also the reverse, on how health can affect work (dis)ability.

David Guest is Emeritus Professor of Organizational Psychology and Human Resource Management at King's Business School, King's College, London. His work addresses HRM, performance and well-being; the psychological contract; the employment relationship; and the evolution of careers. He has extensive publications and journal roles.

Jari Hakanen is Research Professor at the Finnish Institute of Occupational Health, Helsinki. He is also Docent in Social Psychology at the University of Helsinki. His research interests revolve around employee well-being and organizational behaviour, such as work engagement, burnout, job boredom, job crafting and servant leadership.

Johnny Hellgren (PhD) is Associate Professor at the Division of Work and Organizational Psychology, Department of Psychology, Stockholm University, Sweden. His main research interests include job insecurity, organizational development and change, pay setting, motivation, and health and safety in organizations.

Dragoş Iliescu is Professor of Psychology at the University of Bucharest and an Extraordinary Professor at the University of Stellenbosch in South Africa. His research interests group around two domains: psychological and educational assessment, tests and testing (with an important cross-cultural component) and applied psychology. He is the current President of Division 2 (Assessment) of the International Association of Applied Psychology and a Past-President of the International Test Commission.

Kerstin Isaksson is affiliated with Mälardalen University as Emerita Professor in Psychology. Her research has covered areas such as unemployment, retirement, job insecurity and psychological contracts. She was the coordinator of the PSYCONES project (Psychological contracts across employment situations) involving researchers from seven countries supported by the EU Fifth framework programme.

Darja Maslić Seršić is Professor of Psychology and Head of Doctoral Studies at the Department of Psychology, Faculty of Humanities and Social Sciences, University of Zagreb, where she teaches courses in research methodology, organizational psychology and career behaviour. Her research topics include psychology of unemployment, work stress and job insecurity.

Bart Meuleman is Full Professor at the Centre for Sociological Research (CeSO), University of Leuven (Belgium). His main research interests are cross-cultural survey methodology and cross-national comparisons of value and attitude patterns.

Katharina Näswall (PhD) is Professor in the School of Psychology, Speech and Hearing at the University of Canterbury, New Zealand. Her research focuses on employee well-being and factors that lead to psychologically healthy workplaces, with a special focus on how organizations and managers can contribute to employee well-being.

Karina Nielsen is Professor of Work Psychology at Sheffield University Management School, UK. Her main research area concerns participatory, organizational interventions, aiming to improve employee well-being through making changes to the way work is organized, designed and managed. She has developed and tested models for the design, implementation and evaluation of organizational interventions in order to promote employee well-being.

Guy Notelaers (PhD) is Full Professor of Work and Organizational Psychology at the Faculty of Psychology in the University of Bergen, Norway. His lines of research focus on workplace bullying, and on identifying and analysing psychosocial risks at work. Guy has published his academic work in leading journals such as *Journal of Occupational Health Psychology*, *European Journal of Work and Organizational Psychology*, *Work & Stress* and *Journal of Organizational Behavior*.

Tahira M. Probst is Professor of Psychology at Washington State University (United States), where she directs the Coalition for Healthy and Equitable Workplaces lab. Her research focuses on the health, safety and performance-related outcomes of economic stressors (including job insecurity, financial strain and underemployment), as well as multilevel contextual variables influencing these relationships.

Lara C. Roll (PhD) is an EU-funded Marie Curie Fellow in the Research Group Work, Organizational and Personnel Psychology at KU Leuven. Further, she is an Extraordinary Professor in the Optentia Research Unit at North-West University (South Africa). Her research focuses on the impact of automation in the workplace.

Wilmar Schaufeli is Professor Emeritus of Work and Organizational Psychology at Utrecht University, the Netherlands, and distinguished research professor at KU Leuven, Belgium. His main research field is occupational health psychology, originally focusing on job stress, and later on positive occupational health, notably work engagement. He also works as an organizational consultant.

Eva Selenko is Professor of Work Psychology at Loughborough University, UK. Her research focusses on precarious working conditions and how they affect people's identity, well-being, work behaviour and acting in wider society. Eva studied Psychology in the Netherlands (MSc) and Austria (Dr), and is living in Sheffield with her husband.

Akihito Shimazu is Professor of Faculty of Policy Management, Keio University, Japan. His research concerns workplace psychosocial factors and employee well-being, such as work engagement, workaholism, work–life balance, recovery experiences, and wants to bridge between research, practice and policy management. He has served as Chair of the ICOH-WOPS International Commission on Occupational Health-Work Organization and Psychosocial Factors Scientific Committee since 2018.

Mindy Shoss is Professor of Psychology at the University of Central Florida, United States. Her research examines the intersection of the future of work and occupational health psychology. She is Associate Editor of the *Journal of Occupational Health Psychology* and a Fellow of the Society for Industrial/ Organizational Psychology.

Roxana Spinu is PhD student at the Faculty of Psychology and Educational Sciences, University of Bucharest. Her research interests focus on the design of employee assessment reports. In practice, Roxana has collaborated with consulting companies such as SHL and Skill Tests, and was a part of the Research Central project.

Coralia Sulea (PhD) is Associate Professor and Organizational Psychologist. Her teaching activity focuses on occupational health psychology and leadership. Coralia's research studies mainly analyse correlates of employee well-being, organizational and interpersonal misbehaviour, and job insecurity. She has co-authored several articles in journals such as the *Journal of Applied Psychology*, *Learning and Individual Differences*, books and chapters in this field.

Magnus Sverke (PhD) is Professor and Chair of the Division of Work and Organizational Psychology, Department of Psychology, Stockholm University, Sweden. His current research interests include job insecurity, employment relations, organizational change, individualized pay setting, workplace well-being, employee attitudes and behaviour, and union membership.

Anna S. Tanimoto (MSc) is doctoral student at the Division of Work and Organizational Psychology, Department of Psychology, Stockholm University, Sweden. Her research interests include job insecurity, employment relations, health and well-being, and work–life balance.

Jasmina Tomas (PhD) is postdoctoral researcher at the Faculty of Humanities and Social Sciences (University of Zagreb). Her research primarily focuses on topics of economic stressors and well-being at work. She teaches several courses in the realm of W/O psychology and quantitative research methods. Until now, her research has been published in several (inter)national peer-reviewed journals.

Inge Van den Brande holds a PhD in Applied Economics (KU Leuven, 2002). After a career as a researcher and Professor in the field of HRM at KU Leuven, she joined the Pulso Group in 2007. Currently, she is International Director, responsible for sales and the implementation of well-being projects and tools.

Anja Van den Broeck is Professor at the Department of Work and Organization Studies at KU Leuven, Belgium. Her research goal is to examine how, and under which circumstances individuals may thrive at work. In her research, she unravels the interplay between job design, well-being (burnout, engagement) and motivation.

Lore Van den Broeck holds a Master's degree in Research and Experimental Psychology (KU Leuven, 2013). After working as a Research Associate at KU Leuven and Thomas More, she joined the Pulso Group in 2018. As Senior Expert and Data Analyst, she develops tools and offers technical support in surveys, analysis and reporting.

Anahí Van Hootegem (PhD) is currently working at KU Leuven, Belgium. Her research in work psychology focuses on job insecurity and how this affects positive outcomes such as innovative work behaviour and work-related learning. Her more recent work concentrates on the wider societal and political consequences of job insecurity.

Sofie Vandenbroeck is head of the Knowledge, Information and Research Department of IDEWE. She has more than ten years' experience as a project leader in (inter)national research and development projects regarding psycho-social well-being, sustainable employability and return to work. She is also postdoctoral researcher at the Department of Environment and Health at KU Leuven.

Tinne Vander Elst is lecturer and researcher at the Department of Social Psychology at Tilburg University, senior researcher at IDEWE (a Belgian occupational health service), and guest lecturer at the Centre for Environment and Health of the University of Leuven. Her research interests include job insecurity, organizational change, hybrid ways of working and employee well-being.

Maarten Vansteenkiste is Full Professor in the Department of Developmental, Personality and Social Psychology at Ghent University, Belgium. He aims to refine and extend motivational theories such as the self-determination theory by mapping out the reasons that underlie people's behaviour and the goals and ambitions that people pursue throughout their lives.

Introduction: Facts and fables in work psychology: a critical interrogation and future proofing of job insecurity, precarious employment and burnout

Nele De Cuyper, Eva Selenko, Martin Euwema, & Wilmar Schaufeli

WHY THIS BOOK NOW?

There is much to learn when things go wrong at work. If so, work psychology has a bright future ahead. Job insecurity and precarious employment are at an all-time high (OECD, 2022) so it seems, and burnout has been advanced as the new worker pandemic in the popular press and media (Schaufeli et al., this volume). With this book, our aim is to fuel learning in work psychology in two ways: through a *critical interrogation* of what is known and through *future proofing* of the field of work psychology in general, and the areas of *job insecurity, precarious employment and burnout* in particular.

A *critical interrogation* implies looking back at the body of knowledge that is already there. Looking back is essential. With a discipline that is so intertwined with people's daily lives, we need to take stock of what we know and how we can use this knowledge; indeed, work psychology is about understanding *and* improving employee health and well-being. *Future proofing* implies looking ahead. The world of work is rapidly changing in response to – just to name a few – digitalization, globalization and automatization, and following a series of impactful events – such as the Covid pandemic(s) (Guest & Isaksson, this volume; Probst et al., this volume). An obvious but fundamental question then is whether the "typical" occupational health concepts, themes and theories are still relevant. This question is not new (e.g., Gallagher & Sverke, 2005, in their article "Contingent employment contracts: Are existing theories still relevant?") yet it certainly has become more pressing. Looking back and looking ahead both serve to disentangle facts from fables: unlike facts, fables typically narrate a story that is intuitively appealing and brought to life through anecdotic rather than strong empirical evidence. Those stories are inherently meaningful as they give an interpretation about what is happening in society and what is preoccupying people. Or else, "at times of crisis, myths have historical importance" (Winston Churchill). Yet, there are also risks involved, for example, when harmful or inferior interventions are based solely on stories rather than on evidence, or worse even, when proper interventions are contested in spite of the evidence. A blunt example are the recent conspiracy theories around the Covid-19 pandemic and associated fears and concerns around vaccination (De Witte et al., 2021). Looking back and forward helps to uncover the unfolding evidence, what is known and not (yet) known.

We focus upon three themes in particular: job insecurity, precarious employment and burnout. Those themes are deliberately chosen. At the highest aggregate level, work psychology connects work characteristics to worker well-being and strain (De Witte, 2005a). Job insecurity and precarious employment are work characteristics and burnout is a particularly strong indicator of strain; all with strong resonance in today's world of work. *Job insecurity* concerns the employee's perception that one's job is at risk (De Witte, 1999, 2005b; De Witte et al., 2016): essentially, subjective job insecurity implies that the employee does not know what will happen in the near future. *Precarious employment* is typically portrayed as an objective form of job insecurity (De Cuyper & De Witte, 2006; De Witte & Näswall, 2003; Sverke et al., this volume): it refers to employment that deviates from the standard, permanent open-ended labor contract. Job insecurity and precarious employment are obviously related and difficult to disentangle and they both have particular significance against the background of the growing gig economy. *Burnout* is "a work-related state of mental exhaustion which is characterized by extreme tiredness, cognitive and emotional impairment and mental distancing" (Schaufeli et al., 2020). It has attracted much attention, particularly among health care workers (Vandenbroeck et al., 2017) and even more so in the aftermath of the Covid-19 pandemic (Shoss et al., 2022). Burnout is also high on the policy agenda (e.g., Eurofound, 2018). The book is focused but not limited to those themes; it provides a broader view on other work psychology themes such as workplace bullying and the connection between work and other areas of life (e.g., perceived immigrant threat, voting behavior), and on interventions in the broader area of work psychology.

So, why this book now? Because it seems the right time to look back and to look forward and to disentangle facts from fables and fiction in the area of job insecurity and burnout. But also, it is the right time to honor the career of one of the scholarly leaders of the field of work psychology: Hans De Witte. Hans has spent his entire career studying work psychology topics, particularly focusing on job insecurity, precarious employment and burnout. However, his expertise also extended to related topics such as workplace bullying and political attitudes. He is a strong and persistent advocate of facts above fables – for instance, no one dares to suggest that job insecurity may have beneficial effects in his presence, or if they do, they do so only once. The book is being issued as a liber amicorum of colleagues and friends that brings together a group of experts who have worked with Hans throughout his academic career. Remarkably, members of this group originate from many countries and reflect Hans' strong international orientation. With this liber amicorum dedicated to Hans, his academic comrades aim to trigger debate and inspire a new generation.

HOW TO READ THIS BOOK?

The book is structured along five parts, including 13 chapters. Some chapters are more conceptual, others theoretical, while others provide or summarize empirical evidence (Table 0.1). In *Part I*, three chapters look back at what is known about job insecurity, each with a specific lens: conceptual, empirical and theoretical. At the conceptual level, *Fischmann, Corbeanu, Spinu, Sulea and Iliescu* describe how the notion of job insecurity may appear as conceptually clear and straightforward but, in fact, it is not (see also De Witte, 1999, 2005b): there are different dimensions and interpretations of job insecurity. This easily leads to the jingle-jangle fallacy in which concepts and measures are not aligned, which is typical for the broader field of work psychology. Their contribution offers a valuable overview of the different measurements of job insecurity and their definitions, which will be indicative to the senior as well as more uninitiated reader in the area of job insecurity. At the empirical level, *Tomas and Maslić Seršić* summarize the current evidence on the relationship between job insecurity and performance. This relationship is hotly debated (De Cuyper et al., 2020; Nikolova et al., 2022; Piccoli et al., 2021). Some scholars argue that job insecurity may motivate employees to work harder, for example in view of job preservation. However, the strength of opinions is not matched with evidence; overall, job insecurity is bad. But still, this fable is persistent, perhaps as a way to legitimize growing insecurity in organizations. This is an illustrative example of how fables may harm employees: HR policies that are built on the idea that job insecurity has motivating potential may exhaust employees, could hamper goal achievement, and ultimately may harm the organization. At the level of theory, *De Cuyper, Van Hootegem and Roll* argue that job insecurity research is perhaps not the strongest area when it comes to theory use and conceptual development: job insecurity research typically borrows theories from related fields, sometimes in an ad hoc fashion and without much depth. On a slightly more positive note, this also means much potential for theory development and elaboration.

In *Part II*, three chapters look ahead and discuss the future of job insecurity research against the overall rise in different types of non-standard employment. Perhaps the most fundamental question is whether there is a future for non-standard employment; a question that is addressed most sharply in the chapter "Is job insecurity still relevant?" by *Probst, Selenko and Shoss*. Their conclusion is that insecurity certainly remains relevant, but needs to be future-proofed against the background of non-standard work. Non-standard work may rapidly become the norm, and has been so for most people and industries across the globe. The implication is that workers may not worry about their job – they know that jobs are not forever anyway. This does not mean that they have embraced insecurity as a fact of life: they may not worry about their job but about work in general. *Guest and Isaksson* continue along this line, they agree with Probst et al. (this volume) that "job" insecurity may not be the key issue for many workers, but other types of insecurity certainly are. They outline how and in which ways the psychological contract needs rethinking in view of job insecurity (De Cuyper & De Witte, 2006): what meaning, if any, has the psychological contract for gig workers, self-employed or for those for whom employment is mediated by an algorithm? *Sverke, Ferré Hernandez, Tanimoto, Hellgren and Näswall* start from the apparent paradox that non-standard and otherwise insecure workers are most in need of union protection, yet they are less likely to be members of a union (De Witte et al., 2008). There is no easy way out of this paradox; unions deliberately strive to protect employee rights, including security, but they seem to define employees in a "standard" fashion that is perhaps too exclusive and may ultimately undermine unionization. The authors call for a broader and non-standard interpretation of who are core union members, or perhaps a specific union for non-standard employees.

Part III shifts the focus from job insecurity and precarious employment to burnout, with another three chapters. *Schaufeli, Hakanen and Shimazu* address six "burning issues in burnout research", related to the definition, diagnosis, assessment, prevalence, causes and interventions. In doing so, they dismantle two of the most persistent burnout fables. One fable that is heavily fed by popular media is that there is an ongoing burnout epidemic: there is not or at least not as far as empirical evidence is concerned. That is not necessarily good news, it simply means that burnout has always been there. What the fable shows is that burnout has perhaps become more visible in society and is less seen as a taboo or a signal of weakness. Another fable is that burnout is not very different from depression. This is a popular belief and may wrongfully lead to the conclusion that structural changes in job and work design and in HR policy may not prevent or buffer burnout. In this respect, the study by *Vander Elst, Vandenbroeck and Godderis* convincingly shows that the work context does matter: organizational communication and procedural justice attenuated the relationship between job insecurity and burnout (see also Vander Elst et al., 2010). *Antonissen, Eertmans, Van den Brande and L. Van den Broeck* address another popular belief, namely that the level of burnout symptoms differs between generations. As such there is virtually no proof for this. Yet they show that the level of burnout symptoms is higher among younger workers compared with older workers. Also risk factors differ: factors tied to the job seem to form a risk for younger workers and factors tied to the organization for older workers. This naturally leads to the suggestion to invest in the development of age-sensitive HR-strategies.

In *Part IV*, we turn to interventions. As has already been said, work psychology is not only about understanding employee health and well-being, but also about *improving* employee health and well-being, and yet, carefully designed interventions are scarce, as demonstrated for example by Schaufeli et al. (this volume) in the context of burnout. The two chapters in this section provide tools and hands-on advice on how to design successful interventions. *Nielsen and Brough* highlight the critical role of participation processes in all interventions that aim to make structural changes in the workplace, much in line with the evidence provided by Vander Elst et al. (in this volume). They discuss challenges in worker participation in organizational interventions. *A. Van den Broeck and Vansteenkiste* make a theory-based case to use motivational interviewing to bring the group of unemployed individuals back to the labor market (see also Van der Vaart et al., 2022). Motivational interviewing in itself may not be new, yet it is applied to an entirely different target group – the unemployed and particularly those with a fairly large distance to the labor market – for whom it could have particular relevance.

Part V finally shows that method matters in addressing fables and popular beliefs with illustrations coming from different areas: fables often continue to exist because we do not challenge and test them, or because there are many pitfalls when attempting to do so. The chapter by *Billiet and Meuleman* delves into the topic of perceived immigrant threat, a specific ethic threat perception often studied in the form of anti-immigrant sentiments or right-wing voting (see Selenko & De Witte, 2021; Van Hootegem et al., 2021, for studies in the area of work psychology). Work psychological articles often justify their enquiry of political effects of work arguing that right-wing sentiments would be on the rise. While this assumption may reflect a popular discourse, it is unclear whether such ethnic threat perceptions are *really* on the rise. *Billiet and Meuleman* take a longitudinal representative Belgian dataset, including six measurement occasions between 1995 and 2020. Immigrant threat is surprisingly difficult to investigate across time as there are challenging methodological issues around non-response, non-representativeness, biased answering, and measurement change which can easily distort the results. The authors illustrate how to deal with those issues. Their conclusion is a hopeful one: perceived immigrant threat decreased slightly in Belgium over the last 25 years. *Baillien and Notelaers* make a convincing case that lack of social support and work-place bullying are related, yet distinct phenomena as opposed to the belief that lack of social support and workplace bullying are tautological. While this may seem a conceptual and purely academic debate, it does have serious implications. Lack of social support is not the same as workplace bullying but should instead be seen as an antecedent. Hence, facilitating social support can be an important leverage in the prevention of workplace bullying.

So, how to read this book? We structured the book by topic: job insecurity and precarious unemployment in *Parts I* and *II*, burnout in *Part III*, interventions in *Part IV*, and concluding with a view on methods in research applied to perceived immigrant threat and workplace bullying. But an alternative grouping – and reading – other than by topic is also possible as displayed in Table 0.1. Some readers may prefer to focus upon conceptual or theoretical development, others on the empirical body of knowledge. Whatever reading approach is chosen, it fits with Hans' legacy: Hans has delved into different topics, but has also been an advocate of robust conceptualization and rigorous methodology, and has brought theory to the fore in job insecurity research.

FOR WHOM?

The target audience are researchers across all career stages. Early career scholars and PhD students may use this book to get a view on the breadth of the three topic clusters – job insecurity, precarious employment and burnout – and they may find inspiration for new topics and questions and tips for stronger theorizing, accurate methods and well-designed interventions. More established scholars may find the critical perspectives helpful to self-examine and to see potential assumptions based on fables in their own research lines.

But above all, this book is for you, Hans!

Table 0.1   *Overview of the book*

Chapters and authors	Facts, fables, future proofing	Conceptual	Empirical	Theoretical
PART I. Job insecurity: Looking back				
Job insecurity, job security, job future ambiguity? Oh my... a new step towards conceptual clarity Gabriel Fischmann, Andreea Corbeanu, Roxana Spinu, Coralia Sulea, & Dragos Iliescu	Fable Job insecurity is conceptually clear	✓		
Job insecurity and job performance: Why do job-insecure employees not perform better? Jasmina Tomas & Darja Maslić Seršić	Fable Job insecurity motivates workers to perform		✓	
Borrowing trouble? A debate on how social exchange theory is used and can be used in job insecurity research Nele De Cuyper, Anahí Van Hootegem, & Lara C. Roll	Fact Job insecurity research is atheoretical (or in any case not very strong in theory)			✓
PART II. Job insecurity and precarious employment: Looking ahead!				
Is job insecurity still relevant? Unpacking the meaning of "job" and "insecurity" in today's economy Tahira Probst, Eva Selenko, & Mindy Shoss	Future-proof Work insecurity instead of job insecurity	✓		
Is there a future for research on job insecurity and the psychological contract in a changing world of work? David Guest & Kerstin Isaksson		✓		✓

Chapters and authors	Facts, fables, future proofing	Conceptual	Empirical	Theoretical
Can unions represent the interests of insecure workers? Magnus Sverke, Isabelle Ferré Hernandez, Anna S. Tanimoto, Johnny Hellgren, & Katharina Näswall	Future-proof Towards specific or inclusive unions		✓	
PART III. Burnout: Contemporary issues				
Burning issues in burnout research Wilmar Schaufeli, Jari Hakanen, & Akihito Shimazu	Fable Burnout is some sort of depression Fable There is a burnout pandemic	✓	✓	
Contextual factors moderating the relationship between qualitative job insecurity and burnout: A plea for a multilevel approach Tinne Vander Elst, Sofie Vandenbroeck, & Lode Godderis	Fact Organizations also have responsibility in the prevention of burnout		✓	
Age differences in levels and risk factors of burnout in three European countries: a contribution from consultancy practice Dirk Antonissen, Audrey Eertmans, Inge Van den Brande, & Lore Van den Broeck	Fact There are age differences in burnout		✓	
PART IV. Interventions: Getting people on board				
The tricky issue of worker participation in organizational interventions within Occupational Health Psychology Karina Nielsen & Paula Brough	Fact Participation is crucial (but challenging in all organizational interventions)	✓		✓

Chapters and authors	Facts, fables, future proofing	Conceptual	Empirical	Theoretical
Motivating the unemployed: How motivational interviewing may help to tailor interventions to different unemployment profiles Anja Van den Broeck & Maarten Vansteenkiste	Future-proof Motivational interviewing to bring the unemployed back to the labor market		✓	
PART V. Methods matter!				
Methodological challenges for studying trends in perceived immigrant threat Jaak Billiet & Bart Meuleman	Fable Perceived immigrant threat increased in the past decades		✓	
What's in a name! The thin line between being bullied and lacking social support: Are both "just" the same? Elfi Baillien & Guy Notelaers	Fable Workplace bullying is little more than lack of social support	✓	✓	

REFERENCES

De Cuyper, N., & De Witte, H. (2006). The impact of job insecurity and contract type on attitudes, well-being and behavioral reports: A psychological contract perspective. *Journal of Occupational and Organizational Psychology*, 79(3), 395–409. https://doi.org/10.1348/096317905X53660

De Cuyper, N., Schreurs, B., De Witte, H., & Selenko, E. (2020). Impact of job insecurity on job performance: Introduction. *Career Development International*, 25(3), 221–228. https://doi.org/10.1108/CDI-06-2020-332

De Witte, H. (1999). Job insecurity and psychological well-being: Review of the literature and exploration of some unresolved issues. European Journal of Work and Organizational Psychology, 8(2), 155–177. https://doi.org/10.1080/135943299398302

De Witte, H. (2005a). Definitie: Wat is "arbeidspsychologie"? [Definition: What is "workpsychology"?] [Student handbook].

De Witte, H. (2005b). Job insecurity: Review of the international literature on definitions, prevalence, antecedents and consequences. *SA Journal of Industrial Psychology*, 31(4), 1–6. https://doi.org/10.4102/sajip.v31i4.200

De Witte, H., & Näswall, K. (2003). "Objective" vs "subjective" job insecurity: Consequences of temporary work for job satisfaction and organizational commitment in four European countries. *Economic and Industrial Democracy*, 24(2), 149–188. https://doi.org/10.1177/0143831X03024002002

De Witte, H., Pienaar, J., & De Cuyper, N. (2016). Review of 30 years of longitudinal studies on the association between job insecurity and health and well-being: Is there causal evidence? *Australian Psychologist*, 51(1), 18–31. https://doi.org/10.1111/ap .12176

De Witte, H., Roll, L., & Van Hootegem, A. (2021). On the consequences of the corona crisis for occupational insecurity, political powerlessness and beliefs in conspiracy. *Gedrag & Organisatie*, 34(3), 382–406. https://doi.org/10.5117/GO2021.3.005 .WITT

De Witte, H., Sverke, M., Van Ruysseveldt, J., Goslinga, S., Chirumbolo, A., Hellgren, J., & Näswall, K. (2008). Job insecurity, union support and intentions to resign membership: A psychological contract perspective. *European Journal of Industrial Relations*, 14(1), 85–103. https://doi.org/10.1177/0959680107086113

Eurofound (2018). *Burnout in the workplace: A review of data and policy responses in the EU*. Publications Office of the European Union, Luxembourg.

Gallagher, D. G., & Sverke, M. (2005). Contingent employment contracts: Are existing employment theories still relevant? *Economic and Industrial Democracy*, 26(2), 181–203. https://doi.org/10.1177/0143831X05051513

Nikolova, I., Stynen, D., Van Coillie, H., & De Witte, H. (2022). Job insecurity and employee performance: Examining different types of performance, rating sources and levels. *European Journal of Work and Organizational Psychology*, 31(5), 713–726. https://doi.org/10.1080/1359432X.2021.2023499

OECD (2022). *OECD Labor Force Statistics 2021*. OECD Publishing: Paris. https://doi .org/10.1787/177e93b9-en

Piccoli, B., Reisel, W. D., & De Witte, H. (2021). Understanding the relationship between job insecurity and performance: Hindrance or challenge effect? *Journal of Career Development*, 48(2), 1–16. https://doi.org/10.1177/0894845319833

Schaufeli, W. B., Desart, S., & De Witte, H. (2020). Burnout Assessment Tool (BAT) - Development, validity and reliability. *International Journal of Environmental Research and Public Health* 17(24), 9495. https://doi.org/10.3390/ijerph17249495

Selenko, E., & De Witte, H. (2021). How job insecurity affects political attitudes: Identity threat may play a role. *Applied Psychology: An International Review*, 70(3), 1267–1294. https://doi.org/10.1111/apps.12275

Shoss, M., Van Hootegem, A., Selenko, E., & De Witte, H. (2022). The job insecurity of others: On the role of perceived national job insecurity during the COVID-19 pandemic. *Economic and Industrial Democracy.* https://doi.org/10 .1177/0143831X221076176

Van der Vaart, L., Van den Broeck, A., Rothmann, S., & De Witte, H. (2022). Motivational profiles in unemployment: a self-determination perspective. *Frontiers in Public Health, 10*.

Van Hootegem, A., Van Hootegem, A., Selenko, E., & De Witte, H. (2021). Work is political: Distributive injustice as a mediating mechanism in the relationship between job insecurity and political cynicism. *Political Psychology*, 43(2), 375–396. https://doi.org/10.1111/pops.12766

Vandenbroeck, S., Van Gerven, E., De Witte, H., Vanhaecht, K., & Godderis, L. (2017). Burnout in Belgian physicians and nurses. *Occupational Medicine*, 67(7), 546–554. https://doi.org/10.1093/occmed/kqx126

Vander Elst, T., Baillien, E., De Cuyper, N., & De Witte, H. (2010). The role of organizational communication and participation in reducing job insecurity and its negative association with work-related well-being. *Economic and Industrial Democracy*, 31(2), 249–264. https://doi.org/10.1177/0143831X09358372

PART I

JOB INSECURITY: LOOKING BACK

1. Job insecurity, job security, job future ambiguity? Oh my… A new step towards conceptual clarity

Gabriel Fischmann, Andreea Corbeanu, Roxana Spinu, Coralia Sulea, & Dragoş Iliescu

Pinpointed as one of the most prominent emerging psychological risks (European Agency for Safety and Health at Work, 2007), job insecurity (JI) is a widespread phenomenon, affecting millions of people across Europe (De Witte, 2005). Regarded as a danger to the health of populations (Burgard et al., 2009), as well as a driver of health inequalities (Benach et al., 2014), JI is a tipping point phenomenon, potentially leading organizations into irreversible negative spirals by being simultaneously a promoter and an outcome of organizational decline (Greenhalgh & Rosenblatt, 2010). Empirically, it has been associated with bleak mental health, lack of well-being at work, negative job attitudes, and reduced performance, creativity and adaptability (e.g., Cheng & Chan, 2008; De Witte et al., 2016; Fischmann et al., 2018, Sverke et al., 2019). The present chapter provides a critical examination of the construct and measurement of JI.

JOB INSECURITY – ORIGINS AND EVOLUTION OF THE CONSTRUCT

The construct of JI has its roots in the job climate and stress theories of the 1970s (Hackman & Oldham, 1976; Rizzo et al., 1970). At the time, "job security", or "occupational certainty", as it was called, was approached as a single-faceted phenomenon, centred on one's broad disquiet around future employment. The term "job insecurity", as we currently know it, was crystallized in the scientific literature after the publication of the seminal article of Greenhalgh and Rosenblatt (1984), and has started to systematically appear in research ever since (Llosa et al., 2018; Sverke et al., 2006). Greenhalgh and Rosenblatt (1984) are the first to propose a multidimensional approach to the JI construct, as well as to distinguish between the worry of losing current employment and the perception of the threat of losing certain features of their job, or a decrease in the quality of the employment relationship. Hellgren et al. (1999) dubbed the first dimension quantitative JI and the second one qualitative JI, and the terms were used as such in subsequent JI research.

An important distinction regarding the JI construct emerged in the late 1990s and the beginning of the 2000s (Büssing, 1999; De Witte, 1999; De Witte & Näswall, 2003), between objective and subjective JI. The former refers to observable structural variables (such as the economic situation of the company) and relates JI to the literal, directly visible instability of the environment. As such, some jobs can be objectively insecure, such as those involving temporary work arrangements, or those directly affected by organizational layoffs (Van Vuuren et al., 1991). In contrast, subjective JI is centred around employees' perceptions and the way they view and interpret their status within the organization (De Witte, 1999; Probst, 2003).

A second dichotomy was introduced in 1992 by Borg and Elizur, between the cognitive (appraisals regarding the possibility of future job loss), and the affective dimension (worries and fears related to the potential loss). Some JI measures aggregate the two forms, containing both cognitive and affective items (e.g., De Witte, 2000; Fischmann et al., 2022; Reisel & Banai, 2002; Vander Elst et al., 2014). Separate measures, of either cognitive JI or affective JI, can also be found (e.g., Huang et al., 2010; Mauno & Kinnunen, 2002).

To summarize, the majority of the definitions of JI contain at least one, if not all of the following attributes: (1) the employee's subjective perceptions of possible threats to their job (Heaney et al., 1994); (2) the involuntary and unwanted nature of the changes to the employee's job (De Cuyper et al., 2012); and (3) worker apprehension around losing their job, or features of their job as it currently stands (Keim et al., 2014; Vander Elst et al., 2014). JI can be viewed as multidimensional when it distinguishes between quantitative (threats to the person's total job), and qualitative (threats to certain features of one's job). JI has also been viewed as cognitive, involving workers' beliefs around threats to their current job, or affective, referring to the emotional reaction's employees have in the face of these threats (Huang et al., 2010; Jiang & Lavaysse, 2018; Vander Elst et al., 2014). Taking all these aspects into consideration, we offer our critique of the topic in the following sections of this chapter.

CRITICAL CONSIDERATIONS AROUND JI MEASURES

Fostered by and alongside the plethora of JI definitions, many measures of this construct have been developed, each with potential benefits and issues, as discussed in the current section of this chapter. Table 1.1 lists scales that were referenced in the literature as being used to measure JI. We tried to include as many relevant measures as we could find. However, there are scales that we either did not find (e.g., they were either never published, or were published in sources that we could not reach), or we could not find enough information about (e.g., they listed some example items, but not enough for us to understand the complete scale), or were too similar to the included scales (there are probably many variations with one or more items modified, removed or added), and as such did not make the list.

For each scale we included notes which show an unexpected variability on how researchers have been measuring JI. We marked each scale as either *qualitative* or *quantitative* if it can reasonably be assumed to measure qualitative or quantitative JI, respectively. However, this does not mean that results obtained using a qualitative (or quantitative) JI scale are readily comparable with results obtained with other scales labelled similarly, or that the scales measure the construct at the same level of quality (i.e., respecting existing definitions). On the contrary, after the analysis of the listed scales and the difficult process of trying to find out what hundreds of JI articles actually measured, we are more convinced than ever that the JI domain needs a thorough clean-up, more conceptual clarity, and an agreement among researchers on what JI is, what types of JI exist, and how they should be measured. For quantitative JI, we found global measures (Vander Elst et al., 2014), multidimensional measures (e.g., Staufenbiel & König, 2011), and measures containing some JI-related items, together with non-JI items (e.g., viewing JI as part of the larger concept of career instability; Borg, 1992). In the case of qualitative JI, there are scales with only specific items – that is, which list clearly defined valued job features – (e.g., Brondino et al., 2020), only generic items – that is, which do not mention any particular job features – (e.g., Fischmann et al., 2022), as well as a mix of generic and specific items (e.g., Blotenberg & Richter, 2020). To complicate matters even more, some of the instruments measure only the cognitive component of JI (e.g., De Witte et al., 2010), some only the affective component (e.g., Huang et al., 2010), and others include both cognitive and affective items (e.g., Hellgren et al., 1999). Given this variability, it is imperative to clearly understand what a certain study measured before comparing its results with those of other studies and assuming that measurements were equivalent.

In addition to qualitative and quantitative JI scales, we marked some scales as *mixed*, as they either contain both qualitative and quantitative JI items, and they calculate an aggregated score (e.g., Lee et al., 2008), or they contain other types of items besides JI items (e.g., Burr et al., 2019, JI subscale of COPSOQ).

In some instances, we list the same source twice – this is because it contains two different scales. In other cases, we do not list a source twice, even though it describes more than one scale – this is because not all the scales met the criteria to be included in the list, as explained above.

In the next part of this chapter, we describe several issues that JI scales may exhibit, and we offer suggestions regarding how to best measure JI.

Table 1.1   *Source, number of items, type, and specific notes for JI measures*

No.	Source	No. of items	Type of JI	Notes
1.	Arnold & Staffelbach (2012)	7	Qualitative	Respondents are asked to rate how worried they are about changes in seven job features: fewer career opportunities, pay cuts, dislocation, higher workload, less influence over job changes, feeling pressured to work fewer hours, and further restructuring.
2.	Ashford, Lee, & Bobko (1989)	57	Mixed	Multidimensional, measuring both quantitative and qualitative JI. A multiplicative formula is used to calculate the score. Theory-driven, close to original Greenhalgh and Rosenblatt (1984) definition. Twenty-seven of the items repeat, first asking the respondent about the importance of each job feature, including the total job, then asking about the probability for each change to occur. The final three items refer to the responder's ability (or, inversely, powerlessness) to control the changes. There are two shorter versions of this scale, listed in this table.
3.	Blotenberg & Richter (2020)	11	Qualitative	The Qualitative Job Insecurity Measure (QJIM) asks respondents about their agreement with 11 statements regarding assessments or worries about changes to relevant job characteristics, some generic (e.g., the job changing for the worse), some specific (e.g., the ability to influence one's work planning).
4.	Borg (1992)	10	Mixed	The scale measures two dimensions, affective (three items) and cognitive (seven items) JI. The first three items refer to dealing with concerns and feelings of unease about the possibility of losing the job, and the other seven with the perceived job and career instability. It was developed and published in German, with two versions, a preliminary one, and a final one. The first nine items of the preliminary version were listed in English in Borg and Elizur (1992). The second and final version of the scale was evaluated by Staufenbiel and König (2011).

No.	Source	No. of items	Type of JI	Notes
5.	Brondino, Bazzoli, Vander Elst, De Witte, & Pasini (2020)	8	Qualitative	The Multidimensional Qualitative Job Insecurity Scale (MQJIS) reflects a multidimensional model of qualitative JI, with two items (one affective and one cognitive) for each of the following dimensions: social relationships, employment conditions, working conditions, and job content.
6.	Burr, Berthelsen, Moncada, Nübling, Dupret, Demiral, Oudyk, Kristensen, Llorens, Navarro, Lincke, Bocéréan, Sahan, Smith, & Pohrt (2019)	3/2	Mixed	The Copenhagen Psychosocial Questionnaire (COPSOQ) JI scale contains two items in its core version, the first measuring worries about becoming unemployed, and the other worries about employability. In the long version, another item is added, asking the respondent about their worries regarding new technology making them redundant.
7.	Burr, Berthelsen, Moncada, Nübling, Dupret, Demiral, Oudyk, Kristensen, Llorens, Navarro, Lincke, Bocéréan, Sahan, Smith, & Pohrt (2019)	5/3/1	Qualitative	The COPSOQ Insecurity over Working Conditions scale contains one generic and four specific qualitative JI items in its full version, three items in its medium version, and a single item in its core version.
8.	Caplan, Cobb, French, Van Harrison, & Pinneau (1975)	4	Mixed	A scale measuring job future ambiguity, which refers to the amount of certainty regarding future job security and career security. The respondents are asked about their certainty regarding: future career picture, future opportunities for promotion and advancement, future value of current job skills, future responsibilities. It has been referred to as a (sometimes qualitative) JI scale by several articles, although it was not defined as such by its authors (it predates Greenhalgh and Rosenblatt's conceptual clarification paper).
9.	Chirumbolo & Areni (2010)	5	Qualitative	The four items of Hellgren et al.'s qualitative scale (1999), plus one item: "I fear that work in my organization will become less challenging".

No.	Source	No. of items	Type of JI	Notes
10.	De Witte, De Cuyper, Handaja, Sverke, Näswall, & Hellgren (2010)	10	Qualitative	The cognitive qualitative JI scale includes ten job features, concerning four dimensions: job content (autonomy, skill utilization, specific tasks), working conditions (workload, quality of working conditions), employment conditions (wage, working hours, opportunities for promotion), and social relations at work (with colleagues, with supervisors).
11.	Fischmann, De Witte, Sulea, Vander Elst, De Cuyper, & Iliescu (2022)	4	Qualitative	Originally developed by De Witte and De Cuyper (not published) and validated in Fischmann et al. (2022), the Qualitative Job Insecurity Scale (QUAL-JIS) is a generic (i.e., global) measure, including both affective and cognitive items.
12.	Francis & Barling (2005)	5	Mixed	The scale, containing one affective and four cognitive items, includes three reverse-scored items. One of the items refers to retirement security.
13.	Hellgren, Sverke, & Isaksson (1999)	4	Qualitative	Respondents were asked about their agreement with statements regarding the near future improvement (reverse-scoring) of four job features: future career opportunities in the organization, future stimulating job content, future need for the employee's competence, and future pay development.
14.	Hellgren, Sverke, & Isaksson (1999)	3	Quantitative	A brief quantitative JI scale, combining affective and cognitive items. There are several variations of this scale in use, with one item removed and/or added, but since only Chirumbolo and Areni (2010) seemed to have been used more than one time, we did not list the others.
15.	Huang, Lee, Ashford, Chen, & Ren (2010)	7	Quantitative	The scale measures affective JI, by referring to the employees' negative feelings regarding their job security (e.g., "I am unhappy with the amount of job security that I have").
16.	Johnson, Messe, & Crano (1984)	7	Quantitative	The scale measures affective JI, by asking the respondent about their worries and fears of being fired.

No.	Source	No. of items	Type of JI	Notes
17.	Lee, Bobko, Ashford, Chen, & Ren (2008)	37/25	Mixed	Abridged (37-item) and bare-bone (25-item) versions of the Ashford, Lee, and Bobko (1989) scale, whose structure and characteristics it retains.
18.	Mohr (2000)	1	Quantitative	The question is focused on the assessment of the probability of losing one's job in the near future.
19.	O'Neill & Sevastos (2013)	6	Quantitative	The Job Insecurity Measure (JIM), a four-factor scale, includes the job loss insecurity subscale (six items), which measures cognitive quantitative JI.
20.	O'Neill & Sevastos (2013)	6	Mixed	JIM, a four-factor scale, includes the job changes insecurity subscale (six items). The subscale is made of generic (2) and specific (3) qualitative JI items, as well as one item which seems to measure regret relative to how the job used to be.
21.	Oldham, Kulik, Stepina, & Ambrose (1986)	10	Mixed	Meant as a job security scale, it measures mostly the employee's assessment regarding the safety of the total job. However, some items ask about related issues, such as the ability to get a replacement job, or the possibility of forced reduction in the number of worked hours. It mixes normal and reverse-scored items.
22.	Probst (2005)	3	Quantitative	The items describe the perceptions of the future of one's job: "can depend on being here," "stable," "unknown". They are a subset of the Job Security Index (Probst, 2003).
23.	Staufenbiel & König (2011)	7	Quantitative	Based on Borg's (1992) scale, this is an English translation including only affective (3) and cognitive (4) JI items, in two separate dimensions, thus eliminating four of the original items which measured other constructs.
24.	Sverke, Hellgren, Näswall, Chirumbolo, De Witte, & Goslinga (2004)	5	Quantitative	The scale mixes three affective and two cognitive items. One item is reverse-scored.

No.	Source	No. of items	Type of JI	Notes
25.	Van Hootegem, Grosemans, & De Witte (2023)	1	Quantitative	The item measures the uncertainty of whether one's job will continue to exist.
26.	Vander Elst, De Witte, & De Cuyper (2014)	4	Quantitative	Originally developed by De Witte (2000) and validated by Vander Elst et al. (2014), JIS is a global (i.e., one-dimensional) JI measure, including both affective and cognitive items. One item is reverse-scored.

Multidimensionality

At a broad level, two types of measures can be distinguished: multidimensional vs global (Mauno et al., 2001; Sverke et al., 2004). Multidimensional measures incorporate in one instrument multiple subscales and may or may not allow the computation of a total score based on a formula combining scores of each of the subscales. For JI, subscales could be qualitative and quantitative JI (see Ashford et al., 1989), or affective and cognitive JI (see Staufenbiel & König, 2011). In the case of a multidimensional scale, it may be necessary for authors to spend additional effort to justify the structural validity of a more complex definition of the construct, perhaps much more than has been done until now, in the case of JI.

Even when, theoretically, a construct is multidimensional, there is a need for a compelling explanation of how much each dimension is expected to influence the total score, if one is to be computed. Unfortunately, the main approach currently seems to be to compute scores based on the assumption that each item carries the same weight as all other items, and that dimensions also have equal weights. This a priori path may not be justified by empirical data and can be easily verified, for example, through confirmatory factor analyses, or Item Response Theory approaches. For example, in the case of quantitative vs qualitative JI, studies have shown that the two types of JI are associated with different outcomes at specific moments in time (e.g., Fischmann et al., 2015), and, as such, it is justified to measure them separately. It seems, thus, unfit to compute a mixed JI score that assumes the opposite, that is, that the two types of JI bring an a priori defined contribution to outcomes. Hence, regarding the issue of multidimensionality for JI, we recommend that quantitative and qualitative JI should be measured separately, as two separate global constructs.

We do not suggest the same though for affective and cognitive JI. Although the literature is far from reaching a consensus on the need to differentiate between affective and cognitive JI, a meta-analysis by Jiang and Lavaysse (2018) could not find a clear distinctiveness between cognitive and affective

JI, identifying only limited support for this hypothesis. We thus recommend that, without claiming to measure two separate constructs (i.e., affective and cognitive JI), scales should measure either quantitative or qualitative JI, mixing both affective (e.g., "I worry that I will lose my job" for quantitative JI; "I fear that I will lose job features that I really value" for qualitative JI) and cognitive (e.g., "I will probably lose my job" for quantitative JI; "Chances are that my job will change for the worst" for qualitative JI) items.

Scoring

Multiplicative scales (i.e., instruments where total scores are calculated by multiplying the scores of two or more components), such as the scale by Ashford et al. (1989) have raised concerns for several reasons (Evans, 1991; Shoss, 2017). First, correlations are not the proper statistical measure for the relationship between a multiplicative composite and another variable (Evans, 1991). Multiplicative composites can be used in linear regression analyses, and only together with their constituent components. A classic example of a proper usage of a multiplicative variable is in moderation analyses, where the independent variable and the moderator are included in the same linear regression as their interaction effect (i.e., the product of the two variables). Since correlations are used extensively in JI research, and possibly not all researchers are aware about the fact that JI was sometimes measured with a multiplicative scale, they may use the data improperly, by correlating these measurements of JI with other variables, as opposed to using a linear regression analysis and including the components that were used to compute the total JI score. Second, only the maximum and minimum scores on a multiplicative scale are easily interpretable. While it's clear that a maximum score of a multiplicative variable means that all the product components had high values, and a minimum score entails low values for the components, a score in the middle range cannot distinguish between the case when one of the components (e.g., the importance of the total job) has a high value and another one (e.g., the perceived threat to the total job) a lower value, and the other way around (i.e., high perceived threat and low importance). This is because the product (the total score) will be the same, when multiplying the scores of the two components, in both cases. And third, not all total scores are possible, meaning that the multiplicative scale is ordinal, rather than interval or ratio (Shoss, 2017), thus further reducing the usable statistical techniques.

Most qualitative JI scales are both non-generic and non-multiplicative (e.g., Blotenberg & Richter, 2020; Brondino et al., 2020; Hellgren et al., 1999). They list several specific job features and do not measure their relative importance to the respondent. This raises a specificity issue (discussed in detail in its own section, below), and the following scoring issue. Since the scale is not multiplicative (it measures just the perceived threat of losing the job feature, not the feature's importance to the respondent), all listed job features are presumed to be equally important (the total score is usually calculated as the mean of item scores). Obviously, not all job features are similarly important to all respondents, in all possible samples. As such, instead of computing total scores as the mean of item scores, researchers could use a different technique, such as structural equation modelling, where qualitative JI may be represented as a latent variable, with the measured item scores as its indicators, and their factor loadings estimated freely. This way the result would be an assessment of qualitative JI which takes into account each job feature's unique contribution to the total score.

Regarding the scoring issues, we thus recommend avoiding the usage of multiplicative scales. For other scale types, we encourage the computing of the total score based on the items' actual weights, in a latent construct of JI, rather than as the mean of item scores.

Construct Contamination

One fundamental criticism that has been addressed about JI scales is that the measured construct could potentially be contaminated by correlates of JI, such as affective reactions to the possible consequences of losing one's job, power-lessness to resist the change, employability, and so on. Such pooling together of items belonging to different constructs makes it impossible to understand the real cause–effect chain (Huang et al., 2012; Shoss, 2017). To avoid construct contamination, JI measures should follow as close as possible the agreed-upon definitions of JI. At the same time, definitions of JI should reflect the construct properly and plainly, without unnecessary complexity which could lead to con-tamination. Originally, during their conceptual clarification paper, Greenhalgh and Rosenblatt (1984, p. 438) defined JI as a "sense of powerlessness to maintain desired continuity in a threatened job situation". This may have already contaminated the construct by including in the definition, in addition to the question of whether the job was perceived as changing negatively, the requirement that a sense of powerlessness to resist the change should also be present. Because of this, we recommend more recent definitions, such as those provided by Hellgren et al. (1999), which have removed the control component and distinguish between losing the job and losing valued job features. Later in this chapter, we offer updated definitions for qualitative and quantitative JI, and arguments for their continued usage henceforth.

Validity

It is very rare to encounter a "validated" JI scale (i.e., one for which consistent and convincing evidence for validity, preferably stemming from several
sources of validity, has been offered). In their overwhelming majority, JI
scales derive from the conceptual clarification of Greenhalgh and Rosenblatt
(1984), and, except for face validity, lack even basic psychometric evidence.
For a JI scale to be used with confidence, we would expect that evidence exists
regarding the following aspects:

- *Distinguishing between quantitative and qualitative JI.* Given the current
  state of the art, we expect that a JI scale measures either one, or the other,
  and that validity evidence exists that it measures the stated dimension of
  JI, and not the other.
- *Invariance.* Is the scale usable on the available sample? Was it used successfully on comparable samples, in previous research? Most importantly,
  was the scale used in the language that the current study uses?
- *Convergent and discriminant validity evidence.* Was JI measured with the
  scale shown to be related to other constructs, theoretically related to JI, and
  unrelated to constructs that should be theoretically dissimilar to JI?

In addition to the validity questions listed above, there could be additional data
available, such as concurrent, predictive or incremental validity evidence, in
relationship with known JI outcomes. The more validity data exists regarding
a scale, the safer it is to use it in future research. For newly developed scales,
validation studies should be an essential first step before accepting them as
proper instruments to measure JI.

Practical Issues

The size or extent of a scale, that is, the number of items it comprises, may
represent an important practical aspect that needs to be considered when using
the instrument. Depending on the nature of the study, often JI is just one of
many variables that are included in the study. A long JI scale would in such
cases represent an impediment, by taking too much of the total number of
items that can be included in the study. What often happens in such situations
is that researchers try to solve the problem by selecting and using a small
number of items from an existing larger scale, with the hope that they will end
up measuring JI with less effort for the participant. Needless to say, whatever
ends up measured this way may, or may not be closely related to what the
scale designers intended (and provided validity evidence for). To avoid such
approaches, authors of long JI scales (e.g., Ashford et al., 1989) later offered

shorter versions (e.g., Lee et al., 2008), while explaining the effects the shortening may have on the measured construct. Unfortunately, this approach is rare in JI research and is not the norm. We would encourage authors of JI scales to embark on such efforts, with clear explanations about the positive (e.g., utility) and negative (e.g., psychometric characteristics) consequences of shortening measures of JI.

Specificity

When measuring qualitative JI, we must deal with an additional aspect, compared to quantitative JI: genericity vs specificity. Originally, starting with the work of Greenhalgh and Rosenblatt (1984), researchers used to list the most important features a job could have, asking respondents to assess how much each of the job features may be threatened. This approach was the norm and was used in almost all qualitative JI scales (e.g., Brondino et al., 2020; Hellgren et al., 1999). Over time, and in different contexts, researchers varied the job features that they considered important or valued by the participants. However, almost no existing instrument leaves it to the latitude of the participant to assess which exact job features they value most, without starting with a predefined list. In our opinion, this is an important problem, as there are many novel contemporary job aspects that were not present (or important) in past scales. Examples include the ability to work remotely, a flexible working schedule, paid time off for taking care of children, continuous training so as to keep up with an ever-changing job, and many more. None of these features are listed in existing qualitative JI scales, even though they are certainly important to many employees. This problem is discussed in detail by Fischmann et al. (2022).

To conclude, there are still many challenges in the correct measurement of JI. We offer a summary of recommendations, together with definitions for quantitative and qualitative JI, at the end of this chapter.

JI MEASUREMENT RECOMMENDATIONS

We discussed several issues (multidimensionality, scoring, construct contamination, validity, size, and specificity) that might affect the existing measurement of JI, and we highlighted the potential problems in each case. We mentioned that we need an agreement on the definition of JI, before we can check if current or future scales abide by those definitions. We explained what was problematic in previous definitions of JI, and what better definitions might look like. As such, we propose the following definitions to be used for quantitative and qualitative JI:

Quantitative job insecurity is the employee's uncertainty regarding keeping one's job in the near future, and the worries associated with it.

Qualitative job insecurity is the employee's uncertainty regarding keeping valued job features in the near future, and the worries associated with it.

These definitions include the core of the JI construct as it was understood in most recent JI research, while separating the two constructs of qualitative and quantitative JI and including both the cognitive and affective components. When we refer to uncertainty, we mean a cognitive evaluation. Since research is as yet unable to justify the standalone usage of cognitive and affective JI, we propose not to separate the two, but to keep both in the same definition, and to measure them accordingly, with instruments incorporating both types of items. An important part of the definitions is the time-binding to the near future, since otherwise, the question may become meaningless (eventually, one will probably lose their job or some valued job features, if enough time passes).

Measures conforming to these definitions would additionally be short and global (as opposed to long and multidimensional), and in the case of qualitative JI, they would be generic (as opposed to listing specific job features). Examples of existing validated JI scales that are close to what we proposed above are JIS (Vander Elst et al., 2014) for quantitative JI, and QUAL-JIS (Fischmann et al., 2022) for qualitative JI.

There may be cases, however, where some of the qualities we listed as desirable for a JI scale would not apply completely. For example, we may imagine a situation where, while designing an organizational intervention aimed at reducing qualitative JI, a custom set of instruments must be prepared to determine the exact job features that are most valued by employees, and which the employees perceive as being most likely to be in danger of being lost. This intervention's objective could not be reached using a generic scale, and a more specific assessment would need to be done. Nevertheless, in most situations where JI needs to be measured, we expect that scales conforming to our specifications above should be the correct default choice.

CONCLUSIONS

In this chapter, we discussed issues related to the past and current definitions and measurement of JI, and we argued for ways to improve both. We started by briefly reviewing JI's origin and its evolution throughout the last four decades. If, before 1984, organizational researchers were analysing JI either as part of related variables (e.g., a facet of job satisfaction, Hackman & Oldham, 1976) or under different names (e.g., job future ambiguity, Caplan et al., 1975), starting with Greenhalgh and Rosenblatt (1984), the naming and (mostly) the meaning of JI was established and became clear for all future research. We discussed how, over time, definitions of JI reflected objective vs subjective JI, qualitative vs quantitative JI, and affective vs cognitive JI, and how measures of JI did not settle on a "proper" way to assess the construct(s). We provided a list of quantitative, qualitative and mixed JI scales, briefly describing each of them, and we offered a critical assessment of common issues affecting the measurement of JI. Examples of areas where special attention should be paid when measuring JI include: (a) scoring (computing multiplicative scores, computing the total JI score as an average of item scores, or computing the total score of a multidimensional JI scale, as the mean of individual facets); (b) possible construct contamination; (c) the amount and quality of the effort allocated for the validation of the instrument; (d) whether the scale is specific or generic (this applies only for qualitative JI); and (e) other practical issues, such as the size of the JI scale (number of items).

Finally, we offered new definitions of JI, arguing for their future use, given that they offer a clear, simple, complete and symmetric (similarly approaching quantitative and qualitative JI) view of the construct. We also suggested two existing scales, one for each type of JI, as meeting these new definitions, in addition to being brief and generic and, as such, usable in a wide variety of contexts.

We hope that the information provided in this chapter makes it clear that more attention needs to be paid to the field of JI, and that future research will continue to improve our understanding of this constantly evolving, intriguing topic.

REFERENCES

Arnold, A., & Staffelbach, B. (2012). Perceived post-restructuring job insecurity: The impact of employees' trust in one's employer and perceived employability. *Zeitschrift für Personalforschung, 26*(4), 307–330.

Ashford, S., Lee, C., & Bobko, P. (1989). Content, causes, and consequences of job insecurity: A theory-based measure and substantive test. *Academy of Management Journal, 32*(4), 803–829. https://doi.org/10.2307/256569

Benach, J., Vives, A., Amable, M., Vanroelen, C., Tarafa, G., & Muntaner, C. (2014). Precarious employment: Understanding an emerging social determinant of health. *Annual Review of Public Health, 35*, 229–253. DOI: 10.1146/annure v-publhealth-032013-182500

Blotenberg, I., & Richter, A. (2020). Validation of the QJIM: A measure of qualitative job insecurity. *Work & Stress, 34*(4), 406–417. https://doi.org/10.1080/02678373 .2020.1719553

Borg, I. (1992). Überlegungen und Untersuchungen zur Messung der subjektiven Unsicherheit der Arbeitsstelle [Reflections and investigations in the measurement of subjective job uncertainty]. *Zeitschrift für Arbeits- und Organisationspsychologie, 36*(3), 107–116.

Borg, I., & Elizur, D. (1992). Job insecurity: Correlates, moderators and measurement. *International Journal of Manpower, 13*(2), 13–26. https://doi.org/10.1108/01437729210010210

Brondino, M., Bazzoli, A., Vander Elst, T., De Witte, H., & Pasini, M. (2020). Validation and measurement invariance of the Multidimensional Qualitative Job Insecurity Scale. *Quality & Quantity: International Journal of Methodology, 54*(3), 925–942. https://doi.org/10.1007/s11135-020-00966-y

Burgard, S. A., Brand, J. E., & House, J. S. (2009). Perceived job insecurity and worker health in the United States. *Social Science & Medicine, 69*(5), 777–785. DOI: 10.1016/j.socscimed.2009.06.029

Burr, H., Berthelsen, H., Moncada, S., Nübling, M., Dupret, E., Demiral, Y., Oudyk, J., Kristensen, T. S., Llorens, C., Navarro, A., Lincke, H.-J., Bocéréan, C., Sahan, C., Smith, P., & Pohrt, A. (2019). The third version of the Copenhagen Psychosocial Questionnaire. *Safety and Health at Work, 10*(4), 482–503. DOI: 10.1016/j.shaw.2019.10.002

Büssing, A. (1999). Can control at work and social support moderate psychological consequences of job insecurity? Results from a quasi-experimental study in the steel industry. *European Journal of Work and Organizational Psychology, 8*(2), 219–242. https://doi.org/10.1080/135943299398339

Caplan, R. D., Cobb, S., French, J. R. P., Jr., Van Harrison, R. V., & Pinneau, S. R., Jr. (1975). *Job demands and worker health: Main effects and occupational differences.* Washington, DC: US Department of Health, Education, and Welfare.

Cheng, G. H.-L., & Chan, D. K.-S. (2008). Who suffers more from job insecurity? A meta-analytic review. *Applied Psychology: An International Review, 57*(2), 272–303. https://doi.org/10.1111/j.1464-0597.2007.00312.x

Chirumbolo, A., & Areni, A. (2010). Job insecurity influence on job performance and mental health: Testing the moderating effect of the need for closure. *Economic and Industrial Democracy, 31*(2), 195–214. DOI: 10.1177/0143831X09358368

De Cuyper, N., Mäkikangas, A., Kinnunen, U., Mauno, S., & De Witte, H. (2012). Cross-lagged associations between perceived external employability, job insecurity, and exhaustion: Testing gain and loss spirals according to the Conservation of Resources Theory. *Journal of Organizational Behavior, 33*(6), 770–788. https://doi.org/10.1002/job.1800

De Witte, H. (1999). Job insecurity and psychological well-being: Review of the literature and exploration of some unresolved issues. *European Journal of Work and Organizational Psychology, 8*(2), 155–177. https://doi.org/10.1080/135943299398302

De Witte, H. (2000). Arbeidsethos en jobonzekerheid: meting en gevolgen voor welzijn, tevredenheid en inzet op het werk. In *Van groep naar gemeenschap: liber amicorum Prof. Dr. Leo Lagrou* (pp. 325–350). Rotterdam: Garant.

De Witte, H. (2005). Job insecurity: Review of the international literature on definitions, prevalence, antecedents, and consequences. *SA Journal of Industrial Psychology, 31*(4), 1–6.

De Witte, H., & Näswall, K. (2003). "Objective" vs "subjective" job insecurity: Consequences of temporary work for job satisfaction and organizational commitment in four European countries. *Economic and Industrial Democracy, 24*(2), 149–188.

De Witte, H., De Cuyper, N., Handaja, Y., Sverke, M., Näswall, K., & Hellgren, J. (2010). Associations between quantitative and qualitative job insecurity and well-being: A test in Belgian banks. *International Studies of Management & Organization, 40*(1), 40–56. https://doi.org/10.2753/IMO0020-8825400103

De Witte, H., Pienaar, J., & De Cuyper, N. (2016). Review of 30 years of longitudinal studies on the association between job insecurity and health and well-being: Is there causal evidence? *Australian Psychologist, 51*(1), 18–31. https://doi.org/10.1111/ap.12176

European Agency for Safety and Health at Work. (2007). *European risk observatory report: Expert forecast on emerging psychosocial risks related to occupational safety and health (OSH).* Retrieved on 11.01.2023 from https://osha.europa.eu/sites/default/files/report535_en.pdf

Evans, M. G. (1991). The problem of analyzing multiplicative composites: Interactions revisited. *American Psychologist, 46*(1), 6–15. https://doi.org/10.1037/0003-066X.46.1.6

Fischmann, G., De Witte, H., Sulea, C., & Iliescu, D. (2018). Qualitative job insecurity and in-role performance: A bidirectional longitudinal relationship? *European Journal of Work and Organizational Psychology, 27*(5), 603–615. https://doi.org/10.1080/1359432X.2018.1504769

Fischmann, G., De Witte, H., Sulea, C., Vander Elst, T., De Cuyper, N., & Iliescu, D. (2022). Validation of a short and generic Qualitative Job Insecurity Scale (QUAL-JIS). *European Journal of Psychological Assessment, 38*(5), 397–411. https://doi.org/10.1027/1015-5759/a000674

Fischmann, G., Sulea, C., Kovacs, P., Iliescu, D., & De Witte, H. (2015). Qualitative and quantitative job insecurity: Relations with nine types of performance. *Psihologia Resurselor Umane,* 13(2), 152–164.

Francis, L., & Barling, J. (2005). Organizational justice and psychological strain. *Canadian Journal of Behavioral Science, 37*(4), 250–261. https://doi.org/10.1037/h0087260

Greenhalgh, L., & Rosenblatt, Z. (1984). Job insecurity: Toward conceptual clarity. *Academy of Management Review, 9*(3), 438–448. https://doi.org/10.2307/258284

Greenhalgh, L., & Rosenblatt, Z. (2010). Evolution of research on job insecurity. *International Studies of Management and Organization, 40*(1), 6–19. https://www.jstor.org/stable/25704019

Hackman, J. R., & Oldham, G. R. (1976). Motivation through the design of work: Test of a theory. *Organizational Behavior and Human Performance, 16*(2), 250–279. https://doi.org/10.1016/0030-5073(76)90016-7

Heaney, C. A., Israel, B. A., & House, J. S. (1994). Chronic job insecurity among automobile workers: Effects on job satisfaction and health. *Social Science & Medicine, 38*(10), 1431–1437. https://doi.org/10.1016/0277-9536(94)90281-X

Hellgren, J., Sverke, M., & Isaksson, K. (1999). A two-dimensional approach to job insecurity: Consequences for employee attitudes and well-being. *European Journal of Work and Organizational Psychology, 8*(2), 179–195. https://doi.org/10.1080/135943299398311

Huang, G., Lee, C., Ashford, S., Chen, Z., & Ren, X. (2010). Affective job insecurity: A mediator of cognitive job insecurity and employee outcomes relationships. *International Studies of Management and Organization, 40*(1), 20–39. https://doi.org/10.2753/IMO0020-8825400102

Huang, G., Niu, X., Lee, C., & Ashford, S. J. (2012). Differentiating cognitive and affective job insecurity: Antecedents and outcomes. *Journal of Organizational Behavior, 33*(6), 752–769. https://doi.org/10.1002/job.1815

Jiang, L., & Lavaysse, L. M. (2018). Cognitive and affective job insecurity: A meta-analysis and a primary study. *Journal of Management, 44*(6), 2307–2342. https://doi.org/10.1177/0149206318773853

Johnson, C. D., Messe, L. A., & Crano, W. D. (1984). Predicting job performance of low-income workers: The work opinion questionnaire. *Personnel Psychology, 37*(2), 291–299. https://doi.org/10.1111/j.1744-6570.1984.tb01451.x

Keim, A. C., Landis, R. S., Pierce, C. A., & Earnest, D. R. (2014). Why do employees worry about their jobs? A meta-analytic review of predictors of job insecurity. *Journal of Occupational Health Psychology, 19*(3), 269–290. DOI: 10.1037/a0036743

Lee, C., Bobko, P., Ashford, S., Chen, Z. X., & Ren, X. (2008). Cross-cultural development of an abridged job insecurity measure. *Journal of Organizational Behavior, 29*(3), 373–390. https://doi.org/10.1002/job.513

Llosa, J. A., Menéndez-Espina, S., Agulló-Tomás, E., & Rodríguez-Suárez, J. (2018). Job insecurity and mental health: A meta-analytical review of the consequences of precarious work in clinical disorders. *Anales de Psicología, 34*(2), 211–223.

Mauno, S., & Kinnunen, U. (2002). Perceived job insecurity among dual-earner couples: Do its antecedents vary according to gender, economic sector and the measure used? *Journal of Occupational and Organizational Psychology, 75*(3), 295–314. https://doi.org/10.1348/096317902320369721

Mauno, S., Leskinen, E., & Kinnunen, U. (2001). Multi-wave, multi-variable models of job insecurity: Applying different scales in studying the stability of job insecurity. *Journal of Organizational Behavior, 22*(8), 919–937. https://www.jstor.org/stable/3649579

Mohr, G. B. (2000). The changing significance of different stressors after the announcement of bankruptcy: A longitudinal investigation with special emphasis on job insecurity. *Journal of Organizational Behavior, 21*(3), 337–359. https://doi.org/10.1002/(SICI)1099-1379(200005)21:3<337::AID-JOB18>3.0.CO;2-G

O'Neill, P., & Sevastos, P. (2013). The development and validation of a new multidimensional Job Insecurity Measure (JIM): An inductive methodology. *Journal of Occupational Health Psychology, 18*(3), 338–349. https://doi.org/10.1037/a0033114

Oldham, G. R., Kulik, C. T., Stepina, L. P., & Ambrose, M. L. (1986). Relations between situational factors and the comparative referents used by employees. *Academy of Management Journal, 29*(3), 599–608. https://doi.org/10.2307/256226

Probst, T. (2003). Development and validation of the Job Security Index and the Job Security Satisfaction scale: A classical test theory and IRT approach. *Journal of Occupational and Organizational Psychology, 76*(4), 451–467. https://doi.org/10.1348/096317903322591587

Probst, T. M. (2005). Countering the negative effects of job insecurity through participative decision making: Lessons from the demand-control model. *Journal of Occupational Health Psycholollgy, 10*(4), 320–329. https://doi.org/10.1037/1076-

Reisel, W. D., & Banai, M. (2002). Job insecurity revisited: Reformulating with affect. *Journal of Behavioral and Applied Management, 4*(1), 87–91.

Rizzo, J. R., House, R. J., & Lirtzman, S. I. (1970). Role conflict and ambiguity in complex organizations. *Administrative Science Quarterly, 15*(2), 150–163. https://doi.org/10.2307/2391486

Shoss, M. K. (2017). Job insecurity: An integrative review and agenda for future research. *Journal of Management, 43*(6), 1911–1939. https://doi.org/10.1177/014920631769157

Staufenbiel, T., & König, C. J. (2011). An evaluation of Borg's cognitive and affective job insecurity scales. *International Journal of Business and Social Science, 2*(20), 13–26.

Sverke, M., Hellgren, J., & Näswall, K. (2006). *Job insecurity: A literature review* (Vol. 1, pp. 1–30). Stockholm: Arbetslivsinstitutet.

Sverke, M., Hellgren, J., Näswall, K., Chirumbolo, A., De Witte, H., & Goslinga, S. (2004). *Job insecurity and union membership: European unions in the wake of flexible production.* Brussels: P. I. E. Peter Lang.

Sverke, M., Låstad, L., Hellgren, J., Richter, A., & Näswall, K. (2019). A meta-analysis of job insecurity and employee performance: Testing temporal aspects, rating source, welfare regime, and union density as moderators. *International Journal of Environmental Research and Public Health, 16*(14), 1–29. DOI: 10.3390/ijerph16142536

Van Hootegem, A., Grosemans, I., & De Witte, H. (2023). In need of opportunities: A within-person investigation of opposing pathways in the relationship between job insecurity and participation in development activities. *Journal of Vocational Behavior, 140,* 103825. https://doi.org/10.1016/j.jvb.2022.103825

Van Vuuren, T., Klandermans, B., Jacobson, D., & Hartley, J. (1991). Employees' reactions to job insecurity. In J. Hartley, D. Jacobson, B. Klandermans, & T. Van Vuuren (Eds.), *Job insecurity: Coping with jobs at risk* (pp. 79–103). London: Sage.

Vander Elst, T., De Witte, H., & De Cuyper, N. (2014). The Job Insecurity Scale: A psychometric evaluation across five European countries. *European Journal of Work and Organizational Psychology, 23*(3), 364–380. https://doi.org/10.1080/1359432X.2012.745989

2. Job insecurity and job performance: Why do job-insecure employees not perform better?

Jasmina Tomas & Darja Maslić Seršić

One of the most strongly debated topics in job insecurity literature concerns the relationship between job insecurity and employee performance. Job insecurity represents "the perceived threat of job loss and the worries related to that threat" (De Witte, 2005, p. 1). Departing from the premise that good performers are less likely to be laid-off due to their value to the organization, one stream of research has argued that job insecurity may enhance various forms of employee performance. In these studies, job insecurity has been framed as a job preservation strategy or a challenge stressor: job-insecure employees would invest additional efforts into performance to demonstrate their value to the employer and decrease the likelihood of job loss (Shoss, 2017). Following this line of research, a couple of studies have found a positive association between job insecurity and job performance (e.g., Probst, 2002; Probst et al., 2007). Another stream of research argues that job insecurity is a hindrance stressor, which not only drains employees' energy resources, but also interferes with employee progress towards goal achievements (LePine et al., 2005). As such, job insecurity has been framed as a chronic stressor that relates negatively to employee performance (De Witte, 2005). After more than three decades of accumulating research summarized in two recent meta-analyses (Jiang & Lavaysse, 2018; Sverke et al., 2019), we now have conclusive evidence that job insecurity indeed harms employee performance and should not be used as a managerial strategy to motivate employee performance.

Although a debate about the valence of the job insecurity–performance relationship has reached a conclusion, knowledge about its underlying explanatory mechanisms is still relatively scarce and scattered within separate theoretical frameworks (De Cuyper et al., 2020). This hampers the theoretical development of the field, as well as the development of more effective managerial interventions. In response, the aim of this chapter is to review and summarize theories that have been dominantly used to test the mediators underlying the effects of job insecurity on performance. To achieve this aim, we outline the reasoning inherent to each theory, delineate results of empirical tests of corresponding indirect effects and suggest research pathways that could further advance this stream of research. Furthermore, we describe the organizational resources that we believe can serve as successful buffers of the negative indirect effects of job insecurity placing a particular emphasis on organizational justice. Our review incorporates a wide range of performance types including in-role performance, contextual performance, counterproductive work behaviour and innovative work behaviour (cf. Sverke et al., 2019). In sum, we provide an integrative framework (Figure 2.1) that we hope will prompt future studies addressing the question: why is job insecurity bad for employee performance?

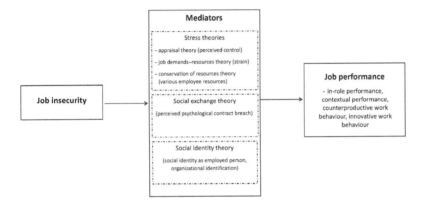

Figure 2.1   *Integrative theoretical framework of mediators linking job insecurity to job performance*

WHY DO JOB-INSECURE EMPLOYEES PERFORM WORSE? REVIEW OF THEORETICAL FRAMEWORKS AND CORRESPONDING EXPLAINING MECHANISMS

Knowing not just whether, but also why job-insecure employees perform worse is key to advancing the theoretical understanding of this relationship and crucial for a research area to evolve (Hayes, 2018). For that reason, the following paragraphs deal with explaining the detrimental effects of job insecurity on employee performance through the lens of: (i) stress theories; (ii) social exchange theory; and (iii) social identity theory. We conclude by outlining several plausible pathways that we see as fruitful for further advancing this line of research.

Job-Insecure Employees are not able to Perform Well: A Perspective from Stress Theories

At the core of all stress theories used to explain the job insecurity–performance relationship lies the notion that job insecurity is a stressful workplace experience draining employees' capacities to perform (Lawrence & Kacmar, 2017; Vander Elst et al., 2016). Hence, the main assumption derived from this set of theories is that job-insecure employees are simply *not able* to perform well, at least not as well as employees who feel relatively secure with regards to the continuity of their current job. In his seminal review of job insecurity literature, De Witte (2005) outlined several aspects of this work stressor that make it particularly harmful for employees' well-being and work behaviour. First, job insecurity, by its definition, represents a perceived threat to something that is regarded as highly valuable for most people, ranging from more obvious, concrete resources (e.g., financial income, social network, opportunities for professional development) to the more abstract ones (e.g., one's identity, sense of higher collective purpose and sense of belonging) (De Witte, 2005; Selenko & Batinic, 2013; Selenko et al., 2017). Therefore, the experience of job insecurity is involuntary and unpleasant (De Witte, 2005; Smet et al., 2016; Vander Elst et al., 2016). Second, defining characteristics of job-insecure situations refer to its inherent uncertainty and unpredictability. As De Witte (2005) pointed out, job-insecure employees are "groping in the dark" (p. 1) because they anticipate loss of an important resource – their employment – but at the same time cannot know when, how and even whether that loss will occur. Such constellation of circumstances should be particularly stressful because it hampers any constructive coping efforts (Vander Elst et al., 2014). Accordingly, job insecurity represents a highly stressful, burdening and energy-draining working condition, which in the long run may severely undermine employees' capacities to deliver desirable performance to their organization.

Following this line of reasoning, researchers have used several more specific theoretical frameworks to explain the job insecurity–performance relationship. Depending on the theory, the conceptualization of the "cannot" perspective has included related, but distinct mediating mechanisms: (i) appraisal theory (Lazarus & Folkman, 1984); (ii) job demands–resources (JD-R) theory (Bakker & Demerouti, 2017); and (iii) conservation of resources (COR) theory (Hobfoll et al., 2018).

Building upon the assumptions of appraisal theory (Lazarus & Folkman, 1984), researchers have argued that job insecurity leads to impaired performance through a perceived lack of situational control (e.g., Vander Elst et al., 2016). Along this line of research, perceived control reflects the extent of subjectively assessed control over one's current work situation (Vander Elst et al., 2014). In particular, job insecurity has been aligned with the primary appraisal of a threat – employees anticipate a harm in terms of the potential job loss (Vander Elst et al., 2014). When the situation is perceived as threatening, people evaluate the resources at their disposal to deal with this threat, a process that denotes a secondary appraisal (Lazarus & Folkman, 1984). As previously noted, any form of coping with job insecurity is likely to be in vain because job-insecure situations usually stem from uncontrollable factors (e.g., decisions at a higher organizational level, country unemployment rate) (Vander Elst et al., 2014). For that reason, job insecurity (i.e., a primary appraisal) is assumed to reduce employees' perceptions of control over their current work situation (i.e., a secondary appraisal). Furthermore, when a threatening situation is perceived as uncontrollable, people tend to withdraw from that situation (Lazarus & Folkman, 1984). For example, when job-insecure employees assess that there is not much they can do to influence the decisions about their jobs, any form of (pro)active coping (i.e., in the form of increased performance) may lose its perceived coping value and distancing oneself from that situation becomes an inevitable alternative. Reduced performance represents one form of behavioural withdrawal (Vander Elst et al., 2016). In sum, job insecurity may impair employee performance due to diminished perceptions of control over that situation. Comporting with appraisal theory, the mediating role of diminished control perceptions in the job insecurity–performance relationship has received empirical support. For example, Vander Elst et al. (2016) demonstrated a negative indirect effect of job insecurity on both in-role performance and innovative work behaviour through perceived control.

According to JD-R theory (Bakker & Demerouti, 2017), job insecurity is framed as a hindrance job demand (e.g., LePine et al., 2005) – an organizational aspect of the job that requires sustained physical and/or psychological effort resulting in physiological and psychological costs (Bakker & Demerouti, 2017). The costs incurred by job insecurity are most often described in terms of energy losses. Job insecurity can impel employees to exert their energy in numerous ways. For example, merely suppressing or altering a negative mood and unpleasant emotions evoked by a job-insecure situation requires one to invest extra energy resources into self-regulatory processes (Lawrence & Kacmar, 2017). The unpredictable nature of such a threat may also prompt employees to monitor external cues and search for information that could clarify their future position within the organization. When added to day-to-day tasks and obligations, these additional efforts cost energy and lead to strain (Bakker & Demerouti, 2017). In line with this reasoning, the results of meta-analysis demonstrate that job insecurity relates to a host of strain indicators, including higher levels of burnout, anger, anxiety and depression, as well as lower levels of psychological, physical and general health (Jiang & Lavaysse, 2018). JD-R theory proposes that strain in turn leads to impaired performance (Bakker & Demerouti, 2017). Accordingly, job insecurity, as a demanding working condition, impairs employees' health and well-being. As a result, employees are not able to reach their work goals and perform well. Supporting these theoretical assumptions, Darvishmotevali and Ali (2020) found that lower levels of subjective well-being explained the negative relationship between job insecurity and supervisor-rated in-role performance. Furthermore, using a time-lagged study, Lawrence and Kacmar (2017) showed that emotional exhaustion explained the effect of job insecurity on increased levels of unethical behaviour measured one month later. Interesting to note is that these authors did not explicitly utilize JD-R theory to guide their hypotheses (instead, they used a self-regulation theory which has a logic complementary to JD-R theory).

The third framework that has been often used to explain the negative relationship between job insecurity and employee performance is COR theory (Hobfoll et al., 2018). According to this theory, employment is considered to be a valuable resource (Hobfoll, 2001). COR theory assumes that stress occurs when peoples' resources are threatened with loss. For that reason, job insecurity, as a threat to a valuable resource, elicits stress (Urbanaviciute et al., 2021). Another assumption of COR theory is that initial resource loss leads to further losses (Hobfoll, 2001). Hence, the initial stress may lead to loss of energy resources, which over time may lead to loss of one's health, as another valuable COR resource (Hobfoll, 2001). When employees find themselves caught in such a loss spiral, they are compelled to limit further resource losses, for example in the form of preserving their remaining energy by refraining from high-level performance (Schreurs et al., 2012). Interestingly, the mediators outlined in appraisal theory (perceived control) and JD-R theory (energy resources) can also be considered valuable resources within COR theory. For that reason, empirical studies of indirect effects through these constructs (e.g., Darvishmotevali & Ali, 2020; Vander Elst et al., 2016) also represent empirical tests of COR theory's explanation of the job insecurity–performance relationship.

Job-Insecure Employees are not Willing to Reciprocate Good Performance: A Perspective from Social Exchange Theory

In contrast to studies using stress theories to explain why job-insecure employees are unable to perform well, studies utilizing social exchange theory place an emphasis on employees' unwillingness to perform (e.g., Piccoli et al., 2017b). The central tenet of this theoretical framework is that there is a perceived (im-)balance in the transaction of resources between an employee and employer (or organization as a whole) (Cropanzano & Mitchell, 2005). Specifically, some of the most often exchanged resources in the employee–employer relationship include loyalty and effort (from the employee side) and job security and rewards (from an employer side) (De Cuyper & De Witte, 2007). Investments from one side generate expectations of returns from the other side (Cropanzano & Mitchell, 2005). Therefore, when confronted with a threat of a potential job loss, employees are prone to perceive an imbalance in this exchange: the employer is not reciprocating the expected levels of security of one's employment in return for the employees' invested effort. As a result, employees do not feel obliged to reciprocate with high-level performance. The most often studied conceptualization of such psychological process refers to the psychological contract breach.

The psychological contract encompasses employees' subjective evaluations of what constitutes mutual obligations between themselves and their employer (Robinson et al., 1994). If there is a discrepancy between what an employee believes they should receive and what they perceive they have received from their employer, a perceived breach of the psychological contract emerges. Job insecurity perceptions represent one source of psychological contract breach (Piccoli & De Witte, 2015). Accordingly, job-insecure employees are no longer willing to invest in their employer or organization because they perceive that their employer has not invested in them. And in more extreme scenarios, they may even try to retaliate against their organization. Comporting these assumptions, studies have demonstrated that psychological contract breach explains the detrimental effects of job insecurity on organizational citizenship behaviour and counterproductive work behaviour (Piccoli et al., 2017b), as well as in-role performance (an effect that was significant even when tested simultaneously with perceived control discussed above; Vander Elst et al., 2016).

Job-Insecure Employees Perform Worse Due to Eroded Self-Concept: A Perspective from Social Identity Theory

A more recent theoretical account of the job insecurity–performance relationship has been derived from the social identity perspective (Tajfel & Turner, 1986). Researchers utilizing this theoretical framework have recognized that underlying mechanisms of the detrimental effects of job insecurity on employee performance span beyond more traditionally studied mediators derived from stress theories and social exchange theory (Selenko et al., 2017). In particular, the main idea rooted in the social identity perspective is that job insecurity erodes valued parts of employees' social identity, which in turn has unfavourable consequences on a wide span of outcomes, including employee performance (Selenko et al., 2017). This process is initiated by the tendency of people to categorize themselves and others into social groups, which enables individuals to define themselves in terms of a membership in a specific group (Piccoli et al., 2017a). In the context of job insecurity, researchers have extracted at least two social groups that are deemed relevant for understanding the harmful effects of this work stressor: a group of employed persons (Selenko et al., 2017) and a group of people belonging to a particular organization (Piccoli et al., 2017a).

In particular, job insecurity signals to employees that in the near future they might no longer have the status of an employed person. Employment represents an important social identity category for most people; therefore, job insecurity poses a threat to a relevant part of their self-concept (Selenko et al., 2017). Moreover, when one's employment situation is perceived as threatened, Selenko et al. (2017) argue that an individual's identity as an employed person gains in salience and affects one's attitudes and behaviours, including job performance. This is because social identities provide multiple identity functions for employees. For example, social identities influence self-esteem and a sense of worth (Haslam et al., 2009), which positively relate to job performance (Judge & Bono, 2001). People who belong to the employed population may draw a positive sense of self from their membership in this valued group. Furthermore, social identities provide people with a sense of belonging (Haslam et al., 2009). For that reason, threatened social identity as an employed person can induce feelings of social exclusion from a group, which provides employees with work-related support crucial for good performance (Selenko et al., 2017). Finally, identifying oneself with an employed population implies having a clearer sense of who one is in a professional sense, which career goals they strive for and how to achieve such goals. For that reason, by threatening their social identity as an employed person, job insecurity may blur employees' identity clarity, making them less likely to invest effort into job performance. Empirical findings support these theoretical claims. Using a three-wave cross-lagged research design, Selenko et al. (2017) showed that job-insecure employees exhibit lower levels of subsequent in-role performance due to reduced social identity as an employed person.

A second stream of research within social identity framework is a bit narrower in scope because it places an emphasis on one's membership in a specific organization, not in an entire working population. A key mediator of the job insecurity–performance relationship is organizational identification – a perceived "oneness" between self and organization (Ashforth et al., 2008). Job insecurity is assumed to undermine such perception of organizational belonginess. In other words, it communicates to employees that they are no longer valued and respected members of their organization because in the near future they might no longer be members at all, or they might lose the valued features of that membership (Piccoli et al., 2017a). As a result, employees may become less motivated to promote the interests of their organization by working hard and well. In line with these predictions, Piccoli et al. (2017a) demonstrated that the negative indirect effect of job insecurity on both in-role performance and organizational citizenship can be explained by employees' organizational identification.

IN SEARCH OF A MORE THEORETICAL INTEGRATION AND MORE RIGOROUS METHODOLOGY

Need for theoretical integration. With few notable exceptions (Piccoli et al., 2017b; Probst et al., 2019; Vander Elst et al., 2016), previous studies have usually relied upon only one theoretical explanation when testing mediators of the job insecurity–performance relationship. Although parsimony should be the leading principle in science, such research efforts potentially oversimplify more complex psychological processes which unravel when employees are confronted with job insecurity in real life. In response, accounting for our three-pathway model (Figure 2.1), we suggest that the more nuanced understanding of the job insecurity–performance relationship can be achieved by integrating two or more theoretical approaches, either within a particular pathway (e.g., stress theories) or between two or more pathways (e.g., social exchange theory and social identity theory). Depending on the theoretical relationship between examined mediators, such a multiple mediator model can be tested either as a parallel mediation or as a serial mediation. The extant study using such a research approach is a study by Probst et al. (2019), who used both Fredrickson's (2004) broaden-and-build theory and Staw et al.'s (1981) threat-rigidity theory to examine whether decreased job-related affective well-being and increased cognitive failures explain the relationship between (quantitative and qualitative) job insecurity and employee creativity. Both mechanisms reflect the logic of the first pathway described in this chapter: job-insecure employees are not able to perform well due to drained (emotional and cognitive) capacities. Probst et al. (2019) found that decreased affective well-being had more explanatory power in the relationship between job insecurity and self-rated creativity, whereas cognitive failures were a more powerful mediator in the relationship between job insecurity and performance on the idea generation task. A second research approach could incorporate mediating effects that contrast different theoretical perspectives, such as appraisal theory (and the corresponding mediator perceived control), social exchange theory (and the corresponding mediator psychological contract breach) and social identity theory (and the corresponding mediator social identity as an employed person). By testing these competing explanations researchers could not only provide more robust evidence that each mediator transmits the effects of job insecurity when tested simultaneously with other mediators, but also establish which one (if either) is relatively more important in explaining the detrimental effects of job insecurity. A research example that has already adopted this approach is a study by Vander Elst et al. (2016). Although framing both mechanisms within appraisal theory, the authors examined whether perceived control and psychological contract breach both mediated the effects of job insecurity on in-role performance and innovative work behaviour when tested simultaneously in a parallel mediation model. They found that perceived control and psychological contract breach were equally powerful mediators of the effects of job insecurity on in-role performance and that only perceived control transmitted the effect of job insecurity on innovative work behaviour. Finally, when mediators are not only related, but causally influence each other, testing serial multiple mediator models may serve as yet another research approach that facilitates theoretical integration of this scattered field. For example, building upon COR theory, future studies could examine a serial causal chain in which job insecurity first decreases employees' perception of control over their work situation, which in turn predicts higher levels of strain (Vander Elst et al., 2014), leading to decreased employee performance.

Need for longitudinal research design. The majority of studies testing the explanatory mechanisms have utilized cross-sectional research designs. However, a more powerful empirical test of proposed mediating effects would be based on experimental design where applicable, or on a full panel correlational research design with a minimum of three measurement occasions. The latter design enables researchers to conclude whether job insecurity relates to subsequent increases/decreases in a mediator and whether a mediator relates to subsequent increases/decreases in job performance (Little, 2013). Full panel research designs also enable explicit statistical comparison with alternative models which suggest the opposite causal order of examined variables, thereby additionally strengthening causal conclusions. A study by Selenko et al. (2017) represents one of the few notable exceptions that have grounded their conclusions about mediating mechanisms using such rigorous research methodology.

Need for establishing boundary conditions. In addition to understanding why job insecurity impairs performance, it is also valuable to understand under which conditions are such effects more or less pronounced. Therefore, a fruitful avenue for future studies, that is already becoming standard in job insecurity literature, includes integrating mediating and moderating mechanisms into one more complex research model. For example, Lawrence and Kacmar (2017) demonstrated that the indirect link between job insecurity and employees' unethical behaviour through emotional exhaustion is more highly pronounced for employees who are highly embedded in their organization. Moderators stemming from employees' work environments represent another set of moderators that could explain why indirect effects of job insecurity are in some cases stronger and in some weaker. Due to their applicability in managerial practices, we discuss them in greater detail next.

HOW CAN WE AMELIORATE THE NEGATIVE EFFECTS OF JOB INSECURITY ON PERFORMANCE? THE MODERATING ROLE OF ORGANIZATIONAL RESOURCES

Relying on eclecticism in the theoretical understanding of the negative impact of job insecurity on performance, several recent studies looked for the contextual factors which buffer the negative impact of job insecurity on performance. In this regard, a novel theoretical approach has been introduced to the field – uncertainty management theory (Lind & Van den Bos, 2002) – which places justice in the focus of HRM as a key factor that breaks the harmful vicious circle in which job insecurity undermines organizational effectiveness, which then further increases experience of job insecurity (Greenhalgh & Rosenblatt, 1984). Research has shown that external resources such as fair treatment and organizational justice moderate the association of job insecurity with job attitudes (Richter & Näsvall, 2019; Silla et al., 2010; Sverke & Hellgren, 2002). In a longitudinal study, Chirumbolo and Areni (2005) found that job satisfaction and organizational commitment moderate the negative impact of job insecurity on job performance and suggested organizational interventions that lead to greater job satisfaction and organizational commitment among employees. The study indirectly confirmed the importance of perceived fairness because research showed that organizational fairness positively relates to these job attitudes (Lavelle et al., 2009; Schumacher et al., 2016). In addition, by influencing attitudes such as job satisfaction and organizational loyalty, external organizational resources have the potential to moderate behavioural outcomes of job insecurity that are directly related to the organizational efficacy, such as job performance, absenteeism or turnover intentions (Chirumbolo & Areni, 2005).

The external resources which moderate the negative impact of job insecurity on performance are of special interest for HRM processes because they present artefacts of organizational culture and as such are more easily influenced by employers and subject to organizational interventions (De Cuyper et al., 2020). These resources are in focus of this paragraph where we analyse research specifically dealing with supportive social behaviour, fairness and justice as moderators of the negative impact of job insecurity on job performance. We discuss psychological mechanisms that define the beneficial nature of these concepts relying on the theory of social exchange (Blau, 2009; Cook et al., 2013) and the uncertainty management theory (Lind & Van den Bos, 2002). In addition, we discuss a relevance of justice for stress theories of job insecurity and present the results of several empirical studies in this area.

Why are Organizational Fairness and Justice Beneficial in the Situation of Job Insecurity?

Organizational justice and fairness models draw directly on social exchange theory (Cropanzano & Mitchell, 2005); specifically, by framing psychological contract breach as a mediator of the job insecurity–performance relationship, this theory also predicts the usefulness of organizational fairness and justice in a job-insecure situation. In short, overall organizational justice facilitates positive exchange relationships between employees and employers (Colquitt, 2012), which are accompanied by employee perceptions that it is worth investing effort in the organization, as well as positive emotions towards work and the organization. In the situation of job insecurity, these cognitions and emotions could increase the employee's willingness to make an effort which might result in greater in-role and extra-role work performance. On the contrary, perceived injustice of organizational procedures (especially those related to layoffs), distribution of resources and information could intensify the negative emotions and frustrations that job insecurity already caused, as well as foster the belief that the organization is not worth employee work engagement. Researchers that focus on justice, fairness, or external resources representing their correlates (e.g., voice, communication, or social support) ground their hypotheses on social exchange theory (e.g., Chirumbolo & Areni, 2005; Schreurs et al., 2012; Silla et al., 2010).

While the cognitive assessment of a job-insecure situation impacts the employee's *willingness* to put an effort into work, negative emotions that accompany this interpretation facilitate energy drain and decrease work-related well-being. Stress-related theoretical explanations are based on these affective mechanisms. Accordingly, relying on the appraisal theory, Piccoli et al. (2011) argue that fairness may shape employees' perception of work control and suggest that "… justice may be a proxy for the secondary appraisal of perceived control, which enables people to determine whether they will be able to neutralize the perceived threats" (p. 41). In line with COR theory, Jiang and Probst (2014) stated that open and relevant communication might serve as an energy resource which can help in gaining and protecting other valued resources. Kausto et al. (2005) demonstrated the interaction effect of procedural and interactional justice and job insecurity on emotional exhaustion and stress symptoms.

How to Manage Work Behaviour in a Situation of Uncertainty? Empirical Examples Testing Moderating Role of Organizational Resources

Previously mentioned uncertainty management theory (Lind & Van den Bos, 2002) deals with the link between uncertainty and justice in the context of organizational behaviour and points to the importance of organizational justice in a situation of job insecurity. Lind and Van den Bos (2002) argued that fairness matters more whenever situational factors increase the salience of uncertainty because it provides strategies that people can use as adaptive coping. As a result, in a situation of job insecurity, employees are particularly sensitive to signs of organizational justice and fairness, they look for them and use them to cope with the stress of uncertainty. For these reasons, uncertainty management theory can be inspiring for both researchers and managers. More specifically, this theory argues that job-insecure employees will spontaneously evaluate organizational processes in terms of their fairness and justice (Lind & Van den Bos, 2002; Van den Bos, 2001). Depending on the results of these judgements, employees will regulate their work behaviour, that is, invest more or less efforts in achieving organizational goals through in-role and extra-role performance. Furthermore, they will use cognitive shortcuts to form justice judgements and use available information about any aspect of justice (e.g., distributive, procedural, or interactional) to make general inferences about the organizational fairness (substitutability effect). Extant experimental studies demonstrated that uncertainty enhances the ability of fairness to decrease negative affect or increase positive affect (Van den Bos, 2001), and field research showed that employees used information about justice to a greater extent when they experienced insecurity in organizations (Thau et al., 2007).

Although there is still a lack of empirical evidence on the moderating effect of organizational justice on the job insecurity–performance relationship, several methodologically sound studies provide initial evidence for its ameliorating effect. Wang et al. (2015) used two-wave and three-wave longitudinal studies and proved the interaction effect of job insecurity and organizational justice on job performance. They found that when employees perceived low levels of organizational justice, job insecurity was significantly, negatively related to job performance. In contrast, it was not related to job performance when levels of organizational justice were high. In addition, the research revealed that work engagement mediated this interaction effect. The results of the mediated moderation analysis revealed that job insecurity was negatively associated with job performance through work engagement when organizational justice was low. Using the perspective of social identity theory (Tajfel & Turner, 1986), the authors framed job insecurity as a threat to the employees' personal identity and a sense of self and concluded that: "Fair treatment of the organization could make them feel self-affirmed in the organization which can attenuate their negative affective reactions to job insecurity" (p. 1254). Sun et al. (2022) also demonstrated the moderated mediation effect in a study in which supervisors' ratings of employees' taking charge behaviour was examined as an outcome of job insecurity and interactional justice as a hypothesized moderator. This longitudinal study on a sample of 194 employees, paired with their immediate supervisors, showed that employees' perception of interactional justice ameliorated the negative effect of job insecurity on their work engagement and, consequently, their supervisor-rated taking charge behaviours. More specifically, the negative relationship between job insecurity and employees' work engagement was weaker when employees perceived high rather than low levels of interactional justice. These studies present a direct empirical test of the moderating role of organizational justice in the relationship between job insecurity and performance. However, it is important to mention that other organizational resources subject to HRM interventions have also proven to be as effective in mitigating the negative effect of job insecurity on performance. In a weekly diary study, Schreurs et al. (2012) showed that supervisor support moderated the intra-individual relationship between job insecurity and in-role performance, and Jiang and Probst (2019) showed buffering effects of positive organizational communication on the increased number of accidents resulting from job insecurity. Finally, when testing a mediation model linking job insecurity with organizational commitment and well-being using a multi-group analysis on a large sample of employees facing organizational change, Schumacher et al. (2016) showed that the negative relationship between job insecurity and fairness gradually decreased across three stages of change. The authors pointed to a relatively more important role of fairness in the early stages of change, a finding that would be worth verifying with longitudinal studies in which the moderating role of fairness would be tested in different phases of organizational change, that is, in which its usefulness would be explored with regards to the duration of the insecurity experience.

CONCLUSION

Extensive research has clearly shown that job insecurity is a hindrance stressor whose detrimental effects on well-being and work motivation can be explained by various theoretical perspectives. Describing the negative consequences of experiencing job insecurity on work motivation and well-being, the same theories also offer explanations for the negative relationship between job insecurity and job performance. In this section, we have described three dominant theoretical frameworks: (i) stress theories that explain why job insecurity impairs employees' capacities to perform; (ii) social exchange theory that explains why job insecurity impairs employees' willingness to perform; and

(iii) social identity theory, which explains why experiencing the threat of job loss and the consequential threat to employees' work-related identity leads to impaired performance.

These theories describe mediating mechanisms that are of a different nature, which potentially has important implications for managing employee work motivation and job performance in a situation of job insecurity. In particular, we suggested that future research may contrast the strength of proposed mediating effects in relation to certain types of employee performance. Such knowledge may inform practitioners to develop more effective interventions which specifically target the underlying detrimental processes caused by job insecurity. If, for example, perceived control is the most important mediator of the relationship between job insecurity and innovative work behaviour, as initial evidence suggests (Vander Elst et al., 2016), organizational interventions may primarily aim to reduce employees' feelings of powerlessness by enabling them more opportunities to participate in organizational decision making and by transparently conveying information relevant to employees' future job situation in their organization. However, if explanations related to employees' social identity are revealed as most important in relation to some performance types, practical interventions may primarily focus on inducing feelings of belongingness, for example, through volunteer work as suggested by Selenko et al. (2017).

On the other hand, utilizing longitudinal full panel research designs to test the models proposed in this chapter may advance future theoretical and practical knowledge in yet another way. Such research may reveal that the relationship between job insecurity and employee performance is not strictly unidirectional; rather, job insecurity may reduce performance through proposed mediators, which in turn may further enhance job insecurity through different mechanisms (Shoss, 2017). Building on this theoretical knowledge, practitioners may not only target the specific mechanisms, but also account for the extent of damage caused by job insecurity. If employees are already deeply caught in a vicious cycle or (in a more negative scenario) spiral composed of perceptions of job insecurity and reduced performance, interventions should also strive to enhance employees' psychological empowerment (Pieterse et al., 2010).

To sum up, throughout this chapter we aimed to structure the knowledge about the mechanisms that explain why job insecurity is harmful for employee performance. We also discussed some of the possible avenues to reduce this detrimental effect. Given the still scarce and scattered knowledge on this topic, we hope that this chapter may provide useful guidelines for future fruitful investigation.

REFERENCES

Ashforth, B. E., Harrison, S. H., & Corley, K. G. (2008). Identification in organizations: An examination of four fundamental questions. *Journal of Management, 34*(3), 325–374. https://doi.org/10.1177/0149206308316059

Bakker, A. B., & Demerouti, E. (2017). Job demands-resources theory: Taking stock and looking forward. *Journal of Occupational Health Psychology, 22*(3), 273–285. https://doi.org/10.1108/02683940710733115

Blau, P. M. (2009). *Exchange and power in social life*. Piscataway, NJ: Transaction Publishers.

Chirumbolo, A., & Areni, A. (2005). The influence of job insecurity on job performance and absenteeism: The moderating effect of work attitudes. *SA Journal of Industrial Psychology, 31*(4), 65–71. https://doi.org/10.4102/sajip.v31i4.213

Colquitt, J. A. (2012). Organizational justice. In S. W. J. Kozlowski (Ed.), *The Oxford handbook of organizational psychology* (Vol. 1, pp. 526–547). New York: Oxford University Press.

Cook, K. S., Cheshire, C., Rice, E. R., & Nakagawa, S. (2013). Social exchange theory. In J. DeLamater & A. Ward (Eds.), *Handbook of social psychology* (pp. 61–88). Dordrecht: Springer.

Cropanzano, R., & Mitchell, M. S. (2005). Social exchange theory: An interdisciplinary review. *Journal of Management, 31*(6), 874–900.

Darvishmotevali, M., & Ali, F. (2020). Job insecurity, subjective well-being and job performance: The moderating role of psychological capital. *International Journal of Hospitality Management, 87*, 102462.

De Cuyper, N., & De Witte, H. (2007). Job insecurity in temporary versus permanent workers: Associations with attitudes, well-being, and behaviour. *Work & Stress, 21*(1), 65–84.

De Cuyper, N., Schreurs, B., De Witte, H., & Selenko, E. (2020). Impact of job insecurity on job performance introduction. *Career Development International, 25*(3), 221–228.

De Witte, H. (2005). Job insecurity: Review of the international literature on definitions, prevalence, antecedents and consequences. *SA Journal of Industrial Psychology, 31*(4), 1–6. https://doi.org/10.4102/sajip.v31i4.200

Fredrickson, B. L. (2004). The broaden-and-build theory of positive emotions. Philosophical Transactions of the Royal Society of London. *Series B: Biological Sciences, 359*(1449), 1367–1377.

Greenhalgh, L., & Rosenblatt, Z. (1984). Job insecurity: Toward conceptual clarity. *Academy of Management Review, 9*(3), 438–448.

Haslam, S. A., Jetten, J., Postmes, T., & Haslam, C. (2009). Social identity, health and well-being: An emerging agenda for applied psychology. *Applied Psychology: An International Review, 58*(1), 1–23. https://doi.org/10.1111/j.1464-0597.2008.00379.x

Hayes, A. F. (2018). *Introduction to mediation, moderation, and conditional process analysis: A regression-based approach (methodology in the social sciences)* (2nd ed.). New York, NY: The Guilford Press.

Hobfoll, S. E. (2001). The influence of culture, community, and the nested-self in the stress process: Advancing conservation of resources theory. *Applied Psychology, 50*(3), 337–421.

Hobfoll, S. E., Halbesleben, J., Neveu, J. P., & Westman, M. (2018). Conservation of resources in the organizational context: The reality of resources and their consequences. *Annual Review of Organizational Psychology and Organizational Behavior*, *5*, 103–128.

Jiang, L., & Lavaysse, L. M. (2018). Cognitive and affective job insecurity: A meta-analysis and a primary study. *Journal of Management*, *44*(6), 2307–2342. https://doi.org/10.1177/0149206318773853

Jiang, L., & Probst, T. M. (2014). Organizational communication: A buffer in times of job insecurity? *Economic and Industrial Democracy*, 35(3), 557–579. https://doi .org/10.1177/0143831X13489356

Jiang, L., & Probst, T. M. (2019). The moderating effect of trust in management on consequences of job insecurity. *Economic and Industrial Democracy*, *40*(2), 409–433. https://doi.org/10.1177/0143831X16652945

Judge, T. A., & Bono, J. E. (2001). Relationship of core self-evaluations traits—self-esteem, generalized self-efficacy, locus of control, and emotional stability—with job satisfaction and job performance: A meta-analysis. *Journal of Applied Psychology*, *86*(1), 80–92. https://doi.org/10.1037/0021-9010.86.1.80

Kausto, J., Elo, A.-L., Lipponen, J., & Elovainio, M. (2005). Moderating effects of job insecurity in the relationships between procedural justice and employee well-being: Gender differences. *European Journal of Work and Organizational Psychology*, 14(4), 431–452. https://doi.org/10.1080/13594320500349813

Lavelle, J. J., Brockner, J., Konovsky, M. A., Price, K. H., Henley, A. B., Taneja, A., & Vinekar, V. (2009). Commitment, procedural fairness, and organizational citizenship behavior: A multifoci analysis. *Journal of Organizational Behavior*, *30*(3), 337–357. https://doi.org/10.1002/job.518

Lawrence, E. R., & Kacmar, K. M. (2017). Exploring the impact of job insecurity on employees' unethical behavior. *Business Ethics Quarterly*, *27*(1), 39–70. https://doi .org/10.1017/beq.2016.58

Lazarus, R. S., & Folkman, S. (1984). *Stress appraisal and coping*. New York, NY: Springer.

LePine, J. A., Podsakoff, N. P., & LePine, M. A. (2005). A meta-analytic test of the challenge stressor-hindrance stressor framework: An explanation for inconsistent relationships among stressors and performance. *Academy of Management Journal*, *48*(5), 764–775.

Lind, E. A., & Van den Bos, K. (2002). When fairness works: Toward a general theory of uncertainty management. In B. M. Staw & R. M. Kramer (Eds.), *Research in organizational behavior* (Vol. 24, pp. 181–223). Boston, MA: Elsevier.

Little, T. D. (2013). *Longitudinal structural equation modeling*. New York, NY: The Guilford Press.

Piccoli, B., Callea, A., Urbini, F., Chirumbolo, A., Ingusci, E., & De Witte, H. (2017a). Job insecurity and performance: The mediating role of organizational identification. *Personnel Review*, *46*(8), 1508–1522. https://doi.org/10.1108/PR-05-2016-0120

Piccoli, B., & De Witte, H. (2015). Job insecurity and emotional exhaustion: Testing psychological contract breach versus distributive injustice as indicators of lack of reciprocity. *Work & Stress*, *29*(3), 246–263.

Piccoli, B., De Witte, H., & Pasini, M. (2011). Job insecurity and organizational consequences: How justice moderates this relationship. *Romanian Journal of Applied Psychology*, *13*(2), 37–49.

Piccoli, B., De Witte, H., & Reisel, W. D. (2017b). Job insecurity and discretionary behaviors: Social exchange perspective versus group value model. *Scandinavian Journal of Psychology, 58*(1), 69–79.

Pieterse, A. N., Van Knippenberg, D., Schippers, M., & Stam, D. (2010). Transformational and transactional leadership and innovative behavior: The moderating role of psychological empowerment. *Journal of Organizational Behavior, 31*(4), 609–623. https://doi.org/10.1002/job.650

Probst, T. M. (2002). Layoffs and tradeoffs: Production, quality, and safety demands under the threat of job loss. *Journal of Occupational Health Psychology, 7*(3), 211–220. https://doi.org/10.1037/1076-8998.7.3.211

Probst, T. M., Chizh, A., Hu, S., Jiang, L., & Austin, C. (2019). Explaining the relationship between job insecurity and creativity: A test of cognitive and affective mediators. *Career Development International, 25*(3), 247–270.

Probst, T. M., Stewart, S. M., Gruys, M. L., & Tierney, B. W. (2007). Productivity, counterproductivity and creativity: The ups and downs of job insecurity. *Journal of Occupational and Organizational Psychology, 80*(3), 479–497. https://doi.org/10.1348/096317906X159103

Richter, A., & Näswall, K. (2019). Job insecurity and trust: Uncovering a mechanism linking job insecurity to well-being. *Work & Stress, 33*(1), 22–40. https://doi.org/10.1080/02678373.2018.1461709

Robinson, S. L., Kraatz, M. S., & Rousseau, M. L. (1994). Changing obligations and the psychological contract: A longitudinal study. *Academy of Management Journal, 37*(1), 137–152. https://doi.org/10.2307/256773

Schreurs, B. H. J., Hetty van Emmerik, I., Günter, H., & Germeys, F. (2012). A weekly diary study on the buffering role of social support in the relationship between job insecurity and employee performance. *Human Resource Management, 51*(2), 259–280. https://doi.org/10.1002/hrm.21465

Schumacher, D., Schreurs, B., Van Emmerik, H., & De Witte, H. (2016). Explaining the relation between job insecurity and employee outcomes during organizational change: A multiple group comparison. *Human Resource Management, 55*(5), 809–827. https://doi.org/10.1002/hrm.21687

Selenko, E., & Batinic, B. (2013). Job insecurity and the benefits of work. *European Journal of Work and Organizational Psychology, 22*(6), 725–736. http://dx.doi.org/10.1080/1359432X.2012.703376

Selenko, E., Mäkikangas, A., & Stride, C. B. (2017). Does job insecurity threaten who you are? Introducing a social identity perspective to explain well-being and performance consequences of job insecurity. *Journal of Organizational Behavior, 38*(6), 856–875. https://doi.org/10.1002/job.2172

Shoss, M. K. (2017). Job insecurity: An integrative review and agenda for future research. *Journal of Management, 43*(6), 1911–1939. https://doi.org/10.1177/0149206317691574

Silla, I., Gracia, F. J., Angel Mañas, M., & Peiró, J. M. (2010). Job insecurity and employees' attitudes: The moderating role of fairness. *International Journal of Manpower, 31*(4), 449–465. https://doi.org/10.1108/01437721011057029

Smet, K., Vander Elst, T., Griep, Y., & De Witte, H. (2016). The explanatory role of rumours in the reciprocal relationship between organizational change communication and job insecurity: A within-person approach. *European Journal of Work and Organizational Psychology, 25*(5), 631–644.

Staw, B. M., Sandelands, L. E., & Dutton, J. E. (1981). Threat rigidity effects in organizational behavior: A multilevel analysis. *Administrative Science Quarterly, 26*(4), 501–524.

Sun, F., Zheng, A., & Lan, J. (2022). Job insecurity and employees' taking charge behaviors: Testing a moderated mediation model. *International Journal of Environmental Research and Public Health, 19*(2), 696.

Sverke, M., & Hellgren, J. (2002). The nature of job insecurity: Understanding employment uncertainty on the brink of a new millennium. *Applied Psychology, 51*(1), 23–42. https://doi.org/10.1111/1464-0597.0077z

Sverke, M., Låstad, L., Hellgren, J., Richter, A., & Näswall, K. (2019). A meta-analysis of job insecurity and employee performance: Testing temporal aspects, rating source, welfare regime, and union density as moderators. *International Journal of Environmental Research and Public Health, 16*(14), 1–29. https://doi.org/10.3390/ijerph16142536

Tajfel, H., & Turner, J. C. (1986). The social identity theory of intergroup behavior. In S. Worchel & L. W. Austin (Eds.), *Psychology of intergroup relations*, pp. 7–24. Chicago: Nelson-Hall.

Thau, S., Aquino, K., & Wittek, R. (2007). An extension of uncertainty management theory to the self: The relationship between justice, social comparison orientation, and antisocial work behaviors. *Journal of Applied Psychology, 92*(1), 250–258. http://dx.doi.org/10.1037/0021-9010.92 .1.250

Urbanaviciute, I., Christina Roll, L., Tomas, J., & De Witte, H. (2021). Proactive strategies for countering the detrimental outcomes of qualitative job insecurity in academia. *Stress and Health, 37*(3), 557–571.

Van den Bos, K. (2001). Uncertainty management: The influence of uncertainty salience on reactions to perceived procedural fairness. *Journal of Personality and Social Psychology, 80*(6), 931–941. https://doi.org/10.1037/0022-3514.80.6.931

Vander Elst, T., De Cuyper, N., Baillien, E., Niesen, W., & De Witte, H. (2016). Perceived control and psychological contract breach as explanations of the relationships between job insecurity, job strain and coping reactions: Towards a theoretical integration. *Stress and Health, 32*(2), 100–116. http://dx.doi .org/100-116. 10.1002/smi.2584

Vander Elst, T., Van den Broeck, A., De Cuyper, N., & De Witte, H. (2014). On the reciprocal relationship between job insecurity and employee well-being: Mediation by perceived control? *Journal of Occupational and Organizational Psychology, 87*, 671–693.

Wang, H., Lu, C., & Siu, O. (2015). Job insecurity and job performance: The moderating role of organizational justice and the mediating role of work engagement. *Journal of Applied Psychology, 100*(4), 1249–1258. doi:10.1037/a0038330

3. Borrowing trouble? A debate on how social exchange theory is used and can be used in job insecurity research

Nele De Cuyper, Anahí Van Hootegem, & Lara C. Roll

INTRODUCTION

There is no such thing as an overall job insecurity theory. Instead, job insecurity research borrows theories from related fields, such as conservation of resources theory (COR; Hobfoll, 2001) and social exchange theory (SET; Cook et al., 2013; Cropanzano et al., 2017). Along the lines of COR, job insecurity is seen as a threat to existing resources, which might lead to poorer well-being (e.g., De Cuyper et al., 2012). Along the lines of SET, job insecurity causes an imbalance in the employment relationship, and hence negative attitudes and behaviour vis-à-vis the organisation (e.g., Piccoli et al., 2017). Theory-borrowing is not problematic per se, and in fact common practice in the field of work and organisational psychology (Whetten et al., 2009). Yet, it can become problematic when not done with great care and caution.

There could be cause for concern in job insecurity research. Our impression – and we will illustrate this in the next section – is that theory is used in an ad hoc and piecemeal fashion in job insecurity studies: some elements within a theory are isolated and then magnified, while other aspects that are equally central to the theory are neglected. This selective use of theory is problematic for two reasons. First, research questions and findings may be more compelling when framed against a stronger theoretical account. Second, better use of theory may also lead to more accurate tests. Methods have become more advanced and allow for sophisticated tests closely aligned with theoretical assumptions (see Halbesleben et al., 2014, for an excellent case on how to align methods with assumptions in COR). Yet, job insecurity research often relies on more traditional methods and analyses, mostly between-person, and on cross-sectional or two-wave designs.

In the following, we will use SET to illustrate the problem with theory-borrowing in job insecurity research. We first show how SET is used and what are missed opportunities. In a next step, we will advance potential routes for better use of SET. SET is exemplary as it is often used in job insecurity research (Shoss, 2017): job insecurity is tied to the relationship with the organisation. It has particular resonance as it is often used to explain performance, both in-role and extra-role behaviour. The relationship between job insecurity and performance is hotly debated (Tomas & Seršić, Chapter 2, this volume): while most job insecurity scholars would agree that the relationship is negative, the idea that job insecurity can boost performance is particularly persistent.

More in general, our aim is to illustrate how theory *is* used and then how it *can* be used. The latter is inspired by the approach for theory elaboration, as described by Fisher and Aguinis (2017). Theory elaboration is typically used to expand and tighten existing theoretical ideas based on empirical research: the base of evidence feeds the theory. Yet, it also offers useful tools to see how theories can be fleshed out in a specific field. This is important because it may bring about novel ideas by adding detail and complexity while at the same time acknowledging the accumulated evidence in the field.

SOCIAL EXCHANGE THEORY IN JOB INSECURITY RESEARCH

SET is a widely used framework to understand behaviour in interpersonal relationships. While originally a sociological theory, it has been used extensively in social psychology in very different areas (e.g., romantic relationships, friendships), in management and in work and organisational psychology (see Cook et al., 2013, for an overview). SET is not a specific theory but rather a collection of theories that share some features: all theories under the SET heading refer to (1) two or more parties; (2) who engage in a reciprocal exchange; and (3) along a cost/benefit analysis (Cropanzano et al., 2017).

How SET is Used

The use of SET in job insecurity research can be summarised in a few words: job insecurity represents a reciprocity deficit between employee and employer (Piccoli & De Witte, 2015). The somewhat longer version requires explanation and comments on two aspects: reciprocity and deficit. First, reciprocity refers to the norm that one party repays the other party in kind for previous behaviour that benefitted the first party. This creates a system of entitlements and obligations (Lam et al., 2015). For example, employees are loyal in exchange for job security provided by the employer and vice versa. Second, deficit refers to the idea that job insecurity violates this norm of reciprocity and induces an imbalance in the employment relationship (Shoss, 2017): the organisation fails to provide job security. This harms the exchange, so that employees no longer feel obligated to reciprocate and withdraw their investments in the employment relationship. Even more, they may reciprocate adverse treatment. This leads to the hypothesis that job insecurity leads to undesirable outcomes. In this respect, SET in job insecurity research is typically, though not exclusively (see e.g., Piccoli & De Witte, 2015, for a study on emotional exhaustion), used to explain attitudes (e.g., organisational commitment) and intentions (e.g., turnover intention) that signal withdrawal from (vs loyalty to) the organisation, or behaviour aimed at hurting (vs benefitting) the organisation (e.g., in-role, extra-role and counterproductive work behaviour).

The notion of reciprocity deficit is often assumed, yet not always tested (e.g., Fischmann et al., 2018). This is unfortunate as it leaves the field meagre in theory development. When tested, studies typically see psychological contract breaches or injustice as indicators of reciprocity deficit. The psychological contract describes a set of mostly implicit – in the head of employees – expectations between employee and employer. Job security is often part of this contract, and accordingly, job insecurity presents a psychological contract breach. Employees tend to bring balance by no longer complying with their part of the deal: they withdraw effort and goodwill in order to restore the imbalanced reciprocity (Piccoli et al., 2017; Shoss, 2017). Similarly, injustice relates to the notion that employees do not receive the outcomes they are/feel entitled to based on their investments. Job insecurity devalues the rewards, and hence employees may reduce investment (Piccoli & De Witte, 2015; Shoss, 2017).

How SET is Not Used

The central idea taken from SET is that employees withdraw from or get back at the employer when they feel insecure: job insecure employees' reactions are contingent upon what they do not get from the employer, and thus negative. This idea is not necessarily wrong, yet it is certainly incomplete. A more comprehensive account would also consider temporal and relational dynamics. Those dynamics are naturally intertwined, but we discuss them separately for the sake of explanation.

Gap 1: Temporal dynamics

A social exchange relationship develops through a series of interactions over time (Cropanzano & Mitchell, 2005) that creates a self-reinforcing cycle of obligations and entitlements, and ultimately cooperation and a high-quality exchange. For example, employees are loyal and hard-working when employers provide them with job security, and vice versa, employers continue to guarantee job security to loyal and hard-working employees. Security can take many forms; some employees may feel more secure because they are granted tenure or a permanent contract, others because they accumulate tenure-based benefits that strengthen their security in the organisation. This leads to a chain in which job security triggers desirable attitudes and behaviour, which consolidates security.

The self-reinforcing cycle binds the parties to the relationship in two ways: backward-looking and forward-looking. Backward-looking means that one party considers what "worked" in the past and then engages in similar actions: this is based on rationality and reinforcement. This is the case when employees have learned that loyalty and hard work is rewarded with security. Forward-looking means that one party anticipates benefits in the future and engages in those actions that lead to those benefits: this is based on instrumentality and is first and foremost self-serving. This is the case when employees (appear to) be loyal and work hard to secure their jobs (Figure 3.1, upper panel).

Job insecurity research does not usually account for such cycles, neither continuous exchange nor the combination of backward- and forward-looking. First, job insecurity research typically isolates a specific and unidirectional exchange "chunk" (Figure 3.1, lower panel): the employer fails to provide job security and this causes the employee to react. The assumption then is that job insecurity caused by the organisation is an immediate deal-breaker for the employee. This is not entirely correct for two reasons. One reason is that the employee could as well be the cause of eroded exchange, for example when the employee does not perform well and the employer reacts accordingly. Shoss (2017) explicitly discusses this possibility, yet without reference to SET, when emphasising that employees may create circumstances that put them at greater risk of job loss. Those dynamics could strengthen each other over time, even to the extent that it becomes difficult to disentangle cause and effect. A second reason is that one "episode" of job insecurity might not necessarily jeopardise the entire exchange. Employees may be more tolerant vis-à-vis job insecurity when they feel embedded in a long-term exchange relationship, in which job insecurity is appraised as "a slip" in an otherwise satisfactory relationship.

Second, job insecurity studies based on SET typically account for backward-looking but not often for forward-looking exchange. This emphasis is not surprising. Anticipated loss is at the heart of job insecurity and central to backward-looking. In addition, anticipated loss affects people more strongly than anticipated gain (Hobfoll, 2001; McGraw et al., 2010). In any case, this emphasis on backward-looking exchange implies that employees are portrayed as reactive: they look back at what the organisation did or did not provide and adapt their reactions accordingly (Lam et al., 2015; Thaker et

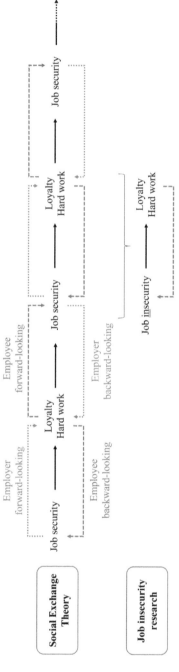

Figure 3.1   Temporal dynamics in social exchange theory and job insecurity research

al., 2021). This passive view is debatable; employees can be proactive agents who shape the relationship according to their needs and preferences, and job insecurity creates a strong motive for doing so. Said differently, job insecure employees may "give" to create an obligation to reciprocate in the future. Such forward-looking dynamics have been acknowledged, yet under the heading of job preservation (Huang et al., 2013; Shoss, 2017), the likelihood of getting fired motivates employees to work harder or in any case motivates them to appear hard-working. To date, social exchange dynamics and job preservation are treated as separate mechanisms, and they lead to conflicting hypotheses, perhaps wrongfully so. More specifically, SET as used to date leads to the hypothesis that job insecurity produces less loyal employees and poorer performance. In contrast, ideas based on job preservation led to the hypothesis that job insecurity triggers performance. These hypotheses are seemingly conflicting, yet they can be reconciled when framed as backward- and forward-looking exchange, respectively.

Gap 2: Relational dynamics
Any social exchange relationship is based on interdependence; both parties engage in reciprocal backward- and forward-looking exchange in view of securing benefits and gains that cannot be achieved alone (Cook et al., 2013; Cropanzano & Mitchell, 2005). Interdependence can take different forms, depending on the level of dependency and mutuality (Fugate et al., 2021). The level of dependency concerns the extent to which one party's actions may affect the other party's outcomes. For example, employees may be more dependent on their employer when their human capital is not needed or valued in the labour market, and they may be quite independent when they can easily secure another job, and vice versa. An employer may be dependent upon the unique expertise of some employees, but independent from employees in the periphery of the organisation. Mutuality refers to the degree to which both parties are equally dependent or independent. The exchange between employee and employer is equal when both parties feel either dependent on each other or independent from each other. The exchange is unequal when the employer has valuable resources to exchange but the employee has little to offer, or vice versa. This leads to different types of exchange, with four prototypes (labels are based on Janssens et al., 2003, and from an employee perspective):

1. Relational exchange, in which there is a high level of dependency from both employee and employer. The employee has or more likely has built expertise that is at the core of the organisation's functioning, and the employer provides security to facilitate the building of expertise and to protect this expertise. This is often the case in the standard employment

relationship in which employees have an open-ended contract with the employer.

2.   Transactional exchange, in which both employee and employer are independent. Such could be the case among employees with "niche" human capital that employers need, yet that is not "core business". The employee brings in unique expertise and the employer makes selective investments (e.g., repeated hiring) and pays for performance. Such exchange can be found among so-called voluntary temporary workers, who willingly and knowingly accept temporary employment (de Jong et al., 2009).

3.   Instrumental exchange, in which the employer but not the employee is dependent. In this type of exchange, the employee has unique capital that is in high and continuous demand in the labour market. The employee is the most powerful party: the employer tries to bind such employees to the organisation by investments in different areas (e.g., pay, training and development...). Such dynamics are illustrated in literature on high potentials (e.g., Kwon & Jang, 2022, for a review).

4.   Investing exchange, in which the employee but not the employer is dependent. The employee has human capital that is easily replaceable and easily found in the labour market, and hence the employer becomes the more powerful party in the employment bargain. An illustration comes from temporary employment research: temporary employees often invest heavily in the employment relationship, or in any case more than they get back, in view of landing a permanent job (de Jong et al., 2009).

Most job insecurity studies remain quite silent about types of exchange relationships. Typically, they sample "standard" employees: employees who have an open-ended (permanent) employment contract with one employer. Those studies start from the – often implicit – assumption of a relational exchange relationship. Studies that have accounted for exchange relationships, mostly compare relational and transactional exchanges. This is illustrated in the stream of job insecurity studies that have focussed upon non-standard employees, mostly employees on temporary (fixed-term) contracts. The argument is that temporary employees, unlike permanent employees, have a transactional exchange relationship (De Cuyper & De Witte, 2006). The different exchange relationships – relational and transactional – explain why and how employees react to job insecurity. Job insecurity breaches the relational but not the transactional psychological contract, and hence permanent compared to temporary workers may react more strongly to job insecurity.

While this reasoning has appeal, it is incomplete. The focus is upon exchange relationships that are equal, be it relational or transactional exchange. What is missing is an account of unequal exchange relationships, in which either the employee or the employer – but not both at the same time – are more dependent or independent. Unequal exchange relationships are not exceptional. Rather to the contrary, they may be the norm among the majority of temporary workers and in so-called new employment types in the gig economy: platform workers, freelance workers, independent contracts, on-call workers, solo self-employed… (e.g., Hamouche & Chabani, 2021). They are sometimes portrayed as extremely independent (e.g., portfolio workers; Neely, 2020) and on other occasions as extremely dependent (e.g., "reluctant entrepreneurs" in the study by Haynes & Marshall, 2017). Job insecurity may be particularly problematic among employees who are extremely dependent on the current employment relationship. Paradoxically, this may go unnoticed (or may be interpreted wrongfully as not being affected), as they may not have much room to react: they cannot afford to withdraw from or to lash out to the organisation.

In short, job insecurity research that is inspired by SET sometimes neglects and in other cases adopts a narrow view on aspects related to time and relational dynamics, in particular continuous exchange, backward- and forward-looking and unequal exchanges. As highlighted earlier, time and relational dynamics are intertwined: exchange relationships are constructed and reconstructed over time. This also means that interdependencies may shift. For example, permanent employees may react particularly strong to job insecurity when they feel their relational exchange is hollowed out and becomes transactional.

Addressing those gaps and issues may lead to a stronger and accurate SET-based understanding of job insecurity; it may bring more depth to the now dominant hypothesis that job insecurity is bad, for everything, always and everyone. The next part on "moving forward" hopefully provides some tools to create this depth.

MOVING FORWARD: A THEORY ELABORATION APPROACH

Theory elaboration is "about improving theories so that they more accurately account for and explain empirical observations" (Fisher & Aguinis, 2017, p. 441). Theory elaboration can be used for different purposes, including theory-borrowing. Here, we use theory elaboration in the context of theory-borrowing to improve how a specific theory (i.e., SET) is used in a specific field (i.e., job insecurity research). Doing so can advance job insecurity research in at least two ways. First, it could help to make sense of the strong basis of evidence that already exists, for example in explaining the variation in strengths in relationships or inconsistencies across studies. Second, it could also help to align theory and methods by tailoring designs and analyses to theoretical assumptions. Fisher and Aguinis (2017) describe three broad approaches to theory elaboration: structuring, contrasting and construct specification. Each approach comes with specific tactics. We will discuss those approaches and a selection of tactics and how they can be used to advance the job insecurity research below (see Figure 3.2). This should be seen as illustrations, among many other potential routes for theory elaboration.

Approach One: Structuring

Structuring means elaborating on potential theoretical relationships. Tactics to do so are adding recursive structures and sequencing. Those tactics have resonance for job insecurity research inspired by SET. Studies to date often focus on a specific chunk within a series of interactions, and this chunk is unidirectional.

Adding recursive structure
This form of theory elaboration goes beyond the cause–effect relationships in current job insecurity research. It connects repeated interactions – the isolated chunks – over time in the form of feedback loops so that ultimately cause and effect are difficult to disentangle. Feedback loops may have different loading, positive and negative, and job insecurity carries different meaning, depending on this loading. Positively reinforcing cycles are at the core of SET through backward- and forward-looking exchanges. Job insecurity here is a disruptive event: it may temporarily slow down the cycle until job security is restored or it could put a hold on otherwise infinite feedback loops. Negatively reinforcing feedback loops are at the core of current job insecurity research. They are often assumed, not so much in studies inspired by SET but more so in studies inspired by COR through the notion of loss spirals. Job insecurity in those studies is seen as a trigger for poorer attitudes and behaviour, which then could lead to even more insecurity and so on, up to the point that an event (e.g., being laid off, leaving the organisation) breaks the cycle. Those negatively reinforcing feedback loops are not so often tested though. If so, tests take the form of mere "reversed causation" (e.g., Fischmann et al., 2018) as a proxy for feedback loops over time (see "vertical contrasting" for more detail on method).

Sequencing
This approach means adding explanations of a specific sequence of events. This brings context to the exchange relationship. Context here should be understood as a view on the history of the exchange relationship and how (through which mechanisms) this exchange relationship develops and is constructed and reconstructed. Consider the example of a long-term relational exchange relationship: employees who pick up first signals of job insecurity may not immediately "blame" the employer, but attribute insecurity to other factors, such as economic recession. This may mean that they do not readily retaliate to the employer. First evidence supports this view. Wong et al.

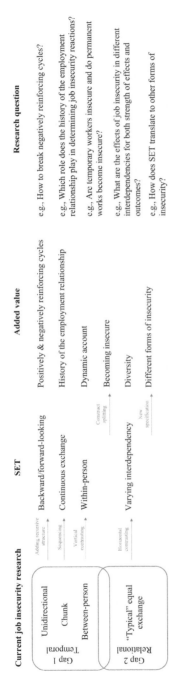

Figure 3.2   Theory elaboration in job insecurity research

(2005) demonstrate that the relationship between job insecurity and extra-role behaviour is not significant in employment relationships characterised by trust, but negative otherwise. In a similar vein, Huang et al. (2017) find that the relationship between job insecurity and both turnover intention and organisational deviance is not significant under the condition of high leader-member exchange (LMX) but positive otherwise. Trust and LMX in those studies bring history to the employment relationship and explains their reactions.

The takeaway message for job insecurity research then is twofold. First, adding recursive structures leads to a richer understanding of the role of job insecurity depending on whether feedback loops are positive or negative. Job insecurity intervenes in positively reinforcing feedback loops, and it can be both cause and effect in negatively reinforcing feedback loops. So far, positive feedback loops have received comparatively little attention, though those are central in SET. Second, sequencing helps to contextualise the employment relationship through adding history and interpretation.

Approach Two: Contrasting

Contrasting in theory elaboration terms concerns applying the theory in different settings, either on different levels of analysis or in different contexts. Different levels of analysis refer to the tactic of vertical contrasting; this is particularly relevant for job insecurity research which has mostly taken the between-person level, or in any case failed to disentangle the between and the within-person level. Adding a within-person level could push a more dynamic view. Horizontal contrasting refers to different contexts and may make researchers aware of the (implicit) focus upon equal exchanges and standard employment relationships. This could push a more diverse view on the impact of job insecurity.

Vertical contrasting
This concerns different levels of analysis, often along with different tests and designs. In terms of unit of analysis, most SET-based job insecurity studies to date are at the between-person level. One compares the level of job insecurity between persons (e.g., employee A is more insecure than person B) and connects those to levels of social exchange perceptions (e.g., person A experiences more psychological breach than person B) and outcomes (person A is less committed than person B). This is not an accurate test of SET: SET describes a within-person process over time. Employee A evaluates the actions of the other party (e.g., employee A is more insecure than usual) and reciprocates based on this evaluation (e.g., employee A is less committed than usual), and so on (Cropanzano et al., 2017). The problem with job insecurity research is

not that hypotheses are wrong – one often assumes within-person processes – the problem is that hypotheses and tests are not aligned.

In terms of methods, aligning hypotheses and methods requires a view on individual processes and the way in which job insecurity and the employment relationship have evolved over time. This can be achieved through qualitative and quantitative designs. Qualitative research designs may lead to employee narratives that account for both past and future expectations. There have been repeated calls for more qualitative designs to probe into the variety of reactions to job insecurity (Bartunek & Seo, 2002), yet so far without much follow-up. Quantitative research designs need to follow up persons to probe intra-individual changes over time. This obviously shows the limits of cross-sectional job insecurity studies, yet it also begets a different way of thinking about longitudinal studies. Most longitudinal job insecurity studies use a general cross-lagged panel design. In doing so, they cannot disentangle between-person and within-person variance and this could lead to erroneous conclusions (Hamaker et al., 2015). A more accurate test accounts for within-individual processes. SET studies doing so are, however, few (for an exception, see Bernhard-Oettel et al., 2020). This is certainly not due to a lack of available methods. Without aiming to be exhaustive, we see much potential in the use of random-intercept cross-lagged panel models (see De Cuyper et al., 2021, for a job insecurity study; Hamaker et al., 2015; RICLPM), growth curve modelling (Wickrama et al., 2016) and growth mixture modelling (Wickrama et al., 2016). Such methods allow better alignment between theory and methods – many psychological theories concern within-person processes – and more complex questions. For example, an intriguing question is whether and how *changes* in job insecurity relate to *changes* in reciprocity deficit and *changes* in attitudes and behaviour. Another question could be whether and how exchange relationships develop over time and how this affects employee's reactions to job insecurity. A plausible assumption is that employees are more forgiving towards their organisation when job insecurity is a one-time deviation compared to when it is part of an unpredictable series.

In terms of design, one needs to invest in data collection over multiple waves with specific attention for time lags. The number of waves is dependent upon the specific research question, yet at least three – or ideally four – waves are necessary for most of the more complex analytical strategies. Time lags in current research are often based on what has been done previously and what seemed "to work", yet this may need a stronger theoretical rationale. For example, when examining changes in job insecurity along with changes in the employment relationships, longer time lags may be necessary. When examining how an abrupt change in job insecurity affects employee reactions, shorter time lags may be suitable. Note that we are very much aware that following up on individuals for a longer time and with higher frequency is challenging and may require a trade-off between practicability and theory.

Horizontal contrasting

This form of contrasting concerns an account of different contexts, with a focus upon contexts that are not typically considered when testing the theory. Different contexts could concern varying industry, organisational or geographic contexts. It could also touch upon the observation that job insecurity research has not often considered exchange relationships that are unequal: instrumental or investing exchange. Adding this SET piece may lead to a richer account of the impact of job insecurity.

Under instrumental exchange, employees are in a powerful position when the employer is dependent but not vice versa. Those employees may react quite strongly to job insecurity in a way that hurts the organisation. The reason is that they have inflated expectations from the employer because they are "worth it", and because they can easily replicate their deal elsewhere. Job insecurity then becomes betrayal and a signal of devaluation. In support of this view, employees who feel more employable are more inclined to leave and to lash out to the organisation (e.g., Huang et al., 2017): employability is an indicator of employee independence.

Under investing exchange, the employee is in a precarious position. The employee may not have many options to react, as it could readily back-fire: poorer attitudes or poorer performance give the employer the final push to dismissal. Accordingly, the employee may not do much, or in any case not much that is visible (e.g., reduced voice), or may instead engage in overcompensation. Shoss (2017) describes very similar dynamics under the notion of "economic vulnerabilities", she refers to earlier studies which show that those employees become strained. She furthermore speculates that those workers may be motivated to work harder in view of job preservation, but ultimately fail and do not do much because they are exhausted or do not have the right set of skills. Sora et al. (2010) provide supporting evidence; job insecurity associates with negative outcomes (lower organisational commitment and higher turnover intention), but particularly among employees who feel dependent (i.e., high financial strain or lack of alternatives). The authors thought this finding was unexpected; they had hypothesised stronger effects for those who are less dependent, yet the results make sense from the perspective of SET.

The takeaway message from vertical contrasting is that SET, like many theories in organisational and applied social sciences, calls for a dynamic approach, but is seldomly analysed in this way (see Ployhart & Vandenberg, 2010, for a general discussion).

The takeaway message from horizontal contrasting is that embracing the diversity in employment relationships may help to understand how job insecurity may have different effects, both in strength and type of outcomes and that those effects should be understood through different mechanisms.

Approach Three: Construct Specification

Construct specification brings more accuracy to the construct, here job insecurity. This too has resonance in job insecurity research. The review by Shoss (2017) and the work by Probst et al. (Chapter 4, this volume) shows that there is an ongoing conceptual debate. Construct splitting could help to add accuracy.

Construct splitting

This means adding detail to existing constructs. This has been done in job insecurity research by using the distinction between quantitative and qualitative job insecurity (Shoss, 2017), also from the viewpoint of SET (e.g., Fischmann et al., 2018). An obvious question then is what affects the exchange relationships most. A stronger account of SET could add more detail. For example, a plausible assumption is that quantitative job insecurity may quickly convert a positive feedback loop into a negative one, while the process is slower when qualitative job insecurity is concerned.

Yet, SET may also point to another splitting, namely between being insecure and becoming insecure. Job insecurity research to date has focussed, implicitly so through the between-person level, upon "being insecure". SET is about "becoming insecure". Being insecure is static, for example, temporary employees are more insecure than permanent employees. Becoming insecure is more dynamic and concerns a change in one's average level of insecurity. This aligns with SET: SET is basically about how a perceived change in the employment relationship shapes further changes; for example, when an employee becomes insecure, this may trigger downward reactions. This ties in with the methodological discussion under vertical contrasting. In short, construct splitting helps to see that being insecure is different from becoming insecure, and that theories may concern either one or the other, but seldom both at the same time.

DISCUSSION

This chapter was written out of concern for theory-borrowing in job insecurity research. We illustrated our point using SET and pointed at two gaps in current research, namely temporal and relational dynamics. We then showed how theory elaboration tactics can help to flesh out theory for use in job insecurity research and to align theory and methods. This is not just a thought experiment or a call for increasingly more advanced analyses and more challenging designs, though this will certainly be the implication for most studies. It is in the first place meant to move job insecurity forward, also in terms of research questions: the more advanced analyses and more challenging designs should deliver the goods.

Consider the following research questions by way of illustration (and certainly not as an exhaustive list; see Figure 3.2 for an overview). First, SET is built around forward- and backward-looking dynamics that together create positively or negatively reinforcing cycles. Job insecurity may intuitively appear as part of a negatively reinforcing cycle, as that is also how it is used in most job insecurity studies. A follow-up question is: How to break this negative cycle? This has received some but not systematic attention. Going one step further, job insecurity may also intervene in positively reinforcing cycles. For example, the employer may invest in training in exchange for employee commitment, and commitment may trigger further investments. Job insecurity could break this cycle. Job insecure employees may no longer feel that commitment is needed and instead see training as a way to market themselves. An interesting question then is at which point positively reinforcing cycles turn into negative ones: What is the tipping point? Second, SET is about continuous exchange, not about "chunks" of exchanges. This means that one needs to place the ongoing exchange within the broader context and history of the employment relationship. This leads to follow-up questions such as: How does the history of the employment relationship affect employees' perceptions of and reactions to job insecurity? Is there perhaps a different "tipping point" depending on such history? Third, the between (i.e., current practice in job insecurity research) vs within (i.e., the SET perspective) person approach instigates conceptual debate: What does it mean to "be" insecure? Are temporary workers insecure and do permanent workers become insecure? And if so, how to compare their experiences and reactions? Finally, SET concerns a variety of interdependencies. Perhaps the most pressing issues here are: What are the effects of job insecurity in different interdependencies in terms of both strength of effects and outcomes? And how to explain those reactions? Bringing in a temporal perspective may lead to even more challenging questions: How do interdependencies change under feelings of job insecurity?

A potential criticism could be that we illustrated our point – theory-borrowing in job insecurity is problematic and theory elaboration can push job insecurity in new directions – using one framework: SET. Yet, we feel confident that similar criticisms apply also for other theories that are often used in the job insecurity field. The reason is that most psychological theories concern within-person dynamics, but most studies apply a between-person design. Or else, the gap related to temporal dynamics and the need for vertical contrasting are not unique to SET. Similarly, theories are often tested based on WEIRD samples, leaving much opportunity for horizontal contrasting.

Another criticism could be that theory elaboration typically works the other way around: one starts from empirical observation and then adds more complexity ("elaborate") to the theory. What we did instead was show the complexity in the theory and then discuss what this could mean for job insecurity research. In a way, we "elaborated on" job insecurity research. This is an absolutely justified criticism. While not the aim of this chapter, we do think that job insecurity research can feed social exchange theory and hence that theory elaboration could be used in many different ways. For example, job insecurity research points at the existence of negatively reinforcing cycles that have not received much attention in SET (cf. "adding recursive structure"). As another example, a recent study highlighted national job insecurity (i.e., the perceived level of job insecurity in one's country; Shoss et al., 2022): national job insecurity was related to the perceptions that the country's government did not comply with their part of the deal. This seems to suggest that SET could also work for institutions that are not typically considered (cfr. "vertical contrasting"). A third example is that job insecurity may urge a more accurate conceptualisation of "social" and "exchange" in SET: job insecurity caused by an "unsocial" trigger (e.g., natural disaster causing the organisation to close) may not have the same effects. Similarly, scholars have recently invested in identifying other types of insecurity against the background of automation (Frey & Osborne, 2017, and the rise of the gig economy; Hamouche & Chabani, 2021; cfr. "construct specification"). Automation may give rise to *occupation insecurity* – the perceived fear that one's occupation may disappear or significantly change (Roll et al., 2022). In contrast to job insecurity, if the occupation is affected, employees cannot work in a similar job at a different organisation. While this without doubt affects the exchange relationship, it cannot be described in terms of interdependency: the employee may no longer feel or be part of the exchange. The gig economy is sometimes seen as a signal that jobs for life are becoming increasingly rare. While this is perhaps an overinterpretation – permanent employment is still the norm in many countries (OECD, 2022) – it does highlight the notion of *career insecurity*: "an individual's thoughts and worries that central content aspects of one's future career might possibly develop in an undesired manner" (Spurk et al., 2022, p. 253). Career insecurity may make the employee extremely dependent on the employer, yet it may also be the trigger for the employee to become more independent; this duality has been the topic of much of the contemporary career literature but is not touched upon in SET.

To conclude, the theory elaboration approach, whether used as we did to make current job insecurity even stronger or the other way around, shows that there are many avenues ahead for future generations of job insecurity scholars!

ACKNOWLEDGEMENTS

The contribution by Anahí Van Hootegem was supported by Research Foundation Flanders (FWO; 1176120N); the contribution by Lara C. Roll was supported by the European Union's Horizon 2020 research and Innovation Programme under the Marie Sklodowska-Curie grant (agreement no. 896341).

REFERENCES

Bartunek, J.M., & Seo, M.-G. (2002). Qualitative research can add new meanings to quantitative research. *Journal of Organizational Behavior, 23*(2), 237–242. https://doi.org/10.1002/job.132

Bernhard-Oettel, C., Eib, C., Griep, Y., & Leineweber, C. (2020). How do job insecurity and organizational justice relate to depressive symptoms and sleep difficulties: A multilevel study on immediate and prolonged effects in Swedish workers. *Applied Psychology: An International Review, 69*, 1271–1300. https://doi.org/10.1111/apps.12222

Cook, K.S., Cheshire, C., Rice, E.R.W., & Nakagawa, S. (2013). Social exchange theory. In J. Delamater & A. Wards (Eds.), *Handbook of social psychology. Handbooks of sociology and social research.* Springer, Dordrecht. https://doi.org/10.1007/978-94-007-6772-0_3

Cropanzano, R., & Mitchell, M. (2005). Social exchange theory: An interdisciplinary review. *Journal of Management, 31*(6), 874–900. https://doi.org/10.1177/0149206305279602

Cropanzano, R., Anthony, E., Daniels, S., & Hall, A. (2017). Social exchange theory: A critical review with theoretical remedies. *The Academy of Management Annals, 11*(1), 479–516. https://doi.org/10.5465/annals.2015.0099

De Cuyper, N., & De Witte, H. (2006). The impact of job insecurity and contract type on attitudes, well-being and behavioural reports: A psychological contract perspective. *Journal of Occupational and Organizational Psychology, 79*(3), 395–409. https://doi.org/10.1348/096317905X53660

De Cuyper, N., Mäkikangas, A., Kinnunen, U., Mauno, S., & De Witte, H. (2012). Cross-lagged associations between perceived external employability, job insecurity, and exhaustion: Testing gain and loss spirals according to conservation of resources theory. *Journal of Organizational Behavior, 33*(6), 770–788. https://doi.org/10.1002/job.1800

De Cuyper, N., Smet, K., & De Witte, H. (2021). I should learn to feel secure but I don't because I feel insecure: The relationship between qualitative job insecurity and work-related learning in the public sector. *Review of Public Personnel Administration, 42*(4), 760–785. https://doi.org/10.1177/0734371X211032391

de Jong, J., De Cuyper, N., De Witte, H., Silla, I., & Bernhard-Oettel, C. (2009). Motives for acceding temporary employment: A typology. *International Journal of Manpower, 30*(3), 237–252. https://doi.org/10.1108/01437720956745

Fischmann, G., De Witte, H., Sulea, C., & Iliescu, D. (2018) Qualitative job insecurity and in-role performance: A bidirectional longitudinal relationship? *European Journal of Work and Organizational Psychology, 27*(5), 603–615. https://doi.org/10.1080/1359432X.2018.1504769

Fisher, G., & Aguinis, H. (2017). Using theory elaboration to make theoretical advancements. *Organization Research Methods, 20*(3), 438–464. https://doi.org/10.1177/1094428116689707

Frey, C.B., & Osborne, M.A. (2017). The future of employment: How susceptible are jobs to computerisation? *Technological Forecasting and Social Change, 114*, 254–280. https://doi.org/10.1016/j.techfore.2016.08.019

Fugate, M., Van der Heijden, B., De Vos, A., Forrier, A., & De Cuyper, N. (2021). Is what's past prologue? A review and agenda for contemporary employability research. *Academy of Management Annals, 15*(1), 266–298. https://doi.org/10.5465/annals.2018.0171

Halbesleben, J.R.B., Neveu, U.-P., Paustian-Underdahl, S.C., & Westman, M. (2014). Getting to the "COR": Understanding the role of resources in conservation of resources theory. *Journal of Management, 40*(5), 1334–1364. https://doi.org/10.1177/0149206314527130

Hamaker, E.L., Kuiper, R.M., & Grasman, R.P.P.P. (2015). A critique of the cross-lagged panel model. *Psychological Methods, 20*(1), 102–116. https://doi.org/10.1037/a0038889

Hamouche, S., & Chabani, Z. (2021). COVID-19 and the new forms of employment relationship: Implications and insights for human resource development. *Industrial and Commercial Training, 53*(4), 366–379. https://doi.org/10.1108/ICT-11-2020-0112

Haynes, J., & Marshall, L. (2017). Reluctant entrepreneurs: Musicians and entrepreneurship in the "new" music industry. *The British Journal of Sociology, 69*(2), 459–482. https://doi.org/10.1111/1468-4446.12286

Hobfoll, S.E. (2001). The influence of culture, community, and the nested-self in the stress process: Advancing conservation of resources theory. *Applied Psychology: An International Review, 50*(3), 337–421. https://doi.org/10.1111/1464-0597.00062

Huang, G.H., Wellman, N., Ashford, S.J., Lee, C., & Wang, L. (2017). Deviance and exit: The organizational costs of job insecurity and moral disengagement. *Journal of Applied Psychology, 102*(1), 26–42. http://dx.doi.org/10.1037/apl0000158

Huang, G.H., Zhao, H.H., Niu, X.Y., Ashford, S.J., & Lee, C. (2013). Reducing job insecurity and increasing performance ratings: Does impression management matter? *Journal of Applied Psychology, 98*(5), 852–862. https://doi.org/10.1037/a0033151

Janssens, M., Sels, L., & Van Den Brande, I. (2003). Multiple types of psychological contracts: A six-cluster solution. *Human Relations, 56*(11), 1349–1378. https://doi.org/10.1177/00187267035611004

Kwon, K., & Jang, S. (2022). There is no good war for talent: A critical review of the literature on talent management. *Employee Relations, 44*(1), 94–120. https://doi.org/10.1108/ER-08-2020-0374

Lam, C.F., Liang, J., Ashford, S.J., & Lee, C. (2015). Job insecurity and organizational citizenship behavior: Exploring curvilinear and moderated relationships. *Journal of Applied Psychology, 100*(2), 499–510. https://doi.org/10.1037/a0038659

McGraw, A.P., Larsen, J.T., Kahneman, D., & Schkade, D. (2010). Comparing gains and losses. *Psychological Science, 21*(10), 1438–1445. https://doi.org/10.1177/0956797610381504

Neely, M.T. (2020). The portfolio ideal worker: Insecurity and inequality in the new economy. *Qualitative Sociology, 43*, 271–296. https://doi.org/10.1007/s11133-020-09444-1

OECD (2022). *OECD Labour Force Statistics 2021*. OECD Publishing, Paris. https://doi.org/10.1787/177e93b9-en

Piccoli, B., & De Witte, H. (2015). Job insecurity and emotional exhaustion: Testing psychological contract breach versus distributive injustice as indicators of lack of reciprocity. *Work & Stress, 29*(3), 246–263. https://doi.org/10.1080/02678373.2015.1075624

Piccoli, B., De Witte, H., & Reisel, W.D. (2017). Job insecurity and discretionary behaviors: Social exchange perspective versus group value model. *Scandinavian Journal of Psychology, 58*(1), 69–79. https://doi.org/10.1111/sjop.12340

Ployhart, R.E., & Vandenberg, R.J. (2010). Longitudinal research: The theory, design, and analysis of change. *Journal of Management, 36*(1), 94–120. https://doi.org/10.1177/0149206309352110

Roll, L.C., De Witte, H., & Wang, H.J. (2022). *Occupation insecurity: Scale development and validation* [Manuscript in preparation]. Department of Work, Organisational and Personnel Psychology, KU Leuven.

Shoss, M.K. (2017). Job insecurity: An integrative review and agenda for future research. *Journal of Management, 43*(6), 1911–1939. https://doi.org/10.1177/0149206317691574

Shoss, M.K., Van Hootegem, A., Selenko, E., & De Witte, H. (2022). The job insecurity of others: On the role of perceived national job insecurity during the COVID-19 pandemic. *Economic and Industrial Democracy (online first)*. https://doi.org/10.1177/0143831X221076176

Sora, B., Caballer, A., & Peiro, J.M. (2010). The consequences of job insecurity for employees: The moderator role of job dependence. *International Labour Review, 149*(1), 59–72. https://doi.org/10.1111/j.1564-913X.2010.00075.x

Spurk, D., Hofer, A., De Cuyper, N., De Witte, H., & Hirschi, A. (2022). Conceptualizing career insecurity: Toward a better understanding and measurement of a multidimensional construct. *Personnel Psychology, 75*(2), 253–294. https://doi.org/10.1111/peps.12493

Thaker, V., Jiang, L., & Xu, X. (2021). A test of competing theoretical models of meaningful work as a moderator in the curvilinear relationship between job insecurity and employee voice. *International Journal of Stress Management, 28*(3), 165–175. https://doi.org/10.1037/str0000229

Whetten, D.A., Felin, T., & King, B.G. (2009). The practice of theory borrowing in organizational studies: Current issues and future directions. *Journal of Management, 35*(3), 537–563. https://doi.org/10.1177/0149206308330556

Wickrama, K., Lee, T.K., Walker O'Neal, C., & Lorenz, F. (2016). *Higher order growth curves and mixture modeling with M-Plus. A practical guide* (1st ed.). Routledge, New York. https://doi.org/10.4324/9781315642741

Wong, Y.-T., Wong, C.-S., Ngo, H-Y., & Lui, H.-K. (2005). Different responses to job insecurity of Chinese workers in joint ventures and state-owned enterprises. *Human Relations, 58*(11), 1391–1418. https://doi.org/10.1177/0018726705060243

PART II

JOB INSECURITY AND PRECARIOUS
EMPLOYMENT: LOOKING AHEAD!

4. Is job insecurity still relevant? Unpacking the meaning of "job" and "insecurity" in today's economy

Tahira M. Probst, Eva Selenko, & Mindy Shoss

The only way to make sense out of change is to plunge into it, move with it, and join the dance.

(Alan W. Watts)

Modern industrial society is in decay (Casey, 1999; McGaughey, 2021). Social observers propose that we have entered an in-between state of post-industrialism, marked by increased automatization, integration and *informatization* of specialized jobs and an expansion of work into the service sector. In the workplace, these changes have been accompanied by organizational restructuring, workplace re-design, downsizing, and a handover of critical job functions to intelligent machines (Casey, 1999; Selenko et al., 2022). At the societal level, these developments are reflected in an erosion of social and employment protection securities, a dismantling of labour unions, and a rise in political populist movements (Kalleberg, 2009; Standing, 2011). Accompanying these changes has been the rise of the so-called "gig-economy", where work is often mediated and managed through online platforms (Kuhn, 2016) such as Uber, Upwork, Fiverr, and TaskRabbit, along with increasing numbers of workers whose income stems from freelancing, independent contracts, and self-employed services, businesses, and consulting. Such shifts away from more traditional forms of employment increase the risks of further precarization and offer even fewer employment protections, as well as lower pay and benefits, and rising income inequality (McGaughey, 2021; Spreitzer et al., 2017). In short, the age of the twentieth-century worker, with life-long employment in a single organization often under highly paternalistic management models, seems to be truly gone (Standing, 2011).

While noting these shifts in the nature of employment, we acknowledge that we lament this apparent loss from a position of privilege, as that idealized standard of "life-long employment in a single organization" has never been the normative employment relationship for many individuals around the globe.

Indeed, over 60 percent of the employed population globally earns a living via the informal economy and outside of the protections of formalized legal, tax, regulatory, and social insurance systems (International Labour Organization (ILO), 2018). Moreover, the percentage of those labouring in the informal economy are unequally distributed among developing (90 percent), emerging (67 percent), and developed (18 percent) economies.

Nevertheless, the rapidly changing context of work, particularly throughout the Global North, poses significant new questions regarding the nature of job insecurity, which has captured the attention of researchers for nearly five decades. In that time, the nature of what is meant by a "job" throughout much of the Global North has shifted (e.g., the rise in gig-economy workers, casual employment, and non-standard work arrangements) with concurrent implications for how we might best conceptualize "insecurity" in those jobs. Thus, in our chapter, we propose to describe some of the most prevalent employment arrangements (i.e., what do we mean by a "job"?) and unpack the meaning of "insecurity" across a range of modern employment contexts. In doing so, we ask: for whom, where and how is job insecurity a relevant stressor? For example, in times of increasingly informal and precarious work, are people constantly insecure? Or is precarity the "new normal", and, if so, how do people adapt? Or have employment contexts changed so fundamentally now that work is no longer the primary source of financial and psychological benefits of many people? Depending on the answers to these questions, what are their conceptual and methodological implications for the future of research on job insecurity? By considering these provocative questions, we hope to stimulate job insecurity research to "join the dance" and offer suggestions for adapting job insecurity research to address the changing meaning of "job" and "insecurity" in today's economy.

WHAT IS MEANT BY A JOB IN TODAY'S SOCIETY?

Approaches to Defining Standard and Non-Standard Forms of Employment

The traditional nine to five job working full-time and long term for a single employer – while still the dominant model of employment in industrialized countries (Bureau of Labor Statistics, 2018; International Labour Organization, 2015) – is increasingly being replaced and supplemented by non-standard employment arrangements, including freelancing, independent contracting, job sharing, and gig-economy work (Eurofound, 2015). Researchers who have been interested in studying the proliferation of these new forms of work have used varying approaches to defining and classifying non-standard employment

(Gig Economy Data Hub, 2022) with a focus on either: (1) the employment contract; (2) legal classifications; and/or (3) nature of the work itself.

Contractual approach. From a contractual perspective, this approach tends to focus on comparing standard workers earning a long-term wage or salary from a single employer to temporary or project-based workers. Such non-standard employment arrangements under this definition would include freelancers, contingent workers, temp agency workers, self-employed workers, and subcontracted work (Gig Economy Data Hub, 2022). In essence, any contractual arrangement that departs from the traditional standard employment relationship involving a long-term employer–employee contract would be considered atypical or non-standard.

Legal approach. From a legal perspective, many countries have specific classifications of income earners based upon the legally binding tax status, rights, and/or benefits afforded to them. For example, in the United States, there are legal distinctions between what constitutes an "employee" vs. a "worker". In the US, an "employee" is an individual who is contractually hired for the benefit of a specific employer that has discretion over how and when the employee does their job and pays the employee wages along with any required benefits, taxes, or other forms of compensation. Employees can be full- or part-time, temporary, seasonal, or "leased" (i.e., hired through a staffing agency but be on the employer's payroll) (e.g., Eurofound, 2017). On the other hand, a "worker" (often referred to as a "contingent worker" or "independent worker") is someone who has a non-permanent and non-employee relationship with a company (or customer), but rather is hired to do a specific task or duty, often part-time, temporary, seasonal, casual, self-employed. Such workers typically are non-salaried, file their own taxes, and are (in theory) in control over how, where, and when they perform their negotiated duties. Using this legal classification system, such workers include (among others) independent contractors, consultants, and freelancers, but also casual workers and seasonal workers (Eurofound, 2017). Other countries have different legal classifications, often using different terminology. For example, in the UK, the term "people in employment" is used. Moreover, there is a clear occupational/class connotation between the terms employee and worker: the term "employee" is often reserved for people in white collar work, while a worker would be a "blue collar worker" (e.g., a steel worker, a factory worker). In some European countries (e.g., Austria), there can be additional legal terms used to denote different occupations stemming from different insurance systems, political party affiliations, and so on. Clearly, from a research standpoint, these differing legal classifications pose challenges to conducting and comparing outcomes of individuals in non-standard vs. standard employment relationships.

The nature of the work approach. The third way in which researchers have emphasized standard vs. non-standard employment focuses on the nature of the work itself, rather than the contractual or legal distinctions noted above. Using this perspective, non-standard employment might be characterized by situations where the worker has discretion over the scheduling and tasks they complete, has flexibility of when, where, and how the work is completed, and lacks direct oversight from a supervisor (Gig Economy Data Hub, 2022). Under this approach, classifications are based more upon the way in which the work is organized rather than the employment contract, content of the work, or legal requirements.

The rise of gig work. A specific non-standard form of employment that has risen in recent years is work in the so-called gig-economy (or platform economy). In gig work, individuals typically use an electronic platform to manage their work relationships by hiring-out their skills, abilities, and talents to one or more businesses (or customers) simultaneously. Such an arrangement offers workers, at least in theory, the flexibility of setting their own work hours, level of workload, and accepting "gigs" of their choosing. However, research (e.g., Rosenblatt & Stark, 2016, in their case study of Uber drivers) suggests that these online platforms often exert imbalanced power differentials where the algorithms used by the online platform indirectly control the flow of work opportunities to the gig worker.

Overlapping employment arrangements. To add complexity, some individuals may be in standard and atypical employment at the same time – or somewhere in between. For example, individuals may have full-time traditional standard employment with an organization while also "moonlighting" to take on additional freelance jobs after hours. Similarly, there can be so-called "diversified" workers (Upwork, 2020) with multiple sources of income (e.g., part-time employment coupled with one or more gig jobs on the side). A Europe-wide mapping exercise conducted by Eurofound in 2015 identified nine different, completely new forms of employment across all member-states that fall outside the standard typical full-time employment: examples of that being employee sharing (where a worker is hired jointly by a group of employers, who are not a temporary work agency), job sharing (where two or more employees are hired to do the same job), and voucher-based work (where workers are paid by vouchers rather than through an employment contract). In all these cases, workers had an employment relationship somewhere between being employed and self-employed (Eurofound, 2015).

Is Non-standard Employment on the Rise? A Challenging Question and Critical Note

Given the myriad of different classifications and definitions of non-standard employment (e.g., contractual work arrangements, tax status, nature of work, mediated by online platforms, etc.), it is not surprising that estimates of the size of the non-standard workforce greatly vary. According to Gallup (2017), 36 percent of all workers in the United States were participating in non-standard arrangements as "self-employed" workers (i.e., obtaining income via some form other than the traditional employee–employer relationship). Similarly, estimates from the EU-15 (McKinsey, 2016) suggest that "independent" workers (defined as individuals who assemble various income streams outside of structured payroll jobs) make up approximately 20–30 percent of the working age population, with this percentage expected to increase over time. Over the next five years, some estimates (MBO Partners, 2020) suggest that a majority (54 percent) of the US adult labour force will be (or have been) independent workers.

While numerous estimates suggest that non-standard employment arrangements are on the rise, it is equally important to note that any discussion as to the occurrence and development of non-standard employment and new forms of employment runs the risk of overlooking the fact that what is considered as "standard" employment has been eroding in safety, employment protection and so on, as well. Also, the presumption that the life-long employment in a single organization with full employment protection would constitute the standard, comes from a position of privilege (Bapuji et al., 2020). In many places, this type of employment was never "standard". A large amount of work across the globe is performed outside of countries' formal legal systems, including tax, regulatory, and social insurance systems (International Labour Organization (ILO), 2013; ILO, n.d.). This informal economy captures a heterogenous variety of jobs, all of which "share a basic vulnerability, namely, their need to be self-supporting and to rely on 'informal' arrangements" (ILO, 2002; ILO, 2013, p. 4; ILO, n.d.). In some economies (e.g., India), the percentage of employment occurring outside of the formal sector averages around 80+ percent (Elgin et al., 2021). Thus, perhaps non-standard employment is actually the more standard employment globally. In that respect, rather than calling it non-standard work, perhaps we need to develop a new label for these contemporary, less protected forms of employment. Perhaps terms like "new standard work" or simply "insecure work" might be more appropriate to capture the unprotected, often unpredictable nature of employment throughout much of the world.

Additionally, while labour force statistics can capture the numbers of individuals in various standard and non-standard employment arrangements, such data does not capture what is the focus of job insecurity research, namely, how do such arrangements impact perceived job insecurity and perceptions of precarity?

What is the Meaning of "Insecurity" in Less Protected Forms of Employment?

Many of the new forms of employment discussed above come with unconventional places of work or work patterns, and irregular provision of work (Eurofound, 2015). While some non-standard forms of employment have a long history and tradition in some professions (e.g., independent doctors, lawyers, shopkeepers) and are not necessarily precarious by definition, there are certainly many forms of atypical employment situations (e.g., casual work, on-call manual work in blue collar professions) that pay too little, offer too much insecurity, and/or assign limited social status, which makes them precarious. Job precarity, according to some understandings (e.g., Creed et al., 2020), consists of a combination of unfavourable job conditions, high job insecurity, financial strain, and low flexibility to plan work. Below, we discuss in greater depth the implications of these new forms of work for research on job insecurity, as well as potential benefits of such non-standard employment arrangements.

Are There Benefits of Non-standard Employment?

It is important to acknowledge that there may be certain benefits to non-standard employment arrangements for individuals and companies. Individuals are increasingly pursuing non-standard forms of work due to enhanced flexibility to work the hours they want and in a location of their choosing. Greater autonomy and control over how they complete their work is also a potential advantage. Non-standard work can also act as a supplemental form of income to top up their income from other more standard sources. Moreover, non-standard work arrangements may allow for greater task and work variety than traditional standard jobs can offer. Finally, while digital platform work per se does not reduce social inequality, it can offer easier and quicker access to work (given the algorithm operates fairly) to those who face discrimination by hiring managers or lack the networks needed to earn money (Graham et al., 2017; Hoang et al., 2020).

Companies are increasingly relying on atypical and gig workers in an effort to reduce recruitment and training costs, save on benefits such as retirement, taxes, or health care coverage, and have more flexibility to scale their workforce up or down as needed (Kalleberg, 2009). Given these potential bottom-line benefits, not surprisingly, a recent report (Intuit, 2020) indicated that 80 percent of large corporations planned to increase their reliance on contingent workers (rather than traditional employees). However, one needs to be cautious that such arrangements are not a trap that makes it difficult for workers to attain good jobs, especially since an implication of this trend is that traditional full-time jobs with benefits will be harder to find. Indeed, even firms like Google, known for lavish benefits, employ more temp workers than full-time employees (Wakabayshi, 2019).

From a scholarly perspective on the topic of job insecurity, this raises the issue of how to best conceptualize and measure job insecurity given these increasing numbers and forms of employment relationships, as well as per-spectives that work in general – regardless of contract type – is increasingly insecure (Hollister, 2011). It also raises the question of how perceptions of job insecurity may vary as a function of these work arrangements. In part, this may depend on what drives workers into such arrangements.

Profiles of Non-standard Workers

A recent report by McKinsey and Company (2016) identified four distinct profiles of independent non-standard workers. The plurality (40 percent) were so-called "casual workers" who use independent work (e.g., via Amazon's Mechanical Turk, Etsy, or other digital or in-person means) as a preferred means to supplement the income derived from their primary employer. Pursuit of such independent work may be to fulfil personal interests or to provide additional income streams to facilitate their income goals. An additional 30 percent were classified as "free agents" who preferentially choose independent work which serves as their primary source of income (e.g., a self-employed electrician). However, a substantial proportion (16 percent) were "financially strapped" individuals who supplement their primary income out of necessity to make ends meet (e.g., a hospitality employee who housecleans on the weekends). Finally, 14 percent are classified as "reluctants" who report that independent work serves as their primary source of income but would prefer a traditional employment arrangement. Based on these classifications, impor-tant distinctions might be made regarding the preferred vs. non-preferred nature of these employment arrangements, as well as the extent to which workers rely on these forms of employment to meet their income needs and/or goals (i.e., primary vs. supplemental income).

Alternatively, it might be useful to instead identify profiles based on the type of non-standard occupation and the quality of the jobs offered by these income streams. For example, Hoang et al. (2020) found different profiles of non-standard workers for different platform economy jobs using a nationally representative US dataset. Notably, disadvantaged groups were less likely to participate in platform work in the first place, but if they did then they per-formed the kinds of platform work that were less beneficial to their economic development (e.g., cleaning, ride sharing). On the other hand, people who engaged in platform-based work to supplement their income tended to often be those in already good jobs and conducted qualitatively different types of platform work (e.g., selling stuff, renting a room or conducting online tasks).

Beyond these considerations, other elements such as the stability of working hours and income, the degree of coverage of employment rights, the degree of certainty around pensions and social security, as well as the access to training and career development are crucial factors that might determine whether non-standard employment will be precarious or not (Eurofound, 2017). Thus, below we delve further into the construct of "job insecurity" and try to answer what it means to be insecure in the context of this changing employment land-scape and the changing nature of jobs today.

HOW CAN WE RECONCEPTUALIZE JOB INSECURITY FOR CHANGED CONTEXTS OF WORK?

To answer this question, it is helpful to understand what we mean by "work" and what work in general means psychologically to people. In this chapter we take Warr's definition of work as an umbrella term that comprises of any kind of activity, that is conducted "…with a purpose beyond enjoyment of the activity itself" (Warr, 2007, p. 3). While this can also include unpaid types of activity, such as family care-work, house work, or volunteer work, for the purpose of this chapter we will primarily focus on paid forms of activities. Psychologically, these types of activities come with several types of important categories of experience for people: they grant access to people outside the private family, provide the opportunity to contribute to something bigger than what one would have achieved alone, structure time, automatically activate people, and may offer recognition and validation by others (e.g., Jahoda, 1982). Even if those experiences are not necessarily always positive, they are essential for human functioning. Work also provides one with a sense of identity, and understanding of who one is in relation to others (Hulin, 2002; Kalleberg, 2009) by providing membership to important groups, the ability to enact identity relevant behaviours and getting social recognition for it. The organization of work thus provides a mechanism through which society creates and reinforces status and distributes rewards (Dijk et al., 2019). As a result, work (via one's "job") shapes where people live, the social circles in which they interact, their financial means and opportunities, the day-to-day stressors of their lives, and so forth. A threat to one's job via job insecurity thus simul-taneously threatens many of these psychological benefits of work. Yet, these psychological benefits may not be tied to an organization or job per se in the context of newer non-standard forms of employment.

Research on job insecurity was in part propelled by Greenhalgh and Rosenblatt's (1984) seminal article appearing in *Academy of Management Review*. At the time, they defined job insecurity as "perceived powerlessness to maintain desired continuity in a threatened job situation" (p. 438). Since then, researchers have come to understand that job insecurity is an umbrella concept that contains multiple different dimensions, different definitions and conceptualizations. While there is still no unified conceptualization of job insecurity available (Probst, 2003; Shoss, 2017), there are some core threats of job insecurity that most job insecurity researchers acknowledge. These include the threat of potential loss (of either the job itself or features of the job) combined with the threat of uncertainty. Moreover, most present-day job insecurity research differentiates between *quantitative* job insecurity (fear of losing one's job) and *qualitative* job insecurity (fear of job quality deterioration) (Lee et al., 2018). In the classic job insecurity literature, the psychological impact of these threats of loss have been argued to be due to the importance of work for people as well as the fact that many benefits of work, both latent and manifest (e.g., identity, status, health insurance in the US), are tied to specific jobs (De Witte, 1999; Sverke et al., 2002).

However, given the changed nature of employment in post-industrialist societies and the rise of new non-standard employment arrangements, are these aspects still relevant? Should the construct of quantitative job insecurity be limited to a potential loss of a "job" or should it be expanded to include the potential loss of "work"? Similarly, might qualitative job insecurity researchers reconceptualize the deterioration of "job" features to refer to "work" features? In other words, in light of the proliferation of new non-standard forms of working, does it make sense to decouple work from job when considering how to expand or modify our conceptualization of "job insecurity"?

Given the psychological and material importance of work in societies across the globe, we argue that threats to current shapes of work*ing* – qualitatively or quantitatively, will continue to affect people. Thus, we argue that such insecurity (traditionally conceptualized as "job" insecurity) might be better understood as *work insecurity*. This is in line with prior work by Wickrama et al. (2018, p. 351) in which they defined work insecurity as "concerns about possible future termination or disruption of work and the associated threats and uncertainties." In using this definition, they deliberately noted that this was in line with a broader conceptualization of work which included both traditional salaried jobs and non-standard self-employment. This makes it distinct from existing, but closely related constructs, such as employability or career insecurity. Self-perceived employability describes people's belief in their ability to secure employment within and between organizations (e.g., Rothwell & Arnold, 2007), but does not capture the insecurity that might occur among individuals working outside of the bounds of employment within an organization. Work insecurity should also not to be confused with career insecurity (Spurk et al., 2022), which captures people's insecurity about multiple aspects of their career (including retirement, unemployment, career goals).

Atypical, non-standard employment rarely offers clear career-paths, let alone a longer-term perspective.

Expanding upon this and drawing from traditional job insecurity research conceptualizations, we can break down such work insecurity along the dimensions of: *quantitative work insecurity* (i.e., threats to one's opportunities for work) as well as *qualitative work feature instability* (i.e., threats that might lead to a deterioration of the qualitative features of one's work). Given the myriad different terminologies and types of non-standard work arrangements reviewed earlier, using the concepts of *work (in)security* (i.e., quantitative work insecurity) and *work feature (in)stability* (i.e., qualitative work insecurity) might help to better categorize and understand the diversity of threats people may experience with regard to the continuity and stability of their income-generating work, regardless of whether they hold a standard employment relationship, a non-standard one, or a mix of both. This conceptualization may also help link the work of psychology literature with other literatures focused on elements of work feature instability, such as research on work hours insecurity and zero hours contracts (Lambert et al., 2019).

In proposing the terms qualitative and quantitative *work* security, we acknowledge that quantitative and qualitative *job* insecurity will still hold relevance to workers in standard employment roles. Yet, by considering both the combination of patterns or profiles of quantitative and qualitative job and work insecurity, we might obtain a more comprehensive understanding of the overall precariousness of people's work, which in turn is likely to have implications for the wide range of outcomes of job insecurity.

For example, certain types of employment opportunities provide *work security* (due to an individual having high-demand knowledge, skills and abilities [KSAs], e.g., cybersecurity, nursing), whereas others, such as jobs requiring fewer KSAs where workers can be more easily replaced (e.g., fast food workers, mortgage brokers), might not. Consider that, early in the pandemic, grocery and food delivery workers were in high demand as cities were placed under lockdown and people were fearful of being exposed to the coronavirus. In that context, these gig workers may have had higher levels of quantitative work security (i.e., a stable and high flow of income-generating opportunities). Yet, as the pandemic has progressed and life has returned to a "new normal", demand for these workers has declined, resulting in less quantitative work security.

In certain types of income-earning roles, it might rather be the *work features* that might be at risk than the work continuity. This could include access to uniform safety standards, training, and personal protective equipment; rights against discrimination; access to fair wages; or sufficient work hours, which can vary within and across professions. While job insecurity researchers have accumulated a relatively large body of evidence on the deleterious effects of qualitative and quantitative job insecurity, workers in non-standard employment arrangements have arguably been left behind. Workers in non-standard employment (e.g., on-call workers, cash-in-hand workers), might not worry about the continuance of their work, but might still be concerned about a change in job features (e.g., working in the one factory might come with a better work environment than working in another). Among non-standard workers, the concept of work (continuance and features) insecurity hence might capture feelings of insecurity better than traditional concepts of job insecurity.

Gig-economy work in particular comes with insecurity of a very special kind: algorithmic insecurity (Wood & Lehdonvirta, 2021), which describes the fears that gig-economy workers experience as a result of working on an unstable and opaque platform that uses customer ratings and algorithms to allocate work (and income) to workers. In some cases, to respond to this insecurity, gig workers have banded together to show resistance by informally policing and self-monitoring their work task platforms. For example, Amazon's Mechanical Turk is an online crowdsourced platform where "requesters" outsource tasks to MTurk "workers". There is no required minimum wage for completion of the Human Intelligence Tasks (HITs) and many workers complete tasks and yet remain unpaid for various reasons. To ensure a minimum level of qualitative work security, MTurkers have created their own websites (e.g., TurkerView, Turkopticon) to identify Requesters and HITs that provide reasonable levels of work feature security. For example, Turkopticon advocates for MTurkers' rights by raising issues regarding account suspensions or poor Requesters to Amazon. TurkerView colour codes Requesters on MTurk according to their aggregated hourly pay range (based on actual task completion time and pay-outs) and provides MTurkers with real-time data regarding reviews of Requesters, approval rates, time to payment, and so on. While these sorts of platforms cannot raise the level of quantitative work security (i.e., increase the number of HITs available on the MTurk platform), they can increase the algorithmic work security of MTurkers by facilitating fair wages and connecting workers with high-quality Requesters. Similar efforts have been observed by workers in other countries and occupational sectors who founded their own unions to fight for better employment rights and protection (e.g., the Independent Workers Union of Great Britain).

As Peter Drucker famously noted, "What gets measured gets managed." Conversely, what cannot be measured cannot be studied. Therefore, in the section below, we consider how our proposed expanded conceptualization of (work and job) insecurity might impact our operationalization and measures currently in wide usage by job insecurity researchers. Only by modifying our existing measures of job security can we properly investigate the antecedents, consequences, mechanisms, and boundary conditions of insecurity prompted by today's unique non-standard forms of employment.

IMPLICATIONS FOR THE MEASUREMENT OF JOB INSECURITY

We believe that despite dramatic changes in employment contexts in post-industrial societies, the psychological experiences that come with work*ing* are of timeless importance to humans (e.g., Eisenberger et al., 2019), even if those activities are no longer called "employment" or "work" in the traditional sense. However, these changes in work and the rise of non-standard work likely necessitate a reconsideration of several aspects of job insecurity operationalizations and measurement to enable the field to capture how a broad variety of workers experience and respond to threats of loss or deterioration of their current working arrangements, whatever they may be.

For job insecurity researchers, this might mean that our definition of job insecurity should be expanded to avoid explicit or implicit assumptions regarding traditional standard forms of employment. For example, quantitative job insecurity might be reconceptualized as perceived instability or potential loss of one's regular or expected "income source(s)" as opposed to one's "job." Another alternative conceptualization might be drawn from the ILO's (2016) treatise on non-standard employment arrangements which refers to "the perceived risk of losing income-earning work." Thus, job insecurity scale items which ask about the "chances of losing one's job" might instead ask about losing one's "work," including perceived uncertainty of obtaining income-generating work tasks, duration of work for payment, amount and timing of work, and so on.

Similarly, while a definition of qualitative work insecurity might require little reconceptualization from qualitative job insecurity (i.e., perceived threat to valued work vs. valued job features), specific items on commonly used measures of qualitative job insecurity might be irrelevant to workers with non-traditional employment arrangements (e.g., "I worry that the values of the organization will change for the worse," Blotenberg & Richter, 2020; or "I worry about my career development in the organization," Hellgren et al., 1999). Instead, researchers might focus on valued job features independent of the source of those job features (i.e., the organization vs. independent forms of work). Many existing scale items could be easily re-worded (e.g., "I worry about my career development in this line of work" rather than "…in this organization"; "I feel insecure about the future content of my work tasks" rather than "…my job"). Of course, with the growing recognition that many jobs lack characteristics associated with decent work (ILO, 2002), perhaps the construct would be better conceptualized and operationalized in terms of deterioration rather than loss given that the latter assumes that one had positive work characteristics to begin with.

Once we have developed and validated scales to measure a broader conceptualization of qualitative and quantitative work insecurity, we can then more fully investigate the extent to which workers perceive the increasing instability of work and their work features, as well as how people understand, desire, and respond to various levels of job security.

FOR WHOM, WHERE, AND HOW IS JOB INSECURITY A RELEVANT STRESSOR?

In unpacking the nature and proliferation of different forms of "jobs" in today's economy, it is clear that the world of work appears highly fluid. Such uncertainty was accelerated by the pandemic when employees and workers were faced with abrupt qualitative changes in who they worked with, where they worked, what tools they had access to (or were required to learn to continue performing their work), and when they completed their work tasks. During that same time, significant quantitative changes occurred as the labour market whiplashed, for example, from a record pre-pandemic low of 3.6 percent unemployment in the US, to staggering job losses affecting nearly one fifth of the entire workforce, and back again to 3.6 percent in a mere two years. The pandemic aside, work is bound to change over the coming years due to increased computational abilities, which will replace, substitute and generate new tasks in almost any occupation (Brynjolfsson et al., 2018).

What is often overlooked is the fact that job losses, dramatic job changes and subsequent harms to workers are not evenly distributed within society. As with traditional conceptualizations of job insecurity, indications are that the most vulnerable and marginalized groups are perhaps most at risk of quantitative and qualitative work insecurity. Not surprisingly, within the US, 80 percent of the jobs lost were experienced by the lowest wage earners (Gould & Kandra, 2021). Moreover, already marginalized and vulnerable worker populations including Black and Hispanic women were among the hardest hit and slowest to recover from the pandemic. Also, digitalization and occupational change will not happen according to what is technologically or economically possible: but people with lower power in organizations – non-standard, contingent workers at the lower end of the power hierarchy – will be more affected (Wajcman, 2017).

On the opposite end of the spectrum are the millions of workers who weathered the pandemic-driven changes and came out on the other side demanding that increased flexibility, remote work options, and other work practices continue beyond the pandemic. The Great Resignation revealed that more workers were willing to quit their current jobs to obtain work and employment that meets their newly identified needs. At the same time, many self-employed, independent, and other non-standard workers reported more positive outcomes and higher levels of security and stability during the pandemic. Unfortunately, prognostications of an impending worldwide economic recession threaten to derail this progress (Gilchrist, 2022). This points to the importance of monitoring employees' work and job insecurity across the spectrum of workers, as well as the importance of considering quantitative and qualitative work insecurity in tandem.

Below we consider the experience of job insecurity among these two very divergent groups and workers, particularly in light of our updated conceptualization of job/work insecurity and the rise in non-standard employment arrangements.

The Marginalized, Powerless, Low Status Precarious Non-standard Workers

Workers in non-standard employment at the lower end of the occupational status hierarchy are likely to be more affected by job change and task replacement by digitalization, as well as eventual job loss (if enough tasks are replaced). This is because they tend to have less of a voice within organizations and in broader society due to their precarious status (Allan et al., 2021). It is hence likely that rather the task of a low-ranking clerk in an organization will be replaced by digitalization than the task of a high-ranking CEO, even if both tasks would be technically equally replaceable.

Non-standard workers at the lower end of the employment hierarchy will also be more threatened by potential unemployment (e.g., due to occupational change). Different from more privileged non-standard workers, many precarious cash-in-hand job workers, workers in the informal sector, or workers in countries or contexts without unemployment protection, simply cannot afford to lose their income. A job loss might force an immediate change of life. This was noticeable in developing economies during the pandemic – vulnerable Indian migrant workers had no alternative than to immediately return to their villages and subsistence farming in response to their loss of income (Khanna, 2020). A similar scenario might be imagined for a sudden change in occupational demand due to digitalization. In short, non-standard precarious workers are not only more greatly affected by employment change (due to less power), but will also more likely suffer worse consequences (due to less financial reserves).

The Bright Side of Non-standard Employment Arrangements: People who Prefer to Work On and Off

While we have primarily discussed the potential drawbacks of non-standard employment arrangements, some emerging data (McKinsey, 2016) suggests that individuals who preferentially choose those forms of work arrangements report being more satisfied and perceive more "stability" and "security" compared to traditional employees or non-standard workers who prefer standard employment. Part of the higher level of satisfaction among these workers was driven specifically by qualitative work features, such as being able to control the amount, price, timing, and content of their work tasks. Thus, while one might assume that non-standard work arrangements would be accompanied by more insecurity, this may not always be the case and can potentially be counteracted by the enhanced qualitative work features.

These early data comport with surveys conducted at the height of the pandemic (e.g., MBO Partners, 2020), which found that a majority of independent workers reported feeling more financially secure than they would in a traditional standard employment position. Similarly, research by Upwork (2020) found that over half of individuals in non-standard employment relationships would not return to traditional employment if it were offered to them. Notably, they cited career ownership, scheduling flexibility, ability to work remotely, and pursuit of meaningful work as key reasons.

A comparison of these two groups (marginalized precarious workers in an informal economy vs. voluntary non-standard workers seeking and finding higher qualitative work security) suggests that there may indeed be significant differences in for whom, where, and how job insecurity remains a relevant stressor. In particular, when unpacking the meaning and experience of insecurity among workers engaged in non-traditional forms of employment, it may be that the critical distinction is whether such employment arrangements have been voluntarily pursued (i.e., the free agents and casual workers) rather than accepted as a means of a last resort (i.e., the reluctants and financially strapped), whether they are well-paid, so that people can build up reserves, or just a precarious form of getting by, and whether they consist of high in demand, non-replaceable work tasks.

CONCLUDING THOUGHTS

In conclusion, work (and insecurity thereof) will continue to be of high relevance to individual workers, no matter what exactly their form of work looks like. We suggest that future job insecurity research might consider the use of work insecurity rather than job insecurity, to allow for the increase in non-standard work that has been predicted. The future brings new challenges to the lives of workers and organizations; in a way, change of work will always be a normal component of innovation and economic development. Therefore, it should be the call for work psychologists to ensure that our research into the causes, consequences, and processes involving these new forms of work also change and adapt as needed. We hope that the ideas set forth in this chapter help future researchers to make sense out of this change and join the dance.

REFERENCES

Allan, B. A., Autin, K. L., & Wilkins-Yel, K. G. (2021). Precarious work in the 21st century: A psychological perspective. *Journal of Vocational Behavior, 126*, 103491. https://doi.org/10.1016/j.jvb.2020.103491

Bapuji, H., Patel, C., Ertug, G., & Allen, D. G. (2020). Corona crisis and inequality: Why management research needs a societal turn. *Journal of Management, 46*(7), 1205–1222. https://doi.org/10.1177/0149206320925

Blotenberg, I., & Richter, A. (2020). Validation of the QJIM: A measure of qualitative job insecurity. *Work & Stress, 34*(4), 406–417. https://doi.org/10.1080/02678373.2020.1719553

Brynjolfsson, E., Mitchell, T., & Rock, D. (2018, May). What can machines learn, and what does it mean for occupations and the economy? *AEA Papers and Proceedings, 108*, 43–47.

Bureau of Labor Statistics. (2018, June 7). Contingent and alternative employment arrangements summary. *US Bureau of Labor Statistics.* Retrieved April 4, 2022 from https://www.bls.gov/news.release/conemp.nr0.htm

Casey, C. (1999). The changing contexts of work. In D. Boud (Ed.) *Understanding learning at work* (pp. 15–28). London: Routledge.

Creed, P. A., Hood, M., Selenko, E., & Bagley, L. (2020). The development and initial validation of a self-report job precariousness scale suitable for use with young adults who study and work. *Journal of Career Assessment, 28*(4), 636–654. https://doi.org/10.1177/1069072720920788

De Witte, H. (1999). Job insecurity and psychological well-being: Review of the literature and exploration of some unresolved issues. *European Journal of Work and Organizational Psychology, 8*(2), 155–177. https://doi.org/10.1080/135943299398302

Dijk, H. van, Kooij, D., Karanika-Murray, M., Vos, A. D., & Meyer, B. (2019). Meritocracy a myth? A multilevel perspective of how social inequality accumulates through work. *Organizational Psychology Review, 10*(3–4), 240–269. https://doi.org/10.1177/2041386620930063

Eisenberger, R., Rockstuhl, T., Shoss, M. K., Wen, X., & Dulebohn, J. (2019). Is the employee–organization relationship dying or thriving? A temporal meta-analysis. *Journal of Applied Psychology, 104*(8), 1036–1057. DOI: 10.1037/apl0000390

Elgin, C., Kose, M. A., Ohnsorge, F., & Yu, S. (2021). Understanding informality. CEPR Discussion Paper 16497. London, UK: Centre for Economic Policy Research.

Eurofound (2015). *New forms of employment.* Luxembourg: Publications Office of the European Union. Retrieved April 1, 2022 from https://www.eurofound.europa.eu/publications/report/2015/new-forms-of-employment

Eurofound (2017). *Aspects of non-standard employment in Europe*. Dublin: Eurofound. Retrieved April 1, 2022 from https://www.eurofound.europa.eu/publications/customised-report/2017/aspects-of-non-standard-employment-in-europe

Gallup (2017). The gig economy and alternative work arrangements. Retrieved April 1, 2022 from https://www.gallup.com/workplace/240878/gig-economy-paper-2018.aspx

Gig Economy Data Hub (2022). What is a gig worker? Retrieved May 27, 2022 from https://www.gigeconomydata.org/basics/what-gig-worker

Gilchrist, K. (May 24, 2022). Great Resignation? Why it's not a good idea to quit just before a possible recession. https://www.cnbc.com/2022/05/24/last-in-first-out-risks-of-joining-great-resignation-in-a-recession.html

Gould, E., & Kandra, J. (2021). Wages grew in 2020 because the bottom fell out of the low-wage labor market. Retrieved May 27, 2022 from https://www.epi.org/publication/state-of-working-america-wages-in-2020/

Graham, M., Hjorth, I., & Lehdonvirta, V. (2017). Digital labour and development: Impacts of global digital labour platforms and the gig economy on worker livelihoods. *Transfer: European Review of Labour and Research, 23*(2), 135–162. https://doi.org/10.1177/1024258916687250

Greenhalgh, L., & Rosenblatt, Z. (1984). Job insecurity: Toward conceptual clarity. *Academy of Management Review, 9*(3), 438–448. https://doi.org/10.2307/258284

Hellgren, J., Sverke, M., & Isaksson, K. (1999). A two-dimensional approach to job insecurity: Consequences for employee attitudes and well-being. *European Journal of Work and Organizational Psychology, 8*(2), 179–195. https://doi.org/10.1080/135943299398311

Hoang, L., Blank, G., & Quan-Haase, A. (2020). The winners and the losers of the platform economy: Who participates? *Information, Communication & Society, 23*(5), 681–700. https://doi.org/10.1080/1369118X.2020.1720771

Hollister, M. (2011). Employment stability in the US labor market: Rhetoric versus reality. *Annual Review of Sociology, 37*(1), 305–324. https://doi.org/10.1146/annurev-soc-081309- 150042

Hulin, C. L. (2002). Lessons from industrial and organizational psychology. In J. M. Brett & F. Drasgow (Eds.), *The psychology of work* (pp. 19–38). Hove: Psychology Press.

International Labour Office (2016). *Non-standard employment around the world: Understanding challenges, shaping prospects.* International Labour Office; Geneva.

International Labour Organization (n.d.). Indicator description: Informality. https://ilostat.ilo.org/resources/concepts-and-definitions/description-informality/

International Labour Organization (2002). Resolution concerning decent work and the informal economy. https://www.ilo.org/public/english/standards/relm/ilc/ilc90/pdf/pr-25res.pdf

International Labour Organization (2013). Measuring informality: A statistical manual on the informal sector and informal employment. https://www.ilo.org/wcmsp5/groups/public/---dgreports/---dcomm/---publ/documents/publication/wcms_222979.pdf

International Labour Organization (2015). Non-standard forms of employment. Retrieved April 4, 2022 from https://www.ilo.org/wcmsp5/groups/public/---ed_protect/---protrav/---travail/documents/meetingdocument/wcms_336934.pdf

International Labour Organization (2018). *Women and men in the informal economy: A statistical picture*, 3rd ed. Geneva: ILO.

Intuit (2020). Intuit 2020 report: Twenty trends that will shape the next decade. Retrieved April 1, 2022 from https://http-download.intuit.com/http.intuit/CMO/intuit/futureofsmallbusiness/intuit_2020_report.pdf

Jahoda, M. (1982) *Employment and unemployment: A social-psychological analysis.* Cambridge: Cambridge University Press.

Kalleberg, A. L. (2009). Precarious work, insecure workers: Employment relations in transition. *American Sociological Review, 74*(1), 1–22. https://doi.org/10.1177/000312240907400101

Khanna, A. (2020). Impact of migration of labour force due to global COVID-19 pandemic with reference to India. *Journal of Health Management, 22*(2), 181–191. https://doi.org/10.1177/0972063420935542

Kuhn, K. M. (2016). The rise of the "gig economy" and implications for understanding work and workers. *Industrial and Organizational Psychology, 9*(1), 157–162. https://doi.org/10.1017/iop.2015.129

Lambert, S. J., Henly, J. R., & Kim, J. (2019). Precarious work schedules as a source of economic insecurity and institutional distrust. *RSF: The Russell Sage Foundation Journal of the Social Sciences, 5*(4), 218–257.

Lee, C., Huang, G. H., & Ashford, S. J. (2018). Job insecurity and the changing workplace: Recent developments and the future trends in job insecurity research. *Annual Review of Organizational Psychology and Organizational Behavior, 5,* 335–359.

MBO Partners (2020). The state of independence in America 2020. Retrieved April 1, 2022 from https://info.mbopartners.com/rs/mbo/images/MBO_Partners_State_of_Independence_2020_Report.pdf

McGaughey, E. (2021). Will robots automate your job away? Full employment, basic income and economic democracy. *Industrial Law Journal, 51,* 511–559. https://doi.org/10.1093/indlaw/dwab010

McKinsey (2016). Independent work: Choice, necessity, and the gig economy. Retrieved April 1, 2022 from https://www.mckinsey.com/~/media/McKinsey/Featured%20Insights/Employment%20and%20Growth/Independent%20work%20Choice%20necessity%20and%20the%20gig%20economy/Independent-Work-Choice-necessity-and-the-gig-economy-Executive-Summary.ashx

Probst, T. M. (2003). Development and validation of the Job Security Index and the Job Security Satisfaction scale: A classical test theory and IRT approach. *Journal of Occupational and Organizational Psychology, 76*(4), 451–467. DOI:10.1348/096317903322591587

Rosenblatt, A., & Stark, L. (2016). Algorithmic labor and information asymmetries: A case study of Uber's drivers. *International Journal of Communication, 10,* 3758–3784. https://doi.org/10.2139/ssrn.2686227

Rothwell, A., & Arnold, J. (2007). Self-perceived employability: Development and validation of a scale. *Personnel Review, 36*(1), 23–41. https://doi.org/10.1108/00483480710716704

Selenko, E., Bankins, S., Shoss, M., Warburton, J., & Restubog, S. L. D. (2022). Artificial intelligence and the future of work: A functional-identity perspective. *Current Directions in Psychological Science, 31*(3), 272-279.

Shoss, M. K. (2017). Job insecurity: An integrative review and agenda for future research. *Journal of Management, 43*(6), 1911–1939. https://doi.org/10.1177/0149206317691574

Spreitzer, G. M., Cameron, L., & Garrett, L. (2017). Alternative work arrangements: Two images of the new world of work. *Annual Review of Organizational*

Psychology and Organizational Behavior, 4, 473–499. https://doi.org/10.1146/annurev-orgpsych-032516-113332

Spurk, D., Hofer, A., Hirschi, A., De Cuyper, N., & De Witte, H. (2022). Conceptualizing career insecurity: Toward a better understanding and measurement of a multidimensional construct. *Personnel Psychology, 75*(2), 253–294. https://doi.org/10.1111/peps.12493

Standing, G. (2011). *The precariat: The new dangerous class*. New York: Bloomsbury.

Sverke, M., Hellgren, J., & Näswall, K. (2002). No security: A meta-analysis and review of job insecurity and its consequences. *Journal of Occupational Health Psychology, 7*(3), 242–264. https://doi.org/10.1037/1076-8998.7.3.242

Upwork (2020). Freelance forward 2020. Retrieved April 1, 2022 from https://www.upwork.com/documents/freelance-forward-2020

Wajcman, J. (2017). Automation: Is it really different this time? *The British Journal of Sociology, 68*(1), 119–127. https://doi.org/10.1111/1468-4446.12239

Wakabayshi, D. (May 28, 2019). Google's shadow work force: Temps who outnumber full-time employees. *The New York Times.* https://www.nytimes.com/2019/05/28/technology/google-temp-workers.html

Warr, P. (2007). *Work, happiness, and unhappiness*. Mahwah: Erlbaum.

Wickrama, K., O'Neal, C. W., & Lorenz, F. O. (2018). The decade-long effect of work insecurity on husbands' and wives' midlife health mediated by anxiety: A dyadic analysis. *Journal of Occupational Health Psychology, 23*(3), 350–360. https://doi.org/10.1037/ocp0000084

Wood, A., & Lehdonvirta, V. (2021). Platform precarity: Surviving algorithmic insecurity in the gig economy. Available at *SSRN 3795375*.

5. Is there a future for research on job insecurity and the psychological contract in a changing world of work?

David Guest & Kerstin Isaksson

Some years ago, we had the privilege and pleasure of collaborating with Hans De Witte on the Psycones project (psychological contracts across employment situations). This was a European-funded study to explore the impact of temporary work compared with permanent employment on a range of employee outcomes in several European countries. At the heart of the study was an exploration of the relationship between types of employment contracts, the psychological contract and employee well-being, with the expectation that the psychological contract would have a mediating role in the relationship. The initial assumption was that those on temporary contracts would be disadvantaged and likely to report poorer outcomes. In the event, the results in all seven countries revealed that temporary workers reported higher well-being than permanent workers. This core finding contradicted the assumptions of economists and policy-makers and, indeed, of the trade unions that had been supportive of our research proposal. In our final report and in our main integrative publication (Guest et al., 2010) we offered a number of possible explanations for our findings. One of these concerned the different psychological contracts of permanent and temporary workers.

At the outset of the Psycones project it had been assumed that job insecurity would be a critical factor related to well-being. By its very nature, temporary work implies lower job security than permanent employment. Furthermore, meta-analyses (Cheng & Chan, 2008; Sverke et al., 2002) demonstrate a clear association between job insecurity and various indicators of poorer well-being. This finding has been confirmed in the more recent systematic review by De Witte et al. (2016) of longitudinal studies exploring the impact of job insecurity on worker well-being. Yet the temporary workers in our study, despite reporting somewhat higher levels of job insecurity, also reported a lower breach of the psychological contract and higher well-being than those in permanent and seemingly more secure jobs. We can begin to unpick the reasons for this unexpected result by analysing the nature of job insecurity and the psychological contract in contemporary employment and the relationship between these two variables.

Leaving aside for a moment the findings of the Psycones project, there are good reasons for reconsidering the role of both job insecurity and the psychological contract as well as the way we view these concepts. One of the major trends in the labour market in the twenty-first century has been the growth in new forms of employment, much of which can be viewed as insecure employment (Eurofound, 2018; Standing, 2011). Looking back 50 years, the typical worker was engaged in full-time permanent employment and even at the start of the twenty-first century had an average tenure of ten years or more (Rodrigues & Guest, 2010). Contemporary employment includes higher numbers of temporary, contract, part-time and self-employed workers. The digital platform economy is transforming the nature of employment and challenging the traditional view of both job security and the psychological contract as well as the relationship between them. A second reason to investigate this relationship is the changing psychological contract of permanent workers where a question is whether job security still has a role as a critical building block in the psychological contract. If a majority of workers are engaged in non-standard contracts of employment or in managing their own careers, what are the implications for the role of job insecurity and for its relationship to the psychological contract and employee well-being?

DEFINING OUR TERMS

Part of the explanation for the absence of a positive association between the seemingly insecure temporary employment and poorer well-being in the Psycones project can be found in the analysis of the meaning of job insecurity. For this, we can look to the expert on the subject – Hans De Witte – with his impressive list of publications dating back over several decades. An initial distinction can be made between objective and subjective job insecurity (De Witte & Näswall, 2003). Objective job insecurity concerns the probability of losing one's job and is likely to be higher among those in temporary employment. Subjective job insecurity concerns feeling insecure about the future of one's job even if the objective probability of losing it is low, and it is this definition that has dominated research by work and organizational psychologists. We would expect objective and subjective job insecurity to be quite highly correlated and there is evidence that especially where unemployment rates are higher (Ellonen & Natti, 2015) this is indeed the case. Nevertheless, the evidence also shows that the same objective situation can be viewed differently by different employees.

A second distinction in the analysis of job insecurity distinguishes between cognitive perception (I think I will lose my job) and affective perception (I fear losing valued aspects of my job) (Pienaar et al., 2013). This distinction is potentially important in distinguishing between those on permanent and temporary contracts. Temporary workers enter a contract knowing, cognitively, that they are likely to lose it before long and that it is inherently objectively insecure. It is only when it concerns them affectively that it potentially affects their well-being. People on permanent contracts have an expectation of long-term job security and therefore any cognitive or affective insecurity is more likely to have an impact on their well-being.

A third distinction described by De Witte et al. (2010) and previously by Ashford et al. (1989), has been drawn between quantitative and qualitative job insecurity where quantitative job insecurity concerns fear of losing a job whereas qualitative insecurity concerns fear of losing valued aspects of the job. For example, qualitative insecurity may be high due to concerns relating to the job such as a new boss or a change in technology, which can create a sense of insecurity about the future without necessarily implying job loss. The study by De Witte et al. (2010) confirmed that both had a negative association with subjective well-being, revealing that the negative impact of job insecurity can extend beyond fear of losing the job.

The conceptual work of Hans De Witte and his colleagues over the years highlights the potential complexity of the concept of job insecurity. In the Psycones project the distinction between temporary and permanent contracts provided an implicit indicator of objective job insecurity. In addition, the study used a standard measure of subjective job insecurity developed by De Witte (2000). Beyond that, we can speculate about the likely impact of temporary employment on these and other different dimensions of job insecurity in the Psycones project. First, looking at objective and subjective job insecurity where we do have the data, temporary workers are likely to have higher objective job insecurity since they have no permanent contracts. The results indicate that temporary workers also reported higher levels of subjective job insecurity which was the focus of the measure used in the study. Temporary workers will have a higher cognitive perception about the likelihood of ending their current employment but their affective perception of insecurity may be lower, especially if they have freely chosen to enter temporary employment, since they are less worried about their insecure employment status. We might expect that temporary workers report lower quantitative job insecurity reflected in fear of losing their job since they know on entering it that it is temporary. And because it is temporary, they are likely to invest less in the content of the job or in embedding themselves in the organization, resulting in lower qualitative job insecurity. When considering these various perspectives of job insecurity, much may depend on the duration of a temporary contract and there was some indication that those with longer fixed-term contracts began, over time, to develop attitudes closer to those of permanent employees, a finding also noted by Chambel and Sobral (2019).

The challenge of the Psycones project is that temporary workers reported higher subjective job insecurity and lower employability but also reported higher scores compared with permanent workers on eight different indicators of well-being, including lower anxiety; depression and irritation; lower sickness absence and presenteeism; better general health and higher job and life satisfaction. To take a specific example, temporary workers reported significantly higher job satisfaction than permanent workers, even after controlling, for many job characteristics as well as for job insecurity and employability. What this suggests is that among temporary workers, job insecurity matters less. While the temporary workers in the Psycones project were employed on several types of contracts such as fixed-term contracts, agency work and seasonal work, these differences had little impact on outcomes compared with the difference between workers with temporary and permanent contracts. On the other hand, motives for engaging in temporary work did have some impact within the temporary workers sample, especially with those who chose temporary employment or viewed it as a stepping stone to either full-time employment or better work displaying more positive outcomes than those who felt compelled to enter temporary employment because they had no other choice. Nevertheless, the findings still leave a puzzle since temporary workers reported higher job insecurity, lower employability but higher well-being, and the various meta-analyses suggest that this should result in lower well-being. To seek explanations, we can turn to the role of the psychological contract.

JOB INSECURITY AND THE PSYCHOLOGICAL CONTRACT

One of the interesting features noted by De Witte et al. (2016) in their systematic review of longitudinal studies of job insecurity and well-being is the relative lack of theory informing the various analyses, although they reported some focus on Jahoda's (1982) distinction between the manifest and latent functions of work, as well as some limited use of primary and secondary appraisal, conservation of resources theory and social exchange theory. A notable omission is the absence of any explicit reference to psychological contract theory.

Work and organizational psychologists have discussed the concept of the psychological contract over many decades. It was given a new lease of life by the work of Denise Rousseau (1995) who initially defined it as "individual beliefs, shaped by the organization regarding terms of an exchange agreement between the individual and their organization" (Rousseau, 1995, p. 9). This definition adopts an employee perspective on the grounds that you cannot anthropomorphize an organization into having a psychological contract. Set against this, the metaphor of a contract inevitably involves two parties and managers, who represent the organization, can have a psychological contract with their subordinates and operate, in effect, as agents of their organization. Indeed, Rousseau (2005, p. 81) modified her view to redefine a psychological contract as "individual belief systems held by workers and employers regarding their mutual obligations. Every employment relationship is subjectively understood and experienced by each participant – the employee, contractor, employee-manager". In the Psycones project we incorporated the psychological contract as the central pillar of our analytic framework and adopted a wider definition that facilitated the incorporation of an employer perspective viewing the psychological contract as "the perception of both parties to the employment relationship – organization and individual – of the reciprocal promises and obligations implied in that relationship" (Guest et al., 2010, p. 17).

In the Psycones project, we chose the psychological contract as the lens through which to analyse the impact of different types of employment contracts on well-being because there was evidence from previous research (De Cuyper et al., 2008; Guest, 2004) that permanent and temporary workers have different and varied expectations about the employment exchange and that these differences would colour their reactions, including their concerns about job insecurity and also their well-being and other outcomes. The choice was also influenced by reported changes in the human resource management (HRM) policies and practices of employers that have affected many employees and led to a continuing number of studies reporting reduced fairness or unfulfilled psychological contracts together with increased workloads as reasons for leaving jobs (Green et al., 2022; Leineweber et al., 2020).

The content of the psychological contract has been a major focus of research over many years (McLean Parks et al., 1998). A long-standing distinction exists between transactional and relational contracts. Transactional psychological contracts are primarily concerned with relatively short-term transactional exchanges, often about substantive issues such as rewards or working arrangements. In contrast, relational contracts are viewed as more long-term and concerned with establishing positive relations and opportunities for development. Allied to this, psychological contracts can be extensive and wide-ranging or narrow and specifically focussed. We would expect contracts of temporary workers to be more transactional and more narrowly focussed. The content of the psychological contract of traditional full-time employees is likely to include both transactional and relational components, including an implicit expectation and occasionally an explicit promise of job security (Costa & Neves, 2017).

The psychological contracts of permanent and temporary workers can be expected to differ in a number of ways that might affect their outcomes.

Because the psychological contracts of temporary workers are more trans-actional and more limited, they are also easier to monitor than the more qualitative relational features found in permanent contracts. As a result, as we found in the Psycones project, they are less likely to be breached or violated. The findings also revealed that the extent to which the psychological contract was fulfilled or breached was an important mediator of the relation between the type of employment contract and outcomes such as well-being, which helps to explain the higher well-being among temporary workers. The results also confirm that the content of the psychological contract is less important than whether the perceived promises are kept. Under these circumstances, job insecurity ceased to be a particularly relevant variable. This raises the question of whether the Psycones project is a sign of things to come and whether we can expect the Psycones findings to be replicated and the influence of job insecurity on well-being to decline as the various forms of contingent work expand.

THE CHANGING NATURE OF EMPLOYMENT: IMPLICATIONS FOR JOB INSECURITY AND THE PSYCHOLOGICAL CONTRACT

A feature of the twenty-first century has been the decline of the traditional standard full-time permanent job with its promise of long-term job security. Standing (2011) has charted what he terms the growth of the "precariat", those working on non-standard contracts. Although the traditional form of employment still dominates the labour market (see Probst et al., Chapter 4, this volume, for a discussion on standard vs non-standard employment), it is the growth of non-standard forms of employment that have been attracting attention. OECD statistics (OECD, 2022) and Eurofound surveys (Eurofound, 2018, 2019, 2021) have charted a growth in all atypical forms of employment in Europe in the decade to 2020, a trend that is expected to continue following some disruptions caused by Covid-19. Figures for the European Union show that in 2020 an average of 14 per cent of workers had temporary contracts, 15 per cent were self-employed and 15 per cent worked part-time (OECD, 2022). The Netherlands provides an extreme example within Europe with 18 per cent working on temporary contracts, 17 per cent self-employed and 37 per cent working part-time. These figures confirm that a sizeable minority of the work-force within Europe are working on non-standard contracts. Kalleberg (2012) and others have pointed out that not all non-standard work is precarious. For example, part-time workers can have permanent contracts. However, all forms of non-standard work seem to be growing in many economies, justifying the call for specific attention to be given to the roles of job insecurity and the psychological contract for this growing part of the workforce.

Perhaps the extreme example of new forms of precarious employment is platform-based work in what has been termed "the gig economy" (see, e.g., Duggan et al., 2020). It is illustrated by firms such as Uber and Deliveroo, but extends to other forms of activity represented by platforms such as Mechanical Turk and Freelancer. For gig workers, interaction with the organization is mediated by an algorithm. Duggan et al. (2020) define algorithmic management as "a system of control where self-learning algorithms are given the responsibility for making and executing decisions affecting labour, thereby limiting human involvement and oversight of the labour process" (2020, p. 119). Platform-based work has been growing rapidly, with the International Labour Organization (ILO) (2021) outlining how the number of employment-related platforms expanded over the decade to 2020, and this growth is expected to accelerate. Sharma (2022) claims that 35 per cent of the US workforce are engaged in or closely affected by the gig economy, while in India an estimated 58 per cent of new jobs can be found in the gig economy. However, in Europe, the proportion of gig workers within the contingent workforce should not be overstated. In Eurofound and other surveys, it accounted for between one to two per cent of the working population although a much higher proportion, including, for example, students, had some experience of this type of work. Furthermore, some countries such as the UK report considerably higher figures. Cropanzano et al. (2023), who adopt a very broad definition of gig work, suggest that it is characterized by contract length (short), compensation structure (piecework) and organizational membership (absent). It therefore serves as an example of work in which there is no pretence of any job security. In other words, job security/insecurity has been taken out of the "employment" relationship. One implication is that although it is an extreme form, it shares with many other forms of atypical work an acceptance that there is no job security. This extends to much casual and temporary employment as well as self-employment. We might also argue that in these contexts, there is, at best, only a very limited psychological contract.

The role of job security may also have been declining among those in traditional full-time, permanent jobs. This has been highlighted in the separate body of literature that initially appeared in the 1990s, signalling the advent of the boundaryless career (Arthur & Rousseau, 1996). It was based on the premise that employers could no longer guarantee the promise of a secure job for life. It was reinforced by the belief that many professional and managerial workers wanted to manage their own career rather than have it controlled by their employer. They have therefore been abandoning the traditional psychological contract of a long-term secure career in return for loyalty to an organization. Instead, they prefer to manage their own careers and career development, the so-called protean career (Hall, 2004) and focus on maintaining their employability. While some workers may be happy to operate in this new boundaryless world, others can see it as more of a challenge. In this context, it is interesting that Hans De Witte and colleagues have identified career insecurity among these workers as increasingly salient and perhaps more salient than job insecurity (Spurk et al., 2022).

The extent to which careers have become boundaryless has been challenged (Rodrigues & Guest, 2010), based on evidence that the average tenure across several countries has hardly changed over three decades. Nevertheless, there are reasons to believe that the erosion of the long-term exchange in the traditional career is gathering pace. For example, research in the Swedish public sector has shown that large numbers of social workers on permanent contracts reported an erosion of trust in their employer to look after their best interests (Welander et al., 2017). This resulted in increased voluntary turnover and a search for new jobs as the only way to improve working conditions and to get a higher salary. Examples like this support indications that the weight given to the traditional concept of job security allied to an internal organizational career may be weakening due to changing organizational policies and practices and to growing career self-management. This trend may have been reinforced by the experience of Covid-19. Time spent away from the main workplace provided the opportunity to reassess careers and it was followed by what has been termed "the great resignation" (Tessema et al., 2022), implying a willingness to take personal control of careers and reflected in increased mobility across employers, across forms of employment and even out of employment.

Gig work also has interesting implications for the psychological contract. Indeed, it might be argued that since there is no traditional employment contract, there is no psychological contract. Furthermore, as those workers interviewed by Duggan et al. (2021) discovered, it is difficult to develop a psychological contract with an algorithm that represents the organization. Rousseau (1995), in justifying her focus on the employee perspective on the psychological contract, had argued that you cannot anthropomorphize an organization; it is even more difficult to anthropomorphize an algorithm which serves as an inhuman agent of the organization.

The role of the algorithm reinforces a belief that gig workers can no longer have a psychological contract based on some notion of reciprocal exchange. However, this view has been challenged. Shanahan and Smith (2021) used participant observation and interviews with food delivery workers to explore power relationships in gig work and their implications for the psychological contract. As they note, there is an implicit exchange in the relationship with autonomy for the workers in exchange for market flexibility for the organization. They show that workers form expectations about the work that evolves into a transactional contract with implicit promises. These expectations can derive from organizational information, any stated policies, the media, from other gig workers and from their own experience. The problem, they found, was that these implicit promises concerning issues such as pay rates, work demands and autonomy about when to work, were readily changed by the algorithm. Any unwillingness to go along with these changes could result in punishments such as reduced access to work or arbitrary dismissal. In psychological contract terms, there was regular violation of the psychological contract by the organization/algorithm and an absence of any norm of reciprocity (Gouldner, 1960) and certainly no social exchange (Blau, 1964; Coyle-Shapiro & Conway, 2004). In practice, workers had a one-way psychological contract with an algorithm. Objections to changes were hard to make since they were mediated by the algorithms, and Shanahan and Smith (2021) note the importance of "non-decision-making power" in the form of the absence of any response. Workers' reactions to perceived violations ranged across exit, voice and loyalty, with voice expressed through usually ineffective complaints and loyalty reflected in extensive emotional rationalization about continuing with the work. Duggan et al. (2020), who agree that gig workers have a form of one-sided psychological contract, characterize this experience as management by algorithm, noting that the traditional tyranny of the clock that characterized the old Tayloristic scientific management has been replaced by the tyranny of the algorithm. If the psychological contracts of temporary workers are restricted and largely transactional, then those of gig workers, if they can be said to exist at all, are even more limited.

While gig-working provides an extreme example of the use of algorithms in employment, Meijerink and Keegan (2019) note that algorithms are increasingly used to address HRM issues. This seems likely to affect the nature of the two-way interaction within the psychological contract of many workers in more conventional employment, and their use may extend to other forms of temporary employment beyond the more extreme example of gig work. It also raises questions of fairness of treatment if algorithms influencing HR systems develop self-learning biases that might, for example, come to influence selection decisions (Meijerink et al., 2021).

If there are no longer expectations of job security for the sizeable proportion of the working population engaged in various forms of temporary or self-employment, what are the implications for research on job insecurity? Has the promise of job security disappeared from the content of their psychological contracts? Were the findings about the temporary workers in the Psycones project a harbinger of things to come? If a new generation of workers is emerging with few expectations about job security and an assumption that they have to manage their own careers, any link between job security and well-being may disappear. Of course, gig workers, like other types of temporary workers, may feel insecure for reasons other than their employment relationship, notably due to economic insecurity, and may also have low well-being for a variety of reasons. Here, the distinction between cognitive and affective job insecurity may become important. Gig workers, like many temporary workers know, cognitively, that their work is insecure but most do not have strong affective concerns about this insecurity to the extent that it affects their well-being. There appears to be a case in the contemporary world of work and employment for reconsidering the role of job (in)security and its relevance for the psychological contract and, indeed, for worker well-being.

IMPLICATIONS FOR THE FUTURE RELATIONSHIP BETWEEN JOB INSECURITY AND THE PSYCHOLOGICAL CONTRACT

The relationship between job insecurity, notably fear of losing the job, and reduced well-being among workers on permanent employment is well-established (De Witte et al., 2016). However, as De Cuyper et al. (2015) among others note, "felt job insecurity is conditional on having a job; thus felt job insecurity is studied among the employed" (p. 163). This presents a challenge for the study of insecurity and its consequences among those who are not employed (see also Probst et al., Chapter 4, this volume). As the Psycones project and other studies of those employed on temporary contracts have shown, the findings about the consequences of job insecurity that apply to those in traditional permanent jobs do not seem to apply in the same way for temporary workers. When it comes to those who are self-employed, and this includes most gig workers as well as a growing proportion of the overall workforce, we need to consider different aspects of security. This is important because many of the self-employed may feel insecure. This may take the form of contract insecurity – will they be able to obtain future contracts? It could also be manifested in development insecurity – will they be able to update their knowledge and skills to remain attractive as contractors? And it can take the form of financial insecurity related to uncertainty about future income streams.

Concerns about the different forms of insecurity were raised in Barley and Kunda's (2004) study of independent contract workers in the US and seems likely to be pervasive among such workers. Murgia and Pulignano (2021) in their study of self-employed workers in Italy note that insecurity is experienced in the forms of lack of social and sometimes legal protection, and felt a need to work in ways that extend working hours and blur boundaries between work and life outside work threatening work–life balance. This takes us away from the traditional study of job insecurity towards the study of work-related insecurity, notably in the expanding world of new forms of work such as gig work and self-employment. This indicates that we need to reconceptualize the meaning of insecurity, looking beyond job insecurity, which will open up a rich research agenda exploring the relationship between forms of work, forms of (in)security and well-being. One of the features of the rapidly changing world of work will be the role of concepts such as employability.

Hans De Witte and his colleagues were quick to spot that employability was likely to become an important concern in the face of growing challenges to job security. Their initial definition addressed the perceived likelihood of finding new employment or maintaining current employment (De Cuyper & De Witte, 2010). Subsequent writing and research has greatly elaborated our understanding of employability (Van Harten et al., 2022). It generally assumes that the worker is currently employed. Those analysing the boundaryless, protean career emphasize the importance of career self-management (DeFillippi & Arthur, 1994; King, 2004) as part of the process to maintain employability, expecting that individuals are in a position to engage in relevant career-enhancing activities. If employability becomes a central feature of individual attempts to minimize a sense of job insecurity in a world of employment that is increasingly temporary and boundaryless, what are the implications for those who are self-employed? Lo Presti et al. (2018) found that in a large sample of Italian, largely professional, freelance workers a protean and boundaryless mindset was associated with higher employability activity and higher professional commitment, which in turn was associated with more positive career attitudes and higher perceptions of career success. This suggests that those with a positive interest in employability and in their profession are in a position to achieve positive career outcomes. For them, security lies in their continued employability. But is this the case for those working in the gig economy? If fewer people engage in traditional forms of employment, perhaps future research needs to focus more on "workability", giving greater emphasis to the knowledge, skills, attitudes and orientations relevant in the emerging world of work.

Kost et al. (2020) asked whether the idea of a boundaryless career in the gig economy is an oxymoron and they concluded that this was indeed the case. This conclusion is reinforced by Duggan et al. (2021), who interviewed 56 gig workers to explore their scope to develop employability, defined in terms of increasing their "knowing what, knowing how and knowing who" competences (De Fillippi & Arthur, 1994), and found that any scope for development was heavily constrained by the algorithms that controlled their work. These gig workers were boundaryless but unable in their work to develop the skills to advance their careers and move on from gig work. A form of security was found in the ability to continue to undertake gig work, perhaps moving to different platforms, but paradoxically this was a bounded and limited world of work. These findings are reinforced by Newlands (2022) who studied the experience of immigrant workers engaged in food delivery gig work. They found it difficult to progress out of gig work both because of the lack of opportunity to develop their employability but also as a result of their location within a disadvantaged immigrant community. A feature of temporary employment for some of the workers in the Psycones project and in other research was its role as a stepping stone, increasing employability and the likelihood of subsequently obtaining a better job (De Cuyper et al., 2009). Much gig work does not appear to provide similar opportunities. These findings highlight the further disadvantage of those sometimes trapped in low-skill work. They also point to the need to rethink both the concepts of insecurity and of employability in future research in the emerging economy.

The analysis of self-employment and gig work in particular points to a need to reflect on the role of the psychological contract. As already noted, in the case of the gig workers, if there is no employment contract there can be no psychological contract concerning job security. This relationship, in theory at least, does not exist. On the other hand, the research does suggest that gig workers can form an implicit psychological contract based on a set of expectations they develop. The evidence also indicates that this can often be perceived by workers to be violated as the algorithms make arbitrary changes. There is also the possibility of losing access to the platform if a worker transgresses rules concerning, for example, refusing work or receiving poor feedback from customers, further reflecting the "tyranny of the algorithm". Like many others working on temporary contracts, cognitive job insecurity may not be a major concern because it is expected as part of the relationship, while breach of the psychological contract can affect job satisfaction and commitment but seems less likely to affect job insecurity. If undertaking paid work without a recognizable employment contract becomes more widespread, the absence of a relation between job insecurity and low well-being may become more common. At the same time, if the role of algorithms to shape HRM practices and increasingly to affect the organization of work grows, and if voice is mediated or blocked by an algorithm, causing frustration, we can expect an increase in the violation of the psychological contract among permanent workers. Furthermore, if the algorithms do not reflect the norm of reciprocity, this is likely to exacerbate the problem. The implication of self-employment and more particularly its extreme form represented by gig work, is that we need to rethink how we understand the psychological contract, who or what any psychological contract is with and in particular the relevance of its relationship to job insecurity. At the same time, research might usefully explore the impact of the growing influence of algorithms, particularly in relation to HRM decisions, on the security and psychological contracts among those in traditional employment.

The role and relevance of job insecurity in non-traditional employment seems likely to be a function of the type of work and of individual differences in orientations to work. Peel and Boxall (2005) compared high- and low-skill contractors in a context where there had been some choice about whether to remain in permanent employment or become self-employed, and found that the high-skilled engineers typically engaged in successful career self-management and reported positive career-related outcomes. In contrast, the sample of self-employed meter-readers were less positive since there was less opportunity to extend their opportunities and increase their employability. However, across both groups, some workers were positive while others were negative, reflecting the priority given to factors such as autonomy, opportunity and preference for stable relationships. While job security seems to have been of importance for those remaining in permanent employment, for those choosing to become self-employed, security was perceived in terms of opportunity, income and relationships rather than continuity of an employment contract. This highlights the need in future research to consider the importance of both the type of work and individual differences in orientations to work.

Analysis of the continuing nature and relevance of job insecurity and the psychological contract linked to work as well as the relationship between them, needs rethinking, as does their link to worker well-being. A contemporary approach needs to be set in the context of changes in technology that are having wider repercussions. The past decade has seen a growing debate about the advent of "Industry 4.0" reflecting the growth of the digital economy and advances in, for example, artificial intelligence (AI), robotics and digital platforms. It was initially suggested that these developments would result in a substantial loss of jobs (Frey & Osborne, 2013). Subsequent evidence indicates it is likely to result in some job loss but also some job creation as well as changes in the content of many jobs. Concerns about the implications for employment and for the quality of work have set alarm bells ringing in the European Commission and the OECD, including advocacy of a swift move to "Industry 5.0" which would move on from the implicit technological determinism of "Industry 4.0" (Bednor & Welch, 2020; Xu et al., 2021) to an approach to the organization of industry based on core principles of human-centricity, sustainability and resilience and reflecting much more of a stakeholder focus. In this context, employees are viewed as assets rather than costs, technology adapts to workers rather than vice versa and workers are involved in the design of work (Breque et al., 2021). It requires some optimism to believe that industry will move on a voluntary basis towards "Industry 5.0", and it is notable that those concerned about the employment trends associated with digitization and "Industry 4.0" have begun to advocate legislation to mandate more secure and better-quality forms of employment (Warhurst & Knox, 2022).

In conclusion, in the new world of work, the relationship between job insecurity, the psychological contract, the boundaryless career and employability seems likely to become ever more complex. We may need to rethink the central significance of job insecurity as the proportion of workers without traditional employment increases; perhaps the focus needs to shift towards different forms of insecurity such as career insecurity, employment insecurity, financial insecurity and, in a world where alienation persists, even identity insecurity. We also need to rethink the nature and relevance of the psychological contract among those who have no employer or for whom any sense of employment is mediated by an algorithm or some form of agency. While we argue that there is a case for rethinking the nature and importance of job insecurity and the psychological contract in the world of digital work and boundaryless careers, we acknowledge that there is still a majority of the workforce in more traditional standard employment, many of whom value job security and for whom fear of job insecurity can damage their well-being. It is important to retain a focus on these workers in research and policy considerations. At the same time, we need a different perspective and perhaps a new discourse about work-related insecurity and its role in the psychological contract to explore the experiences of those engaged in new forms of contemporary work and employment. To address these challenges we need another generation of researchers to continue the admirable tradition of scholarship set by Hans De Witte and colleagues in his research group.

REFERENCES

Arthur, M., & Rousseau, D. (1996). *The boundaryless career: A new employment principle for a new organizational era.* New York: Oxford University Press.

Ashford, S., Lee, C., & Bobko, P. (1989). Content, causes and consequences of job insecurity: A theory-based measure and substantive test. *Academy of Management Journal, 32*(4), 803–829.

Barley, S., & Kunda, G. (2004). *Gurus, hired guns, and warm bodies.* Princeton, NJ: Princeton University Press.

Bednor, P., & Welch, C. (2020). Socio-technical perspectives on smart working: Creating meaningful and sustainable systems. *Information Systems Frontiers, 22,* 281–298. https://doi.org/10.1007/s10796-019-09921-1

Blau, P. (1964). *Exchange and power in social life.* New York: Wiley.

Breque, M., De Nul, L., & Petridis, A. (2021). *Industry 5.0: Towards a sustainable human-centric and resilient European industry.* Brussels: European Director-General for Research and Innovation.

Chambel, M., & Sobral, F. (2019). When temporary agency work is not so temporary. *Economic and Industrial Democracy, 40*(2), 238–256. https://doi.org/10.1177/0143831X188059

Cheng, G., & Chan, D. (2008). Who suffers more from job insecurity? A meta-analytic review. *Applied Psychology: An International Review, 57*(2), 272–303. https://doi.org/10.1111/j.1464-0597.2007.00312.x

Costa, S., & Neves, P. (2017). Job insecurity and work outcomes: The role of psychological contract breach and positive psychological capital. *Work & Stress, 31*(4), 375–394. https://doi.org/10.1080/02678373.2017.1330781

Coyle-Shapiro, J., & Conway, N. (2004). The employment relationship through the lens of social exchange. In J. Coyle-Shapiro, L. Shore, S. Taylor & L. Tetrick (Eds.), *The employment relationship: Examining psychological and contextual perspectives* (pp. 5–28). Oxford: Oxford University Press.

Cropanzano, R., Keplinger, K., Lambert, B., Caza, B., & Ashford, S. (2023). The organizational psychology of gig work: An integrative conceptual review. *Journal of Applied Psychology, 108*(3), 492–519. https://doi.org/10.1037/apl0001029.

De Cuyper, N., & De Witte, H. (2010). Temporary employment and perceived employability: Mediation by impression management. *Journal of Career Development, 37*(3), 635–652. https://doi.org/10.1177/0894845309357051

De Cuyper, N., De Jong, J., De Witte, H., Isaksson, K., Rigotti, T., & Schalk, R. (2008). Literature review of theory and research on the psychological impact of temporary employment: Towards a conceptual model. *International Journal of Management Reviews, 10*(1), 25–51. https://doi.org/10.1111/j.1468-2370.2007.00221.x

De Cuyper, N., Notelaers, G., & De Witte, H. (2009). Transitioning between temporary and permanent employment: A two-wave study on the entrapment, the stepping stone and the selection hypothesis. *Journal of Occupational and Organizational Psychology, 82*(1), 67–88. https://doi.org/10.1348/096317908X299755

De Cuyper, N., Van den Broeck, A., & De Witte, H. (2015). Perceived employability in times of job insecurity: A theoretical perspective. In A. De Vos & B. Van der Heijden (Eds.) *Handbook of research on sustainable careers* (pp. 161–174). Cheltenham, UK and Northampton, MA, USA: Edward Elgar Publishing.

DeFillippi, R., & Arthur, M. (1994). The boundaryless career: A competency-based perspective. *Journal of Organizational Behavior, 15*(4), 307–324. https://doi.org/10.1002/job.4030150403

De Witte, H. (2000). Arbeidsethos en Jobonzekerheid: Meting en gevolgen voor Welzijn, tevredenheid en inzet op het wek (Work ethic and job insecurity: Measurement and consequences for well-being, satisfaction and work performance"). In R. Bouwen, K. De Witte, H. De Witte & T. Taillieu (eds.), *Van Groep naar Gemeenschap* (pp. 325-350). (Liber Amicorum Prof Dr. Leo Lagrou). Leuven, Belgium: Garant.

De Witte, H., & Näswall, K. (2003). "Objective" vs "subjective" job insecurity: Consequences of temporary work for job satisfaction and organizational commitment in four European countries. *Economic and Industrial Democracy, 24*(2), 149–188. https://doi.org/10.1177/0143831X03024002002

De Witte, H., Handaja, Y., Sverke, M., Näswall, K., & Hellgren, J. (2010). Associations between qualitative and quantitative job insecurity and well-being: A test in Belgian banks. *International Studies of Management and Organization, 40*(1), 40–56. https://doi.org/10.2753/IMO0020-8825400103

De Witte, H., Pienaar, J., & De Cuyper, N. (2016). Review of 30 years of longitudinal studies on the association between job insecurity and health and well-being. Is there causal evidence? *Australian Psychology, 51*(1), 18–31. https://doi.org/10.1111/ap.12176

Duggan, J., Sherman, U., Carbery, R., & McDonnell, A. (2020). Algorithmic management and app-work in the gig economy: A research agenda for employment relations and HRM. *Human Resource Management Journal, 30*(1), 114–132. https://doi.org/10.1111/1748-8583.12258

Duggan, J., Sherman, U., Carbery, R., & McDonnell, A. (2021). Boundaryless careers and algorithmic constraints in the gig economy. *International Journal of Human Resource Management, 33*(22), 4468–4498. https://doi.org/10.1080/09585192.2021.1953565

Ellonen, N., & Natti, J. (2015). Job insecurity and the unemployment rate: Micro- and macro-level predications of perceived job insecurity among Finnish employees. *Economic and Industrial Democracy, 36*(1), 51–71. https://doi.org/10.1177/0143831X13495720

Eurofound (2018). *Non-standard forms of employment: Recent trends and future prospects.* Luxembourg: European Union.

Eurofound (2019). *Automation, digitisation and platforms: Implications for work and employment.* Luxembourg: European Union.

Eurofound (2021). *The digital age: Implications of automation, digitisation and platforms for work and employment.* Luxembourg: European Union.

Frey, C., & Osborne, M. (2013). *The future of employment: How susceptible are jobs to computerization?* Oxford Martin Programme on Technology and Employment: University of Oxford.

Gouldner, M. (1960). The norm of reciprocity: A preliminary statement. *American Sociological Review, 25*(2), 161–178.

Green, F., Felstead, A., Gallie, D., & Henseke, G. (2022). Working still harder. *ILR Review, 75*(2), 458–487. https://doi.org/10.1177/00197939209778

Guest, D. (2004). Flexible employment contracts, the psychological contract and employee outcomes: An analysis and review of the evidence. *International Journal of Management Reviews, 5/6*, 1–19. https://doi.org/10.1111/j.1460-8545.2004.00094.x

Guest, D., Isaksson, K., & De Witte, H. (Eds.) (2010). *Employment contracts, psychological contracts, and employee well-being.* Oxford: Oxford University Press.

Hall, D. (2004). The protean career: A quarter-century journey. *Journal of Vocational Behavior, 65*(1), 1–13. https://doi.org/10.1016/j.jvb.2003.10.006

International Labour Organization (ILO) (2021). *Work, employment and social outlook: The role of digital labour platforms in transforming the world of work.* Geneva: ILO.

Jahoda, M. (1982). *Employment and unemployment – A social psychological analysis.* Cambridge: Cambridge University Press.

Kalleberg, A. (2012). Job quality and precarious work: Clarification, controversies and challenges. *Work and Occupations, 39*(4), 427–448. https://doi.org/10.1177/0730888412460533

King, Z. (2004). Career self-management: Its nature, causes and consequences. *Journal of Vocational Behavior, 65*(1), 112–133. https://doi.org/10.1016/S0001-8791(03)00052-6

Kost, D., Fieseler, C., & Wang, I. (2020). Boundaryless careers in the gig economy – an oxymoron? *Human Resource Management Journal, 30*(1), 100–113. https://doi.org/10.1111/1748-8583.12265

Leineweber, C., Peristera, P., Bernhard-Oettel, C., & Elb, C. (2020). Is interpersonal justice related to group and organizational turnover? Results from a Swedish panel study. *Social Science and Medicine, 265*, 113526. DOI: 10.1016/j.socscimed.2020.113526

Lo Presti, A., Pluviano, S., & Briscoe, J. (2018). Are freelancers a breed apart? The role of protean and boundaryless career attitudes in employability and career success. *Human Resource Management Journal, 28*(3), 427–442. https://doi.org/10.1111/1748-8583.12188

McLean Parks, J., Kidder, D., & Gallager, D. (1998). Fitting square pegs into round holes: Mapping the domain of contingent work onto temporary psychological contracts. *Journal of Organizational Behavior, 19*, 697–730. https://www.jstor.org/stable/3100285

Meijerink, J., & Keegan, A. (2019). Conceptualising human resource management in the gig economy: Toward a platform ecosystem perspective. *Journal of Managerial Psychology, 34*(4), 214–232. https://doi.org/10.1108/JMP-07-2018-0277

Meijerink, J., Boons, M., Keegan, A., & Marler, J. (2021). Algorithmic human resource management: Synthesizing developments and cross-disciplinary insights on digital HRM. *International Journal of Human Resource Management, 32*(12), 2545–2562. https://doi.org/10.1080/09585192.2021.1925326

Murgia, A., & Pulignano, V. (2021). Neither precarious nor entrepreneur: The subjective experience of hybrid self-employed workers. *Economic and Industrial Democracy, 42*(4), 1351–1377. https://doi.org/10.1177/0143831X19873966

Newlands, G. (2022). "This isn't forever for me": Perceived employability and migrant gig work in Norway and Sweden. *EPA Economy and Space.*

OECD (2022). *Employment and labour market statistics: Employment by permanency of job and Incidence.* Paris: OECD.

Peel, S., & Boxall, P. (2005). When is contracting preferable to employment? An exploration of management and worker perspectives. *Journal of Management Studies, 42*(8), 1675–1697. https://doi.org/10.1111/j.1467-6486.2005.00562.x

Pienaar, J., De Witter, H., Hellgren, J., & Sverke, M. (2013). The cognitive/affective distinction of job insecurity: Validation and differential relations. *South African Business Review, 17*(2), 1–22.

Rodrigues, R., & Guest, D. (2010). Have careers become boundaryless? *Human Relations, 63*(8), 1157–1175. https://doi.org/10.1177/0018726709354344

Rousseau, D. (1995). *Psychological contracts in organizations: Understanding written and unwritten agreements.* Thousand Oaks, CA: Sage.

Rousseau, D. (2005). *I-Deals: Idiosyncratic deals employees bargain for themselves.* Armonk, NY: Sharpe.

Shanahan, G., & Smith, M. (2021). Fair's fair: Psychological contracts and power in platform work. *International Journal of Human Resource Management, 32*(19), 1–32. https://doi.org/10.1080/09585192.2020.1867615

Sharma, P. (2022). Digitisation and precarious work practices in alternative economies: Work organisation and work relations in e-cab services. *Economic and Industrial Democracy, 43*(2), 559–584. https://doi.org/10.1177/0143831X20924461

Spurk, D., Hofer, A., Hirsch, A., De Cuyper, N., & De Witte, H. (2022). Conceptualizing career insecurity: Toward a better understanding and measurement of a multi-dimensional construct. *Personnel Psychology, 75*(2), 253–294. https://doi.org/10.1111/peps.12493

Standing, G. (2011). *The Precariat: The new dangerous class.* London: Bloomsbury Press.

Sverke, M., Hellgren, J., & Näswall, K. (2002). No security: A meta-analysis and review of job insecurity and its consequences. *Journal of Occupational Health Psychology, 7*(3), 242–264. https://doi.org/10.1037/1076-8998.7.3.242

Tessema, M., Tesfom, G., Faircloth, M., Tesfagiorgis, M., & Teckle, P. (2022). The "great resignation": Causes, consequences and creative human resource strategies. *Journal of Human Resource Management and Sustainability Studies, 10*(1), 161–178. DOI: 10.4236/jhrss.2022.101011

Van Harten, J., De Cuyper, N., Knies, E., & Forrier, A. (2022). Taking the temperature of employability research: A systematic review of interrelationships across and within conceptual strands. *European Journal of Work and Organizational Psychology, 31*(1), 145–159. https://doi.org/10.1080/1359432X.2021.1942847

Warhurst, C., & Knox, A. (2022). Manifesto for a new quality of working life. *Human Relations, 75*(2), 304–321. https://doi.org/10.1177/0018726720979348

Welander, J., Astvik, W., & Isaksson, K. (2017). Corrosion of trust: Violation of psychological contracts a reason for turnover amongst social workers. *Nordic Social Research, 7*(1), 67–79.

Xu, X., Lu, Y., Vogel-Hueser, B., & Wang, L. (2021). Industry 4 and Industry 5 – Inception, conception and perception. *Journal of Manufacturing Systems, 61*, 530–535. https://doi.org/10.1016/j.jmsy.2021.10.006

6. Can unions represent the interests of insecure workers?

Magnus Sverke, Isabelle Ferré Hernandez, Anna S. Tanimoto, Johnny Hellgren, & Katharina Näswall

INTRODUCTION

Working life is continuously undergoing changes and poses new challenges to organizations through changing competitive conditions (e.g., globalization/ nationalization), economic changes (e.g., recessions/booms, trade tariffs), and technological development (e.g., automatization). One aspect of working life that has undergone major changes since the early 1990s concerns the increase in different forms of employment contracts (De Cuyper & De Witte, 2006; Kalleberg, 2000; Nordic Council of Ministers, 2021), moving away from the traditional permanent contracts. The trend of an increasing number of insecure, temporary employment arrangements has been suggested to be one of the most significant changes the labour market has undergone in a long time (De Cuyper et al., 2008). Nowadays, employment types which deviate from permanent, open-ended contracts account for about a quarter of all employment within the OECD countries (Visser, 2019), and it is forecasted that the proportion of fixed-term employment will increase in the future (ILO, 2016; OECD, 2019). Contractual insecurity has been shown to have negative consequences for both the individual and the organization (Bernhard-Oettel et al., 2017; De Cuyper et al., 2008).

Another characteristic of contemporary working life concerns perceptions of job insecurity – the perceived risk of, or worry about, losing one's job (De Witte, 1999). Perceived job insecurity has accompanied the structural labour market changes and has increased over the past decades (De Witte et al., 2015; OECD, 2019; Probst et al., 2015). Numerous reviews (e.g., De Witte, 1999, 2005; De Witte et al., 2016; Probst et al., 2015; Shoss, 2017) and meta-analyses (e.g., Cheng & Chan, 2008; Jiang & Lavaysse, 2018; Sverke et

al., 2002, 2019) indicate that experiencing job insecurity has negative consequences for individuals and organizations.

A third trend is represented by a decline in the degree of unionization in most
industrialized countries, especially among employees with temporary, or insecure, employment contracts (Jansen & Lehr, 2022; Visser, 2019). For
example, Leschke and Vandaele (2018) noted that employees with insecure
employment contracts tend to work in organizations where the union presence
is weak or even non-existent. The probability of becoming a union member
is 50 percent lower among employees on temporary contracts compared to
employees on permanent contracts (OECD, 2019). This is somewhat paradoxical, given that insecure employment would call for union representation.
Traditionally, trade unions have fought for good working conditions, worked
to reduce hazards and risks in workplaces, and been especially active when
it comes to advocating for secure employment conditions. Empirical evidence suggests that union presence and influence in the workplace may have
a positive effect on the amount of permanent positions in the organization
and on reducing the degree of perceived job insecurity (Fullerton et al., 2011;
Newman et al., 2019).

The legitimacy of unions depends on the degree of unionization and on the
commitment and engagement among union representatives (Barling et al.,
1992). Declining unionization may jeopardize the legitimacy of unions in the
labour market. With the increase in insecure work (contractual and perceived),
the scope of unions to bring about positive changes for employees may need
to look different from what it traditionally has been. However, research is
limited when it comes to how unions can represent employees with insecure
contractual arrangements, and whether unions are able to prevent the impact of
the uncertainty associated with contractual and perceived job insecurity.

This chapter presents a review of research on the role of unions in supporting insecure workers. We focus on two aspects of insecure work: insecure
employment contracts and perceived job insecurity. The chapter begins with
a brief review of research on the characteristics and consequences of insecure
employment, before providing a similar brief review of research on perceived
job insecurity. The remainder of the chapter focuses on addressing the following questions:

1. How do insecure workers view union membership and what are their
    unionization behaviours (joining and leaving)?
2. Can union membership and union support buffer the negative effects that
    insecure work may have on work-related and health-related outcomes?
3. How can unions represent the interests of insecure workers?

INSECURE EMPLOYMENT CONTRACTS

The need for flexibilization has impacted the ways in which employers conduct their business and, perhaps now more than ever, the ability to quickly adapt to economic fluctuations is a necessity. Flexibility practices including numerical and functional flexibility (Atkinson, 1984; Kalleberg, 2001; Reilly, 1998) are utilized by organizations (ILO, 2016). Numerical flexibility in particular allows organizations to increase or decrease staffing based on current demands. Organizations can achieve greater numerical flexibility by making use of various alternative employment contracts, and scholars suggest that flexibilization is an important driver of the increase in insecure employment in today's labour market (Guest et al., 2010; Spreitzer et al., 2017), since these contract types are associated with greater uncertainty for individual employees.

One aspect of insecure work thus concerns employment contracts that may be characterized by uncertainty regarding the continuity of the job and, hence, by employment insecurity (De Cuyper & De Witte, 2006). Such contractual arrangements are often referred to as *insecure employment*, but other terminology exists in the literature, including non-standard (Bernhard-Oettel et al., 2017; Tanimoto et al., 2021), precarious (Standing, 2011), atypical (Goslinga & Sverke, 2003), and contingent employment (McLean Parks et al., 1998). The past few decades have witnessed a number of different contractual arrangements evolve, which fall under insecure employment, for instance, various types of temporary or fixed-term contracts (Bernhard-Oettel et al., 2017; De Cuyper et al., 2008). These differ from permanent, open-ended employment, which might be regarded as *secure employment* if referring to security based solely on contract type. Permanent, open-ended employment is traditionally characterized by a relationship between an employee and an employer, where work is typically carried out on the premises of the employer organization (De Cuyper et al., 2008; McLean Parks et al., 1998), but as a result of the Covid-19 pandemic and the resulting dramatic increase in remote work, this characteristic may now be considered an old-fashioned criterion for secure employment. The "standard" type of permanent employment also tends to consist of full-time work, about 35 to 40 hours a week (Bernhard-Oettel et al., 2017; Kalleberg, 2000), whereas permanent part-time employment is typically included among the insecure contractual arrangements (Nordic Council of Ministers, 2021; Tanimoto et al., 2021). Recent years have seen insecure employment gaining traction across the labour market. In 2015, insecure employment accounted for around 30 percent of employment in the Nordic countries (ranging from 26 percent in Sweden to 32 percent in Iceland; Nordic Council of Ministers, 2021). Among OECD countries, insecure employment makes up around 25 percent of all employment (Visser, 2019).

Insecure employment includes all types of employment contracts which are not open-ended and on a full-time basis (see Tanimoto et al., 2021, for a recent typology of employment forms). Some examples, including project workers, substitutes, and on-call workers are considered temporary and provide numerical flexibility for employers as these workers perform their work on an as-needed basis (Bernhard-Oettel et al., 2017; Tanimoto et al., 2021). Whereas project workers and substitutes may have consistent work schedules, on-call workers must be prepared to work if summoned by their employer. Other types of insecure employment include so-called floats, temporary agency workers and platform workers. Floats may be permanent or temporary and provide organizations with functional flexibility in that they can perform a range of tasks throughout various departments of an organization (McLean Parks et al., 1998). Temporary agency workers are employed by a temporary agency firm (on a permanent or temporary basis) and perform work for one or more client organizations (De Cuyper et al., 2009). Platform workers carry out services via digital platforms on behalf of customers for pay (Schoukens et al., 2018). Platform work is a type of labour exchange characteristic of the gig economy, and its prevalence across the labour market is increasing rapidly (Friedman, 2014).

Although there exist many different types of insecure employment, they appear to share some demographic characteristics. An overrepresentation by age, gender, and foreign or minority status is evident among those with such employment. In 2019, almost 50 percent of young workers in the EU (aged 15 to 24), were in temporary employment (Eurostat, 2019). Although these numbers may reflect a student lifestyle, where studies and part-time or temporary work are combined, many young workers are in fact unable to obtain permanent jobs (Klug, 2020). In addition to young workers, women are overrepresented in insecure employment: part-time contracts are predominantly held by women. In fact, 75 percent of part-time work is done by women (Eurofound, 2020). In the Nordic countries, women are disproportionally represented in fixed-term employment (Nordic Council of Ministers, 2021; Skedinger, 2018). In contrast, men are overrepresented when it comes to self-employment (Eurofound, 2020). Foreign-born or ethnic minorities are another demographic group with overrepresentation in insecure employment (ILO, 2016). In Europe, those who are foreign-born are more likely to have fixed-term employment than native-born workers (Eurofound, 2019).

While organizations use insecure employment to achieve flexibility, the advantages of such arrangements for employees are typically framed as allowing individuals greater flexibility to manage or balance their work and private lives. That said, a number of consequences of insecure employment have been identified, including implications for individual health and safety (Landsbergis et al., 2014; Virtanen et al., 2005) and work-related outcomes (Wilkin, 2013).

Reviews of empirical findings reveal that temporary employment is associated with higher levels of psychological ill-health (Virtanen et al., 2005), poor physical health and more occupational injuries (Landsbergis et al., 2014), and job dissatisfaction (Wilkin, 2013). Yet challenges arise when attempting to draw straightforward, overarching conclusions about the impact of contract type. For example, the heterogeneity of contract types which fall under insecure employment challenges the assumption that all insecure employment has adverse effects. Indeed, research indicates that consequences for health and work-related attitudes and behaviour may differ between different contractual arrangements (Bernhard-Oettel et al., 2017; De Cuyper et al., 2009). Additionally, research suggests that contract volition and motives may play an important role in relationships between insecure employment and various work-related outcomes (De Cuyper & De Witte, 2008).

PERCEIVED JOB INSECURITY

Another aspect of insecure work is perceived job insecurity, which reflects the experience that one's job is at risk (Shoss, 2017; Sverke & Hellgren, 2002). Perceived job insecurity thus characterizes "people at work who fear they might lose their jobs and become unemployed" (De Witte, 1999, p. 156). Similarly, job insecurity has been defined as "an employee's perception of a potential threat to continuity in his or her current job" (Heaney et al., 1994, p. 1431), thus emphasizing the threat to the job. Other scholars have defined job insecurity as "a discrepancy between the level of security a person experiences and the level he or she might prefer" (Hartley et al., 1991, p. 7), to emphasize that the uncertainty about the future is undesired. Another definition highlights that job insecurity is a perceptual phenomenon by defining it as "a worker's perception or concern about involuntary job loss" (De Cuyper et al., 2012, p. 770). Job insecurity has also been defined as "the perceived powerlessness to maintain desired continuity in a threatened job situation" (Greenhalgh & Rosenblatt, 1984, p. 438), which accentuates the vulnerability that may accompany the perceived risk of job loss. Common to these definitions is the perception that there is a potential threat to the future of the job as it is known, that it is outside of the individual's control to counteract this threat, and that the potential loss of the job is something unwanted.

While some studies use a general conceptualization of perceived job insecurity, other research distinguishes between different dimensions of the construct. One of these distinctions concerns cognitive vs. affective job insecurity (De Witte & Näswall, 2003; Probst, 2003). Cognitive job insecurity reflects the perceived probability or risk of involuntary job loss, whereas affective job insecurity refers to the affective reaction accompanying this perception in terms of anxiety and worry. Another distinction is made between quantitative and qualitative job insecurity (De Witte et al., 2010; Hellgren et al., 1999). Quantitative job insecurity refers to threats to the job itself, while qualitative job insecurity relates to threats to valuable features of the job. Such threats to qualities in the employment relationship can include the potential impairment of working conditions, career opportunities, and salary development (Fischmann et al., 2021; Hellgren et al., 1999). Numerous studies by De Witte and colleagues (De Witte et al., 2010; Pienaar et al., 2013; Van Hootegem et al., 2022) show that the different types of job insecurity may have somewhat different associations with outcomes, suggesting that the type of perceived job insecurity is important to consider.

Job insecurity has been described as a stressor in accordance with the transactional stress framework (Lazarus & Folkman, 1984): the individual perceives a threat to their job, and it is unclear how, and whether, this threat can be counteracted, resulting in stress perceptions. Numerous research studies, meta-analyses, and literature reviews have documented the negative impact of perceived job insecurity, including individuals forming negative attitudes towards the organization, experiencing reduced mental and physical health, having increased intentions to leave the organization, and reporting lower levels of job performance (Cheng & Chan, 2008; De Witte, 2005; Lee et al., 2018; Shoss, 2017; Sverke et al., 2002, 2019). Overall, perceived job insecurity is a detrimental experience with negative consequences for both individuals and organizations. This has also been supported in a review of longitudinal research on the association between job insecurity and health and well-being, where the results showed that the impact of job insecurity on psychological well-being and somatic health is lasting (De Witte et al., 2016).

It is important to differentiate perceived job insecurity from actual job loss in that job loss has already occurred, and as such is no longer a threat but a reality. Research has found that those facing the certainty of job loss in some instances tend to report lower stress levels than those experiencing job insecurity (Dekker & Schaufeli, 1995). Despite this difference, the consequences of job insecurity and unemployment are fairly similar and the two phenomena have been described as "surprisingly identical twins" (De Witte et al., 2019, p. 45).

Research on job insecurity in the context of insecure contractual arrangements has shown that those with temporary employment contracts tend to report higher levels of perceived job insecurity than those in permanent employment (De Cuyper & De Witte, 2007; De Witte & Näswall, 2003). This would suggest that those who experience perceived job insecurity, in insecure contractual arrangements, would be the most vulnerable to suffer the consequences of insecure work. In contrast, it has been found that perceived job insecurity tends to be more negative for permanent workers than for temporary workers. Permanent workers with high perceived job insecurity tend to report lower levels of job satisfaction and organizational commitment than permanent workers with low job insecurity, while perceived job insecurity appears not to affect the relation between temporary employment and these work attitudes (De Cuyper & De Witte, 2007; De Witte & Näswall, 2003). This may be explained by the fact that those in insecure types of contracts often expect the uncertainty and are prepared to deal with it and, moreover, that the association between insecure contracts and outcomes depends on whether the reason for being in such a contract is voluntary or involuntary (Bernhard-Oettel et al., 2017; De Cuyper et al., 2008).

INSECURE WORKERS AND UNION MEMBERSHIP

As we have seen, insecure work may result in negative consequences for health, attitudes, and behaviour. Such consequences may arise from insecure contractual arrangements as well as from perceived job insecurity. While unions can play an instrumental role in improving working conditions for individuals with insecure employment contracts (Hughes & Bell, 2015; Ikeler, 2019; Pulignano & Doerflinger, 2013), individuals with insecure employment are less likely to unionize than permanent employees (Gumbrell-McCormick, 2011; OECD, 2019). There exists a scholarly interest to better understand the union-related attitudes and behaviours of individuals with insecure employment. Specifically, what drives these individuals to join unions (in the exceptional cases that they do)? And, among those who are union members, what are the factors which contribute to the abandonment of their union membership (i.e., union turnover)?

Only a few studies have investigated union joining attitudes and behaviours among workers with insecure contractual arrangements. One could argue that workers with insecure employment contracts are in more need of union representation, while at the same time they are in fact less likely to be unionized. This paradoxical relationship could be attributed to different factors, including financial obstacles such as high membership fees in relation to potentially limited salaries (Mayer & Noiseux, 2015), or organizational resistance towards unions (Legault & Weststar, 2015). Another possible explanation is that workers with insecure contracts may not "see the point" of joining a union. In a recent study from the Netherlands, where fixed-term employees and the solo self-employed were compared with permanent employees, the results revealed that those with insecure employment were less inclined to join unions than permanent employees, resulting from a lack of perceived representation (Jansen & Lehr, 2022). Relatedly, union representation in the workplace has been found to be important for union joining: the presence of a union representative at the workplace may motivate employees to join, as was the case in a study of retail workers holding insecure employment contracts (Mayer & Noiseux,

2015). Similarly, results from a fast-food chain in Japan have revealed the union status of the store manager to be a deciding factor for union membership among those with insecure employment (Royle & Urano, 2012). Willingness to unionize may also result from insecure workers' previous experience with union membership, where those who previously felt the union did not do a good job of representing their contract types were less willing to join a union in a new role (MacKenzie, 2010).

Given that workers in insecure employment arrangements are underrepresented when it comes to union membership (OECD, 2019), it is important to elucidate the factors which motivate them to give up their union membership (after having joined a union in the first place). However, little empirical research addresses union turnover among workers with insecure employment contracts. One union specifically dedicated to workers in insecure employment saw, on average, a shorter union membership duration compared to other unions which represented permanent employees (Vaona, 2010), suggesting that insecure employment may lead workers to resign membership when they secure a permanent position. Other possible reasons may be due to early dissatisfaction with the union, as suggested by Leschke and Vandaele (2018), after their study findings revealed a negative relationship between union membership duration and union turnover. The lack of empirical research on unionization behaviours among workers with insecure employment underscores a gap in the current research concerning an increasingly large segment of the labour force.

When it comes to union membership among employees experiencing perceived job insecurity, Anderson and Pontusson (2007) found that union members reported lower levels of job insecurity than non-members, in a sample from 15 countries. This indicates that there is some merit to the idea that union membership itself contributes to lower job insecurity levels. On the other hand, research has also suggested and supported (De Cuyper et al., 2014) that union membership is higher among those who experience higher levels of job insecurity, since those with higher levels of job insecurity seek out union membership to redress the uncertainty they feel (see also Sverke et al., 2004).

CAN UNION MEMBERSHIP AND UNION SUPPORT BUFFER THE NEGATIVE EFFECTS OF INSECURE WORK?

Union membership as a way of reducing insecure work (contractual as well as perceived job insecurity), or its negative effects, has been discussed in the literature for decades, especially in the case of perceived job insecurity. For example, Greenhalgh and Rosenblatt (1984) listed union membership as a potential means to reduce feelings of powerlessness that are a key component of the job insecurity experience. Furthermore, union membership may provide employees with a sense of control that counteracts perceptions of job insecurity (Hartley et al., 1991).

Reducing the levels of perceived job insecurity may be the most desirable strategy, as this would mean that the stressor will have less of an effect. But, in many instances, job insecurity perceptions will still arise, because the world of work is changing, and many workers have insecure employment. Union membership has been proposed as a potential buffer against negative outcomes of job insecurity, since union membership serves as a resource helping individuals cope with job insecurity perceptions (Dekker & Schaufeli, 1995). In addition, union support, which reflects "members' global beliefs concerning the extent to which the union values their contributions and cares about their well-being" (Shore et al., 1994, p. 971), has been suggested as a potential buffering factor. However, there is a lack of empirical evidence demonstrating a buffering effect of union membership or support on job insecurity outcomes (Goslinga et al., 2005; Hellgren & Chirumbolo, 2003). Sverke et al. (2004) is one exception, showing that union support buffered against physical health complaints related to job insecurity, and that higher union support was associated with higher well-being levels and lower levels of turnover intentions.

An important aspect of union membership that has been investigated less in the context of perceived job insecurity is whether members think that the union can actually do something to alleviate their job insecurity or its negative consequences, that is, perceived union instrumentality (Newman et al., 2019). Union instrumentality concerns the perception of whether the union is capable of obtaining benefits, like wages, for their members (Fuller & Hester, 2001), and has been linked to positive attitudes including union loyalty (Tetrick et al., 2007). It is plausible that perceived instrumentality could play a moderating role in the relationship between job insecurity and its outcomes. If employees perceive that their union has the ability to affect working conditions, it is likely that the union will support employees coping with job insecurity – which could lead to less detrimental outcomes of job insecurity.

While the moderating role of union instrumentality on the effect of perceived job insecurity has not been studied to date, there is some research exploring the main effect of union instrumentality. Newman et al. (2019) proposed, and found support for, the idea that the extent to which employees perceive the union as useful (i.e., union instrumentality) contributes to employees perceiving higher levels of job *security*. Perceptions of instrumentality make it more likely that employees will also perceive union support, which acts as a resource reducing stressors like uncertainty (Newman et al., 2019). These results suggest that employee perceptions of the degree to which unions are supportive are important for how much impact union membership will have in protecting against stressors and stress-related outcomes.

Most of the research on union membership and support in the context of job insecurity is conducted on permanent workers (De Cuyper et al., 2014), but the research that includes insecure employment contracts typically finds few or no differences between permanent and non-permanent workers regarding the impact of union membership and support on the association between insecure work and its consequences. However, results from the ESENER project (European Survey of Enterprises on New and Emerging Risks) show that working conditions are typically more favourable in workplaces where there is employee representation in occupational health and safety work (EU-OSHA, 2017). As insecure employment is becoming more common (Visser, 2019), research on how unions can better serve employees with insecure employment is needed, but it is plausible that this category of workers will benefit from union membership and support to the same extent as permanent employees do, if not more.

Furthermore, as workplaces around the world are experiencing rapid change because of the Covid-19 pandemic, the role of unions in supporting employees and organizations through such change may be significant. For example, unions have played an important role in the Covid-19 pandemic, where organizations have struggled with fluctuating demands and firm closures have resulted in layoffs (Vo-Thanh et al., 2022). Unions have an important role in turbulent times to ensure that employee rights are protected (Näswall & Sverke, 2014). As rapid technological advancements lead to jobs changing or sometimes becoming obsolete, resulting in uncertainty about future employment, unions can support their members by ensuring they receive skill development and training to increase their employability (Kristensen & Rocha, 2012; Stroud, 2012). Moving forward, it is important for unions to go beyond their traditional roles, and for research to explore the role of unions beyond perceptions of union support.

WHAT DO UNIONS DO TO REPRESENT THE INTERESTS OF INSECURE WORKERS?

There are different ways in which unions represent the interests of insecure workers. Unions may approach workers in insecure employment by trying to represent all workers equally, such as opting to achieve equal working conditions, regardless of employment status (Carver & Doellgast, 2021; Oh, 2012). Other approaches include altering their strategies to target workers with insecure contractual arrangements specifically (Webster & Bischoff, 2011). There are some examples of this, including cases in Italy (Marino et al., 2019; Pulignano et al., 2016) and the Independent Workers' Union of Great Britain (Woodcock, 2020), where new unions have been formed to specifically target workers with insecure employment contracts. Another example concerns the unionization of platform workers in African and Asian countries (Wood et al., 2018).

There are several ways unions have worked to improve the working conditions of workers with insecure contracts, one example being engaging in the regulation of insecure employment. This includes limiting companies' use of temporary workers (MacKenzie, 2010; Pulignano & Doerflinger, 2013), promoting *conversion rights* (i.e., allowing workers with insecure contracts to request permanent employment after a given time period) (Markey & McIvor, 2018), or trying to eliminate some of the most insecure employment contracts, such as zero-hour contracts, through legislative changes (Murphy et al., 2019). Unions may also assist unionized workers with insecure employment contracts in matters including grievance procedures (Charlesworth & Howe, 2018). The presence of unions in the workplace has been positively related to different aspects of insecure employment, including increased wages, better working conditions, improved access to employer-paid training, more fringe benefits, and more secure working arrangements (e.g., Adolfsson et al., 2022; Fervers & Schwander, 2015; Hughes & Bell, 2015; Ikeler, 2019; Pulignano & Doerflinger, 2013).

While there are several examples of how unions represent the interests of insecure workers, unions are not always successful in this respect. There are examples where unions have failed to address the needs of workers with insecure employment contracts despite efforts for doing so, or where they have failed to represent them altogether (Carver & Doellgast, 2021). This could simply be due to prioritizing permanent, full-time workers first (Baranowska & Gebel, 2010; Pulignano et al., 2016), or even actively excluding workers with insecure employment contracts by means of protecting their "core" members (Oh, 2012; Webster & Bischoff, 2011). Other reasons why unions may fail to represent the interests of insecure workers include difficult-to-meet eligibility requirements for joining the union, thus excluding workers in insecure employment by default (Oh, 2012). It has been suggested that some unions view non-permanent employment arrangements as something to be discouraged (Webster & Bischoff, 2011), possibly making unions less willing to advocate on behalf of workers in other types of contractual arrangements. This, of course, could prove counterproductive, resulting in lost influence over growing numbers of workers that unions could represent. In fact, some evidence suggests that due to the low unionization rates amongst workers with insecure employment, organizations may make use of insecure employment contracts as a way of weakening union power (Böheim & Zweimüller, 2013; Ikeler, 2019). This means that excluding workers with insecure employment contracts from becoming union members could actually become problematic for unions and their members.

Despite what the unions are (or are not) doing, they also face several challenges. One challenging scenario for unions is when employers are opposed to unionization. Workers in insecure employment in particular may fear suffering repercussions if they were to join a union (Legault & Weststar, 2015; Massimo, 2020). One current example is the case of Amazon, which has been widely criticized for providing sub-optimal working conditions and inherently banning unions from the workplace (Massimo, 2020). However, as Amazon expands globally, maintaining an anti-union stance has proven difficult. In some European contexts, where union presence is overall stronger than in the U.S., Amazon ultimately has had to acknowledge unions in the workplace, which has resulted in union actions such as strikes taking place across Amazon branches in several European countries (Massimo, 2020). This suggests that representing workers in insecure employment is not only a union matter, but also dependent on societal structures which allow (or disallow) union influence.

Another challenge faced by unions in the current labour market is the rise of platform work, or the "gig economy", as this type of work deviates even further from the standard employer–employee relationship. Platform work is typically performed by individuals in vulnerable socioeconomic positions (Pesole et al., 2018). Although platform work may lower the threshold to the labour market, making work more accessible to individuals otherwise struggling to find other employment, there is also a risk of these individuals getting stuck in precarity. Research shows that workers with precarious employment and hazardous working conditions often face a dilemma between having a job and having good health (an "employment–health dilemma"; Kößler et al., 2022). Because they are in a vulnerable situation, they may be forced to accept, or retain, a job that is risky in order to secure an income – or they may be forced to turn down, or quit, a risky job to avoid threats to their own health, and thus lose their income.

Several actions that could be beneficial to help regulate platform work have been suggested (Stewart & Stanford, 2017), in which unions could play an important role. These actions include enforcing legislation such as negotiating that platform work should be paid according to minimum wage standards, redefining employment by legally recognizing platform work as comparable to other employment, or by forming new legislation that specifically encompasses platform work (Stewart & Stanford, 2017). Recent examples suggest that extending traditional union structures, including legislation and collective bargaining, to include platform workers could be a successful approach, as demonstrated in the case of unionizing Foodora couriers in Canada (Gebert, 2021).

CONCLUDING REMARKS

This chapter set out to review the literature on insecure work (both contractual and perceived) and unions. The first question addressed in our review concerned insecure workers' unionization behaviours (joining and leaving). It is clear that the unionization rate is low among workers with insecure employment arrangements, in comparison to workers with permanent, open-ended contracts, and there seem to be many obstacles for workers with insecure contracts to join unions, despite often having a need for protection. As for the other type of insecure work discussed in this chapter – perceived job insecurity– it seems that perceptions of job insecurity may lead to either higher rates, or lower rates, of unionization, making it difficult to draw any set conclusions about how job insecurity affects union membership. It is clear that union membership behaviours are affected by insecure work (as well as by union representation at the workplace), but more research is needed to understand unionization behaviours among insecure workers.

Our second question concerned whether union membership and union support buffer negative effects of insecure work on work-related and health-related outcomes. Regardless of whether an employee holds an insecure employment contract or experiences job insecurity for another reason, unions may help decrease feelings of insecurity at work (Fullerton et al., 2011; Newman et al., 2019). Findings based on British panel data suggest that union members are less likely to be dismissed than non-union members (Colonna, 2010), thus indicating that union membership may have a positive effect on employment security. Others have found that a combination of experiencing job insecurity and holding a temporary employment contract increases the probability of becoming a union member (De Cuyper et al., 2014), implying that both feeling insecure and actually holding an insecure contract creates incentives to seek union support. Yet, union membership is still significantly lower amongst workers with insecure employment than amongst those with permanent contracts (OECD, 2019). An important implication for unions would be to take an inclusive stance towards workers with insecure employment contracts, and to adopt strategies that are well adapted for representing them.

The reviewed research on how union membership and support can mitigate the negative impact of perceived job insecurity is mixed. This may be attributable to research studies not being very specific about how employees perceive unions to be able to address their job insecurity perceptions. Therefore, we may not yet know the full extent to which unions can support employees in coping with job insecurity. Research explicitly examining employee perceptions of unions' efficacy to address uncertainty, and the factors contributing to perceptions of such efficacy, will be useful in elucidating what unions can do to support employees experiencing job insecurity. Research addressing union views on their own role in alleviating negative effects of insecure work would also be valuable, as it would provide insight into union priorities.

Our third question concerned what unions do to represent the interests of insecure workers. While the protection of employee rights, including both working conditions and employment security, is at the heart of unions, it appears that unions struggle to ascertain how best to represent the interests of workers with insecure employment contracts. Some unions strive to represent the interests of permanent workers with the intention to reduce the proportion of insecure employment arrangements. Given the development in the labour market, with increasing numbers of workers with arrangements that deviate from permanent work on a full-time basis, preventing insecure contracts does not appear to be a good strategy as it effectively ignores a large proportion of the labour force. Additionally, those with insecure contracts may find it difficult to know which union they should join, were they interested, as they may switch to a different job in a different sector in the near future. One solution might be to have specific unions organizing workers with insecure employment contracts. Another solution might be for unions to represent workers that do not fall precisely within their jurisdiction.

Our review raises some important questions for research as well as for unions and policy. Is it possible to reverse the ongoing trend of increasing insecure work (including both contractual insecurity and perceived job insecurity)? How can insecure workers get better opportunities to signal when working conditions are dissatisfactory? Who should represent the interests of insecure workers? In times when many jobs resemble old times' day labourers (platform work, zero-hour contracts, etc.), can unions attract insecure workers? Unions have a unique role in the labour market, but they must stay relevant for *all* workers, and we propose that to do this they need to advocate for good working conditions regardless of employment arrangement, and for employers to ensure that their staff are well taken care of, despite the increasing turbulence that all organizations face.

REFERENCES

Adolfsson, M., Baranowska-Rataj, A., & Lundmark, A. (2022). Temporary employment, employee representation, and employer-paid training: A comparative analysis. *European Sociological Review* (online first). https://doi.org/10.1093/esr/jcac021

Anderson, C. J., & Pontusson, J. (2007). Workers, worries and welfare states: Social protection and job insecurity in 15 OECD countries. *European Journal of Political Research, 46*(2), 211–235. https://doi.org/10.1111/j.1475-6765.2007.00692.x

Atkinson, J. (1984). Manpower strategies for flexible organizations. *Personnel Management, 16*(8), 28–31.

Baranowska, A., & Gebel, M. (2010). The determinants of youth temporary employment in the enlarged Europe: Do labour market institutions matter? *European Societies, 12*(3), 367–390. https://doi.org/10.1080/14616690903165434

Barling, J., Fullagar, C., & Kelloway, K. K. (1992). *The union and its members: A psychological approach.* New York: Oxford University Press.

Bernhard-Oettel, C., De Cuyper, N., Murphy, M., & Connelly, C. E. (2017). How do we feel and behave when we're not permanent full-time employees? The case of the diverse forms of non-standard work. In N. Chmiel, F. Fraccaroli, & M. Sverke (Eds.), *An introduction to work and organizational psychology: An international perspective* (3rd ed., pp. 258–275). Chichester: Wiley. https://doi.org/10.1002/9781119168058.ch14

Böheim, R., & Zweimüller, M. (2013). The employment of temporary agency workers in the UK: For or against the trade unions? *Economica, 80*(317), 65–95. https://doi.org/10.1111/j.1468-0335.2012.00935.x

Carver, L., & Doellgast, V. (2021). Dualism or solidarity? Conditions for union success in regulating precarious work. *European Journal of Industrial Relations, 27*(4), 367–385. https://doi.org/10.1177/0959680120978916

Charlesworth, S., & Howe, J. (2018). The enforcement of employment standards in Australia: Successes and challenges in aged care. *International Journal of Comparative Labour Law and Industrial Relations, 34*(2), 111–140. https://doi.org/10.1177%2F0959680120978916

Cheng, G. H.-L., & Chan, D. K.-S. (2008). Who suffers more from job insecurity? A meta-analytic review. *Applied Psychology: An International Review, 57*(2), 272–303. https://doi.org/10.1111/j.1464-0597.2007.00312.x

Colonna, F. (2010). Does union membership increase job security? Evidence from British panel data. Bank of Italy.

De Cuyper, N., & De Witte, H. (2006). The impact of job insecurity and contract type on attitudes, well-being and behavioural reports: A psychological contract perspective. *Journal of Occupational and Organizational Psychology, 79*(3), 345–409. https://doi.org/10.1348/096317905X53660

De Cuyper, N., & De Witte, H. (2007). Job insecurity in temporary versus permanent workers: Associations with attitudes, well-being, and behaviour. *Work & Stress, 21*(1), 65–84. https://doi.org/10.1080/02678370701229050

De Cuyper, N., & De Witte, H. (2008). Volition and reasons for accepting temporary employment: Associations with attitudes, well-being, and behavioural intentions. *European Journal of Work and Organizational Psychology, 17*(3), 363–387. https://doi.org/10.1080/13594320701810373

De Cuyper, N., de Jong, J., De Witte, H., Isaksson, K., Rigotti, T., & Schalk, R. (2008). Literature review of theory and research on the psychological impact of temporary employment: Towards a conceptual model. *International Journal of Management Reviews, 10*(1), 25–51. https://doi.org/10.1111/j.1468-2370.2007.00221.x

De Cuyper, N., De Witte, H., Sverke, M., Hellgren, J., & Näswall, K. (2014). Felt job insecurity and union membership: The case of temporary workers. *Drustvena Istrazivanja/Journal for General Social Issues, 23*(4), 577–591. https://doi.org/10.5559/di.23.4.02

De Cuyper, N., Mäkikangas, A., Kinnunen, U., Mauno, S., & De Witte, H. (2012). Cross-lagged associations between perceived external employability, job insecurity, and exhaustion: Testing gain and loss spirals according to the Conservation of Resources Theory. *Journal of Organizational Behavior, 33*(6), 770–788. https://doi.org/10.1002/job.1800

De Cuyper, N., Notelaers, G., & De Witte, H. (2009). Job insecurity and employability in fixed-term contractors, agency workers, and permanent workers: Associations with job satisfaction and affective organizational commitment. *Journal of Occupational Health Psychology, 14*(2), 193–205. https://doi.org/10.1037/a0014603

Dekker, S. W. A., & Schaufeli, W. B. (1995). The effects of job insecurity on psychological health and withdrawal: A longitudinal study. *Australian Psychologist, 30*(1), 57–63. https://doi.org/10.1080/00050069508259607

De Witte, H. (1999). Job insecurity and psychological well-being: Review of the literature and exploration of some unresolved issues. *European Journal of Work and Organizational Psychology, 8*(2) 155–177. https://doi.org/10.1080/135943299398302

De Witte, H. (2005). Job insecurity: Review of the international literature on definitions, prevalence, antecedents and consequences. *SA Journal of Industrial Psychology, 31*(4), 1–6. https://doi.org/10.4102/sajip.v31i4.200

De Witte, H., & Näswall, K. (2003). Objective vs. subjective job insecurity: Consequences of temporary work for job satisfaction and organizational commitment in four European countries. *Economic and Industrial Democracy, 24*(2), 149–188. https://doi.org/10.1177%2F0143831X03024002002

De Witte, H., De Cuyper, N., Handaja, Y., Sverke, M., Näswall, K., & Hellgren, J. (2010). Associations between quantitative and qualitative job insecurity and well-being: A test in Belgian banks. *International Studies of Management and Organization, 40*(1), 40–56. https://www.jstor.org/stable/25704021

De Witte, H., Pienaar, J., & De Cuyper, N. (2016). Review of 30 years of longitudinal studies on the association between job insecurity and health and well-being: Is there causal evidence? *Australian Psychologist, 51*(1), 18–31. https://doi.org/10.1111/ap.12176

De Witte, H., Selenko, E., & De Cuyper, N. (2019). Unemployment and job insecurity: Surprisingly identical twins. In T. Taris, M. Peeters, & H. De Witte (Eds.), *The fun and frustration of modern working life: Contributions from an occupational health psychology perspective* (pp. 45–57). Kalmthout: Pelckmans Pro.

De Witte, H., Vander Elst, T., & De Cuyper, N. (2015). Job insecurity, health and well-being. In J. Vuori, R. Blonck, & R. H. Price (Eds.), *Sustainable working lives: Aligning perspectives on health, safety, and well-being* (pp. 109–128). Dordrecht: Springer.

EU-OSHA (2017). *Worker participation in the management of occupational safety and health: Qualitative evidence from ESENER-2.* Luxembourg: European Agency for Safety and Health at Work.

Eurofound (2019). *How your birthplace affects your workplace.* Luxembourg: Publications Office of the European Union.

Eurofound (2020). *Labour market change: Trends and policy approaches towards flexibilization (challenges and prospects in the EU).* Luxembourg: Publications Office of the European Union. https://www.eurofound.europa.eu/publications/flagship-report/2020/labour-market-change-trends-and-policy-approaches-towards-flexibilisation

Eurostat (2019). Temporary employment in Q2 2019. November 20. https://ec.europa.eu/eurostat/en/web/products-eurostat-news/-/ddn-20191120-1

Fervers, L., & Schwander, H. (2015). Are outsiders equally out everywhere? The economic disadvantage of outsiders in cross-national perspective. *European Journal of Industrial Relations, 21*(4), 369–387. https://doi.org/10.1177%2F0959680115573363

Fischmann, F., De Witte, H., Sulea, C., Vander Elst, T., De Cuyper, N., & Iliescu, D. (2021). Validation of a short and generic Qualitative Job Insecurity Scale (QUAL-JIS). *European Journal of Psychological Assessment* (online first). https://doi.org/10.1027/1015-5759/a000674

Friedman, G. (2014). Workers without employers: Shadow corporations and the rise of the gig economy. *Review of Keynesian Economics, 2*(2), 171–188. https://doi.org/10.4337/roke.2014.02.03

Fuller, J. J. B., & Hester, K. (2001). A closer look at the relationship between justice perceptions and union participation. *Journal of Applied Psychology, 86*(6), 1096–1105. https://doi.org/10.1037/0021-9010.86.6.1096

Fullerton, A. S., Robertson, D. L., & Dixon, J. C. (2011). Reexamining the relationship between flexibility and insecurity. In D. Brady (Ed.), *Comparing European workers part a* (pp. 9–41). Bingley: Emerald.

Gebert, R. (2021). The pitfalls and promises of successfully organizing Foodora couriers in Toronto. In J. Drahokoupil & K. Vandaele (Eds.), *A modern guide to labour and the platform economy* (pp. 274–289). Cheltenham, UK and Northampton, MA, USA: Edward Elgar Publishing.

Goslinga, S., & Sverke, M. (2003). Atypical work and trade union membership: Union attitudes and union turnover intention among traditional versus atypically employed union members. *Economic and Industrial Democracy, 24*(2), 290–312. https://doi.org/10.1177/0143831x03024002007

Goslinga, S., Hellgren, J., Chirumbolo, A., De Witte, H., Näswall, K., & Sverke, M. (2005). The role of union support in coping with job insecurity: A study among union members from three European countries. *SA Journal of Industrial Psychology, 31*(4), 72–78. https://doi.org/10.4102/sajip.v31i4.215

Greenhalgh, L., & Rosenblatt, Z. (1984). Job insecurity: Toward conceptual clarity. *Academy of Management Review, 9*(3), 438–448. https://doi.org/10.5465/amr.1984.4279673

Guest, D., Isaksson, K., & De Witte, H. (2010). *Employment contracts, psychological contracts, and employee well-being: An international study.* Oxford: Oxford University Press.

Gumbrell-McCormick, R. (2011). European trade unions and "atypical" workers. *Industrial Relations Journal, 42*(3), 293–310. https://doi.org/10.1111/j.1468-2338.2011.00628.x

Hartley, J., Jacobson, D., Klandermans, B., & Van Vuuren, T. (1991). *Job insecurity: Coping with jobs at risk.* London: Sage.

Heaney, C. A., Israel, B. A., & House, J. S. (1994). Chronic job insecurity among automobile workers: Effects on job satisfaction and health. *Social Science & Medicine, 38*(10), 1431–1437. https://doi.org/10.1016/0277-9536(94)90281-X

Hellgren, J., & Chirumbolo, A. (2003). Can union support reduce the negative effects of job insecurity on well-being? *Economic and Industrial Democracy, 24*(2), 271–289. https://doi.org/10.1177%2F0143831X03024002006

Hellgren, J., Sverke, M., & Isaksson, K. (1999). A two-dimensional approach to job insecurity: Consequences for employee attitudes and well-being. *European Journal of Work and Organizational Psychology, 8*(2), 179–195. https://doi.org/10.1080/135943299398311

Hughes, J., & Bell, D. (2015). Bargaining for contract academic staff at English Canadian universities. *Working USA, 18*(3), 377–394. https://thekeep.eiu.edu/jcba/vol0/iss10/35

Ikeler, P. (2019). Precarity's prospect: Contingent control and union renewal in the retail sector. *Critical Sociology*, *45*(4–5), 501–516. https://doi.org/10.1177 %2F0896920517749706

ILO (2016). Non-standard employment around the world: Understanding challenges, shaping prospects. International Labour Office. http://ilo.org/global/publications/ books/WCMS_534326/lang%2D%2Den/index.htm

Jansen, G., & Lehr, A. (2022). On the outside looking in? A micro-level analysis of insiders' and outsiders' trade union membership. *Economic and Industrial Democracy*, *43*(1), 221–251. https://doi.org/10.1177%2F0143831X19890130

Jiang, L., & Lavaysse, L. M. (2018). Cognitive and affective job insecurity: A meta-analysis and a primary study. *Journal of Management*, *44*(6), 2307–2342. https://doi.org/10.1177%2F0149206318773853

Kalleberg, A. L. (2000). Nonstandard employment relations: Part-time, temporary and contract work. *Annual Review of Sociology*, *26*(1), 341–365. https://doi.org/10.1146/ annurev.soc.26.1.341

Kalleberg, A. L. (2001). Organizing flexibility: I flexible firm in a new century. *British Journal of Industrial Relations*, *39*(4), 479–504. https://doi.org/10.1111/1467-8543 .00211

Klug, K. (2020). Young and at risk? Consequences of job insecurity for mental health and satisfaction among labor market entrants with different levels of education. *Economic and Industrial Democracy*, *41*(3), 562–585. https://doi.org/10.1177/ 0143831x17731609

Kößler, F. J., Wesche, J. S., & Hoppe, A. (2022). In a no-win situation: The employment–health dilemma. *Applied Psychology: An International Review* (online first). https://doi.org/10.1111/apps.12393

Kristensen, P. H., & Rocha, R. S. (2012). New roles for the trade unions. *Politics & Society*, *40*(3), 453–479. https://doi.org/10.1177/0032329211424863

Landsbergis, P. A., Grzywacz, J. G., & LaMontagne, A. D. (2014). Work organization, job insecurity, and occupational health disparities. *American Journal of Industrial Medicine*, *57*(5), 495–515. https://doi.org/10.1002/ajim.22126

Lazarus, R. S., & Folkman, S. (1984). *Stress, appraisal, and coping*. New York: Springer.

Lee, C., Huang, G.-H., & Ashford, S. J. (2018). Job insecurity and the changing work-place: Recent developments and the future trends in job insecurity research. *Annual Review of Organizational Psychology and Organizational Behavior*, *5*(1), 335–359. https://doi.org/10.1146/annurev-orgpsych-032117-104651

Legault, M. J., & Weststar, J. (2015). The capacity for mobilization in project-based cultural work: A case of the video game industry. *Canadian Journal of Communication*, *40*(2), 203–221. https://doi.org/10.22230/cjc.2015v40n2a2805

Leschke, J., & Vandaele, K. (2018). Explaining leaving union membership by the degree of labour market attachment: Exploring the case of Germany. *Economic and Industrial Democracy*, *39*(1), 64–86. https://doi.org/10.1177%2F0143831X15603456

MacKenzie, R. (2010). Why do contingent workers join a trade union? Evidence from the Irish telecommunications sector. *European Journal of Industrial Relations*, *16*(2), 153–168. https://doi.org/10.1177%2F0959680110364829

Marino, S., Bernaciak, M., Mrozowicki, A., & Pulignano, V. (2019). Unions for whom? Union democracy and precarious workers in Poland and Italy. *Economic and Industrial Democracy*, *40*(1), 111–131. https://doi.org/10.1177%2F0143831X18780330

Markey, R., & McIvor, J. (2018). Regulating casual employment in Australia. *Journal of Industrial Relations, 60*(5), 593–618. https://doi.org/10.1177%2F0022185618778084

Massimo, F. (2020). Struggle for bodies and souls: Amazon management and union strategies in France and Italy. In J. Alimahomed-Wilson & E. Reese (Eds.), *The cost of free shipping: Amazon in the global economy* (pp. 129–144). London: Pluto Press.

Mayer, S., & Noiseux, Y. (2015). Organizing at Walmart: Lessons from Quebec's women. *Global Labor Journal, 6*(1), 4–23. https://doi.org/10.15173/glj.v6i1.2455

McLean Parks, J., Kidder, D. L., & Gallagher, D. G. (1998). Fitting square pegs into round holes: Mapping the domain of contingent work arrangements onto the psychological contract. *Journal of Organizational Behavior, 19*(S1), 697–730. https://doi.org/10.1002/(SICI)1099-1379(1998)19:1+%3C697::AID-JOB974%3E3.0.CO;2-I

Murphy, C., Turner, T., O'Sullivan, M., MacMahon, J., Lavelle, J., Ryan, L., Gunnigle, P., & O'Brien, M. (2019). Trade union responses to zero hours work in Ireland. *Industrial Relations Journal, 50*(5–6), 468–485. https://doi.org/10.1111/irj.12271

Näswall, K., & Sverke, M. (2014). Unions and changes in working life: New challenges – new opportunities. In A. Day, E. K. Kelloway, & J. Hurrell (Eds.), *Workplace well-being: Building positive and psychologically healthy workplaces* (pp. 245–263). Chichester: Wiley.

Newman, A., Cooper, B., Holland, P., Miao, Q., & Teicher, J. (2019). How do industrial relations climate and union instrumentality enhance employee performance? The mediating effects of perceived job security and trust in management. *Human Resource Management, 58*(1), 35–44. https://doi.org/10.1002/hrm.21921

Nordic Council of Ministers. (2021). *Non-standard work in the Nordics: Troubled waters under the still surface.* https://pub.norden.org/temanord2021-503/#

OECD. (2019). *OECD employment outlook 2019: The future of work.* Paris: OECD Publishing. https://doi.org/10.1787/9ee00155-en.

Oh, H. S. (2012). The unionization of part-time workers in Japan. *Journal of Industrial Relations, 54*(4), 510–524. https://doi.org/10.1177%2F0022185612449132

Pesole, A., Brancati, U., Fernández-Macías, E., Biagi, F., & Gonzalez Vazquez, I. (2018). *Platform workers in Europe.* Luxembourg: Publications Office of the European Union.

Pienaar, J., De Witte, H., Hellgren, J., & Sverke, M. (2013). The cognitive/affective distinction of job insecurity: Validation and differential relations. *Southern African Business Review, 17*(2), 1–22. https://hdl.handle.net/10520/EJC141544

Probst, T. M. (2003). Development and validation of the job security index and the job security satisfaction scale. A classical test theory and IRT approach. *Journal of Occupational and Organizational Psychology, 76*(4), 451–467. https://doi.org/10.1348/096317903322591587

Probst, T. M., Jiang, L., & Benson, W. (2015). Job insecurity and anticipated job loss: A primer and exploration of possible interventions. In U.-C. Klehe & E. A. JU. Van Hooft (Eds.), *The Oxford handbook of job loss and job search* (pp. 31–54). Oxford: Oxford University Press.

Pulignano, V., & Doerflinger, N. (2013). A head with two tales: Trade unions' influence on temporary agency work in Belgian and German workplaces. *The International Journal of Human Resource Management, 24*(22), 4149–4165. https://doi.org/10.1080/09585192.2013.845446

Pulignano, V., Ortiz Gervasi, L., & De Franceschi, F. (2016). Union responses to precarious workers: Italy and Spain compared. *European Journal of Industrial Relations, 22*(1), 39–55. https://doi.org/10.1177%2F0959680115621410

Reilly, P. A. (1998). Balancing flexibility: Meeting the interests of employer and employee. *European Journal of Work and Organizational Psychology, 7*(1), 7–22. https://doi.org/10.1080/135943298398934

Royle, T., & Urano, E. (2012). A new form of union organizing in Japan? Community unions and the case of the McDonald's "McUnion". *Work, Employment and Society, 26*(4), 606–622. https://doi.org/10.1177/0950017012445093

Schoukens, P., Barrio, A., & Montebovi, S. (2018). The EU social pillar: An answer to the challenge of the social protection of platform workers? *European Journal of Social Security, 20*(3), 219–241. https://doi.org/10.1177/1388262718798393

Shore, L. M., Tetrick, L. E., Sinclair, R. R., & Newton, L. A. (1994). Validation of a measure of perceived union support. *Journal of Applied Psychology, 79*(6), 971–977. https://psycnet.apa.org/doi/10.1037/0021-9010.79.6.971

Shoss, M. K. (2017). Job insecurity: An integrative review and agenda for future research. *Journal of Management, 43*(6), 1911–1939. https://doi.org/10.1177 %2F0149206317691574

Skedinger, P. (2018). Non-standard employment in Sweden. *De Economist, 166*(4), 433–454. https://doi.org/10.1007/s10645-018-9317-z

Spreitzer, G. M., Cameron, L., & Garrett, L. (2017). Alternative work arrangements: Two images of the new world of work. *Annual Review of Organizational Psychology and Organizational Behavior, 4*(1), 473–499. https://doi.org/10.1146/annurev-orgpsych-032516-113332

Standing, G. (2011). *The precariat: The new dangerous class.* London: Bloomsbury Academic.

Stewart, A., & Stanford, J. (2017). Regulating work in the gig economy: What are the options? *The Economic and Labour Relations Review, 28*(3), 420–437. https://doi .org/10.1177%2F1035304617722461

Stroud, D. (2012). Organizing training for union renewal: A case study analysis of the European Union steel industry. *Economic and Industrial Democracy, 33*(2), 225–244. https://doi.org/10.1177/0143831x11404577

Sverke, M., & Hellgren, J. (2002). The nature of job insecurity: Understanding employment uncertainty on the brink of a new millennium. *Applied Psychology: An International Review, 51*(1), 23–42. https://doi.org/10.1111/1464-0597.0077z.

Sverke, M., Hellgren, J., & Näswall, K. (2002). No security: A meta-analysis of job insecurity and its consequences. *Journal of Occupational Health Psychology, 7*(3), 242–264. http://dx.doi.org/10.1037/1076-8998.7.3.242

Sverke, M., Hellgren, J., Näswall, K., Chirumbolo, A., De Witte, H., & Goslinga, S. (2004). *Job insecurity and union membership: European unions in the wake of flexible production.* Brussels: P.I.E.-Peter Lang.

Sverke, M., Låstad, L., Hellgren, J., Richter, A., & Näswall, K. (2019). A meta-analysis of job insecurity and employee performance: Testing temporal aspects, rating source, welfare regime, and union density as moderators. *International Journal of Environmental Research and Public Health, 16*(14), 1–29. https://doi.org/10.3390/ijerph16142536

Tanimoto, A. S., Ferré Hernandez, I., Hellgren, J., & Sverke, M. (2021). Non-standard employment contracts: Characteristics and consequences of new ways of working. In C. Korunka (Ed.), *Flexible working practices and approaches: Psychological and social implications* (pp. 191–211). Cham: Springer Nature. https://doi.org/10.1007/978-3-030-74128-0_10

Tetrick, L. E., Shore, L. M., McClurg, L. N., & Vandenberg, R. J. (2007). A model of union participation: The impact of perceived union support, union instrumentality, and union loyalty. *Journal of Applied Psychology, 92*(3), 820–828. https://doi.org/10.1037/0021-9010.92.3.820

Van Hootegem, A., Sverke, M., & De Witte, H. (2022). Does occupational self-efficacy mediate the relationships between job insecurity and work-related learning? A latent growth modelling approach. *Work & Stress, 36*(3), 229–250. https://doi.org/10.1080/02678373.2021.1891585

Vaona, A. (2010). A survival analysis approach to the duration of union membership in Italy. *Applied Economics Letters, 17*(11), 1089–1093. https://doi.org/10.1080/00036840902817482

Virtanen, M., Kivimäki, M., Joensuu, M., Virtanen, P., Elovainio, M., & Vahtera, J. (2005). Temporary employment and health: A review. *International Journal of Epidemiology, 34*(3), 610–622. https://doi.org/10.1093/ije/dyi024

Visser, J. (2019). Trade unions in the balance. ILO ACTRAV Working Paper. Bureau for Workers' Activities. https://www.ilo.org/actrav/pubs/WCMS_722482/lang--en/index.htm

Vo-Thanh, T., Vu, T.-V., Nguyen, N. P., Nguyen, D. V., Zaman, M., & Chi, H. (2022). COVID-19, frontline hotel employees' perceived job insecurity and emotional exhaustion: Does trade union support matter? *Journal of Sustainable Tourism, 30*(6), 1159–1176. https://doi.org/10.1080/09669582.2021.1910829

Webster, E., & Bischoff, C. (2011). New actors in employment relations in the periphery: Closing the representation gap amongst micro and small enterprises. *Relations industrielles/Industrial Relations, 66*(1), 11–33. https://ssrn.com/abstract=1802679

Wilkin, C. L. (2013). I can't get no job satisfaction: Meta-analysis comparing permanent and contingent workers. *Journal of Organizational Behavior, 34*(1), 47–64. https://doi.org/10.1002/job.1790

Wood, A. J., Lehdonvirta, V., & Graham, M. (2018). Workers of the Internet unite? Online freelancer organisation among remote gig economy workers in six Asian and African countries. *New Technology Work and Employment, 33*(2), 95–112. https://doi.org/10.1111/ntwe.12112

Woodcock, J. (2020). How to beat the boss: Game Workers Unite in Britain. *Capital & Class, 44*(4), 523–529. https://doi.org/10.1177/0309816820906349

PART III

BURNOUT: CONTEMPORARY ISSUES

7. Burning questions in burnout research

Wilmar Schaufeli, Jari Hakanen, & Akihito Shimazu

Burnout has been around for about half a century as a metaphor that refers to a specific psychological state that is characterized by mental exhaustion. It first appeared in the United States (US) in the late 1970s and soon spread across the globe, first to Europe and then beyond (Schaufeli, 2017). Meanwhile, a myriad of scientific publications has appeared, not to mention the attention burnout received in the popular press. For instance, entering "burnout" in Google Scholar (November 2022) yields over 1.4 *million* hits, whereas the psychological research database *Psycinfo* includes over 18 *thousand* peer-reviewed papers on the subject. Despite this overwhelming number of scholarly publications some issues are still hotly debated. With this chapter we hope to clarify some major issues in burnout research. In doing so we intend to separate the wheat from the chaff since a lot of unsubstantiated claims and assertions about burnout exist. This is important because we feel that, for decades, scholars, practitioners, managers, and policymakers are not always on the same page.

The overwhelming number of publications necessitates using a big broom instead of a small brush. That means that we do not discuss all we know about burnout, which would be impossible anyway given the sheer quantity of publications. Rather, we focus on six burning questions which refer to some major issues in current burnout research. These questions deal with four topics: the concept of burnout itself (sections 1 and 2); its assessment and prevalence (sections 3 and 4); its relationship with personality and the body (section 5); and burnout interventions (section 6). In the final part (section 7) we present an outlook and discuss avenues of future research.

WHAT IS THE NATURE OF BURNOUT?

Much has been written about the nature of burnout and it is commonly concluded that a generally accepted definition is lacking. Basically, this is correct because, as usual in psychology, different views on the phenomenon exist. Nevertheless, there seems to be an almost universal agreement that burnout refers to a state of mental exhaustion. For instance, Canu et al. (2021) identified 13 different definitions of burnout and found that ten of them included exhaustion as a constituting element. However, disagreements revolve around additional constituting burnout symptoms, the seriousness of the symptoms and their work-relatedness.

Constituting Symptoms

Using the Delphi method in a panel of 50 experts from 29 countries, the following consensual definition of burnout was proposed: "In a worker, occupational burnout or occupational physical and emotional exhaustion state is an exhaustion due to prolonged exposure to work-related problems" (Canu et al., 2021, p. 95). Effectively, this definition reduces burnout to mere work-related exhaustion, or to put it more bluntly, the notion of burnout is simply replaced by exhaustion. This straightforward, one-dimensional approach to define burnout is contrasted by a multi-dimensional approach. For instance, recently, burnout has been described by the World Health Organization in the International Classification of Diseases (ICD-11; WHO, 2019) as an "occupational phenomenon" which is characterized by: "1) feelings of energy depletion or exhaustion; 2) increased mental distance from one's job, or feelings of negativism or cynicism related to one's job; and 3) reduced professional efficacy". This definition is commensurate with the three-dimensional conceptualization of Maslach and Jackson (1981). This definition has been criticized because, rather than being based on theoretical considerations, it resulted from factor analysis of a set of questionnaire items that were supposed to measure burnout and which did yield three factors (Schaufeli & Enzmann, 1998). This procedure reminds one of the fairytale of Baron Von Münchhausen who pulled himself out of the swamp by pulling his own bootstraps.

Drawing on the work of the grand old man of psychological fatigue research, Edward Thorndike (1894–1949), who argued that the basic tenet of fatigue is the intolerance of any effort, Schaufeli and Taris (2005) theorized that burnout is the combination of the inability and the unwillingness to no longer spend the necessary effort at work for proper task completion. In their view, "inability" manifests itself in lack of energy and "unwillingness" in mental distancing from work, representing the energetic and motivational dimension of burnout, respectively. By the way "unwillingness" does not refer to volition (i.e., a conscious decision) but to a motivating process that takes place unconsciously, almost as if it were behind the person's back. Based on this theoretical notion a new conceptualization of burnout was recently proposed: "a work-related state of exhaustion that occurs among employees, which is characterized by extreme tiredness, reduced ability to regulate cognitive and emotional processes, and mental distancing" (Schaufeli, 2021, p. 4). Because all energy has been drained one not only feels extremely tired, but also lacks the energy to

Table 7.1   *Burnout complaints vs. burnout disorder*

	Complaints	Disorder
Discipline	(Occupational health) Psychology	(Occupational) medicine
Assessment	(Multi)dimensional	Diagnosis
Tool	Questionnaire	Clinical interview
Work role	Still working	Sick-listed
Drivers	Primarily work-related	Also non-work-related
Type of intervention	Prevention	Treatment, return to work
Intervention focus	Organization	Individual

effectively regulate cognitive and emotional processes, resulting in cognitive and emotional impairment, respectively. This manifests itself, for instance, in attention and concentration deficits (cognitive impairment) and the inability to control feelings of anger and sadness (emotional impairment). The final constituting element that denotes the motivational dimension of burnout is mental distance, referring to mental withdrawal and psychological detachment from the job. This can be seen as a dysfunctional coping strategy to deal with exhaustion; instead of reducing, it exacerbates exhaustion because it makes the job more stressful.

Seriousness

The fact that burnout may refer to relative mild complaints, which do not prevent employees from working, as well as a chronic disorder, which causes long-term sickness absence, creates quite some confusion. The underlying assumption is that mild complaints will develop into serious symptoms and hence an inability to work. However plausible this assumption may be, scientific evidence for this continuity is lacking. Notably, in a unique prospective cohort among 5,000 workers, burnout scores failed to predict future long-term sickness absence (Roelen et al., 2015). Hence it seems that mild burnout complaints do *not* automatically develop into more serious complaints that lead to long-term sickness absence, most likely because workers recover spontaneously. So, it makes sense to distinguish between burnout *complaints* and burnout as a mental *disorder*. Rather than a continuum, burnout may refer to different phenomena (see Table 7.1).

As shown in Table 7.1 both approaches to burnout differ regarding various aspects and below, we demonstrate that disregarding this distinction may lead to wrong conclusions, for instance about the prevalence of burnout (see the section: "Is there a burnout pandemic?"). Recently, this distinction was also made by Van Dam (2021), who considers complaints to be the result from short-term stress and proposes to use the term "clinical burnout" for the disorder resulting from chronic stress. Moreover, and in line with the study of Roelen et al. (2015), he argues that the development of clinical burnout should not be regarded as a linear process but – like many biological processes – as a process with qualitative different phases. Finally, he maintains that most research – and hence most of our knowledge on burnout – is based on survey research on mild burnout complaints in relatively healthy, working samples. In conclusion, the fact that the same label "burnout" is used for rather different phenomena is confusing and results in a conceptual muddle.

Work-relatedness

Originally, by definition burnout was considered to be a work-related syndrome, but over time the concept of "work" has been stretched. Currently, burnout is also studied among athletes, volunteers, and students, for instance. Although economically speaking these groups do not work, their activities satisfy the psychological definition of work. That is, they engage in meaningful, structured, goal-directed, and mandatory activities. In contrast, this is not the case for pensioners, homecarers or the unemployed, for instance. Hence, also according to the extended definition they cannot burn out (unless they engage, for instance, in volunteer work). Yet, something keeps nagging because pensioners, homecarers and unemployed people can feel dead tired too. However, this does not result from the *activities* they are engaged in but because they experience a lack of meaning, purpose, structure, and social contacts in their social *role*.

The recently introduced concept of parental burnout, defined as "as a state of intense exhaustion related to one's parental role" (Mikolajczak et al., 2019, p. 1319) seems to occupy the middle ground. Clearly, parents do not work in an economic sense since they are not paid for bringing up their offspring. But although they occupy a social role their parental "job" may also be characterized as work in psychological terms, as it is a meaningful, structured, goal-directed, and mandatory activity. Even though parental activities vary widely, and goals are usually implicit and long-term in nature instead of explicit and short-term. So, it seems that parents may also feel mentally exhausted, not because they play the parental role as such, but because they engage in parental activities that can be understood as work in a psychological sense.

Seen from a different perspective, it seems that *job* burnout is mainly related to work-related stressors and not to private life stressors, such as negative life-events, as layman discourse sometimes states. Non-work-related stressors are likely to have only a minor role in job burnout but the risk for burnout increases when there are simultaneously chronic stressors both at work and at home (Hakanen & Bakker, 2017). As a state of energy depletion, burnout actually may increase home-related demands (Hakanen et al., 2008).

Universal

Burnout is not only studied in Western countries but also in the Middle East, Africa, Asia, and Latin America. Interestingly, the order in which the interest in burnout spread around the world seems to correspond to the socio-economic developments of the countries involved, for instance, it emerged in India and China before Africa. Most studies in non-Western countries use the original conceptualization of burnout that was developed in the US. So basically, non-Western burnout studies are replications of those that have been conducted in Western countries and also yielding similar results. Yet, at a more fundamental level Rösing (2003) criticized the concept of burnout as being ethnocentric. She argues that burnout is inherently linked to a job or profession and that these two notions are culture-specific constructs. They only exist in modern industrialized societies and not in traditional, rural, agricultural communities. Therefore, job or professional burnout is intrinsically connected with the former and not the latter. Furthermore, drawing upon the original three-dimensional conceptualization of burnout (Maslach & Jackson, 1981) Rösing (2013) argues that particularly mental distance (depersonalization) and reduced professional efficacy are ethnocentric concepts. The former assumes a typical Western distinction between "me" and "you", whereas the latter presupposes a Western-style notion of personal achievement. By contrast, exhaustion seems to occur universally. For instance, Rösing (2013) observed in her anthropological field studies among the Quechua and Aymaria Indians from the Andes (Bolivia) and the Ladakhs in the Himalaya (Tibet) that what they called "loss of soul" comes very close to mental exhaustion.

Conclusion

The nature of burnout is still debated beyond the fact that almost universally mental exhaustion is considered its hallmark. Some restrict burnout exclusively to this hallmark, so that its specificity is lost (Schaufeli, 2021). Others in contrast favor a multi-dimensional definition, whereby disagreement exists about the additional constituting elements of burnout. We favor a deductive, theory-based rather than an inductively derived definition because of the inevitable arbitrariness of the nature and number of burnout dimensions that is involved in the latter. In addition, it seems important to discriminate between mild and serious burnout symptoms because instead of a continuum (quantitative difference) it is likely that we are talking about different phenomena (qualitative difference). Finally, in our view burnout is always work-related, albeit not in the narrow economical but in the broader psychological sense. However, ultimately, the work-relatedness of burnout is a matter of definition as the case of parental burnout illustrates. Taken together, we define burnout as a work-related state of mental exhaustion which is characterized by extreme tiredness, cognitive and emotional impairment, and mental distancing.

IS BURNOUT A MEDICAL DIAGNOSIS?

The answer to this question differs whether it is answered in North America or Europe. Originally, the term burnout was deliberately introduced in North America to avoid medical stigmatization. Burnout was regarded as a normal reaction to an abnormal, demanding work situation. Therefore, in North America burnout is considered in terms of complaints rather than a disorder (see Table 7.1). However, in Europe burnout became part of the socio-medical discourse. The reason is that European welfare states require formal diagnoses as an entrance ticket for social and medical services, such as sickness and work incapacitation pensions, and prevention and treatment programs, which are funded by public resources. Despite the fact that burnout is not included in the Diagnostic and Statistical Manual (DSM-V), an official catalogue that lists all mental disorders, it is officially recognized as an occupational disease in nine European countries, namely: Denmark, Estonia, France, Hungary, Latvia, the Netherlands, Portugal, Slovakia, and Sweden (Lastovkova et al., 2018). Soon this will be the case in Belgium as well. As we have seen above burnout was recently included in the ICD-11, but curiously enough *not* as a medical condition but as an occupational phenomenon. Hence, it seems that the WHO takes neither side in the transatlantic debate; burnout is included in its official list of diseases, but as an occupational phenomenon instead of a medical diagnosis.

Some countries, notably Sweden[1] (Glise et al., 2010) and the Netherlands (Van der Klink & Van Dijk, 2014), issued detailed, officially sanctioned guidelines for health professionals on the assessment, treatment, and prevention of burnout. Healthcare professionals in these countries are assumed to use these guidelines so that burnout patients have access to public medical and social services. The criteria for burnout that are used in these guidelines are discussed in greater detail below and not only include the nature of the symptoms, but also their duration, and the loss of social roles.

From the onset, the relationship between burnout, seen as a disorder ("clinical burnout") and depression has been debated and this debate still continues. In a way, burnout and depression are considered rival diagnoses. This is not surprising because mental exhaustion plays a prominent role in mood disorder, whereas a depressed mood – the hallmark of mood disorder – is often found in burnout. Roughly, two opposing schools of thought exist; those who believe that burnout and mood disorder are two distinct entities, and those who believe that both are identical. The latter would imply that the notion of burnout is redundant. It is important to realize that different mood disorders exist; for instance, DSM distinguishes between melancholic, catatonic, and atypical types of mood disorders. It is claimed that burnout would mostly resemble the atypical type (Bianchi et al., 2014). Interestingly, both schools of thought claim scientific evidence for their view. But what are the facts? Almost all psychometric studies show that burnout and depression questionnaires measure something different; technically speaking both load on separate factors (e.g., Glass & McKnight, 1996). Nevertheless, an overlap of 20–50 percent is observed, which is by far not enough to conclude that both concepts are *identical*. For instance, after meta-analyzing 67 studies on burnout and depression (and 34 with anxiety) Koutsimani et al. (2019, p. 14) conclude: "Overall, according to our results burnout and depression and burnout and anxiety appear to be different constructs that share some common characteristics and they probably develop in tandem, rather they fall into the same category with different names being used to describe them". Indeed, longitudinal studies that follow employees across time either showed that burnout leads to depression and not the other way around (Hakanen & Schaufeli, 2012), or that both influence each other mutually and develop simultaneously in tandem (Hatch et al., 2019). The first finding agrees with the popular generalization hypothesis that initially burnout symptoms are work-related and then spill over to other life domains, resulting in a more generalized depressed mood. The second finding agrees with the notion that burnout and mood disorder are intertwined.

Please note that the previous studies used workers with mild burnout symptoms, rather than those who suffer from burnout disorder. What about the latter? A Finnish study by Ahola and colleagues (2014) showed that 53 percent of burnout patients also satisfied the diagnostic criteria for mood disorder. At first glance this co-morbidity seems to be quite high, yet a systematic review showed that half of primary care patients with a mood disorder also suffer from an anxiety disorder, and vice versa (Hirschfeld, 2001). So rather than an exception, co-morbidity seems to be a quite common psychiatry.

Conclusion

Although burnout was deliberately not introduced as a diagnostic label, it is, in fact, used as an official diagnosis in European welfare states such as Sweden and the Netherlands. We welcome this because by using burnout as a medical diagnosis employees who suffer from it are eligible for specialized treatment, sickness and disability pensions, and welfare programs. Clearly using burnout as a medical diagnosis that refers to a serious, chronic mental condition may cause some miscommunication because in North America "burnout" signifies relatively mild job stress. On balance, it seems that burnout and depression overlap, but this psychometric, temporal, and clinical overlap is not strong enough to conclude that they are identical. This also meshes with personal communications from numerous health professionals for whom it is obvious that burnout differs from depression (Schaufeli & Verolme, 2022).

HOW TO ASSESS BURNOUT?

As noted earlier, it is essential to distinguish between burnout *complaints* and burnout as a *disorder*. The former can be assessed by self-report question-naires, whereas for the latter a clinical interview is necessary.

Questionnaires

Various burnout questionnaires exist, of which the Maslach Burnout Inventory (MBI) is by far the most popular; it is estimated that it is used in about 90 percent of all scientific publications (Boudreau et al., 2015). Unfortunately, the MBI does not allow discrimination between burnout cases and non-cases because validated cut-offs for high scores are lacking. This is not surprising since the MBI was developed as a research tool and not as an assessment instrument. Another complication is that instead of a single burnout score, the MBI produces three scores for each of its dimensions: exhaustion, cynicism, and reduced efficacy. Tellingly, the MBI test manual explicitly states: "Note that responses to MBI items should not be combined to form a single 'burnout' score" (Maslach et al., 2017, p. 44). In fact, this is odd since burnout is con-sidered a syndrome in the same test manual, which – by definition – denotes a set of related symptoms that refer to the *same* entity. Finally, the MBI is based on an outdated conceptualization of burnout as, on the one hand, it does not include cognitive and emotional impairment (see the section: "What is the nature of burnout?"), whereas on the other hand it includes reduced efficacy, which, rather than being a constituting element, seems to be the consequence of burnout (Schaufeli & Taris, 2005). These are the main reasons that an alternative burnout inventory has been introduced by a team at KU Leuven in which Hans de Witte plays a key-role; the Burnout Assessment Tool (BAT; Schaufeli et al., 2020).

The BAT is based on the conceptualization of burnout that was discussed earlier (see "What is the nature of burnout?") and includes four subscales: exhaustion, cognitive and emotional impairment, and psychological distanc-ing. So compared with the MBI, the BAT includes two new subscales (i.e., cognitive and emotional impairment), whereas reduced efficacy was deleted. In addition to the original Dutch version, Brazilian, Ecuadorian, Italian, Polish, Japanese, Korean, Portuguese, and Romanian versions have been validated, and the BAT is being used in many more countries.[2] Most importantly, it

Table 7.2   *Diagnostic criteria for clinical burnout*

1	Physical and mental exhaustion after minimal effort
2	Reduced mental energy, which is expressed by a lack of initiative and the inability for perseverance, poor endurance, and inability to recover
3	Loss of control or ineffectiveness of the usual coping systems
4	Loss of social/work roles for at least 50 percent
5	Distress symptoms (daily) in the following areas Cognitive (lack of concentration, memory deficits, inefficient thinking) Emotional (irritability, instability)
6	Supplemented by (daily) distress symptoms in at least one of the following areas: Sleep Psychosomatic (e.g., chest pain, palpitations, muscle aches, gastro-intestinal problems) Psychological (e.g., dizziness, oversensitivity to stimuli like sounds, tension, nervousness, worrying, inability to relax, gloomy mood)
7	These symptoms should be present for at least six months

appears that the subscales of the BAT are invariant across seven national samples, meaning that they can be used in similar ways across countries (De Beer et al., 2020). Moreover, it appears that the BAT fulfills the measurement criteria according to the Rasch model so that the four subscales can be combined into one overall burnout score (Hadžibajramović et al., 2021). Recently, also a shortened, time-saving 12-item version of the BAT was introduced, which like the original 23-item version works invariantly for older and younger age, women and men, and across countries (Hadžibajramović et al., 2022).

Clinical Interview

For diagnosing burnout as a disorder, a clinical interview is used that might be based on specific guidelines, that are, for instance, available in Sweden and the Netherlands (see the section: "Is Burnout a Medical Diagnosis?"). The diagnostic criteria for burnout in both countries largely overlap and are displayed in Table 7.2.

If employees satisfy the criteria that are shown in Table 7.2, they are considered to suffer from burnout disorder.[3] The first two criteria are seen as the most distinctive for burnout. In addition to the inclusion criteria listed in Table 7.2, two additional exclusion criteria are used: (1) psychiatric disorder such as mood disorder, anxiety disorder, PTSD, chronic fatigue syndrome, or fibromyalgia; and (2) the symptoms should not be due to substance abuse, medication, or a somatic disease (e.g., diabetes, hyperthyroidism, or arthritis). These diagnostic inclusion and exclusion criteria were also used for establishing clinically validated cut-off scores of the BAT. More specifically, cut-off values were determined in such a way that they differentiate optimally between a healthy group without burnout symptoms and a group with burnout disorder that satisfies the diagnostic criteria for clinical burnout (Schaufeli et al., 2020).

Conclusion

Although burnout complaints can be measured by the MBI at group level, this tool cannot be used to assess burnout at the individual level because clinically validated benchmarks are lacking. Moreover, because the MBI is outdated the BAT has been introduced as an alternative burnout measure. The first psychometric results with the BAT are very promising but more research on the concurrent validity vis-à-vis the MBI is needed. Diagnostic criteria for severe burnout exist that are being used in some countries in clinical interviews to assess burnout disorder. It seems that – as expected – those who suffer from burnout disorder have higher scores on the BAT than, for instance, those with mood disorder (Schaufeli et al., 2022).

IS THERE A BURNOUT PANDEMIC?

The term "burnout" appeared on the scene in the late 1970s, although many examples of burnout *avant-la-lettre* exist. Particularly interesting is the resemblance with neurasthenia – literally "nerve weakness" – that emerged at the end of the nineteenth century and was seen at the time as the result of modern, hectic life (Schaufeli, 2017). Continuous overstimulation by phone, telegraph, newspapers, and trains, weakened the nerves and resulted in mental exhaustion, it was reasoned. The parallel with burnout is striking because today's burnout is thought to result from modern, hectic life as well embodied by the 24/7 economy, social media, mobile phones, and the internet. If the popular media are to be believed, currently a burnout pandemic exists. But is that true?

Burnout Complaints

Unfortunately, no trustworthy data exists that documents the prevalence and development of burnout over the years. For instance, using the MBI with various thresholds and definitions in a sample of nearly 7,000 US surgical residents, Hewitt et al. (2020) found that between 3.3 percent and 91.4 percent suffered from burnout. In a similar vein, a meta-analysis of 56 MBI-studies among European physicians found that between 2.5 percent and 72 percent suffered from burnout (Hiver et al., 2022). Such results are not credible for two reasons because; (1) the variation is too high for a reliable estimation of the burnout prevalence; and (2) these high prevalences are unlikely because healthcare would collapse when most physicians would suffer from burnout.

Once more, these studies illustrate that the MBI cannot be used for estimating the prevalence of burnout complaints since it depends on the chosen arbitrary threshold.

When it comes to the development of burnout across time, virtually no information exists. The closest we can get involves data from the Dutch annual working conditions survey that monitors levels of work-related exhaustion since 1997, using a national representative sample of the national workforce. In the first decade or so the rate of exhaustion fluctuated around 10 percent, after which an increase is observed amounting to 17 percent in 2019 (Schaufeli & Verolme, 2022). The increase has particularly occurred in women aged between 25 and 35 years. It is interesting to note that during the Covid pandemic in 2020 exhaustion rates *fell* by 1.3 percent compared to the pre-Covid year before. The highest prevalence was observed in education (21 percent), information and communication (18 percent), and healthcare and social services (17 percent). Although it is clear that burnout complaints – or more precisely feelings of exhaustion – are steadily increasing over the years, the true prevalence of burnout remains unclear. First, instead of burnout only work-related exhaustion is assessed and second, a rather liberal and not clinically validated cut-off is used identifying cases. Using the BAT with more rigorous and clinically validated cut-offs it is estimated that 12–13 percent of the Dutch working population suffers from more severe burnout complaints (Schaufeli et al., 2020).

In Finland the prevalence of burnout in the general working population was assessed in 1997, 2000 and 2011 with the MBI, and starting from 2019 with the BAT. Burnout was more common in 1997 than in 2000 and 2011. In 1997, 7 percent reported severe burnout and 48 percent mild burnout, whereas the corresponding figures in 2000 and 2001 were around 2.5 percent and 25 percent, respectively. It may be that the higher prevalence of burnout in the late 1990's was due to the economic recession that hit Finland harder than most other Western countries. An ongoing follow-up study with the BAT that started in 2019 investigates the impact of the Covid pandemic. Preliminary results suggest that 6.6 percent of the Finnish working population suffers from severe burnout and 12 percent from mild burnout complaints. Moreover, levels of burnout did not increase up to 1.5 years after the outbreak of the pandemic (Kaltiainen & Hakanen, 2022).

Burnout Disorder

Another source of information are reports by occupational physicians of burnout as an occupational disease (Schaufeli & Verolme, 2022). From 1999 till 2011 the rate of occupational mental disease remained rather stable at about 20 percent, but then it increased to over 60 percent of all occupational diseases in 2020. Currently, mental disorders are the most common occupational disease, followed by musculoskeletal diseases and hearing disorders, respectively. However, despite the relative increase of mental diseases compared to other diseases in the past decade, the *proportion* of burnout remains relatively stable among those with mental diseases at 75–80 percent. In absolute numbers 1,329 burnout cases were reported by occupational physicians in 2020 – 25 percent *less* than in the pre-Covid year 1999. Most likely this is the tip of the iceberg because not all employees have an occupational physician and not all occupational physicians report burnout cases to the national register – although by law they should. Taking underreporting into account, it has been estimated that the annual number of employees suffering from burnout disorder is about 6,000, which corresponds with less than 1 percent of the Dutch workforce (Houtman, 2020).

Strictly speaking, there is little to nothing to say about the occurrence of burnout across countries. To be able to make a meaningful comparison, the same reliable and valid instrument must be used in various nationally representative samples with the same cut-off value. To date no such research exists. In Scandinavian countries such as Norway, Sweden and Finland, large-scale surveys on burnout have been conducted, but these focus on specific regions or professional groups and use different questionnaires and cut-off values. Nonetheless, it is striking that one of the better designed studies estimates the prevalence of burnout in Northern Sweden at 13 percent, slightly lower but in the same range as in the Netherlands (Norlund et al., 2010).

Conclusion

Burnout is *not* typical of our time, as suggested by the historical parallel with neurasthenia. Contrary to what the popular press wants us to believe there is *no* burnout pandemic and studies that suggest otherwise are untrustworthy. The most reliable estimates come from the Dutch annual working conditions survey, which shows an increase in burnout complaints during the last decade. Currently 17 percent of Dutch and 12 percent of Finnish employees report mild burnout complaints, which is too low to speak of a pandemic, particularly because the threshold for burnout complaints is rather low. Besides it is estimated that only about 1 percent of the Dutch workforce suffers from burnout disorder (occupational disease) which comes close to the 2.5 percent in Finland that experiences severe burnout. Tellingly, it seems burnout complaints as well as burnout disorders did *not* increase during Covid (2020). To date, with the exception of Finland and the Netherlands, virtually nothing can be said with certainty about the occurrence of burnout across countries. In fact, this is quite astonishing 40 years after the introduction of the concept.

IS BURNOUT ROOTED IN THE PERSON AND THE BODY?

From the onset it was hypothesized that burnout is related to personality, as it was observed that those suffering from burnout complaints were characterized by diligence and perfectionism, for instance. Also, particularly laymen assume that burnout is – in one way or another – rooted in the body. The debate about the biological nature of burnout is intimately linked with legitimacy of the concept itself. For many, burnout exists to the extent that it is associated with objective biological features. They have internalized biomedical thinking that doesn't allow them to accept that people may suffer from psychological distress unless it can be objectified by the readings of any instruments. It is therefore not surprising that the general opinion is that with burnout the biological balance is disturbed; it is argued that burnout is not so much mental, but mainly physical.

Personality

There have been quite a few studies on the relationship between burnout and personality. A meta-analysis comprised over 100 studies, from which a fairly consistent picture emerges; the Big Five personality traits explain 25–30 percent of the variance in burnout (Swider & Zimmerman, 2010). By far the most important trait is neuroticism, also called emotional instability, followed by extraversion and to a lesser degree conscientiousness. The remaining two traits, agreeableness and openness to experience, hardly matter. Hence, those with burnout complaints are emotionally unstable and not extraverted. Another meta-analysis (Alarcon et al., 2009) adds that those high in burnout also have low levels of self-esteem and self-efficacy and feel dependent from others or from the situation (external locus of control). This meta-analysis also found positive relationships of burnout with perfectionism, and negative relationships with optimism and personal initiative.

The Body

Large epidemiological studies suggest a link between burnout complaints and cardio-vascular disease (Melamed et al., 2006) and common infections (Mohren et al., 2003), for instance. This could indicate an underlying biological mechanism, such as an excessive production of blood lipids and a less effective immune system, respectively. However, a recent meta-analysis of over 30 studies that included almost 40 different biomarkers, including blood lipids and immune parameters, concluded that, "… no potential biomarkers for burnout were found" (Danhof-Pont, 2011, p. 505). For instance, in spite of the popular belief, no difference was found in the level of the stress hormone cortisol in those with and without burnout. These disappointing results were corroborated in a more recent review that focused on the dysregulation of the hypothalamus-pituitary-adrenal (HPA) axis (Jonsdottir & Dahlman, 2019). This review concludes likewise that: "… research cannot confirm any homologous reliable endocrinological or immunological changes related to burnout" (p. 147).

However, indications have been found in some fMRI studies of reduced activity of certain areas of the brain in people with burnout complaints (e.g., Tei et al., 2014). This concerns areas of the brain that have to do with empathy or with certain cognitive functions. Apart from the fact that there are still very few studies on the subject, the chicken-or-the-egg problem remains unresolved: is burnout caused by impaired brain activity or does burnout cause certain areas of the brain to work differently?

Conclusion

When it comes to burnout personality matters, particularly less emotionally stable people are more likely to develop burnout complaints. However, lack of emotional stability is not specific for burnout, as it is also a risk factor for all sorts of other problems such as addiction, psychoses, affective disorders, and medically unexplained symptoms. Furthermore, it seems premature to assume that there is a biological substrate of burnout, albeit that burnout can lead to certain diseases. Some indications exist that burnout symptoms are associated with reduced activity in certain areas of the brain, but cause and effect still need to be disentangled.

ARE BURNOUT INTERVENTIONS SUCCESSFUL?

Throughout the years, an entire burnout industry emerged with countless suppliers of various, sometimes the most esoteric interventions, such as Tibetan singing bowls. Compared to the size of this industry, the evidence base of burnout interventions is relatively limited.

In principle, burnout can be targeted at the individual, team, and organization level. The vast majority of interventions are aimed at the individual, probably because interventions are more difficult to implement at both other levels since they interfere with organizational practices. Moreover, by far, most interventions focus on the prevention of burnout complaints among working employees, rather than the treatment or rehabilitation of those with a burnout disorder. In addition to the relatively small number of intervention studies, they often lack a proper design; for instance, a non-intervention control group is lacking.

Burnout Complaints

Among the thousands of burnout studies, at most a few dozen well-designed intervention studies exist that qualify for meta-analyses. Yet, the results from various meta-analyses are highly consistent, though; burnout interventions have a statistically significant, yet small *positive* effect, with effect sizes around 0.20. For instance, a meta-analysis of Maricuțoiu and colleagues (2014), including almost 50 studies, showed the strongest effect for relaxation, followed by learning new role behaviors and cognitive-behavioral interventions, such as changing dysfunctional thinking patterns and gradual exposure to demanding situations. Another meta-analysis (Iancu et al., 2018) found positive effects in teachers for mindfulness, stimulating professional development, and learning to organize social support. Generally speaking, effects of person-centered interventions are stronger than for organization-centered interventions. Typically, both meta-analyses focused on those with mild burnout symptoms who are still at work.

Burnout Disorder

Today, only a single review is available of interventions for those with burnout disorder that includes almost 20 studies, of which only four are adequately designed and qualify for a meta-analysis (Ahola et al., 2017). Unfortunately, none of these studies showed a significant decrease in burnout symptoms in the intervention group compared to the control group.

Return to Work

In addition to a decrease in burnout symptoms it is, of course, also important that burned-out employees return to work. A meta-analysis also shows a somewhat disappointing picture regarding work resumption (Perski et al., 2017). First, only eight eligible studies could be included that satisfied quality criteria and second, *no* intervention effect was observed for full return to work. Whether employees received specific burnout treatment, were on the waiting list, or received "treatment as usual" did not matter for *full* resumption of work. However, compared to the control group, those who received burnout treatment *partially* returned to work somewhat sooner. Strikingly, burnout, anxiety and depression complaints did *not* significantly decrease as a result of the intervention, which indicates that work resumption and symptom reduction are two different things that do not necessarily go together.

Recently, a systematic review of ten interventions studies that focused on return to work *as well as* symptom reduction drew a somewhat more optimistic picture (Pijpker et al., 2020). Most likely this is because half of the studies did not include a proper non-intervention control group. It appeared that *all* interventions were effective – at least to a certain extent – in facilitating return to work. With regard to symptom reduction, the combined interventions also led to greater improvement in both the short term (after four months) and the long term (after 12 months).

Conclusion

Most striking is the paucity of high-quality intervention studies, which are predominantly aimed at the person and not at the job, the team, or the organization. Relatively mild burnout complaints seem to decrease as a result of person-centered interventions, such as relaxation, mindfulness, and cognitive-behavioral approaches. For people with severe burnout complaints, things look less promising, though. Interventions that exclusively focus on work resumption are successful in promoting partial instead of full return to work. There are some indications that combined interventions which focus on symptom reduction as well as work resumption might be successful in achieving both goals. Yet, some caution is warranted because many of the reviewed combined interventions did not include a control group.

OUTLOOK – HOW TO SOLVE THE PARADOX?

In spite of the countless scientific publications on burnout that have appeared in the past half century, most burning questions could only be answered preliminarily. Table 7.3 below displays an overview that also includes proposed actions, particularly as far as future research is concerned.

The fact that plentiful research on burnout exists but that many questions still wait for a final answer illustrates the paradox of burnout between quantity and quality. How is it possible that so much research about burnout has been carried out over the years and yet relatively little is known? We believe that three reasons can be identified for that.

First, there is no agreement about what burnout really is, except that it refers to a state of mental exhaustion (see the section: "What is the nature of burnout?"). In the absence of a credible alternative, the definition that is implied in the MBI came to be *the* definition of burnout. But this circularity does not solve the problem, despite the fact that the WHO recently adapted the definition of burnout that is implied in the MBI. What adds to the confusion is that this tool does not yield a total burnout score so that as a stopgap measure, work-related exhaustion is often used as *pars pro toto* for burnout. However,

Table 7.3   *Summary of burning questions, answers, and actions*

Burning question	Preliminary answer	Proposed action
What is the nature of burnout?	No agreement exists beyond that burnout is a state of mental exhaustion.	Full agreement may be an illusion, yet a theory-based conceptualization was proposed that might spur future research.
Is burnout a medical diagnosis?	The scientific community is not completely convinced that burnout can – and should – be considered a psychological disorder as well.	Practitioners in Europe consider burnout as a disorder and scholars should follow suit.
How to assess burnout?	Burnout complaints can be assessed with questionnaires, and burnout disorder with a clinical interview.	Research should focus more on the use of diagnostic guidelines and clinical interviews.
Is there a burnout pandemic?	No burnout pandemic exists, particularly not when it comes to burnout disorder.	Improvement of deteriorating working conditions is key for prevention of mild burnout complaints.
Is burnout rooted in the person and the body?	Burnout is related to personality characteristics but not to biomarkers.	Instead of research on popular personality models (Big 5), brain research and rigorous psychophysiological research.
Are burnout interventions successful?	Individual-based interventions for mild burnout complaints are successful.	Strong focus on team- and organization-based interventions and on interventions for burnout disorder.

this is a dead-end street since burnout is more than mere occupational fatigue or exhaustion, as was argued above. As a result, much of our knowledge of burnout is limited to exhaustion. For instance, the distinctive annual Dutch Working Conditions survey has monitored work-related exhaustion and not burnout for more than two decades. Future research using the BAT might increase our knowledge of burnout.

Second, virtually all research focuses on burnout complaints and not on burnout as a psychological disorder. As is illustrated throughout this chapter, both are very different phenomena that should not be interchanged. The former refers to work-related stress symptoms, from which most people recover spontaneously or continue to work with. The latter refers to severe, chronic, and disabling symptoms that are associated with long-term sickness absence. Historically speaking the metamorphosis from job stress to disorder occurred when the concept of burnout crossed the Atlantic. As a result, almost all research on severe burnout was carried out in Europe, most notably in Scandinavia and the low countries (the Netherlands and Belgium). However, European findings on burnout disorder are also interesting for North America. Severe burnout also exists there but may be less visible than in Europe because no public welfare and healthcare system exists for which an entry ticket is required in the form of an officially sanctioned medical diagnosis.

Finally, there is a pragmatic and perhaps even trivial reason why many questions about burnout have not been answered conclusively so far. Researchers often choose the path of least resistance. Carrying out prospective longitudinal research using representative samples or controlled intervention studies among those suffering from clinical burnout, takes much more time and effort than cross-sectional research on burnout symptoms using readily available convenience samples of healthy employees. There is plenty of such easy-to-do burnout research so that we propose a moratorium on one-shot studies about possible antecedents and consequences of burnout because that does not add to our knowledge. In a similar vein, we should also stop studying the prevalence of burnout using unvalidated cut-off values and convenience samples. Epidemiological research only makes sense when clinically validated test norms and representative samples are used. The time and effort that is saved by refraining from this type of easy-to-do research can be much better spent by investigating burnout disorder – including its assessment, biological substrate, epidemiology, and interventions.

How do we solve the quantity–quality paradox of burnout research? We feel that this can only be done by returning to the drawing board, and armed with our current empirical and theoretical knowledge, reflect on the concept of burnout and its assessment, as we have tried to do in this chapter. In doing so it is crucially important to acknowledge the distinction between mild burnout complaints and burnout disorder.

NOTES

1. Clinical burnout is referred to as "stress-related exhaustion disorder".
2. For more information see: www.burnoutassessmenttool.be.
3. In the Dutch guidelines two other, less severe diagnoses are distinguished; job stress and overstrain (surmenage). The former does not include criteria four and seven and instead of distinctive core symptoms, exhaustion and reduced mental energy are considered on equal terms with other distress symptoms. The latter does not include criterion seven.

REFERENCES

Ahola, K., Hakanen, J., Perhoniemi, R., & Mutanen, P. (2014). Relationship between burnout and depressive symptoms: A study using the person-centered approach. *Burnout Research, 1*, 29–37. https://doi.org/10.1016/j.burn.2014.03.003

Ahola, K., Toppinen-Tanner, S., & Seppänen, J. (2017). Interventions to alleviate burnout symptoms and to support return to work among employees with burnout: Systematic review and meta-analysis. *Burnout Research, 4*, 1–11. https://doi.org/10.1016/j.burn.2017.02.001

Alarcon, G., Eschleman, K. J., & Bowling, N. (2009). Relationships between personality variables and burnout: A meta-analysis. *Work & Stress, 23*, 244–263. https://doi.org/10.1080/02678370903282600

Bianchi, R., Schonfeld, I. S., & Laurent, E. (2014). Is burnout a depressive disorder? A reexamination with special focus on atypical depression. *International Journal of Stress Management, 21*, 307–324. https://doi.org/10.1037/a0037906

Boudreau, R. A., Boudreau, W. F., & Mauthe-Kaddoura, A. J. (2015). *From 57 for 57: A bibliography of burnout citations.* Presentation at the 17th Conference of the European Association of Work and Organizational Psychology (EAWOP), Oslo, Norway.

Canu, G., Marca, S., ... Wahlen, A. (2021). Harmonized definition of occupational burnout: A systematic review, semantic analysis, and Delphi consensus in 29 countries. *Scandinavian Journal of Work, Environment & Health, 47*, 95–107. doi: 10.5271/sjweh.3935.

Danhof-Pont, M. B., van Veen, T., & Zitman, F. G. (2011). Biomarkers in burnout: A systematic review. *Journal of Psychosomatic Research, 70*, 505–524. doi: 10.1016/j.jpsychores.2010.10.012.

De Beer, L. T., Schaufeli, W. B., De Witte, H., Hakanen, J., Shimazu, A., Glaser, J., Seubert, C., Bosak, J., Sinval, J., & Rudnev, M. (2020). Measurement invariance of the Burnout Assessment Tool (BAT) across seven cross-national representative samples. *International Journal of Environmental Research and Public Health, 17*, 5604. doi:10.3390/ijerph17155604.

Glass, D. C., & McKnight, J. D. (1996). Perceived control, depressive symptomatology, and professional burnout: A review of the evidence. *Psychology & Health, 11*, 23–48. https://doi.org/10.1080/08870449608401975

Glise, K., Hadzibajramovic, E., Jonsdottir, I. H., & Ahlborg, G. (2010). Self-reported exhaustion: A possible indicator of reduced work ability and increased risk of sickness absence among human service workers. *International Archives of Occupational and Environmental Health, 83*, 511–520. DOI: 10.1007/s00420-009-0490-x

Hadžibajramović, E., Schaufeli, W., & De Witte, H. (2021). A Rasch analysis of the Burnout Assessment Tool (BAT). *PlosONE, 15*, e0242241. https://doi.org/10.1371.

Hadžibajramović, E., Schaufeli, W., & De Witte, H. (2022). Shortening of the Burnout Assessment Tool (BAT) – From 23 to 12 items using content and Rasch analysis. *BMC Public Health, 22*, 560. https://dio.org/10.1186/s12899-022-12946-yhttps://doi.org/10.1186/s12889-022-12946-yhttps://doi.org/10.1186/s12889-022-12946-yhttps://doi.org/10.1186/s12889-022-12946-y

Hakanen, J. J., & Bakker, A. B. (2017). Born and bred to burn out: A life-course view and reflections on job burnout. *Journal of Occupational Health Psychology, 22*, 354–364. https://doi.org/10.1037/ocp0000053

Hakanen, J. J., & Schaufeli, W. B. (2012). Do burnout and work engagement predict depressive symptoms and life satisfaction? A three-wave seven-year prospective study. *Journal of Affective Disorders, 141*, 415–424. doi: 10.1016/j.jad.2012.02.043

Hakanen, J. J., Schaufeli, W. B., & Ahola, K. (2008). The job demands-resources model: A three-year cross-lagged study of burnout, depression, commitment, and work engagement. *Work & Stress, 22*, 224–241. https://doi.org/10.1080/02678370802379432

Hatch, D. J., Potter, G. G., Martus, P., Rose, U., & Freude, G. (2019). Lagged versus concurrent changes between burnout and depression symptoms and unique contributions from job demands and job resources. *Journal of Occupational Health Psychology, 24*, 617–628. https://doi.org/10.1037/ocp0000170

Hewitt, D. B., Ellis, R. J., Hu, Y. Y., Cheung, E. O., Moskowitz, J. T., Agarwal, G., & Bilimoria, K. Y. (2020). Evaluating the association of multiple burnout definitions and thresholds with prevalence and outcomes. *JAMA Surgery, 155*, 1043–1049. DOI: 10.1001/jamasurg.2020.3351

Hirschfeld, R. M. A. (2001). The comorbidity of major depression and anxiety disorders: Recognition and management in primary care. *Journal of Clinical Psychiatry, 3*, 244–254. DOI: 10.4088/pcc.v03n0609

Hiver, C., Villa, A., Bellagamba, G., & Lehucher-Michel, M. P. (2022). Burnout prevalence among European physicians: A systematic review and meta-analysis. *International Archives of Occupational and Environmental Health, 95*, 259–273. DOI: 10.1007/s00420-021-01782-z

Houtman, I. (2020). De epidemiologie van werkgerelateerde psychische aandoeningen en klachten [The epidemiology of work-related mental disorders and complaints]. In W. B. Schaufeli & A. B. Bakker (Eds.), *De psychologie van arbeid en gezondheid* (pp. 259–278). Houten: Bohn Stafleu van Loghum.

Iancu, A. E., Rusu, A., Măroiu, C., Păcurar, R., & Maricuţoiu, L. P. (2018). The effectiveness of interventions aimed at reducing teacher burnout: A meta-analysis. *Educational Psychology, 30*, 373–396. https://doi.org/10.1007/s10648-017-9420-

Jonsdottir, I. H., & Dahlman, A. S. (2019). Mechanisms in endocrinology: Endocrine and immunological aspects of burnout: A narrative review. *European Journal of Endocrinology, 180*, 147–158. DOI: 10.1530/EJE-18-0741

Kaltiainen, J., & Hakanen, J. J. (2022). Changes in occupational well-being during COVID-19: The impact of age, gender, education, living alone, and telework in a Finnish 4-wave population sample. *Scandinavian Journal of Work, Environment & Health, 48*, 457–467. doi: 10.5271/sjweh.4033.

Koutsimani, P., Montgomery, A., & Georganta, K. (2019). The relationship between burnout, depression, and anxiety: A systematic review and meta-analysis. *Frontiers in Psychology, 10*, 1–19. https://doi.org/10.3389/fpsyg.2019.00284.

Lastovkova, A., Carder, M., ..., & Pelclove, D. (2018). Burnout syndrome as an occupational disease in the European Union: An exploratory study. *Industrial Health, 56*, 160–165. doi: 10.2486/indhealth.2017-0132

Maricuţoiu, L. P., Sava, F. A., & Butta, O. (2014). The effectiveness of controlled interventions on employees' burnout: A meta-analysis. *Journal of Occupational and Organizational Psychology, 89*, 1–27. https://doi.org/10.1111/joop.12099

Maslach, C., & Jackson, S. E. (1981). The measurement of experienced burnout. *Journal of Organizational Behavior, 2*, 99–113.

Maslach, C., Leiter, M. P, & Jackson, S. E. (2017). *Maslach Burnout Inventory Manual* (4th ed.). Mind Garden, Inc.: Palo Alto.

Melamed, S., Shirom, A., Toker, S., Berliner, S., & Shapira, I. (2006). Burnout and risk of cardiovascular disease: Evidence, possible causal paths, and promising research directions. *Psychological Bulletin, 132*, 327–353. DOI: 10.1037/0033-2909.132.3. 327

Mikolajczak, M., Gross, J. J., & Roskam, I. (2019). Parental burnout: What is it, and why does it matter? *Clinical Psychological Science, 7*, 1319–1329. https://doi.org/10.1177/216770261985843

Mohren, D. C. L., Swaen, G. M. H., Kant, I., Van Amelsvoort, L. G. P. M., Borm, P. J. A., & Galama, J. M. D. (2003). Common infections and the role of burnout in a Dutch working population. *Journal of Psychosomatic Research, 55*, 201–208. https://doi.org/10.1016/S0022-3999(02)00517-2

Norlund, S., Reuterwall, C., Höög, J., Lindahl, B., Janlert, U., & Birgander, L. S. (2010). Burnout, working conditions and gender: Results from the northern Sweden MONICA Study. *BMC Public Health, 10*, 326. DOI: 10.1186/1471-2458-10-326

Perski, O., Grossi, G., Perski, A., & Niemi, M. (2017). A systematic review and meta-analysis of tertiary interventions in clinical burnout. *Scandinavian Journal of Psychology, 58*, 551–561. DOI: 10.1111/sjop.12398

Pijpker, R., Vaandrager, L., Veen, E. J., & Koelen, M. A. (2020). Combined interventions to reduce burnout complaints and promote return to work: A systematic review of effectiveness and mediators of change. *International Journal of Environmental Research and Public Health, 17*, 55. https://doi.org/10.3390/ijerph17010055.

Roelen, C. A. M., Van Hoffen, M. F. A., Groothoff, J. W., De Bruin, J., Schaufeli, W. B., & Van Rhenen, W. (2015). Can the Maslach Burnout Questionnaire and the Utrecht Work Engagement Scale be used to screen for risk of long-term sickness absence? *International Archives for Occupational and Environmental Health, 88*, 467–475. DOI: 10.1007/s00420-014-0981-2

Rösing, I. (2003). *Ist die Burnout-Forschung ausgebrannt? Analyse und Kritik der internationalen Burnout-Forschung* [Has burnout research burned out? Analysis and criticism of international burnout research]. Heidelberg: Asanger.

Schaufeli, W. B. (2017). Burnout: A short socio-cultural history. In S. Neckel, A. K. Schaffner & G. Wagner (Eds.), *Burnout, fatigue, exhaustion: An interdisciplinary perspective on a modern affliction* (pp. 105–127). Cham: Springer.

Schaufeli, W. B. (2021). The burnout enigma solved? *Scandinavian Journal for Work Environment and Health, 47*, 169–170. doi: 10.5271/sjweh.3950

Schaufeli, W. B., & Enzmann, D. (1998). *The burn-out companion to study and practice*. London: Taylor Francis.

Schaufeli, W. B., & Taris, T. W. (2005). The conceptualization and measurement of burnout: Common ground and worlds apart. *Work & Stress, 19*, 256–262. https://doi.org/10.1080/02678370500385913

Schaufeli, W. B., & Verolme, J. J. (2022). *De burnout bubble* [The burnout bubble]. Houten: Bohn Stafleu van Loghum.

Schaufeli, W. B., De Witte, H., & Desart, S. (2020). *Manual Burnout Assessment Tool (BAT) – Version 2.0*. Intern report; KU Leuven. www.burnoutassessmenttool.be.

Schaufeli, W. B., De Witte, H., & Kok, R. (2022). Inzet van vragenlijsten bij stressgerelateerde aandoeningen: Het verschil maken met BAT en 4DKL [The use of questionnaires for stress-related disorders: Making a difference with the BAT and 4DSQ]. *Tijdschrift voor Bedrijfs- en Verzekeringegeneeskunde (TBV), 30*, 41–45.

Swider, B. W., & Zimmerman, R. D. (2010). Born to burnout: A meta-analytic path model of personality, job burnout, and work outcomes. *Journal of Vocational Behavior, 76*, 487–506. https://doi.org/10.1016/j.jvb.2010.01.003

Tei, S., Becker, C., Kawada, R., Fujino, J., Jankowski, K. F., Sugihara, G., ... Takahashi, H. (2014). Can we predict burnout severity from empathy-related brain activity? *Translational Psychiatry, 4*(6), e393. https://doi.org/10.1038/tp.2014.34.

Van Dam, A. (2021). A clinical perspective on burnout: Diagnosis, classification, and treatment of clinical burnout. *European Journal of Work and Organizational Psychology, 30*, 732–741. https://doi.org/10.1080/1359432x.2021.1948400.

Van der Klink, J. T. L., & Van Dijk, F. T. H. (2014). Dutch practice guidelines for managing adjustment disorders in occupational and primary health care. *Scandinavian Journal of Work, Environment & Health, 29*, 478–487. doi: 10.5271/sjweh.756.

WHO (2019). *International statistical classification of diseases and related health problems, ICD–11*. Geneva: World Health Organization. https://icd.who.int/en.

8. Contextual factors moderating the relationship between qualitative job insecurity and burnout: A plea for a multilevel approach

Tinne Vander Elst, Sofie Vandenbroeck, & Lode Godderis

Work psychology is the study of the impact of work (at the level of functions and tasks) on the working person, with the ultimate goal of adapting work to the person so that they can function more optimally (De Witte, 2005a). Work stress takes a prominent place in work psychology. It is an umbrella term referring to stressful work characteristics ("stressors"), stress reactions ("strain"), as well as to an imbalance between the demands of the work situation and the ability of the individual to deal with these demands (stress as an interaction between the context and the person). These three meanings of work stress can be reduced to one fairly straightforward model of work psychology – the basic model of work psychology – which was presented by De Witte in his Work Psychology course (part 1), organized at the University of Leuven from 2000 to 2023 (De Witte, 2005a). Central to this model is the prediction that the perceived work situation affects workers' psychological functioning. De Witte conceives of the job situation as aspects of the job content, the working conditions, the employment conditions, working relationships and the work organization, aligned with the "five aspects of work" described in the Belgian legislation regarding the prevention of psychosocial risks at work. Workers' psychological functioning reflects well-being (e.g., burnout), attitudes (e.g., organizational commitment) and performance. In addition, the model predicts that the relationship between the work situation and the employees' functioning is moderated by personal characteristics (e.g., negative affectivity) as well as contextual factors (e.g., social support, organizational communication). As such, it is a simplified version of multiple work stress theories that have been presented during the last decades, such as the Job Demands–Resources model (Bakker & Demerouti, 2007).

The basic model of work psychology has significance for theory development on work psychological phenomena as well as for identifying focal points for stress prevention and well-being policy. Although Hans De Witte has invested greatly and has significantly enhanced our theoretical knowledge on various work psychological phenomena (e.g., job insecurity, workplace bullying, technostress) and its underlying processes (De Witte, 2016; Sparidans et al., 2023; Van den Brande et al., 2020), he never forgot the essential importance of transferring and applying this knowledge to the working field. By redesigning the job and the work context, practitioners may change "bad work" into "good work" and enhance the beneficial impact of work on workers' well-being (De Witte, 2005a). In this chapter, we will specifically focus on the prediction of contextual factors moderating the relationship between stressors and strain. These contextual factors offer valuable input for secondary prevention directed at the work environment, that is, preventing employees who already show signs of stress (in terms of experienced stressors) from getting sick by improving the work environment (Kompier, 2003).

Although many of those moderating factors (e.g., leadership, organizational communication) are situated at the group or organizational level, these relationships have been studied primarily from an individual perspective (Bliese & Jex, 1999). Researchers have focused on how individual employees perceive and react to the work situation and how moderators at the individual level might moderate these stressor–strain processes. However, it is inaccurate to make inferences about contextual factors situated at the organizational level based on individual-level data (Bliese, 2000; Bliese & Jex, 1999). After all, there might be non-independence among individuals of the same organization: their perceptions and reactions may depend on similar environmental factors and this may influence how they experience and react to the work situation, leading to bias in individual-level results (Bliese & Jex, 1999). Moreover, the non-independence might lead to different results when investigating moderators at the individual level instead of the organizational level. For instance, it is possible that contextual factors buffer the effect of stressors on strain outcomes based on individual-level but *not* on organizational-level results, or the other way round. So, implementing interventions at the organizational level based on individual-level moderators might lead to wrong policy decisions with potentially large financial implications (Bliese & Jex, 1999). Rather, policymakers should base their organizational-level interventions on organization-level moderators.

Hence, the aim of this chapter is to examine whether, in addition to individual-level factors, contextual factors at the organizational level might moderate stressor–strain relationships at the individual level using a multi-level framework (i.e., a cross-level interaction). We will do this within one of the research domains in which Hans De Witte can be considered one of the pioneers, namely the domain of job insecurity. We will specifically focus on the potential buffering effect of the contextual factors of organizational communication and procedural justice in the individual-level relationship between qualitative job insecurity and risk of burnout. To illustrate, we will test our predictions using a large-scale sample by IDEWE (a Belgian occupational health service) of 35,558 employees clustered within 83 organizations from various sectors.

ORGANIZATIONAL COMMUNICATION AND PROCEDURAL JUSTICE AS MODERATORS OF THE RELATIONSHIP BETWEEN QUALITATIVE JOB INSECURITY AND BURNOUT

Job insecurity refers to the "subjectively perceived likelihood of involuntary job loss" (i.e., quantitative job insecurity; De Witte, 2016, p. 99), as well as to the perceived threat of losing valued job features (Fischmann et al., 2022). The latter is called qualitative job insecurity and will be our focus. Although qualitative job insecurity, compared to quantitative job insecurity, is under-explored in job insecurity research, it might be relevant during organizational changes without jobs being at risk, and in countries like Belgium with strong employment legislation and solid social security systems. Relying on the Transactional Theory of Stress and Coping (Lazarus & Folkman, 1984), qualitative job insecurity can be conceived as an appraisal of one's job situation where individuals evaluate the stakes with respect to their goals, motives and well-being. Specifically, qualitative job insecurity could be considered a primary threat appraisal: employees anticipate losing valued job characteristics without having already suffered harm or loss (Vander Elst et al., 2016). Based on the idea that the anticipation of losing something of value might have just as severe consequences as the loss itself (Lazarus & Folkman, 1984), qualitative job insecurity has been presented as an important work stressor with implications for both employees and organizations. It has been related to various negative outcomes for employee well-being, including burnout and depressive symptoms. In addition, it increases employees' intentions to leave the organization and lowers their work motivation and job performance (De Witte et al., 2010; De Witte et al., 2016; Hellgren et al., 1999).

A next important step is to investigate moderators of the relationship between the stressor of qualitative job insecurity and strain. Indeed, although scholars agree on the aversive impact of (qualitative) job insecurity on employee well-being, multiple studies have found non-significant or weak results (Sverke et al., 2002). This suggests that individual and contextual factors that vary across studies might alter the relationship between qualitative job insecurity and its outcomes. In addition, initial feelings of job insecurity might not always be avoided and primary prevention might not be possible, and therefore there is a need to think of ways to prevent job insecurity from further resulting in these outcomes or at least attenuate its negative impact.

In this regard, we believe organizational communication and procedural justice (covering the concept of employee participation) would be particularly relevant as buffers of the relationship between job insecurity and strain, as was also highlighted by other scholars (e.g., Ashford et al., 1989; De Witte, 2005b), for two reasons. First, they are both characteristics of the organization and can thus be conceived as contextual factors. Organizational communication refers to the extent to which employees receive adequate information about the functioning of the organization (Stoter, 1997). It concerns both the quantity and the quality, or the information value of the communication. It is conceived as a formal and intentional type of communication governed by management that proceeds via predetermined communication structures in the organization (Koeleman, 2012). Although organizational communication closely relates to informational justice, it is not the same. Accurate organizational communi- cation is crucial in order to establish (and thus predict) informational justice or fairness, which more specifically refers to the transparency, adequacy and candidness of explanations individuals receive about procedures and decisions (Kernan & Hanges, 2002). Next, procedural justice is the fairness of the process that leads to decision outcomes in the organization (Colquitt, 2001). It refers to having a voice or being able to participate in organizational decision-making as well as to the adherence to fair process criteria (e.g., consistency of apply- ing procedures, lack of bias). Second, organizational communication and procedural justice might be particularly relevant in insecure situations where the outcome is not clear (yet) and where the most valuable information on the controllability and fairness of the situation can be taken from the information and decision-making process (Van den Bos, 2005).

The buffering roles of organizational communication and procedural justice can be conceived based on the Transactional Theory of Stress and Coping (Lazarus & Folkman, 1984). This theory describes secondary appraisals as evaluations of one's resources to deal with the stressful situation (control appraisals) and the fairness of that situation. We believe that organizational communication and procedural justice might increase individuals' secondary appraisals of control and fairness in insecure situations, thereby protecting them against strain reactions (see also Ashford et al., 1989; De Witte, 2005b; Konovsky, 2000). First, organizational communication is a crucial resource for employees to gain insight into what is going on in the organization, which may increase their feeling of control (DiFonzo & Bordia, 1998; Rotter, 1966). In the context of qualitative job insecurity, organizational communication may help employees to understand when, where and in what way possible changes in the work situation will occur, and as a result, employees will get a better understanding of the stressful situation. This may help them to cope better with qualitative job insecurity (DiFonzo & Bordia, 1998). Moreover, organizational communication may increase the employees' feeling that management is not intentionally withholding information from them and can be trusted (Colquitt & Rodell, 2011), thus reducing the strain when being insecure (Helliwell & Huang, 2011). As such, organizational communication may buffer the positive relationship between qualitative job insecurity and strain. Second, we reason that procedural justice (including the component of employee participation) offers control to employees in insecure situations, enabling them to better deal with qualitative job insecurity (Vander Elst et al., 2010). In addition, when experiencing threats to valued aspects of the job (high qualitative job insecurity), procedural justice may reassure employees that decisions are made in a fair way and that individuals are respected and valued, protecting them against strain (Le et al., 2018). Hence, we predict that procedural justice buffers the positive relationship between qualitative job insecurity and strain.

To our knowledge, there are no studies that have investigated organizational communication and procedural justice as moderators of the relationship between qualitative job insecurity and *strain*, although some evidence is available for quantitative job insecurity in relation to diverse outcomes (strain, attitudes, behaviours). Regarding organizational communication (as well as the closely related concept of informational justice), results seem rather mixed. While there is research pointing to a buffer effect of organizational communication or informational justice in the relationship between quantitative job insecurity and poor health/attitudes/performance (e.g., Jiang & Probst, 2014; Schumacher et al., 2021), there are also studies that could not find a moderation effect (e.g., Vander Elst et al., 2010), or only found a moderation effect under certain conditions (e.g., König et al., 2010). For instance, in a cross-sectional study with 3,881 Belgian employees (Vander Elst et al., 2010), organizational communication did not moderate the relationships between quantitative job insecurity and both work engagement and need for recovery. However, in an intra-individual study by Schumacher et al. (2021), employees reported lower levels of contextual performance and productivity in weeks when quantitative job insecurity was higher than usual, unless employees perceived high informational justice. With regard to procedural justice (as well as employee participation, a closely related concept), previous research highlights its potential in buffering the relationship between quantitative job insecurity and negative outcomes, although not all moderation effects proved to be significant or were in the expected direction (e.g., Park et al., 2020; Piccoli et al., 2011; Vander Elst et al., 2010). While Piccoli et al. (2011) found that procedural justice buffered the relationship between quantitative job insecurity and both affective organizational commitment and citizenship behaviours, high procedural justice unexpectedly exacerbated the negative relationship between job insecurity and performance.

Given the inconclusive evidence, the moderating roles of both organizational communication and procedural justice should receive further examination. In doing so, we select burnout as the indicator of strain. Burnout is conceptualized as an occupational syndrome characterized by feelings of energy depletion or exhaustion, increased mental distance from one's job, and reduced professional efficacy (WHO, 2019). It is one of the most frequently investigated indicators of occupational mental health (Schaufeli et al., 2009) and has been related to job insecurity (De Witte et al., 2010; De Witte et al., 2016). We thus hypothesize:

Hypothesis 1: Organizational communication moderates the relationship between qualitative job insecurity and burnout, so that the positive relationship between qualitative job insecurity and burnout would be lower for individuals with higher values of organizational communication.
Hypothesis 2: Procedural justice moderates the relationship between qualitative job insecurity and burnout, so that the positive relationship between qualitative job insecurity and burnout would be lower for individuals with higher values of procedural justice.

BRINGING COMMUNICATION AND PROCEDURAL JUSTICE TO THE ORGANIZATIONAL LEVEL

Hypotheses 1 and 2 align with the vast majority of previous research examining these moderating processes at the individual level (e.g., Piccoli et al., 2011; Schumacher et al., 2021; Vander Elst et al., 2010). That is, all variables where self-reports by employees and relationships were tested at the individual level. However, both organizational communication and procedural justice are defined as characteristics of the organization (Colquitt, 2001; Stoter, 1997), and they are influenced at the organizational level, for instance, by organizational policies, procedures and norms, the manager's actions, and information exchanges (for a general discussion, see Bliese & Jex, 1999). As such, *collective* rather than individual perceptions of the employees would better fit their conceptualization, and could equally buffer the relationship between job insecurity and burnout. Organizational-level communication and procedural justice could provide employees with the general idea that their organization is supportive and is treating them in a fair and respectful way, which in turn might protect employees against the harm of qualitative job insecurity. To make correct inferences about the moderating role of organizational communication and procedural justice as contextual factors at the organizational level, we should therefore investigate their role at that very level (Bliese, 2000; Bliese

& Jex, 1999). This assumes the testing of organization-level moderators on the relationship between qualitative job insecurity and burnout at the individual level (i.e., cross-level interaction). By doing so, we may examine whether the individual-level relationships identified in previous research can be generalized to the organizational level, that is, the level on which organizational interventions are implemented. Indeed, our final concern is prevention of the harm from qualitative job insecurity. Answering the question "Is the relationship between qualitative job insecurity and burnout weaker in organizations that score higher on organizational communication and procedural justice?" would correctly inform policymakers when deciding on implementing interventions directed at these factors at the organizational level.

We are aware of only one relevant study conducting a multilevel analysis on organizational justice moderating the quantitative job insecurity–outcome relationship using a multilevel perspective. Sora et al. (2010) introduced organizational justice climate (including informational and procedural justice, in addition to distributive and interactional justice) as a moderator at the organizational level; an aggregated variable whereby individuals showed high agreement within organizations (i.e., high interrater agreement). They theorized that justice perceptions of an organization's employees may be shared through social interaction, organizational socialization and the use of social information to develop one's own judgements. Organizational justice climate was predicted to buffer the relationship between quantitative job insecurity and detrimental outcomes by providing certainty and stability to the threatened job situation. Sora et al. (2010) found evidence for an organizational justice climate in terms of interrater agreement in 29 out of 47 Spanish organizations (61.7 percent). In these organizations, organizational justice climate attenuated the relationships between quantitative job insecurity, and job satisfaction and turnover intentions, but not in relation to affective well-being.

We take a similar approach by conceiving organizational communication and procedural justice as collective phenomena and model these variables at the organizational level. However, we do not necessarily expect the individuals of an organization to agree in terms of their scores on these moderators and thus we do not assume a culture of organizational communication and procedural justice. Although organizational communication and procedural justice may depend on organizational-level factors (e.g., actions of the manager, organization's policy and procedures), individuals' perceptions may also be influenced by contextual factors at lower levels of the organization (especially in large organizations with a tall hierarchical structure, see e.g., Bliese & Halverson, 1998) and by individual characteristics and experiences creating variability within organizations. Hence, we employ an additive conceptualization; organizational communication and procedural justice are summations of the individual scores within an organization regardless of whether individuals differ much from one another within organizations (Chan, 1998) (for a similar approach, see e.g., Jex & Bliese, 1999). We predict:

Hypothesis 3: Organization-level organizational communication is a contextual variable that moderates the relationship between qualitative job insecurity and burnout, so that the positive relationship between qualitative job insecurity and burnout would be lower in organizations with higher values of organizational communication.

Hypothesis 4: Organization-level procedural justice is a contextual variable that moderates the relationship between qualitative job insecurity and burnout, so that the positive relationship between qualitative job insecurity and burnout would be lower in organizations with higher values of procedural justice.

INDIVIDUAL AND COLLECTIVE ORGANIZATIONAL COMMUNICATION AND PROCEDURAL JUSTICE AS DIFFERENT BUT COMPLEMENTARY PERCEPTIONS

While individual-level perceptions of organizational communication and procedural justice might play a part in how individuals appraise and react to the job-insecure situation ("individual difference model"), organizational-level or collective perceptions of organizational communication and procedural justice could protect employees against strain in job-insecure situations by fostering a general sense that the organization cares about and respects their employees ("contextual model"). Although the latter model best fits the conceptualization of organizational communication and procedural justice as characteristics of the organization, both models might be meaningful for a complete understanding of their interplay in the relationship between qualitative job insecurity (stressor) and burnout (strain). Our predictions are summarized and displayed in the hypothesized models in Figure 8.1.

To substantiate our predictions, we tested our hypothesized models using multilevel data from 35,558 Belgian employees clustered within 83 organizations from various sectors.

An Empirical Test to Ground our Models

Data was collected in 2021 among the employees of 83 Belgian organizations (N = 35,558). For a detailed description of the procedure of data collection, the measurements and the statistical analyses, we refer to the Appendix.

Table 8.1 shows the descriptive statistics and the individual-level correlations for the study variables. As expected, qualitative job insecurity correlated positively with emotional exhaustion and detachment, two dimensions of

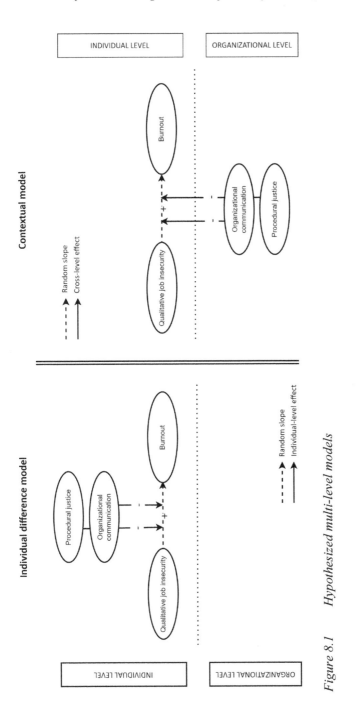

Figure 8.1   *Hypothesized multi-level models*

Table 8.1   *Descriptive statistics and correlations for study variables at the individual level*

Variable	n	M	SD	1	2	3	4	5	6	7	8
1. Age (45 years or older)	35,008	0.47	0.50	—							
2. Gender (Men)	34,483	0.56	0.50	0.03***	—						
3. Education (Higher studies)	35,139	0.61	0.49	0.09***	-0.09***	—					
4. Qualitative job insecurity	35,395	2.55	1.03	0.02***	0.04***	-0.01*	—				
5. Emotional exhaustion	35,394	3.20	1.52	-0.03***	-0.01	0.02**	0.46***	—			
6. Detachment	35,333	2.66	1.48	-0.05***	0.04***	0.03***	0.54***	0.72***	—		
7. Organizational communication	35,387	3.27	0.89	0.01*	0.003	0.03***	-0.42***	-0.34***	-0.43***	—	
8. Procedural justice	35,173	3.42	0.81	-0.02***	0.02***	0.05***	-0.40***	-0.33***	-0.42***	0.46***	—

Note : * p < .05. ** p < .01. *** p < .001

burnout. Organizational communication and procedural justice were negatively related to qualitative job insecurity and the burnout dimensions.

The hypothesized models were tested by running multilevel path analyses in MPlus 8.7 (Muthén & Muthén, 2013), using the Bayesian estimator with diffuse or non-informed priors (Muthén, 2010). Table 8.2 presents the results of the path models in which the relationships between qualitative job insecurity and both emotional exhaustion and detachment at the individual level were investigated, and where the moderation effect by organizational communication and procedural justice at the individual or organizational level was introduced in a stepwise manner. First, the results show that qualitative job insecurity was positively related to emotional exhaustion and detachment, when modelling fixed intercepts (of emotional exhaustion and detachment) and slopes (of the relationships from job insecurity to emotional exhaustion and detachment), and after controlling for age (0 = *younger than 45 years*; 1 = *45 years or older*), gender (0 = *female*; 1 = *male*) and education (0 = *non higher education*; 1 = *higher education*) (Model 1). Allowing the intercepts and the slopes to vary at the organizational level (i.e., random intercepts and slopes; Model 2) increased model fit ($DIC_{Model\ 2} = 207,934.90 < DIC_{Model\ 1} = 208161.24$). The positive relationships between qualitative job insecurity, and emotional exhaustion and detachment remained significant in this main effect model with random intercepts and slopes (Model 2). Further, DIC comparisons of models with and without random slopes (by constraining the variance of the slope to 0) showed that model fit decreased, suggesting that the qualitative job insecurity–outcomes relationships varied across organizations (emotional exhaustion: $DIC_{Model\ 2\ with\ fixed\ slope} = 207964.48$; $\Delta DIC_{comparison\ with\ Model\ 2} = -29.58$; detachment: $DIC_{Model\ 2\ with\ fixed\ slope} = 207974.21$; $\Delta DIC_{comparison\ with\ Model\ 2} = -39.31$). This is an important prerequisite for investigating cross-level interactions.

Table 8.2   *Results of multilevel path models*

Predictor	DIC	Emotional exhaustion		Detachment	
		β	*95% CI*	β	*95% CI*
Model 1: Main effect model with fixed intercepts and slopes	208,161.24				
Individual level:					
Age (45 years or older)		−0.04	−0.05 to −0.03	−0.06	−0.07 to −0.05
Gender (Men)		−0.02	−0.03 to −0.02	0.02	0.02 to 0.03
Education (Higher studies)		0.03	0.02 to 0.04	0.05	0.04 to 0.06
Qual. JIS		0.46	0.46 to 0.47	0.55	0.54 to 0.55
Model 2: Main effect model with random intercepts and slopes	207,934.90				

Predictor	DIC	Emotional exhaustion		Detachment	
		β	*95% CI*	β	*95% CI*
Individual level:					
Qual. JIS (i.e., mean slope at organizational level)		6.62	4.36 to 9.49	7.22	5.47 to 9.79
Model 3: Individual level interaction model with random intercepts and slopes ("individual difference model")					
Model 3a: Individual level:	204,969.78				
Organiz. comm.		−0.18	−0.19 to −0.17	−0.25	−0.26 to −0.24
Organiz. comm. * Qual. JIS		0.001	−0.01 to 0.01	−0.04	−0.05 to −0.03
Model 3b Individual level:	203,751.07				
Procedural justice		−0.17	−0.18 to −0.16	−0.24	−0.25 to −0.23
Procedural justice * Qual. JIS		−0.02	−0.03 to −0.01	−0.05	−0.06 to −0.05
Model 4: Cross-level interaction model with random intercepts and slopes ("contextual model")					
Model 4a: Organizational level:	207,946.92				
Organiz. comm		−0.25	−0.41 to −0.08	−0.17	−0.35 to −0.01
Organiz. comm. * Qual. JIS (slope)		−0.31	−0.48 to −0.12	−0.17	−0.37 to −0.01
Model 4b: Organizational level:	207,945.43				
Procedural justice		−0.34	−0.50 to −0.16	−0.41	−0.59 to −0.16
Procedural justice * Qual. JIS (slope)		−0.20	−0.39 to −0.004	−0.27	−0.46 to −0.07

Note: DIC = Deviance Information Criterion; β = STDY Standardized coefficient; *95% CI =* Bayesian 95% Credibility Interval

Next, we tested the moderating role of organizational communication and procedural justice at the *individual* level (Hypotheses 1 and 2) by adding one of these moderators and its interaction term with qualitative job insecurity to the individual level of Model 2 (i.e., "individual difference model"; Model 3). This increased model fit (see Table 8.2). The results show direct relationships from both organizational communication (Model 3a; shown in the upper left in Figure 8.2) and procedural justice (Model 3b; shown in the bottom left in Figure 8.2) to both emotional exhaustion and detachment at the individual level. Hypothesis 1 was partly confirmed: while we found that organizational communication moderated the relationship between qualitative job inse-curity and detachment, it did *not* moderate the relationship with emotional exhaustion. Hypothesis 2 was fully supported: procedural justice moderated the relationship between qualitative job insecurity and both dimensions of burnout. Although three out of four interactions proved to be significant, they only explained a very small proportion of the variance in emotional exhaustion and detachment. The proportion of explained variances for the individual-level interactions involving organizational communication was 0.1 percent and 0.2 percent for emotional exhaustion and detachment, respectively. The interactions for procedural justice also explained 0.1 percent and 0.2 percent of the variance in emotional exhaustion and detachment at the individual level. Figure 8.3 presents the relationship between qualitative job insecurity and detachment as a function of organizational communication: the slope for the relationship between qualitative job insecurity and detachment was slightly less steep for high (+ 1 *SD*) in comparison with low levels (–1 *SD*) of organizational communication, demonstrating the buffering role of organizational communication. The interactions for procedural justice showed a similar pattern.

Finally, we tested whether organizational communication and procedural justice at the organizational level (i.e., individual perceptions aggregated at the organizational level) moderate the relationship between qualitative job insecurity and both emotional exhaustion and detachment at the individual level (Hypotheses 3 and 4) by adding a cross-level interaction effect to the main effect model with random intercepts and slopes (i.e., "contextual model"; Models 4a and 4b) (based on example 9.2 in the MPlus User Guide; Muthén & Muthén, 2013). The results in Table 8.2 and Figure 8.2 (right section) show that collective organizational communication and procedural justice were negatively related to both burnout dimensions at the organizational level. Furthermore, and in line with Hypotheses 3 and 4, collective organizational communication and procedural justice significantly moderated the relationships between qualitative job insecurity and both emotional exhaustion and detachment at the individual level. This was illustrated by the significant relationship between the moderator under consideration and the qualitative job insecurity–outcome slope. The interaction for collective organizational communication was estimated to explain 9.6 percent (Bayesian 95 percent CI = [1.5 percent; 22.8 percent]) and 2.7 percent (Bayesian 95 percent CI = [0.0 percent; 13.6 percent]) of the variance in the slopes among organizations for both emotional exhaustion and detachment, respectively. Furthermore, the interaction for collective procedural justice was estimated to explain 4.2 percent (Bayesian 95 percent CI = [0.1 percent; 15.1 percent]) and 7.2 percent (Bayesian 95 percent CI = [0.5 percent; 21.3 percent]) of the variance in the slopes among organizations for both emotional exhaustion and detachment, respectively. As an example, Figure 8.4 displays the relationship between qualitative job insecurity and emotional exhaustion as a function of collective procedural justice: high (1 *SD* above the mean) collective procedural justice

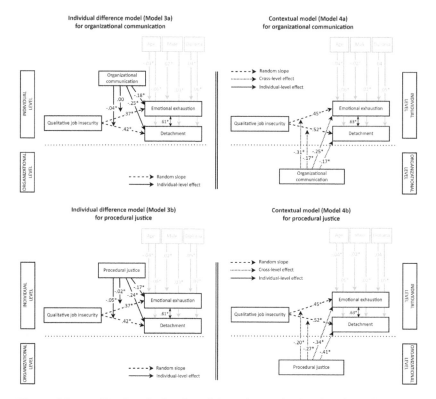

Figure 8.2   Final multi-level models with standardized path coefficients

Note: * reflects a relationship for which 0 did not belong to the Bayesian 95% Credibility Interval.

was associated with a slightly weaker relationship between qualitative job insecurity and emotional exhaustion as predicted. The other interactions showed a similar pattern.

In summary, our tests demonstrated that both individual-level perceptions and organizational-level or collective perceptions of organizational communication and procedural justice buffered the relationship between qualitative job insecurity and two dimensions of burnout at the individual level. In this way, we supported the "individual difference model" and the "collective model" as displayed in Figure 8.1. However, there was one exception; individual per-

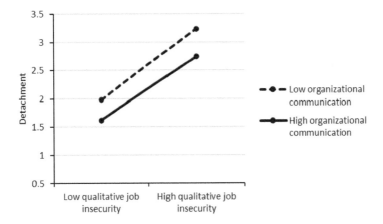

Figure 8.3   Individual level interaction between qualitative job insecurity and organizational communication in relation to detachment

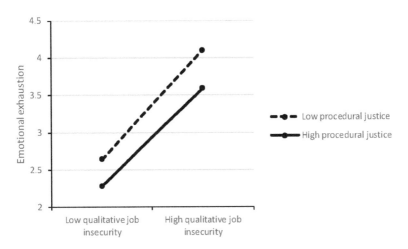

Figure 8.4   Cross-level interaction between individual qualitative job insecurity and collective procedural justice in relation to individual emotional exhaustion

ceptions of organizational communication did *not* moderate the relationship between qualitative job insecurity and emotional exhaustion.

DISCUSSION

In this chapter, we aimed to tap into contextual variables moderating the stressor–strain relationship as presented in the basic model of work psychology by De Witte (2005a). To this end, we specifically examined whether organizational communication and procedural justice buffered the relationship between qualitative job insecurity and burnout, using a multilevel framework. Both individual and collective or organizational-level (i.e., aggregated) perceptions of organizational communication and procedural justice were investigated and as expected, organizational communication and procedural justice were found to attenuate the positive relationship between qualitative job insecurity and burnout. For respondents and organizations with higher levels of organizational communication and procedural justice, the positive relationship between qualitative job insecurity and burnout was somewhat weaker than for respondents and organizations with lower levels of organizational communication and procedural justice. There was only one exception: individual perceptions of organizational communication did *not* moderate the relationship between qualitative job insecurity and emotional exhaustion (a dimension of burnout). These results demonstrate that it is not sufficient to look only at individual perceptions of contextual factors (e.g., organizational communication, procedural justice). We need to consider these contextual factors at a group and organizational level as well. As such, we contributed to previous research in the domain of work psychology which investigates stressor–strain relationships mainly from an individual perspective (Bliese & Jex, 1999).

Individual and Collective Perceptions of Contextual Factors

Along with scholars such as Bliese and Jex (1999) and supported by our own findings, we want to highlight the different but complementary conceptualizations of individual and collective perceptions of contextual factors and their potentially differential impact on stressor–strain relationships. Building on the Transactional Theory of Stress and Coping (Lazarus & Folkman, 1984), we theorized that *individual* perceptions of organizational communication and procedural justice buffer the relationship between qualitative job insecurity (a primary threat appraisal), and both emotional exhaustion and detachment (strain outcomes), by increasing individuals' secondary appraisals of control and fairness of the insecure job situation. Indeed, individual perceptions of organizational communication and procedural justice might help employees in understanding when, where and in what way possible changes in the work situation will occur, providing employees with a sense of control and enabling them to better cope with their job insecurity (Ashford et al., 1989; De Witte,

2005b; Konovsky, 2000). In addition, both organizational communication and procedural justice may increase employees' feelings that management has their best interests at heart and can be trusted, and this belief may protect them against strain (Colquitt & Rodell, 2011; Helliwell & Huang, 2011; Le et al., 2018). In addition, we conceptualized *collective* organizational communication and procedural justice as characteristics of the organization (along with Colquitt, 2001; Stoter, 1997) that are influenced at the organizational level by organizational policies, procedures and norms, and the manager's actions (Bliese & Jex, 1999). We argued that collective or organizational-level communication and procedural justice could provide employees with the general feeling that their organization is supportive and is treating them in a fair and respectful way. This may provide certainty and stability in the threatened work situation, thereby protecting employees against the harm of job insecurity in terms of strain (Sora et al., 2010). Our results show that both types of conceptualizations matter in moderating the relationship between qualitative job insecurity and burnout.

However, there may also be differences in the effects of individual and collective perceptions of contextual factors, illustrated by the lack of a buffer effect of individual-level organizational communication in the relationship between qualitative job insecurity and emotional exhaustion (whereas collective perceptions did buffer this relationship). First, in such cases, interpreting individual-level results at the organizational level might lead to wrong substantive conclusions on the potential buffering role of contextual factors (e.g., incorrectly concluding that the organization cannot buffer the relationship between qualitative job insecurity and emotional exhaustion by establishing good communication). Second, such incorrect conclusions might also lead to erroneous decisions regarding actions and interventions in the work field with potentially serious financial implications (Bliese & Jex, 1999). While individual-level results could meaningfully inform interventions directed at the individual (e.g., a training course to teach individual employees to voice their opinion adequately), only results concerning collective or organizational-level phenomena can be meaningfully used to inform collective interventions at the organizational level (i.e., a communication training course for managers, enabling them to create and propagate a better communication policy within the organization) (Bliese, 2000; Bliese & Jex, 1999). When designing interventions, it is thus important that the level of analysis matches the level of inference (Bliese & Jex, 1999). Otherwise, there is a risk of investing a great deal of resources without seeing any effect at the respective level.

Implications for Work Psychological Research

Next, we want to highlight some implications of this chapter for the *basic model of work psychology* by De Witte (2005a). Our findings regarding the organizational-level moderators align with the model's prediction that contextual factors (e.g., organizational communication, procedural justice) may moderate the relationship between job stressors (e.g., qualitative job insecurity) and strain (e.g., burnout). By aggregating and modelling organizational communication and procedural justice at the organizational level, we investigated these factors as contextual factors rather than merely examining them from an individual perspective. Our results suggest that relationships in the basic model of work psychology (De Witte, 2005a) concerning the contextual factors may be conceived from an organizational perspective too: employees belonging to organizations that are (on average) characterized by good communication and procedural justice suffer less from the effects of job insecurity. This implies that individual perceptions of qualitative job insecurity and burnout are shaped within an organizational context and cannot be understood without taking this context into account. However, we realize that more multilevel research with other moderators, stressors and strain variables is needed to generalize our findings to include all kinds of contextual factors moderating the general stressor–strain relationship. Hence, we would like to join Bliese and Jex (1999) in their call for using this type of multilevel approach in studying contextual factors.

Contributions to Job Insecurity Research

Our results extend existing knowledge on the moderating roles of organizational communication and procedural justice (including participation in decision-making) in the relationship between job insecurity and outcomes (e.g., Jiang & Probst, 2014; Piccoli et al., 2011; Schumacher et al., 2021; Vander Elst et al., 2010) in two ways. First, although there have been studies on these moderation effects for quantitative job insecurity (i.e., threat of job loss) and various outcomes (e.g., Jiang & Probst, 2014; Piccoli et al., 2011; Schumacher et al., 2021; Vander Elst et al., 2010), to the best of our knowledge no previous studies investigated whether these results could be replicated for qualitative job insecurity, referring to the threat of losing valued job characteristics. We found that the buffering role of organizational communication and procedural justice in the quantitative job insecurity–outcome relationship could indeed be generalized to qualitative job insecurity.

Second, we were among the first to investigate the moderating roles of organizational communication and procedural justice as contextual moderators at the organizational level (for another example, see Sora et al., 2010).

As such, our analyses were more congruent with the theory of presenting these constructs as contextual variables or characteristics of the organization. Previous studies using an individual perspective offered mixed evidence on the buffering roles of organizational communication and procedural justice in the relationship between quantitative job insecurity and outcomes (e.g., Jiang & Probst, 2014; Piccoli et al., 2011; Schumacher et al., 2021; Vander Elst et al., 2010). Similarly, we also identified that the results were slightly less consistent for individual-level perceptions than for organizational-level aggregates of communication and procedural justice (e.g., we did not find organizational communication at the individual level to moderate the relationship between qualitative job insecurity and emotional exhaustion). Hence, in future studies, it might be worthwhile exploring whether effects are more consistent when investigating them at the organizational level rather than merely at the individual level. Collective or organizational-level perceptions (in comparison with individual perceptions) might be less subject to short-term or altering situational appraisals and characteristics of the individual, making their protective role in the relationship between job insecurity and strain more stable.

Limitations and Critical Considerations

As in any study, this research has some limitations and several critical considerations can be made. First, given the cross-sectional research design, we cannot make causal inferences. Although longitudinal research can address this shortcoming, it seems difficult to achieve in practice given the magnitude of such a study in a multilevel framework incorporating the intra-individual (across time), inter-individual and organizational levels. Second, all measurements were based on self-reports, possibly increasing common method bias (Podsakoff et al., 2012). Although common method bias is known to attenuate rather than to strengthen interaction effects, one could include other kinds of measurements, such as quality ratings of organizations' communication and procedural justice as provided by external evaluators (e.g., a prevention officer).

Next, in preliminary analyses, we did not find sufficient evidence for a high interrater agreement on organizational communication and procedural justice within organizations ($r_{WG(J)} < .70$ and $AD_{M(J)} > 0.80$ for only 34 percent of the organizations). For most organizations in this study, employees of the same organization thus differed in their individual ratings on organizational communication and procedural justice; they did not have a similar or shared view of their environments in terms of organizational communication and procedural justice. This seems to contradict previous research assuming that there would be something like a shared *climate* of organizational communication and procedural justice (Colquitt et al., 2002; Ehrhart, 2004; Sora et al., 2010).

Although many scholars have introduced strong interrater agreement as an important requisite of multilevel analysis and argued that "aggregation bias" might occur when these requirements are not met (LeBreton & Senter, 2008), others believe that "(a) it is equally erroneous to make group-level inferences from individual-level data (an example of the 'atomistic fallacy'; ...), and (b) that it is appropriate to use aggregate variables to make aggregate-level inferences" (Bliese & Jex, 1999, p. 4). Moreover, scholars have presented additive conceptualizations of contextual factors for which high interrater agreement is not a requirement (Chan, 1998). We followed this current of research, although we realize that this is open for debate. In addition, it is possible that our level of interference (i.e., the organization) is too high and that communication and justice perceptions are shared at a lower level in the organization (i.e., at the team level) (as in e.g., Colquitt et al., 2002; Walumbwa et al., 2008). Future research should illuminate this further.

Finally, despite the many significant interaction effects, we must acknowledge their small effect sizes. At the individual level, effect sizes of the interaction terms ranged between 0.01 percent and 0.02 percent of the variance explained in emotional exhaustion and detachment. At the organizational level, the interaction between qualitative job insecurity and either collective organizational communication or procedural justice explained between 2.7 percent and 9.6 percent of the variability in the slopes for emotional exhaustion and detachment across organizations. Clearly, a possible reason why these interaction effects were still significant is the large sample size used in this study. The small effect sizes raise the question of whether the buffering effects have practical significance. This is further reinforced by the interaction plots, showing only small differences between the slopes. However, we still want to advocate investing in organizational communication and procedural justice, as even small moderation effects may be meaningful (Evans, 1985), and because these variables were also directly associated with strain. In this respect, we advise organizations to invest in realistic communication programmes (Schweiger & Denisi, 1991) and an open and collective planning process (DiFonzo & Bordia, 1998) when implementing changes that create uncertainty among employees.

CONCLUSION

To conclude, this chapter provides theoretical arguments and empirical evidence that organizational communication and procedural justice – both at the individual and organizational level – attenuate the positive relationship between qualitative job insecurity and burnout. These effects were demonstrated in a large-scale and heterogenous sample of employees clustered within organizations and using multilevel path analysis. Our results can inform managers about how to design interventions targeting both individuals and groups of workers to prevent burnout caused by qualitative job insecurity.

REFERENCES

Ashford, S. J., Lee, C., & Bobko, P. (1989). Content, cause, and consequences of job insecurity: A theory-based measure and substantive test. *Academy of Management Journal, 32*(4), 803–829. https://doi.org/10.5465/256569

Bakker, A. B., & Demerouti, E. (2007). The job demands–resources model: State of the art. *Journal of Managerial Psychology, 22*(3), 309–328. https://doi.org/10.1108/02683940710733115

Bliese, P. D. (2000). Within-group agreement, non-independence, and reliability: Implications for data aggregation and analysis. In K. J. Klein and S. W. J. Kozlowski (Eds.), *Multilevel theory, research, and methods in organizations: Foundations, extensions, and new directions* (pp. 349–381). Jossey-Bass/Wiley.

Bliese, P. D., & Halverson, R. R. (1998). Group consensus and psychological well-being: A large field study 1. *Journal of Applied Social Psychology, 28*(7), 563–580. https://doi.org/10.1111/j.1559-1816.1998.tb01720.x

Bliese, P. D., & Jex, S. M. (1999). Incorporating multiple levels of analysis into occupational stress research. *Work & Stress, 13*(1), 1–6. https://doi.org/10.1080/026783799296147

Chan, D. (1998). Functional relations among constructs in the same content domain at different levels of analysis: A typology of composition models. *Journal of Applied Psychology, 83*(2), 234–246. https://doi.org/10.1037/0021-9010.83.2.234

Colquitt, J. A. (2001). On the dimensionality of organizational justice: A construct validation of a measure. *Journal of Applied Psychology, 86*(3), 386–400. https://doi.org/10.1037//0021-9010.86.3.386

Colquitt, J. A., & Rodell, J. B. (2011). Justice, trust, and trustworthiness: A longitudinal analysis integrating three theoretical perspectives. *Academy of Management Journal, 54*(6), 1183–1206. https://doi.org/10.5465/amj.2007.0572

Colquitt, J. A., Noe, R. A., & Jackson, C. L. (2002). Justice in teams: Antecedents and consequences of procedural justice climate. *Personnel Psychology, 55*(1), 83–109. https://doi.org/10.1111/j.1744-6570.2002.tb00104.x

De Witte, H. (2005a). *Definitie: Wat is "arbeidspsychologie"? [Definition: What is "work psychology"?]* [Student handbook].

De Witte, H. (2005b). Job insecurity: Review of the international literature on definitions, prevalence, antecedents and consequences [Job insecurity; International literature; Definitions; Prevalence; Antecedents; Consequences]. *SA Journal of Industrial Psychology, 31*(4), 1–6. http://sajip.co.za/index.php/sajip/article/view/200

De Witte, H. (2016). On the scarring effects of job insecurity (and how they can be explained). *Scandinavian Journal of Work, Environment & Health, 42*(2), 99–102. https://www.jstor.org/stable/43999205

De Witte, H., De Cuyper, N., Handaja, Y., Sverke, M., Näswall, K., & Hellgren, J. (2010). Associations between quantitative and qualitative job insecurity and well-being: A test in Belgian banks. *International Studies of Management & Organization, 40*(1), 40–56. https://doi.org/10.2753/IMO0020-8825400103

De Witte, H., Pienaar, J., & De Cuyper, N. (2016). Review of 30 years of longitudinal studies on the association between job insecurity and health and well-being: Is there

causal evidence? *Australian Psychologist, 51*(1), 18–31. https://doi.org/10.1111/ap
.12176

DiFonzo, N., & Bordia, P. (1998). A tale of two corporations: Managing uncertainty during organizational change. *Human Resource Management: Published
in Cooperation with the School of Business Administration, The University of
Michigan and in alliance with the Society of Human Resources Management,
37*(3–4), 295–303. https://doi.org/10.1002/(SICI)1099-050X(199823/24)37:3/
4<295::AID-HRM10>3.3.CO;2-V

Ehrhart, M. G. (2004). Leadership and procedural justice climate as antecedents of
unit-level organizational citizenship behavior. *Personnel Psychology, 57*(1), 61–94.
https://doi.org/10.1111/j.1744-6570.2004.tb02484.x

Evans, M. G. (1985). A Monte Carlo study of the effects of correlated method variance
in moderated multiple regression analysis. *Organizational Behavior and Human
Decision Processes, 36*(3), 305–323. https://doi.org/10.1016/0749-5978(85)90002-0

Fischmann, G., De Witte, H., Sulea, C., Vander Elst, T., De Cuyper, N., & Iliescu, D.
(2022). Validation of a short and generic qualitative job insecurity scale (QUAL-JIS).
European Journal of Psychological Assessment, 38(5), 397–411. https://doi.org/10
.1027/1015-5759/a000674

Geldhof, G. J., Preacher, K. J., & Zyphur, M. J. (2014). Reliability estimation in
a multilevel confirmatory factor analysis framework. *Psychological Methods, 19*(1),
72–91. https://doi.org/10.1037/a0032138

Hellgren, J., Sverke, M., & Isaksson, K. (1999). A two-dimensional approach to job
insecurity: Consequences for employee attitudes and well-being. *European Journal
of Work and Organizational Psychology, 8*(2), 179–195. https://doi.org/10.1080/
135943299398311

Helliwell, J. F., & Huang, H. (2011). Well-being and trust in the workplace. *Journal
of Happiness Studies, 12*(5), 747–767. https://doi.org/10.1007/s10902-010-9225-7

Jex, S. M., & Bliese, P. D. (1999). Efficacy beliefs as a moderator of the impact of
work-related stressors: A multilevel study. *Journal of Applied Psychology, 84*(3),
349–361. https://doi.org/10.1037/0021-9010.84.3.349

Jiang, L., & Probst, T. M. (2014). Organizational communication: A buffer in times
of job insecurity? *Economic and Industrial Democracy, 35*(3), 557–579. https://doi
.org/10.1177/0143831X13489356

Kernan, M. C., & Hanges, P. J. (2002). Survivor reactions to reorganization:
Antecedents and consequences of procedural, interpersonal, and informational
justice. *Journal of Applied Psychology, 87*(5), 916–928. https://doi.org/10.1037/
0021-9010.87.5.916

Koeleman, H. (2012). *Interne communicatie als managementinstrument: strategieën,
middelen en achtergronden [Organizational communication as managers' instrument: Strategies, channels and backgrounds].* Kluwer.

Kompier, M. (2003). Job design and well-being. In M. J. Schabracq, J. A. M. Winnubst,
& C. L. Cooper (Eds.), *The handbook of work and health psychology* (pp. 429–454).
Wiley. https://doi.org/10.1002/0470013400

König, C. J., Debus, M. E., Häusler, S., Lendenmann, N., & Kleinmann, M. (2010).
Examining occupational self-efficacy, work locus of control and communication
as moderators of the job insecurity–job performance relationship. *Economic and
Industrial Democracy, 31*(2), 231–247. https://doi.org/10.1177/0143831X09358629

Konovsky, M. A. (2000). Understanding procedural justice and its impact on business
organizations. *Journal of Management, 26*(3), 489–511. https://doi.org/10.1016/
S0149-2063(00)00042-8

Lazarus, R. S., & Folkman, S. (1984). *Stress, appraisal, and coping*. Springer.

Le, H., Jiang, Z., Fujimoto, Y., & Nielsen, I. (2018). Inclusion and affective well-being: Roles of justice perceptions. *Personnel Review, 47*(4), 805–820.

LeBreton, J. M., & Senter, J. L. (2008). Answers to 20 questions about interrater reliability and interrater agreement. *Organizational Research Methods, 11*(4), 815–852. https://doi.org/10.1177/109442810629664

Maslach, C., Schaufeli, W. B., & Leiter, M. P. (2001). Job burnout. *Annual Review of Psychology, 52*(2), 397–422. https://doi.org/10.1146/annurev.psych.52.1.397

Muthén, B. (2010). Bayesian analysis in Mplus: A brief introduction. In Citeseer.

Muthén, L. K., & Muthén, B. O. (2013). *Mplus: Statistical analysis with latent variables. User's guide (version 7.11)*. Muthén and Muthén.

Park, K.-H., Youn, S.-J., & Moon, J. (2020). The effect of workforce restructuring on withdrawal behavior: The role of job insecurity, career plateau and procedural justice. *The Journal of Asian Finance, Economics and Business, 7*(7), 413–424. https://doi.org/10.13106/jafeb.2020.vol7.no7.413

Piccoli, B., De Witte, H., & Pasini, M. (2011). Job insecurity and organizational consequences: How justice moderates this relationship. *Romanian Journal of Applied Psychology, 13*(2), 37–49. http://www.rjap.psihologietm.ro/Download/rjap132_1 .pdf

Podsakoff, P. M., MacKenzie, S. B., & Podsakoff, N. P. (2012). Sources of method bias in social science research and recommendations on how to control it. *Annual Review of Psychology, 63*(8), 539–569. https://doi.org/10.1146/annurev-psych-120710 -100452

Rotter, J. B. (1966). Generalized expectancies for internal versus external control of reinforcement. *Psychological Monographs: General and Applied, 80*(1), 1–18. https://doi.org/10.1037/h0092976

Schaufeli, W. B., & Van Dierendonck, D. (2000). *UBOS Utrechtse Burnout Schaal: Handleiding*. Swetz & Zeitlinger B.V.

Schaufeli, W. B., Leiter, M. P., & Maslach, C. (2009). Burnout: 35 years of research and practice. *Career Development International, 14*(2–3), 204–220. https://doi.org/ 10.1108/13620430910966406

Schumacher, D., Schreurs, B., De Cuyper, N., & Grosemans, I. (2021). The ups and downs of felt job insecurity and job performance: The moderating role of informational justice. *Work & Stress, 35*(2), 171–192. https://doi.org/10.1080/02678373 .2020.1832607

Schweiger, D. M., & Denisi, A. S. (1991). Communication with employees following a merger: A longitudinal field experiment. *Academy of Management Journal, 34*(1), 110–135. https://doi.org/10.2307/256304

Sora, B., Caballer, A., Peiró, J. M., Silla, I., & Gracia, F. J. (2010). Moderating influence of organizational justice on the relationship between job insecurity and its outcomes: A multilevel analysis. *Economic and Industrial Democracy, 31*(4), 613–637. https://doi.org/10.1177/0143831X10365924

Sparidans, Y., Vander Elst, T., & De Witte, H. (2023). Technostress en verloopintentie: gemedieerd door burn-out? Een cross-sectioneel onderzoek bij Belgische werknemers. *Gedrag & Organisatie, 36*(1), 1-31. https://doi.org/10.5117/GO2023.1.001 .SPAR

Stoter, A. (1997). *De communicerende organizatie: communicatie in relatie tot organizatieverandering [The communicating organization: Communication in relationship with organizational change]*. Boom Koninklijke Uitgevers.

Sverke, M., Hellgren, J., & Näswall, K. (2002). No security: A meta-analysis and review of job insecurity and its consequences. *Journal of Occupational Health Psychology, 7*(3), 242–264. https://doi.org/10.1037/1076-8998.7.3.242

Van den Bos, K. (2005). What is responsible for the fair process effect? In J. Greenberg & J. A. Colquitt (Eds.), *Handbook of organizational justice: Fundamental questions about fairness in the workplace* (pp. 273–300). Lawrence Erlbaum Associates Publishers.

Van den Brande, W., Baillien, E., Vander Elst, T., De Witte, H., & Godderis, L. (2020). Coping styles and coping resources in the work stressors–workplace bullying relationship: A two-wave study. *Work & Stress, 34*(4), 323–341. https://doi.org/10.1080/02678373.2019.1666433

Van den Broeck, A., Van Ruysseveldt, J., Vanbelle, E., & De Witte, H. (2013). The job demands–resources model: Overview and suggestions for future research. In A. B. Bakker (Ed.), *Advances in positive organizational psychology* (pp. 83–105). Emerald Group Publishing Limited. https://doi.org/10.1108/S2046-410X(2013)0000001007

Van Veldhoven, M., & Meijman, T. (1994). *Het meten van psychosociale arbeidsbelasting met een vragenlijst: de vragenlijst beleving en beoordeling van de arbeid (VBBA) [The measurement of psychosocial job demands with a questionnaire: The Questionnaire for Perception and Judgement of the Work (VBBA)].* Amsterdam: NIA.

Vander Elst, T., Baillien, E., De Cuyper, N., & De Witte, H. (2010). The role of organizational communication and participation in reducing job insecurity and its negative association with work-related well-being. *Economic and Industrial Democracy, 31*(2), 249–264. https://doi.org/10.1177/0143831x09358372

Vander Elst, T., De Cuyper, N., Baillien, E., Niesen, W., & De Witte, H. (2016). Perceived control and psychological contract breach as explanations of the relationships between job insecurity, job strain and coping reactions: Towards a theoretical integration. *Stress Health, 32*(2), 100–116. https://doi.org/10.1002/smi.2584

Walumbwa, F. O., Wu, C., & Orwa, B. (2008). Contingent reward transactional leadership, work attitudes, and organizational citizenship behavior: The role of procedural justice climate perceptions and strength. *The Leadership Quarterly, 19*(3), 251–265. https://doi.org/10.1016/j.leaqua.2008.03.004

WHO. (2019). *Burn-out an "occupational phenomenon": International Classification of Diseases.* https://www.who.int/news/item/28-05-2019-burn-out-an-occupational-phenomenon-international-classification-of-diseases

APPENDIX: METHOD

Sample

Data was collected in 2021 among the employees of 83 Belgian organizations from various sectors (services: $N_{organization}$ = 16, $N_{employees}$ = 12,636, 35.5 percent; trade: $N_{organization}$ = 6, $N_{employees}$ = 8,530, 24.0 percent; construction: $N_{organization}$ = 2, $N_{employees}$ = 4,576, 12.9 percent; industry: $N_{organization}$ = 15, $N_{employees}$ = 3,358, 9.4 percent; the public sector: $N_{organization}$ = 17, $N_{employees}$ = 3,163, 8.9 percent; healthcare: $N_{organization}$ = 11, $N_{employees}$ = 1,561, 4.4 percent; education: $N_{organization}$ = 7, $N_{employees}$ = 743, 2.1 percent; other sectors: $N_{organization}$ = 9, $N_{employees}$ = 961, 2.8 percent), and of various sizes (ranging from 17 to 13,000 employees, $M_{organizations}$ = 793.64 employees). In total, 35,558 employees completed the questionnaire (overall response rate of 53.9 percent). There were slightly more respondents younger than 45 years (52.7 percent) compared to respondents of 45 years or older (45.8 percent). The majority were male (54.3 percent) and there were 42.7 percent women. Finally, 60.5 percent completed higher studies (i.e., Bachelor's degree or higher; 38.3 percent without higher studies).

Procedure

Organizations relied on the services of IDEWE, a Belgian occupational health service of which its main activities rely on the Belgian legislation to perform a risk assessment of psychosocial aspects. Respondents filled out the questionnaire either online (via a hyperlink in an invitation e-mail, or on an online platform) or using a paper and pencil method.

The risk assessments were approved by ethical commission OG117 and were carried out according to the Belgian and international privacy and ethical legislation.

Measurements

All variables were measured using internationally validated scales. For qualitative job insecurity and organizational communication, a shortened version of the original scales was used to limit completion time. For these scales, the original Likert-type scale was also altered to increase consistency throughout the entire questionnaire.

Qualitative job insecurity was measured using three items from the Qualitative Job Insecurity Scale (i.e., "I think that my job will change for the worse in the near future"; "I am worried about what my job will look like in the future"; "Chances are, my job will change in a negative way") (Fischmann et al., 2022). Items were rated on a five-point Likert-type scale from (1) *(Almost) never* to (5) *(Almost) always*. Omega coefficients (ω) were 0.86 ($p < 0.001$) and 0.99 ($p < 0.001$) at the individual and organizational level, respectively (calculations following Geldhof et al., 2014).

Organizational communication was measured with three items from the Questionnaire for Perception and Judgement of the Work by Van Veldhoven and Meijman (1994) (e.g., "I am kept well-informed of important issues within the organization"). A five-point Likert-type scale from (1) *Strongly disagree* to (5) *Strongly agree* was used to rate the items. Omega coefficients (ω) were 0.83 ($p < 0.001$) and 0.97 ($p < 0.001$) at the individual and organizational level. The ICC(1) and ICC(2) were 0.47 and 0.99, respectively. As we also aimed to investigate this variable as a collective phenomenon, we aggregated individuals' ratings at the organizational level.

Procedural justice was measured with the original six-item scale by Colquitt (2001). Example items are: "To what degree do you feel that you can influence the decisions that are made by your supervisor?" and "To what degree do you feel that these procedures are applied consistently by your supervisor?", and items were rated on a scale from (1) *To a very small degree* to (6) *To a very large degree*. This scale was reliable both at the individual ($\omega = 0.85$, $p < 0.001$) and organizational level ($\omega = 0.74$, $p < 0.001$). The ICC(1) and ICC(2) were 0.19 and 0.95, respectively. Individuals' ratings were aggregated at the organizational level to arrive at a measurement of collective procedural justice.

Burnout was measured using the original emotional exhaustion (five items, e.g., "I feel mentally exhausted because of my work") and detachment scales (four items, e.g., "I notice I've taken too much distance from my work") of the general version of the Utrecht Burnout Scale (UBOS-A) by Schaufeli and Van Dierendonck (2000). Emotional exhaustion and detachment are considered to be the most important dimensions of burnout (Van den Broeck et al., 2013). Items were rated on a scale from (1) *Never* to (7) *Always/daily*. Omega coefficients (ω) for emotional exhaustion were 0.90 ($p < 0.001$) and 0.79 ($p < 0.001$) at the individual and organizational level, respectively. Omega coefficients (ω) for detachment were 0.86 ($p < 0.001$) and 0.82 ($p < 0.001$).

Multilevel Measurement Model. Multilevel Confirmatory Factor Analysis (MCFA) (in MPlus 8.7; using the MLR estimator; Muthén & Muthén, 2013) confirmed the expected dimensionality of the study scales. As the hypothesized multilevel measurement model with five factors was under-identified due to a lack of data (too few clusters/organizations), separate MCFAs were conducted for qualitative job insecurity, organizational communication and procedural justice, and for emotional exhaustion and detachment. First, the MCFA for qualitative job insecurity, organizational communication and procedural justice showed a good fit (CFI = 0.91; NNFI = 0.89; RMSEA = 0.04; SRMR-within/-between = 0.04/0.06) and fitted the data better than a one-factor model in which all items loaded on the same factor (model could not converge). Equally, the MCFA with emotional exhaustion and detachment showed a good fit (CFI = 0.95; NNFI = 0.94; RMSEA = 0.03; SRMR-within/-between = 0.02/0.05) and fitted the data better than a one-factor model (Δ-$2LL$(2) = 607.10, p < 0.001; CFI = 0.84; NNFI = 0.79; RMSEA = 0.05; SRMR-within/-between = 0.06/0.13).

Control variables. We selected gender (0 = *female*; 1 = *male*), age (0 = *younger than 45 years*; 1 = *45 years or older*) and education (0 = *no higher studies*; 1 = *higher studies*) as control variables, as they might predict burnout (Maslach et al., 2001) and results might be biased when they are not controlled for.

Statistical Analyses

Hypotheses were tested by running multilevel path analyses in MPlus 8.7 (Muthén & Muthén, 2013). First, we ran a main effect model with fixed intercepts and slopes, including relationships from qualitative job insecurity to both emotional exhaustion and detachment at the individual level (Model 1). Second, we tested a main effect model with random intercepts and slopes, where the intercepts of emotional exhaustion and detachment as well as the slopes of the relationships from job insecurity to emotional exhaustion and detachment were allowed to vary at the organizational level (Model 2). Third, we added one of the two moderators and its interaction term with qualitative job insecurity to the individual level of the previous model, to test for the moderating role of organizational communication/procedural justice at the individual level (Hypotheses 1 and 2). The moderating role of organizational communication and procedural justice was evaluated in separate models (Models 3a and 3b), because we wanted to examine their independent effect. Finally, we added a cross-level interaction effect to the main effect model with random intercepts and slopes (Models 4a and 4b) to test whether organizational communication and procedural justice at the organizational level could moderate the relationship between qualitative job insecurity and both emotional exhaustion and detachment at the individual level (Hypotheses 3 and 4) (based on example 9.2 in the MPlus User Guide; Muthén & Muthén, 2013). Significant interactions were plotted to interpret the direction of the moderation effect. In all models, age, gender and education were entered as covariates of emotional exhaustion and detachment at the individual level. Emotional exhaustion and detachment were allowed to covary.

All exogenous variables were centred. While we group-mean centred all variables at the individual level (i.e., qualitative job insecurity, individual organizational communication, individual procedural justice and the covariates), variables at the organizational level were grand-mean centred (i.e., group-level aggregated organizational communication, group-level aggregated procedural justice).

We used the Bayesian estimator with diffuse or non-informed priors to avoid convergence problems when testing random slopes using the MLR estimator (Muthén, 2010). Although it does not provide fit indices to evaluate model fit, it provides standardized results (unlike the MLR estimator) and the Deviance Information Criterion (DIC) can be used to compare neighbouring models (a smaller value indicates a better fit). Relationships were tested using the Bayesian 95 percent Credibility Intervals (CI; a 95 percent CI including 0 reflects that, given the observed data, there is a 95 percent probability that the parameter falls within this interval. The effect sizes for the predictors were estimated by comparing the overall proportion explained variance (R^2) of the endogenous variables in nested models with and without the predictor under consideration.

9. Age differences in levels and risk factors of burnout in three European countries: A contribution from consultancy practice

Pulso Group: Dirk Antonissen, Audrey Eertmans, Inge Van den Brande, & Lore Van den Broeck

INTRODUCTION

Burnout is recognized as a major problem for today's workforce, and prompts some interesting questions. In human resource management (HRM), the idea of generations, and more specifically generational differences, is a hot topic. Within the generational framework Millennials are often called the "burnout generation", which indicates a higher prevalence of burnout in this group of employees. Typically, it is assumed that specific characteristics attributed to a particular generation remain in place as this generation ages. However, age groups will differ as they progress through successive life stages. There is, therefore, some confusion between the approach that focuses on generations rather than age differences, and this can prove complex. Is the Millennial *generation* more prone to burnout or is this specific *age group* more vulnerable to burnout? The first major question we – as a team from Pulso – want to tackle is whether the prevalence of burnout is indeed higher for some age groups that we use as proxy for generation. Pulso works with managers, employees and partners, to build vibrant, healthy organizations, where everyone is passionate about their work (https://pulso-group.com). This includes the prevention of burnout by developing and implementing integrated and targeted well-being policies. In this chapter, we will build the case that these policies could be age (i.e., generation) specific.

When indeed – as assumed – differences exist in the prevalence of burnout across age groups (i.e., generations), the subsequent question arises: what potential risk factors are related to burnout in particular age groups (i.e., generations)? In other words, are different risk factors related to burnout as employees age and progress through their careers? The answer might provide us with some significant information that can improve prevention strategies for burnout, a topic we will discuss in the final paragraphs of this chapter.

In short, the aim of this chapter is twofold:

1. To test whether the level of burnout differs across age groups (i.e., generations).
2. To identify the specific burnout risk factors in the workplace (in terms of demands and lack of resources) for each age group (i.e., generation).

SETTING THE STAGE: GENERATION VS AGE

Mannheim's (1952) sociological theory of generations proposes that members of each generation share a common identity because of their shared historical experiences or prominent events. Together with influences of upbringing that vary according to the zeitgeist, this means that people from the same generation share certain personal aspects such as motives, attitudes towards work, abilities and needs (Cennamo & Gardner, 2008).

It is assumed that today five different generations are at work in the workplace. However, there is no consensus about the year of birth that is used to define these generations (Lu & Gursoy, 2013). Generally speaking, Traditionalists, Baby Boomers, Generation X, Millennials and Generation Z are distinguished (Table 9.1). For the US workforce, about two-thirds of the current workforce consists of Generation X and Millennials (https://web.uri .edu/worklife/homepages/workplaceproblemspages/age_generation/).

Table 9.1   Five generations at work

	Label	Prevalence in US workforce	Current age	Characteristics
1	Traditionalists Born between 1925 and 1945	2%	77–97	Dependable, straightforward, tactful, and loyal
2	Baby Boomers Born between 1946 and 1964	25%	58–76	Optimistic, competitive, workaholic, and team-oriented
3	Generation X Born between 1965 and 1980	33%	42–57	Flexible, informal, sceptical, and independent

	Label	Prevalence in US workforce	Current age	Characteristics
4	Millennials Born between 1981 and 2000	35%	22–41	Competitive, civic- and open-minded, and achievement-oriented
5	Generation Z Born between 2001 and now	5%	Up to 21	Global, entrepreneurial, progressive, and less focused

Because employees from different generations are simultaneously employed in the same organization, generational differences exist on the shopfloor. At work, such differences might be reflected in attitudes towards work itself, hierarchy and management styles, but also towards work–life and work–family balance, loyalty, need for training or professional development, reliance on (versus resistance to) technology and social media, workplace flexibility, and so on.[1]

On the other hand, one might question whether differences between younger and older employees in the workplace are in fact generational differences or a mere difference in age. Indeed, as time passes, people evolve and change and so do their values, needs, intentions and dreams. What we value and prioritize in our early twenties, might not be what we value a decade later and this will also have an impact on us at the workplace. A clear example is that of starting a family: when evolving into parenthood, most people become more focused on stability and career development as they want to be good caregivers and providers for their family. To take this a step further, we do not all evolve at the same pace, first-time parents range from teens to people in their forties and even beyond. This example illustrates that rather than chronological age (or generation) people's current stage in life matters most (Cennamo & Gardner, 2008).

Let's now have a closer look at how generational differences have been researched. So-called generational research generally relies on cross-sectional studies (e.g., Emory et al., 2022; Huber & Schubert, 2019; Lyons & Kuron, 2013). However, contrasting different age groups at the same point in time is merely an age comparison, and thus not suitable for a generational comparison. As indicated, what distinguishes one generation from another is the shared history and events by the members of that cohort throughout their lives. As such, generations are about trajectories which – by definition – cannot be measured at one point in time. Hence, cross-sectional studies cannot uncover whether differences are specific for a particular generation or can also be found in other generations. Namely, it is also possible that the differences are due to the age of the respondents rather than to the generation they are supposed to belong to (Twenge & Campbell, 2008). The relevant comparisons for generations involve the points of view and behaviours of different cohorts *at comparable ages*. For instance, a proper generational comparison of Generation Z versus Millennials does not involve comparing Generation Z versus Millennials today but rather, comparing Generation Z and Millennials *at the same ages*. Obviously, this implies a longitudinal research design.

Of course, generation, age and stage of life are intrinsically related. In addition, a lot of confounding variables, such as changes in society and culture, and emerging technologies play a role, making it even more difficult to split the impact of generation or age. In the rest of the chapter, we will not separate generation and age, but rather use age as a proxy variable for generation.

Overall, if differences in the personal factors, work attitudes and work motives are related to generation, age or stage of life, research indicates they are rather small to moderate (Costanza et al., 2012; Fairlie, 2013). But even though age and intergenerational differences at the work floor are limited, they do exist and are worth a closer look.

One area where the question about age (i.e., generation) differences is hotly debated is in the field of burnout. Particularly in the popular press it is often said that we are currently going through a *burnout epidemic* and that particularly Millennials are the *"burnout generation"*. Let us dive a little deeper into this issue and investigate this claim.

A BRIEF OVERVIEW OF AGE DIFFERENCES IN BURNOUT

An important question is whether burnout is more *common* in certain age groups or generations as compared to others (see Schaufeli et al., Chapter 7, this volume). A meta-analysis of Lim et al. (2010) investigated personal (including age) and work-related factors as possible correlates of burnout and concludes that overall a significant negative correlation can be found between age and burnout. That means the younger the more and the older the less burned-out. Moreover, age appeared to be the most important factor that discriminates between those with high and low burnout symptoms. Another meta-analysis, based on 36 data samples, corroborated these results and confirmed that younger employees experience more burnout symptoms than older employees (Brewer & Shapard, 2004). In addition, this meta-analysis shows that experienced employees who have worked in the same job for a longer period of time (which of course overlaps with age) report less burnout than less experienced employees, suggesting an effect of job seniority. More recently, De Maeyer and Schoenmakers (2019) showed that 25 percent of young employees (aged 21–35 years) suffered from burnout against 16 percent of those aged 35–50 years and 18 percent of those aged 51–60 years. The authors suggest that this might have to do with high performance pressure, difficulties with making existential choices, and waning tradition. In a similar vein Marchand et al. (2018) found that young employees aged between 20 and 35 are most vulnerable to burnout and that burnout symptoms gradually decrease with more advanced life stages (with the exception of women over 55, showing an increase in burnout levels).

Hence, overall, young employees seem to be particularly susceptible to burnout complaints and the risk thereof decreases as age increases.

THE PULSO STUDY, USING THE WOD® QUESTIONNAIRE

Sample and Questionnaire

The European database of Pulso contains data from representative samples of the working population of Belgium (N = 1,615), France (N = 2,021), and Germany (N = 2,014) (overall N = 5,650). National samples are representative of their national working populations in terms of language, gender, age, education, industry and staff category.

Data was collected using the WOD® questionnaire (*Well-being and Organisational Dynamics*), which is the standard tool of Pulso Europe for measuring psychosocial well-being in the workplace and the organizational dynamics that influence well-being. The WOD® features 100 items, which relate to: (1) the work situation of employees (60 items; work characteristics and individual resources, or "drivers" of well-being at work); (2) their well-being (27 items; measuring eight well-being "indicators"; job engagement, job satisfaction, organizational commitment, loyalty, stress, undesirable behaviour, risk of burnout and absenteeism); and (3) their socio-demographic characteristics (13 items, including age and gender). All drivers and well-being indicators are assessed using a seven-point rating scale ranging from "totally disagree" (1) to "totally agree" (7), or from "never" (1) to "always – daily" (7).

We measured burnout using five items, which tap into the so-called core symptoms as defined by Schaufeli, Desart and De Witte (2020): exhaustion (i.e., "I feel burnt out because of my job"), emotional impairment (i.e., "I find it hard to control my emotions at work"), cognitive impairment (i.e., "I am distracted or find it hard to concentrate on my work"), mental distance (i.e., "I have less interest in my work than I used to") and reduced feeling of competence (i.e., "I feel I can no longer handle my assignments"). The internal consistency (Cronbach's alpha) of this burnout scale is good (0.86). We emphasize that by using these items, we merely measure symptoms of burnout (or "burnout complaints") rather than burnout as a disorder (or "clinical burnout").

Results

Differences in age groups (generations)

When looking at the average burnout score of different age groups, the highest scores are found for the youngest respondents (aged less than 25 years and 25–34 years). As depicted in Figure 9.1, a gradual decline can be seen in the average burnout score as age increases, with the lowest scores for the oldest respondents (aged over 55 years). This trend is found across countries, as well as within each of the three countries individually. Generation Z, roughly corresponding to ages less than 25 years, and Millennials, roughly corresponding to ages between 25 and 44 years, generally have a higher score on burnout than older generations. A formal statistical test (ANOVA) revealed that across all countries age group 1 (less than 25 years – "Generation Z") as well as age groups 2 and 3 (25–44 years – "Millennials") have indeed higher burnout scores than older generations (groups 4 and 5 – aged 45 and more; see Appendix for details). The same picture is found for Germany with the exception that the difference between age groups 1 and 4 is not significant. In addition, in France also the difference between age group 3 on the one hand and age groups 4 and 5 on the other is not significant. Finally, in Belgium "Generation Z" but not the "Millennials" have significantly higher burnout scores as compared to the older generations. So taken together the expected difference in burnout levels between age groups (i.e., generations) was found in the composite pooled sample and with only a few exceptions in each of the three countries. Only one exception appeared in Germany. In France, three exceptions were found, whereas the "Millennials" in Belgium did not differ from older generations. Overall, 16 out of 24 expected differences between age groups were significant (i.e., 66.6 percent; see Appendix 1).

An alternative explanation for this gradual decrease in burnout symptoms with age, is the so-called "healthy worker effect" that is well known in occupational epidemiology (Li & Sung, 1999). This effect refers to a kind of "natural selection" that takes place in the workplace whereby workers with ill health or ill-being drop out over the years so that the most healthy and vital employees remain. Even though this is a plausible alternative explanation for the observed differences between age groups, other counteracting factors may be in play as well. For instance, as employees get older, they develop better and more diverse coping strategies, mature emotionally, and gain a better understanding of their own boundaries (Fairlie, 2013). Hence, it is likely that our results are not adequately explained by the healthy worker effect alone and that age or generational differences play a role in decreasing burnout levels.

Risk factors for burnout

As (slight) differences in burnout occur for different age groups, the question may arise as to which factors are related to these differences. It is important to note that age as such doesn't explain differences in levels of burnout, meaning that the mere fact of being younger or older does not cause burnout complaints (Schaufeli & Verolme, 2022). Instead, factors related to work itself that vary with age are likely to act as drivers for burnout. Likewise, biographical and personal characteristics may impact vulnerability for developing burnout complaints.

The Job Demands–Resources-model (Schaufeli & Taris, 2014) maintains that both stressors (i.e., high job demands) as well as lack of job resources – independently, as well as in concert – pave the way to burnout. Job demands may include, for instance, work overload and task interruption. Also more qualitative job demands, such as work–life imbalance and emotional demands have been found to impact burnout (Schaufeli & Verolme, 2022). In addition, lack of job resources, such as social support, appreciation, role clarity and social climate may act as risk factors for burnout. Apart from these work characteristics, personal factors may also make employees more or less vulnerable to burnout, such as poor resilience and lack of optimism.

Taking this one step further, these potential risk factors of burnout might change over the course of life, as job and personal characteristics evolve. However, research on correlates of burnout across different age groups is rather sparse. A review of the literature reveals that – amongst others – the fol-

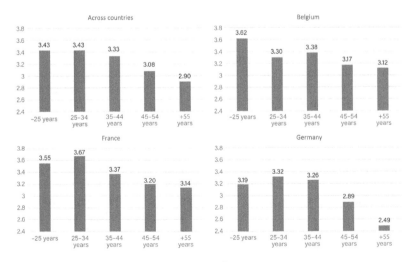

Figure 9.1   Average burnout score of age groups

lowing variables have been identified as correlates of burnout in different age groups: career opportunities, job control, decision making, mismatch between personal and organizational values, and poor person–job fit (Jiang & Yang, 2016; Mockaitis & Butler, 2020; Nakagawa & Yellowlees, 2020; Saber et al., 2018; Widjanarko, 2021). However, overall findings tend to be inconsistent and sample specific (e.g., for nurses or teachers).

To get a more comprehensive picture of age-specific risk factors, we analysed the 60 items from the WOD® questionnaire that tap the work situation of employees. We structured these drivers according to the level of intervention:

1. Person (e.g., resilience, optimism, fear of change, capacity to change)
2. Task (e.g., work complexity, meaningfulness of work)
3. Team (e.g., collaboration, mutual respect)
4. Management (e.g., constructive feedback, support in performing the job)
5. Organization (e.g., procedural fairness, support during change).

In terms of the Job Demands–Resources-model, these drivers assess many job demands and job resources. For the personal factors, the main focus of the WOD® questionnaire is on the concepts of psychological capital (Steeneveld, 2017) and employability (Römgens et al., 2020).

In our study, we calculated the correlations between each of the 60 drivers on the one hand, and burnout on the other hand, for each age category. The "top five" drivers, that are most strongly correlated to burnout per age group can be found in Table 9.2. Inspection of the results from this table indicates that *work complexity* is moderately correlated ($0.41 < r < 0.49$) with burnout in all age groups (albeit somewhat lower in the oldest group). Also, *emotional demands* is included in the top five correlations across all age groups, except the oldest one. Hence, work complexity and emotional demands seem to be common potential risk factors for burnout across all age groups; perhaps with the exception of the oldest group.

Besides these common factors, different age-specific drivers show significant correlations with burnout complaints. For the youngest age group, the *amount of work* (work overload as well as underload) and *interruptions* during work are most important. For 25–34 years old, also too much work (overload) has an impact on burnout, as well as *responsibility* and *fear of change*. For the middle age category (35–44 years), *role clarity* and *appreciation from their manager* is important as well as a *social climate* ("The atmosphere in my team is pleasant"). For the 45–54 years old, the most important factor that is related to burnout is *fear of change* ("I worry that my job will change significantly in the near future"). Also, *resilience* (i.e., the capacity to adapt to difficult or challenging circumstances) plays an important role. For the oldest employees (aged over 55), the organization's *vision for the future* ("I support my organization's plans for the future") correlates highest with burnout complaints. Also, the *physical aspects* of the workplace and *support during change* are important correlates of burnout for the oldest age group.

The most notable finding is the shift in importance of particular risk factors in the work situation for burnout with increasing age. Generally speaking we see an evolution from task-related factors being represented in the top five risk factors for burnout in the youngest employees towards organizational factors being prominent for the oldest employees. Along with this shift, the importance of task-related characteristics gradually declines, whereas in its place other characteristics (related to the person, team, management, and organization) come to the fore. Tellingly, only in the oldest age group are the physical aspects of the job related to burnout, reflecting the decreased physical capacity of older employees.

Table 9.2   *"Top five" correlations with burnout for each age category*

	–25 years	25–34 years	35–44 years	45–54 years	+55 years
1	Work complexity *Task* My job is too complicated	Work overload *Task* I think I have to work too hard	Work complexity *Task* My job is too complicated	Fear of change *Individual* I worry that my job will change significantly in the near future	Vision for the future *Organization* I support my organization's plans for the future
2	Work overload *Task* I think I have to work too hard	Demanding responsibility *Task* My job entails too many responsibilities	Emotional demands *Task* In my work I come across situations that are emotionally difficult for me	Work complexity *Task* My job is too complicated	Physical aspects of the workplace *Organization* I am generally satisfied with the physical aspects of my workplace
3	Interruptions *Task* I am interrupted too often while I work (e.g., by phone calls, emails, enquiries etc.)	Work complexity *Task* My job is too complicated	Role clarity *Task* I know exactly what others expect from me at work	Role clarity *Task* I know exactly what others expect from me at work	Support during change *Organization* I feel supported during the implementation of organizational changes

	−25 years	25–34 years	35–44 years	45–54 years	+55 years
4	Emotional demands *Task* In my work I come across situations that are emotionally difficult for me	Emotional demands *Task* In my work I come across situations that are emotionally difficult for me	Appreciation manager *Management* I feel appreciated by my manager	Emotional demands *Task* In my work I come across situations that are emotionally difficult for me	Work organization *Team* In my team work is well organized
5	Work underload *Task* I do not have enough work to do	Fear of change *Individual* I worry that my job will change significantly in the near future	Social climate *Team* The atmosphere in my team is pleasant	Resilience *Individual* I can usually handle difficulties at work well	Work complexity *Task* My job is too complicated

Note: See Appendix 2 for correlations.

Instead of being merely an effect of age, this age-related shift in importance of risk factors for burnout is likely to be related to a gradual change in perceived job content (from task-related to organizational factors), which might also coincide with other age-related changes such as increased responsibility. This meshes with the finding that job seniority, which clearly is strongly related with age, correlates negatively with burnout (Brewer & Shapard, 2004).

It is important to note that correlations do not imply causality, which can only be established with a longitudinal research design, as explained above. This means that, strictly speaking, we identified *potential* risk factors for burnout.

DIFFERENCES IN HR POLICIES

As we have seen, the most important workplace factors that correlate with burnout change with age. This finding offers some challenges as well as opportunities for human resource management (HRM) and burnout prevention programmes in organizations.

Currently, we witness dramatic demographic changes as the workforce is aging rapidly; the relatively large cohort of Baby Boomers is now retiring and the number of employees aged between 40 and 64 is higher than the number of younger employees aged between 15 and 39. In fact, the number of young people entering the labour market is gradually decreasing (FOD, 2012). This results in a more age-diverse workforce. If, as shown in the previous section, different risk factors for burnout seem to exist for different age groups this suggests a need for age-related HRM and burnout prevention strategies.

The importance of burnout prevention is further highlighted by research showing that prevention programmes are effective, particularly for those with mild symptoms. According to various systematic reviews and meta-analyses, burnout prevention programmes have a small, but consistent positive effect (Dreison et al., 2018; Maricuţoiu et al., 2014; Panagioti et al., 2017). Another meta-analysis on the effectiveness of treatment for severe clinical burnout, leading to long-term sick leave, found no significant effects on burnout symptoms (Ahola et al., 2017). Burnout interventions differ widely and may focus on the individual, the work team or the organization and no consensus exists on which interventions are most effective. In order to prevent severe, clinical burnout and the associated sickness absence, organizations are well advised to fully invest in burnout prevention programmes.

This seamlessly fits with the core idea of an age-conscious HR policy. This is a policy that aims to design HR-practices in order to tackle age barriers and promote age-diverse well-being at the work floor. The goal is to provide a sustainable work environment where employees, irrespective of their age, can realize their full potential, stay vital, motivated, and employable throughout their entire working life (Rožman et al., 2017). To optimize such an age-conscious HR policy it seems appropriate to *further examine the interplay between age, work characteristics and burnout complaints so that targeted burnout prevention strategies can be implemented.*

It is important to focus on specific age-related risk factors for burnout in the workplace that have been identified above. It can be expected that a tailor-made approach to redesign work practices that addresses such specific, age-related risk factors is more successful in preventing burnout than a more general one size fits all solution. Besides, burnout symptoms should be tackled at different levels of intervention: person, task, team, management and organization as our results show. Unfortunately, in practice, most interventions target the person, whereas task-, team- and organization-focused interventions are relatively rare (Maricuţoiu et al., 2014).

Age-conscious HR policies to prevent burnout are still in the early stages, and further research is necessary on age diversity and the associated new challenges for HRM and leadership in organizations. In this chapter we have demonstrated that research that focuses on age differences in burnout may produce valuable insights for designing better workplaces for employees so that instead of burning out, employees and their organizations may thrive.

STRENGTHS AND LIMITATIONS

First, an important issue is to bear in mind that burnout ranges from rather mild burnout symptoms to a full-blown chronic disorder, also called "clinical burnout" (Van Dam, 2021). In the public debate and in organizations these two are often confused. Usually, mild burnout complaints are measured using self-report questionnaires, but the results of such studies are often interpreted in terms of clinical burnout (Schaufeli & Verolme, 2022; Schaufeli et al., Chapter 7, this volume). However, a prevalence of, say, 15 percent burnout complaints does not imply that 15 percent in that sample suffers from a chronic burnout disorder. In fact, this indicates that 15 percent are at risk of developing clinical burnout in the future. In our study we assessed mild burnout complaints and not severe, clinical burnout for which a diagnostic interview by a mental health professional should be used. Nevertheless, also mild burnout symptoms should be taken seriously.

Second, the WOD® questionnaire only maps personal characteristics to a very limited degree, as it is designed to measure psychosocial well-being in the workplace and the organizational dynamics that are involved. Since we know that many personal characteristics, such as personality traits, can act as vulnerability factors for burnout (Swider & Zimmerman, 2010), we might be missing some (important) personal factors across different age groups.

Third, we analysed different age groups, which only provides some circumstantial evidence for differences in burnout across generations. To adequately study generational differences, a longitudinal cohort study should be carried out that compares different generations *at the same age*. Needless to say, that this kind of research takes a very long time and hence consumes significant resources. So it is not surprising that – to the best of our knowledge – longitudinal cohort research on generational differences in burnout has not been published so far. Our preliminary study results might be used as hypotheses that can be tested in future prospective cohort research.

A final remark concerns the issue of causality: we assessed different covariates of burnout across different age groups, using correlation coefficients. As indicated before, the fact that burnout complaints decrease with age, does not indicate that younger age *causes* burnout symptoms. The same holds for age-specific risk factors related to burnout. In order to disentangle cause and effect, longitudinal research should be done that measures burnout and its risk factors in multiple waves across time.

FINAL CONCLUSIONS

The question whether Millennials are the "burnout generation", seems to hold some truth, as we see that the corresponding age groups (between 25–34 years and 35–44 years), show higher levels of burnout complaints compared to the older generations. This result, which is found in the pooled sample, is replicated with a few exceptions in the three different countries that constitute the overall sample. This adds to the robustness of our findings.

When zooming in on possible age-specific risk factors for burnout in the work situation we found that particularly task-related factors are important drivers of burnout for the youngest age groups, whereas predominantly organizational factors are the most important drivers for the oldest age groups. So it seems that the importance of task-related characteristics gradually declines with age, whereas the importance of characteristics from other levels (person, team, management and organization) increases.

Taken together these findings create interesting opportunities and challenges for management and HRM to install age-specific preventative burnout programmes in organizations.

NOTE

1. See: https://web.uri.edu/worklife/homepages/workplaceproblemspages/age_gen eration/

REFERENCES

Ahola, K., Toppinen-Tanner, S., & Seppänen, J. (2017). Interventions to alleviate burnout symptoms and to support return to work among employees with burnout: Systematic review and meta-analysis. *Burnout Research, 4*, 1–11. https://doi.org/10 .1016/j.burn.2017.02.001

Brewer, E. W., & Shapard, L. (2004). Employee burnout: A meta-analysis of the relationship between age or years of experience. *Human Resource Development Review, 3*, 102–123. https://doi.org/10.1177/1534484304263335

Cennamo, L., & Gardner, D. (2008). Generational differences in work values, outcomes and person–organisation values fit. *Journal of Managerial Psychology, 23*, 891–906. https://doi.org/10.1108/02683940810904385

Costanza, D. P., Badger, J. M., Fraser, R. L., Severt, J. B., & Gade, P. A. (2012). Generational differences in work-related attitudes: A meta-analysis. *Journal of Business and Psychology, 27*, 375–394. https://doi.org/10.1007/s10869-012-9259-4

De Maeyer, C., & Schoenmakers, B. (2019). Exploring intergenerational differences in burnout and how they relate to work engagement, norms, and values: A mixed-methods study. *BJGP Open, 3*, 1–9. https://doi.org/10.3399/bjgpopen18X101637

Dreison, K. C., Luther, L., Bonfils, K. A., Sliter, M. T., McGrew, J. H., & Salyers, M. P. (2018). Job burnout in mental health providers: A meta-analysis of 35 years of intervention research. *Journal of Occupational Health Psychology, 23*, 18–30. https://doi .org/10.1037/ocp0000047

Emory, J., Lee, P. B., Kippenbrock, T., Boyd, T., Chen, L., & Harless, L. (2022). Commitment, job satisfaction and personality: A cross sectional study of generational cohorts in nursing students. *Journal of Professional Nursing, 40*, 42–47. https://doi.org/10.1016/j.profnurs.2022.02.010.

Fairlie, P. (2013). Age and generational differences in work psychology: Facts, fictions, and meaningful work. In J. Field, R. J. Burke, & C. L. Cooper (Eds.), *The SAGE Handbook of Aging, Work and Society* (pp. 186–208). London: Sage Publications. https://doi.org/10.13140/2.1.3711.2968

FOD (2012). *Leeftijdsbewust personeelsbeleid aanpakken – Psychosociale risico's* (Age-sensitive HR – Psychosocial risks). Brussels: Federale Overheidsdienst. https://werk.belgie.be/nl/publicaties/leeftijdsbewust-personeelsbeleid-aanpakken -psychosociale-risicos

Huber, P., & Schubert, H. (2019). Attitudes about work engagement of different generations – A cross-sectional study with nurses and supervisors. *Journal of Nursing Management, 27*, 1341–1350. https://doi.org/10.1111/jonm.12805

Jiang, X., & Yang, H. (2016). Impacts of optimism and job characteristics on job burnout among the millennial generation: Evidence from a survey of community service workers in Shaanxi, China. *Revista de Cercetare si Interventie Sociala, 53*, 185–212. ISSN: 1584-5397

Li, C. L., & Sung, F. C. (1999). A review of the healthy worker effect in occupational epidemiology. *Occupational Medicine, 49*, 225–229. https://doi.org/10.1093/ occmed/49.4.225

Lim, N., Kim, E. K., Kim, H., Yang, E., & Lee, S. M. (2010). Individual and work-related factors influencing burnout of mental health professionals: A meta-analysis. *Journal of Employment Counselling, 47*, 86–96. https://doi.org/10.1002/j.2161-1920.2010 .tb00093.x

Lu, A. C. C., & Gursoy, D. (2013). Impact of job burnout on satisfaction and turnover intention: Do generational differences matter? *Journal of Hospitality & Tourism Research, 40*, 1–26. https://doi.org/10.1177/1096348013495696

Lyons, S., & Kuron, L. (2013). Generational differences in the workplace: A review of the evidence and directions for future research. *Journal of Organizational Behavior, 35*, 139–157. https://doi.org/10.1002/job.1913

Mannheim, K. (1952). The problem of generations. In P. Kecskemeti (Ed.), *Essays on the Sociology of Knowledge* (pp. 276–320). London: Routledge and Kegan Paul.

Marchand, A., Blanc, M.-E., & Beauregard, N. (2018). Do age and gender contribute to workers' burnout symptoms? *Occupational Medicine, 68*, 405–411. https://doi.org/ 10.1093/occmed/kqy088

Maricuţoiu, L. P., Sava, F. A., & Butta, O. (2014). The effectiveness of controlled interventions on employees' burnout: A meta-analysis. *Journal of Occupational and Organizational Psychology, 89*, 1–27. https://doi.org/10.1111/joop.12099

Mockaitis, A. I., & Butler, C. L. (2020). *Coping during the pandemic: What a difference a generation makes!* https://mockaitis.com/2020/06/11/coping-during-the -pandemic-what-a-difference-a-generation-makes/

Nakagawa, K., & Yellowlees, P. (2020). Inter-generational effects of technology: Why millennial physicians may be less at risk for burnout than baby boomers. *Current Psychiatry Reports, 22*, 1–7. https://doi.org/10.1007/s11920-020-01171-2

Panagioti, M. et al. (2017). Controlled interventions to reduce burnout in physicians: A systematic review and meta-analysis. *JAMA Internal Medicine, 177*, 195–205. https://doi.org/10.1001/jamainternmed.2016.7674

Römgens, I., Scoupe, R., & Beausaert, S. (2020). Unraveling the concept of employability, bringing together research on employability in higher education and the workplace. *Studies in Higher Education, 45*, 2588–2603. https://doi.org/10.1080/ 03075079.2019.1623770

Rožman, M., Treven, S., Čančer, V., & Cingula, M. (2017). Burnout of older and younger employees – The case of Slovenia. *Organizacija, 50*. https://doi.org/10 .1515/orga-2017-0005

Saber, A., Abbas, T., & El-Monem, A. A. (2018). The effects of the generations' differences on job burnout in Sharm El-Sheikh resorts: Managers' view. *International*

Journal of Heritage, Tourism and Hospitality, 12, 1–33. https://doi.org/10.21608/ijhth.2018.32005

Schaufeli, W. B., & Taris, T. W. (2014). A critical review of the job demands–resources model: Implications for improving work and health. In G. F. Bauer & O. Hämmig (Eds.), *Bridging Occupational, Organizational and Public Health: A Transdisciplinary Approach* (pp. 43–68). Cham: Springer Science + Business Media. https://doi.org/10.1007/978-94-007-5640-3_4

Schaufeli, W. B., & Veroime, J. J. (2022). *De burn-out bubbel (The Burnout Bubble).* Houten: Bohn stafleu van loghum.

Schaufeli, W. B., Desart, S., & De Witte, H. (2020). The Burnout Assessment Tool (BAT) – Development, validity and reliability. *International Journal of Environmental Research and Public Health, 17,* 1–22. https://doi.org/10.3390/ijerph17249495

Steeneveld, M. (2017). *Optimisme Hoop Veerkracht Zelfvertrouwen (Optimism, Hope, Resilience, Confidence).* Amsterdam: Boom.

Swider, B. W., & Zimmerman, R. D. (2010). Born to burnout: A meta-analytic path model of personality, job burnout, and work outcomes. *Journal of Vocational Behavior, 76* (3), 487–506. https://doi.org/10.1016/j.jvb.2010.01.003

Twenge, J. M., & Campbell, S. M. (2008). Generational differences in psychological traits and their impact on the workplace. *Journal of Managerial Psychology, 23,* 862–877. https://doi.org/10.1108/02683940810904367

Van Dam, A. (2021). A clinical perspective on burnout: Diagnosis, classification, and treatment of clinical burnout. *European Journal of Work and Organizational Psychology, 30,* 732–741. https://doi.org/10.1080/1359432x.2021.1948400

Widjanarko, T. (2021). The influence of organizational culture and employee engagement to job burnout on generation Z working at e-commerce. *Journal of Business and Management, 12,* 86–96. https://doi.org/10.19184/bisma.v15i2.26167

APPENDIX 1

Table 9A.1   *P-values from ANOVA's contrasting burnout levels between different age groups across countries and for each country individually**

Age	Age	Across countries	Belgium	France	Germany
1	2	1.000	0.372	1.000	1.000
	3	1.000	1.000	1.000	1.000
	4	0.000	0.032	0.088	0.248
	5	0.000	0.026	0.022	0.000
2	1	1.000	0.372	1.000	1.000
	3	0.495	1.000	0.003	1.000
	4	0.000	1.000	0.000	0.000
	5	0.000	0.981	0.000	0.000
3	1	1.000	1.000	1.000	1.000
	2	0.495	1.000	0.003	1.000
	4	0.000	0.126	0.430	0.000
	5	0.000	0.149	0.065	0.000
4	1	0.000	0.032	0.088	0.248
	2	0.000	1.000	0.000	0.000
	3	0.000	0.126	0.430	0.000
	5	0.004	1.000	1.000	0.000
5	1	0.000	0.026	0.022	0.000
	2	0.000	0.981	0.000	0.000
	3	0.000	0.149	0.065	0.000
	4	0.004	1.000	1.000	0.000

*The mean difference is significant at the 0.05 level; 1 = less than 25 years; 2 = 25–34 years; 3 = 35–44 years; 4 = 45–55 years; 5 = over 55 years.

APPENDIX 2

Table 9A.2   *Correlation coefficients, linking burnout with potential risk factors for different age groups**

	–25 years N=322	25–34 years N= 1345	35–44 years N= 1432	45–54 years N= 1491	+55 years N= 1060
1	Work complexity 0.49	Work overload 0.42	Work complexity 0.43	Fear of change –0.44	Vision for the future –0.47
2	Work overload 0.48	Demanding responsibility 0.41	Emotional demands 0.40	Work complexity 0.43	Physical aspects of workplace –0.46
3	Interruptions 0.37	Work complexity 0.41	Role clarity –0.39	Role clarity –0.42	Support during change –0.46
4	Emotional demands 0.35	Emotional demands 0.36	Appreciation manager –0.37	Emotional demands 0.42	Work organization –0.46
5	Work underload 0.34	Fear of change –0.34	Social climate –0.37	Resilience –0.41	Work complexity –0.46

*All correlations are significant at $p < 0.001$.

PART IV

INTERVENTIONS: GETTING PEOPLE ON BOARD

10. Organizational interventions within occupational health psychology

Karina Nielsen & Paula Brough

INTRODUCTION

Participatory organizational interventions are workplace programmes that aim to change the way work is organized, designed and managed, via the close collaboration and involvement of workers, managers, and other key stakeholders. Within Occupational Health Psychology, participatory organizational interventions commonly focus on changing work practices and procedures and the policies that support these, with the overall objective of improving workers' health and well-being (Brough & O'Driscoll, 2010; Nielsen, 2013). Such interventions often take a participatory approach where workers and managers collectively decide on both the content (what to do) and process (how to do it) of the intervention (Nielsen & Noblet, 2018). Participation is at the core of the main bodies' approaches for the effective promotion of worker's health and well-being (EU-OSHA, 2010; European Commission, 1989; World Health Organization, 1986). A key consideration within these participatory organizational interventions is who really stands to gain from the planned changes (Wilkinson et al., 2010). Participation potentially has mutual gains for both management and workers. Management is the key driver of participatory processes, as it is seen as an opportunity to gain ownership and make use of workers' expertise. However, benefits also apply to workers as they can directly influence their working conditions. These dual key benefits are also known as the mutual gains perspective (Wilkinson et al., 2010).

Professor Hans de Witte has throughout his career made a significant contribution to the field of job insecurity and in 2010 found that participation was associated with a decrease in job insecurity (Vander Elst et al., 2010). Indeed, a recent study supported that job insecurity can be reduced through organizational interventions (Abildgaard et al., 2018b).

The European Directive 1989/391 on the introduction of measures to improve the health and safety of workers states that workers or their representatives should be consulted and involved in all discussions about workplace health and safety. One study of psychosocial risk management within Europe revealed participation to be one of the main drivers of this risk management process (Houtman et al., 2017). Despite this, the actual form of participation remains understudied (Nielsen & Noblet, 2018). In European countries, approximately 65 percent of workers report they contribute to designing and establishing measures to address workplace environment issues (Irastorza et al., 2016). To categorize this participation, Abildgaard et al. (2018a) proposed a four-dimensional participation framework, classifying participation as: determining the content; determining the process of the intervention; directness of participation; and participation as a means to an end. Despite this useful framework, Abildgaard et al. (2018a) failed to discuss the challenges of participation in organizational interventions. We address this shortcoming in this chapter by identifying common challenges concerning participation in the process of changing working conditions. We discuss three main challenges associated with this participatory change process: namely forms of workplace participation, a lack of theoretical frameworks, and participation in different contexts. These challenges and the research questions that may arise from these challenges are summarized in Table 10.1.

DEFINING WORKPLACE PARTICIPATION

Workplace participation is defined as "a process which allows workers to exert some influence over their work and the conditions under which they work" (Heller et al., 1998, p. 15). According to Marchington and Wilkinson (2005), participation can be divided into four categories: direct communication; upward problem-solving; representative participation (also known as indirect participation); and financial participation. Both direct communication and upward problem-solving are *direct methods* of workplace participation, hence all workers are to some extent involved in these types of participatory intervention programmes. These two forms of direct workplace participation are unsurprisingly, the most effective methods of involving workers in successful changes to their work environments. Direct participation informs workers about key business issues and enables them to provide feedback on decisions made and on their working conditions within an objective consultation process. However, the vital final decision-making process for any workplace changes ultimately rests with management (Wilkinson et al., 2010). Upward decision-making entails consulting with workers about which work practices and procedures to change and how. *Indirect participation* involves worker representatives such as union representatives and/or health and safety representatives exerting influence on behalf of their colleagues (Wilkinson et al., 2010). Finally, financial participation commonly consists of financial

Table 10.1   Key challenges in organizational participatory interventions

Key challenge	Key issues	Key future research questions
What should participation look like?	Direct participation ensures voice but may not be feasible in large organizations, may lead to work intensification and lure workers into accepting undesirable work practices. Indirect participation may hamper sense-making and buy-in. Participation may take different forms during the different phases of intervention. Internal project champions could be both workers and line managers.	What type of participation is important in the different phases of intervention? What roles can be assigned to workers to ensure their active participation? What forms of participation are effective at different phases of intervention? Who are effective internal project champions in different organizational contexts?
Why is participation important?	Lack of theories underpinning participation.	How may collective job crafting during interventions support the participatory process? How may trust facilitate engagement in the participatory process? How may sense-making processes be facilitated to ensure participation is effective?
How do we ensure participation in diverse workplaces?	Workers in cross-cultural organizations may hold different knowledge, values and attitudes towards work and participation. National legislation may influence how participation is managed. Outsourcing has made health and safety responsibility unclear. Workers do not share preferences for remote working.	How may we develop intervention processes that consider diverse workplaces? What type of interventions can be developed that improve working conditions and worker health and well-being in diverse workplaces?

compensation, such as profit sharing and worker share ownership. We discuss direct and indirect forms of participation in more detail below.

Participatory Organizational Intervention

Participatory organizational intervention is a specific form of participation where workers and managers engage in a collaborative process to improve working conditions and worker health and well-being. Participation can either consist of a group process involving work teams and their managers, or an individual process involving specific workers directly making decisions about their work contents and contexts (Wilkinson et al., 2010). For participatory organizational interventions, participation is most successful as a *collective process* where workers and managers work together (Nielsen et al., 2021a). Participatory organizational interventions usually employ a systematic, problem-solving approach commonly existing of five phases (Nielsen & Noblet, 2018):

- *Phase 1*: Preparation. In the first phase, a steering group consisting of workers and managers is established. The steering group decides on a communication strategy to ensure those not directly involved in the intervention are kept up to date about its process, progress, and content, together with the vision of the intervention.
- *Phase 2*: Screening. Key strengths and problematic areas of the working environment and existing work policies and practices are identified. The results of this screening are fed back to workers and managers and discussions are held to understand the results and prioritize areas of action.
- *Phase 3*: Action planning. Workers and managers collaborate to develop areas for improvement, through the development of action plans.
- *Phase 4*: Implementation. Action plans are implemented and monitored, to ensure they are implemented according to the plan.
- *Phase 5*: Evaluation. Evaluation should include both the effect of the implemented action plans, that is, improvements in working conditions and worker health and well-being, and the process of the implementation, in terms of whether the intervention was implemented according to plan and the extent to which the process successfully facilitated the intervention outcomes (Biggs & Brough, 2015a). The evaluation phase also identifies any unintended side effects and produces recommendations for how the intervention will inform future health and safety management processes within the organization (Nielsen & Noblet, 2018).

Despite the consensus that participation is important, there is little consensus of what form workplace participation in organizational interventions should take. In the following sections we discuss direct versus indirect participation and the importance of workers being allocated a specific responsibility in leading change.

Direct and Indirect Participation

The specific form of participation that is most effective is currently difficult to identify. Direct participation, where all employees are involved in the planning and implementation of the interventions, is easier to achieve in some contexts than others, for example with small organizations employing ten workers or less. In this situation, direct participation can easily occur throughout all phases of the intervention. Workers can agree on the process and contribute their opinions via various methods, including for example, an interactive screening method using cognitive mapping tools. Workers and management can establish both the good and problematic aspects of their workplace. This mapping tool can then be used to develop and prioritize action plans that can be agreed in a plenary session. Implementation of these action plans can be monitored via meetings and progress reports.

Direct participation, however, does not come without its challenges. Critics have raised the issue of work intensification and luring workers into accepting management practices which may not be in their best interest (Wilkinson et al., 2010). Direct participation is also more challenging to conduct well in larger organizations, for example inviting 3,000 workers to agree to the process for an intervention. In these cases, a *steering group* representing key stakeholders is crucial (indirect participation, where worker representatives represent the interests of workers). Often safety representatives or shop stewards who have been elected by colleagues may already possess a formal role in managing employee health and well-being (Abildgaard et al., 2018b), and they may therefore also be tasked with representing workers in participatory interventions. The tasks of the steering group where managers, workers and other key stakeholders with a responsibility for managing worker mental health and well-being must be clearly defined and agreed. Nielsen et al. (2013) highlighted two key responsibilities of such steering groups.

Strategic tasks refer to the direction of the intervention and include:

- Identification of which departments may benefit from intervention.
- Integration of the intervention into existing practices and procedures.
- Consideration of long-term changes to the company's health and safety policies and practices based on learnings from the intervention.

Operational tasks of a steering group consist of:

- Provision of practical support for the intervention.
- Follow-up on progress of the intervention phases.
- Implementation of strategies to ensure a high response rate in surveys.
- Agreement and delivery of survey feedback.
- Planning and implementation of action planning activities.

In larger organizations, strategic and operational tasks may be split into several groups, however, it is crucial that worker representation occurs at all levels.

A study conducted by the INAIL (National Institute for Insurance against Accidents at Work, the national approach to managing psychosocial risks in Italy) found that 32 percent of the 124 organizations studied used direct participation and 39 percent used indirect participation methods (Di Tecco et al., 2015). However, the authors did not evaluate whether one method was better than the other, nor did they identify in which types of organizations one type may be more appropriate than others. Furthermore, the authors did not identify during which stage of the intervention, either direct or indirect participation was particularly crucial. Tafvelin et al. (2019) examined the role of direct participation at three time points: pre-intervention; during; and post-intervention. They employed a measure of generic participation capturing whether workers felt they were an important part of how a health promotion intervention was being addressed within their organization. Tafvelin et al. (2019) reported that at pre-intervention direct participation was positively related to job satisfaction at both the early stages of the intervention and participation in the later phases of the intervention, that is, the action planning and implementation phases predicted higher levels of job satisfaction 12 months post-intervention. Interestingly, a positive spiral effect was also observed: pre-intervention participation predicted line managers' active involvement in the early stages of the intervention, which in turn, predicted worker participation in the later phases of intervention (Tafvelin et al., 2019). These results demonstrated the importance of direct participation by workers and call for a greater understanding of what types of participation is feasible at different stages of the intervention process.

The divide between direct and indirect participation has received relatively little attention in organizational intervention research (Nielsen & Noblet, 2018). As mentioned above, indirect participation usually consists of a small group of selected workers who represent the interests of the wider workforce and are directly involved in the intervention process and content (Wilkinson et al., 2010). However, the most effective approach remains unclear. On the one hand, in a qualitative study, Framke and Sørensen (2015) found that workers felt indirect participation was sufficient as long as worker representatives kept them informed. On the other hand, in a qualitative study of small and medium-sized enterprises, Poulsen et al. (2015) found that workers who had not participated in action planning workshops felt little ownership over the recommended action plan and did not engage in later stages of the process. More research is needed to understand what forms of participation are most effective during which phase of intervention.

The Role of Workplace Champions

Although rarely discussed and researched in organizational interventions, some research has identified the value of identifying specific workers as "project or intervention champions" and as internal drivers of the organizational change process (Brough & Biggs, 2015). Advantages of internal champions have been argued in terms of the creation of ownership, cost-effectiveness, sustainability and integration beyond the project period and that intervention activities are more likely to be implemented when (jointly) led by an internal advocate (Brough & Biggs, 2015). Other benefits have been found in terms of internal champions being sensitive to the specific organizational context and that it was possible to appoint internal champions without necessarily providing them with formal training (Ipsen, 2019).

It is also clear that the role of an effective supervisor or manager readily lends itself to being an advocate of workplace changes and improvement, including those changes implemented by a formal intervention programme. Thus, an effective supervisor or manager is often a good choice as an internal champion. The role of supervisors as a "gatekeeper" between workers and formal organizational policies has long been established (e.g., Thompson et al., 2006), and similarly, the provision of effective supervisor support clearly serves to protect workers from occupational stress and burnout, including stress caused by organizational changes (Brough et al., 2018). Thus, the value of a highly regarded supervisor being a champion for advocating changes via a workplace intervention programme can be extremely effective. Certainly in our own experiences of interventions within large, hierarchical organizations, such a champion is highly beneficial: contributing their knowledge of both formal and informal internal decision-making channels, knowledge of the most appropriate personnel for intervention engagement, ensuring the intervention progress and results are regularly placed on senior executive meeting agendas, and embedding the changes and recommendations into organizational policies (Biggs & Brough, 2015b; Brough & Biggs, 2015).

Consideration should also be taken of the project champions' own levels of well-being. It is possible that being the project champion may be stressful, both in terms of the added workload (Wilkinson et al., 2010) and the potential mismatch between the person's competencies and the demands of the role. Nielsen et al. (2021b) examined the impact on internal project champions who had received specific training in this role. The role of the internal project champions in this study was to conduct "dialogue workshops" where workers were given the opportunity to communicate about and influence the change process. Nielsen et al. (2021b) found that these internal champions reported increased job satisfaction post-intervention and the improvements in job satisfaction were particularly strong for champions who felt they were a good fit to the champion role and who were dissatisfied with their jobs prior to the intervention. These findings suggest that the positive effects of participation may be stronger when workers are given a formal role in change processes.

EXPLANATIONS OF THE WORKPLACE PARTICIPATION PROCESS: UNDERPINNING THEORETICAL EXPLANATIONS

There is no single theoretical explanation which completely describes the multiple antecedents and consequences of a successful workplace participation process (Nielsen, 2013). Indeed, a recent review of published occupational health interventions identified that 53 percent of these interventions were not explicitly theory based and their outcomes were poorly defined (Burgess et al., 2020). Burgess et al. (2020) suggested recommendations to remedy these issues. In this section, we review three common approaches which purport to explain specific components of this participation process. These approaches include collaborative job crafting, developing a change culture and workplace trust, and workers' sense-making.

Collaborative Job Crafting

Collaborative job crafting is defined as the adaptive changes workers make to their work to fulfil their needs (Leana et al., 2009) and is, therefore, a suitable mechanism to explain the positive effects of participatory interventions (Nielsen, 2013). A key aspect of participatory organizational interventions is the collective process. Through the discussions of both the good and problematic issues at work, be it through interactive cognitive mapping tools or the discussion of survey results, members of the work team develop a shared mental model of their workplace (Weick, 1995), enabling them to collectively develop action plans. Through the collective process, they not only collectively craft a job that fits their needs but also craft a work environment that brings about positive change for the entire work team.

Through the process of collectively job crafting the intervention content, workers may perceive the members of their work team as valuable players in creating an optimal work environment, hence increasing individual levels of work engagement. Rosskam (2009) argued that collective workplace participation is an effective method to improve communications, create opportunities for workers to shape their jobs collectively, and enhance the fit between workers' needs and their jobs. The collective process, when conducted successfully, is effective in preventing workers individually benefiting at the expense of others, for example, when one worker removes a job task from their own work profile to add to a colleague's work profile. Collective participation can, therefore, have a significant impact: by working together workers can implement powerful changes through the generated action plans.

One potential pitfall of the collective team-level approach to developing and implementing workplace participation action plans, is that issues occurring at higher levels of the organization may not be addressed. To remedy this concern, *a multi-level action planning approach* is recommended. In their meta-analysis, Nielsen et al. (2017) found that resources at four levels are associated with both performance and worker well-being, suggesting the IGLO (individual, group, leader or organizational) model of intervention. Day and Nielsen (2017) adopted this IGLO model in a workplace intervention process and reported actions to improve the psychosocial work environment and worker well-being were needed to be undertaken at all four levels. At the individual level, characteristics of the individual (e.g., self-efficacy and job crafting) can be trained. At the group level, interventions focusing on improving the team climate or enhancing decision-making processes may be appropriate. At the leader level, leaders may need training to change their behaviours; for example, adopting a health-promoting leadership style. At the organizational level, changes to policies and practices may be required.

This IGLO model therefore has useful implications for Human Resource policies on work context (e.g., work–life balance policies and increasing decision latitude; Day & Nielsen, 2017). At the team level, team members may reflect and develop action plans at the individual and group level, for example, *what do I and my team need to do differently to address the problem?* Teams may also identify issues that need to be addressed higher up at the leader or organizational levels. It is crucial that systems are in place to ensure that these action plans are developed at the appropriate level, and that the actions undertaken are communicated to the team and individual levels to ensure that all workers feel heard and have their concerns taken seriously.

Developing a Workplace Culture of Change and Trust

A second key explanation of how workplace participatory interventions work, is the development of a change culture, whereby work practices and procedures are critically reviewed and revised. An important component of change culture is trust (Wilkinson et al., 2010). Trust is obviously a dual process flowing between managers and workers. Thus, management trusts workers to have the necessary skills and knowledge to input to the participatory process and to make decisions that benefit the bottom line (Wilkinson et al., 2010). Equally, workers trust management to allow for the necessary changes to be made and to support the recommended change suggestions. However, workplace trust is not necessarily this simple and is not a naturally occurring phenomenon. Some workplaces are relatively low on trust, especially workplaces structured by hierarchical ranks, including the military, police (Brough et al., 2016a), correctional services (Brough et al., 2016b), and hospitals (Links et al., 2021).

Sense-making in Workplaces

A final mechanism to explain workplace participation is workers' cognitive processes of sense-making. From a sense-making perspective (Maitlis & Christianson, 2014), participation and active involvement in the intervention process can be perceived as organizational members actively seeking information and acting to make sense of the intervention. Weick (1988) argued that organizational members come to understand the world by taking action and then observing the outcomes of this action. The sense-making perspective is a useful approach to understand workplace participation, as sense-making actions generate stimuli and cues which enable workers to better understand the intervention (Weick, 1988). Sense-making can be a particularly powerful mechanism during action planning and implementation. For workers to understand why a certain action is important to implement and how it may bring about the intended outcomes, workers must understand what the problem is, the different ways a problem can be addressed, and why a particular solution is prioritized over other possible actions. Once workers and line managers understand *why* a certain action plan has been chosen and *what* its potential benefits are, they are more likely to adopt changes in behaviours to implement the action plan and to actively support actions as they understand the potential of the action.

The sense-making approach is particularly effective when a team-level approach to action planning is adopted, as described above. Rather than having steering groups develop action plans without the involvement of impacted workers, more effective action plans are developed at the team level, giving all affected workers a voice (Nielsen et al., 2013).

Enabling worker sense-making in all stages of workplace intervention programmes can, however, also be a challenge. The collective sense-making process and the development of shared mental models are not necessarily practical or feasible in large organizations. Often standardized surveys such as the HSE Indicator Tool which measures six dimensions of the psychosocial work environment (job demands, control, managerial and peer support, roles, relationships, and changes; Edwards et al., 2008) is utilized (Nielsen & Noblet, 2018). These standardized survey tools suffer from two limitations. First, they rest on the assumption of an objective work environment remote from the worker's appraisal of whether an aspect of the work environment is a problem or a positive aspect of work (Nielsen et al., 2014). However, research has demonstrated that workers do not rate their work environment in the same way. Recent work for example, has highlighted how objective job demands may be perceived as either (positive) challenges, and/or (negative) hindrances or threats by different workers or at different points in time, dependent on the broader work/non-work contexts (Raper & Brough, 2021; Searle et al., 2022).

Standardized work environment survey tools typically adopt a benchmarking approach, allowing organizations to compare themselves with national and/or industry averages (Persechino et al., 2013). However, an organizational score below a certain level does not necessarily imply that workers perceive this aspect of their work environment to be problematic, as this is highly dependent on the job context. Some occupations for example, are naturally quite low in worker autonomy, where individual workers have little control over their work hours or work tasks, including postal service workers (Nielsen et al., 2014), police and other emergency service workers (e.g., Brough, 2004; Raper et al., 2020), mine workers (Morrow & Brough, 2019), and veterinary workers (Deacon & Brough, 2017). Workers' sense-making and interpretations of their working conditions is crucial to identifying suitable changes to improve well-being.

Standardized work environment surveys also may not capture occupational-specific work demands or local aspects of the work environment that significantly influence worker well-being (Brough et al., 2020). The impact of occupational-specific work demands such as frequently dealing with fatal road traffic accidents as a police officer, or the daily exposure to abusive prisoners or patients as a corrections officer or a healthcare worker, have been demonstrated to have as much or even a greater impact upon these workers' well-being over time as compared to common standardized job demands (Brough et al., 2016b).

One solution to these problems is to develop tailored questionnaires in workshops where researchers, workers and their managers are involved in identifying specific problematic aspects of their work environment and then developing the relevant questionnaire content. In a qualitative study, Nielsen et al. (2014) found that the three main advantages of the tailored questionnaire approach were: (a) the ability to detect issues with the work environment that workers felt were important to them; (b) the identified problematic issues were prioritized; and (c) these specific issues were included in the questionnaire. The tailored questionnaire approach allows workers an opportunity to directly influence what the content of the questionnaire should be, which may facilitate sense-making and hence the quality of this well-being assessment tool.

This method, however, is not without its limitations as it is both time-consuming and requires specialist skills in survey methods (Nielsen et al., 2014). A less time-consuming alternative may be to enhance sense-making through questionnaires that adopt a middle way, for example by incorporating standardized scales relevant to the local context. Examples include the *ARK survey*, in which job context scales are incorporated for the university sector

(Innstrand et al., 2015), and the *police work hassles and uplifts scales*, which assess job demands frequently encountered by police officers, such as making arrests and delivering death messages (Brough, 2004; Brough et al., 2016b).

Ideally, all workers in the affected intervention areas should be offered the opportunity to provide feedback on the tailored survey. However, how workers should be involved in developing and implementing action plans is more of a challenge, primarily due to the increased time, costs, and logistics required. Sense-making is, therefore, an effective approach that can help us address the challenges and the balance of direct and indirect worker participation.

Evaluations of Organizational Interventions

Evaluations of organizational interventions commonly occur as outcome evaluations at the end of the intervention period (Nielsen & Miraglia, 2017). However, understanding how the intervention processes influence these outcomes is also important (Biggs & Brough, 2015a; Nielsen & Abildgaard, 2013). Hence, *process evaluations* provide an important learning opportunity both for organizational members and for the scientific community. How organizational members make sense of the intervention may be as important to the sustainability of the intervention, compared to the scientific evaluation (Nielsen et al., 2021a). In one study, Ipsen et al. (2020) explored the impact of using a visible evaluation tool (e.g., using building blocks building a wall to indicate the level of progress) to encourage dialogue about the progress of the intervention and the extent to which action plans were being implemented. Visibility tools are an effective method to externalize tacit individual knowledge about the intervention to explicit individual knowledge (through individual ratings of progress), and from explicit knowledge to explicit collective knowledge (through dialogue about individuals' rating). Ipsen et al. (2020) found that the visibility tool was indeed successful in increasing awareness and visibility of the intervention progress, and it was perceived as a signal to workers that management valued workers' opinions. The challenges of the tool related to the definition of progress, for example it was not clear how much progress warranted one building block being added to the wall and workers found it hard to imagine the end goal, that is, how much did a building block count towards achieving the final goal. Overall, the tool was found useful but was not well implemented in all participating organizations. In summary, ongoing evaluations may promote sense-making and ensure continued commitment to implementing changes beyond the duration of the intervention programme (Nielsen et al., 2021a).

WORKPLACE PARTICIPATION WITHIN DIFFERENT CONTEXTS

Exactly how workplace participation operates within different contexts is a highly pertinent issue that is often ignored by most of the research. It is easier to assume and adopt a "one size fits all" approach when considering worker participation in an organizational intervention. This assumption is, however, highly erroneous and is unlikely to produce optimal results. Research clearly identifies the differences in how work is conducted under different national contexts (i.e., culture and legislation), different types of workers (including local and international workers), different characteristics of workers (i.e., demographic diversity), the complexity of today's workplaces with out-sourcing and complex supply chains, and increasingly, the impact of remote or virtual workers versus on-site workers (Brough et al., 2022b). In a recent review of expatriate workers for example, Gai et al. (2022) discussed how glo-balization has increased the prevalence of cross-cultural workers, especially within multinational corporations, and how their psychological adjustment to work in a new host country is directly influenced by their experiences of pre-departure workplace training and/or post-arrival workplace training. The likelihood of these workers responding to subsequent calls for their participa-tion with an organizational intervention is, therefore, likely to be influenced by their levels of psychological adjustment, the impact of their supervisors' influence, and their own original work experiences and cultural norms.

A five-stage participatory invention framework that encourages migrant workers' participation was recently proposed (Le et al., 2021). Based on Nielsen and Noblet (2018), this framework focuses on improving the moti-vation of migrants to participate in workplace changes and to increase their confidence in expressing their voice (knowledge, skills, and confidence) about workplace issues relevant to themselves. The five phases consist of:

- *Initiation phase:* establishing ground rules, steering group, communica-tion mechanisms, readiness for change, ensuring participation of migrant workers.
- *Screening phase:* identifying problematic issues in the work environment, proposal of solutions, generation of feedback with an explicit focus on cultural differences.
- *Action planning phase:* production of targeted and feasible initiatives considering migrant workers' needs, change management plan, monitoring changes.
- *Implementation phase:* conducting and embedding the planned changes with the involvement of migrant workers.

- *Evaluation phase:* assessment of intervention effectiveness, also for migrant workers, identification of any subsequent intervention refinements.

The framework was informed by social exchange theory (Blau, 1964), suggesting that reciprocal communications between migrant workers and their managers build trust and encourage migrant workers' honest participation throughout each phase of the intervention (Le et al., 2021).

Impact of National Legislation

The impact of different types of national legislation on workers' legal rights is also often an overlooked feature of workplace participation and can directly influence the content of interventions, especially about national workplace health and safety legislation. See, for example, a discussion on the influence of different national legislation for a worker's ability to voice dissent and formally report observed internal wrongdoing (i.e., "whistleblowing") by Brough et al. (2022c). The specific workplace legislation context clearly had a flow-on effect upon work behaviours at all other levels, including workers' perceptions of the organizational culture, their trust in management, and thus, their willingness to directly engage in any workplace intervention process. We acknowledge here that the impact of national workplace legislation is rarely considered in organizational intervention research. This is unfortunate and our recommendation is for their formal discrete consideration within organizational intervention research, particularly to improve our understanding of how and why interventions differ across countries and regions.

We have also previously documented the call for (theory-testing) research to be more widely applied to non-European and non-USA contexts (Brough et al., 2013). The differing impact of national cultures on key workplace behaviours, including trust, participation, and behavioural norms, has been documented by numerous cross-cultural researchers. Brough et al. (2013) for example, observed that testing Western-derived organizational behaviour theories among workers employed in Asia, was a highly pertinent issue, especially regarding the increasing "Westernization" of many Asian organizations and their workers. Similarly, Timms et al. (2015) noted workers in Asian countries are often more sensitive to such issues as workplace interpersonal conflict compared to Western workers, due to a higher value placed on social affiliation by many Asian cultures. This for example, has implications for the participation and engagement of Asian workers with organizational interventions and training programmes.

Impact of COVID-19

The organizational landscape has changed considerably in the last decades, and especially within the last few years. Organizations are often only one link in complex supply chains, which often limit their levels of participation in organizational interventions. Sorensen et al. (2021) described an example of such limitations. In a study of industrial canteens, they discussed how participation was limited in terms of workers' opportunities to participate in the intervention activities due to extreme time pressures: competition in the food service industry is harsh and host organizations were only willing to cover meal delivery not developmental activities. Furthermore, participation in what changes to make were also limited as host organizations were unwilling to invest in improvements of the work environment, e.g., providing ergonomically appropriate workspaces.

The widespread practice of remote working resulting from the COVID-19 pandemic, has highlighted differences between workers in terms of who is and is not able to conduct their work remotely (Chan et al., 2022). This has produced additional pressures for bringing workers together in one physical location for their participation in formal training and interventions. Before the COVID-19 pandemic "remote workers" generally referred to those workers geographically isolated by distance from their central work base. Brough et al. (2020) for example, discussed the occurrence of additional stressors reported by workers based in rural and remote communities within Australia, who are geographically isolated from towns and their colleagues. Brough et al. (2020) also discussed the "fly-in fly-out" (FIFO) mining and construction workers in Australia, who commute long distances to rural inland work sites by aeroplane, living and working intensively on-site for several weeks, followed by one or two weeks leave when they commute back to their homes and families. Although these FIFO workers are not isolated from their site colleagues, the changing rotational intensive shift systems they work under does pose difficulties for their participation in organizational interventions, particularly programmes conducted over a lengthy period.

The COVID-19 pandemic increased the isolation experienced by many workers during enforced lockdowns and working from home periods. These workers found themselves suddenly categorized as "remote workers" and reliant on technology for social and participatory interactions with their colleagues. For most workers, these remote work experiences highlighted the value of having regular physical meetings with colleagues, particularly for creative problem-solving, to promote a psychological sense of belonging, and to feel a connection with co-workers (Brough et al., 2021). This period of approximately two years also caused the pausing of most participatory invention work. Some interventions did continue via video meetings and via mobile "apps", and such technology is also utilized by geographically isolated workers. The efficacy of using virtual technology, as opposed to physical co-location training, for the long-term adoption of workplace changes by workers is yet to be fully assessed.

RECOMMENDATIONS AND CONCLUSIONS

Although a participatory, collaborative approach to designing and implementing the content and process of organizational interventions is widely recommended, we argue that several key issues impacting this participation remain unanswered. In this chapter, we have discussed the three key challenges which reduce participation in organizational interventions. First, we discussed what type of participation should occur, including the importance of direct and indirect participation and whether workers need to be given special roles in ensuring intervention implementation. We call for more research on the impact of this participation to develop our understanding of how workers should be involved to reap the benefits of participation. Second, in extension of Nielsen (2013) we argued the need to understand the theory underpinning participation. We propose the mechanisms that may explain why participation works in promoting successful intervention implementation: specifically enabling workers to proactively craft a healthy work environment, as a method to develop trust and participation as a sense-making process, and to enable workers to better understand what and why changes are required. We recommend that researchers develop and test the mechanisms and theories of why participation works in more detail.

Third, we argued that participation needs to be tailored to the specific organizational context. The COVID-19 pandemic has brought about challenges for how we conduct interventions, as face-to-face interactions have been limited and some organizations have changed their work policies enabling, or requiring, workers to work from home. This also impacts the content of organizational interventions. For a large proportion of workers, remote working has increased their loneliness and decreased social interactions. Thus, new interventions need to consider these changes in working conditions, especially as organizations now move to a "hybrid" model of work locations (Brough et al., 2021; Chan et al., 2022). We also recommend that the organizational context, in terms of cross-cultural demographics, organizational embeddedness in other organizations, and national contexts, also need to be more carefully considered for organizational interventions to be most effective. We urge researchers to carefully consider how these broader contexts may hinder or facilitate workers' participation in organizational interventions. In conclusion, it is our hope that we have inspired researchers to explore further the nature of participation in organizational interventions.

REFERENCES

Abildgaard, J. S., Hasson, H., von Thiele Schwarz, U., Løvseth, L., Ala-Laurinaho, A., & Nielsen, K. (2018). Forms of participation – The development and application of a conceptual model of participation in work environment interventions. *Economic and Industrial Democracy, 41*(3), 746–769. https://doi.org/10.1177/0143831X17743576

Abildgaard, J. S., Nielsen, K., & Sverke, M. (2018). Can job insecurity be managed? Evaluating an organizational-level intervention addressing the negative effects of restructuring. *Work & Stress, 32*(2), 105–123. https://doi.org/10.1080/02678373.2017.1367735

Biggs, A., & Brough, P. (2015a). Explaining intervention success and failure: What works, when, and why? In M. Karanika-Murray & C. Biron (Eds.), *Derailed Organizational Stress and Well-Being Interventions: Confessions of Failure and Solutions for Success.* (pp. 237–244). Springer, London.

Biggs, A., & Brough, P. (2015b). Challenges of intervention acceptance in complex, multifaceted organisations: The importance of local champions. In M. Karanika-Murray & C. Biron (Eds.), *Derailed Organizational Stress and Well-Being Interventions: Confessions of Failure and Solutions for Success.* (pp. 151–158). Springer, London.

Blau, P. M. (1968). Social exchange. *International encyclopedia of the social sciences, 7*(4), 452–457.

Brough, P. (2004). Comparing the influence of traumatic and organizational stressors upon the psychological health of police, fire and ambulance officers. *International Journal of Stress Management, 11*(3), 227–244. Doi: 10.1037/1072-5245.11.3.227

Brough, P., & Biggs, A. (2015). The highs and lows of occupational stress intervention research: Lessons learnt from collaborations with high-risk industries. In M. Karanika-Murray & C. Biron (Eds.), *Derailed Organizational Stress and Well-Being Interventions: Confessions of Failure and Solutions for Success.* (pp. 263–270). Springer, London.

Brough, P., & O'Driscoll, M. (2010). Organisational interventions for balancing work and home demands: An overview. *Work & Stress, 24*(3), 280–297. doi: 10.1080/02678373.2010.506808

Brough, P., Brown, J., & Biggs, A. (2016b). *Improving Criminal Justice Workplaces: Translating Theory and Research into Evidence-Based Practice.* Routledge, London.

Brough, P., Chataway, S., & Biggs, A. (2016a). "You don't want people knowing you're a copper!" A contemporary assessment of police organisational culture. *International Journal of Police Science & Management, 18*(1), 28–36. DOI: 10.1177/1461355716638361

Brough, P., Drummond, S., & Biggs, A. (2018). Job support, coping and control: Assessment of simultaneous impacts within the occupational stress process. *Journal of Occupational Health Psychology, 23*(2), 188–197. http://dx.doi.org/10.1037/ocp000007428

Brough, P., Gardiner, E., & Daniels, K. (Eds.). (2022b). *Handbook on Management and Employment Practices.* Springer, London.

Brough, P., Kinman, G., McDowall, A., & Chan, X. C. (2021). "#Me too" for work–life balance. *British Psychological Society Work–life Balance Bulletin, 5*(1), 4–8.

Brough, P., Lawrence, S., Tsahuridu, E., & Brown, A. J. (2022c). The effective management of whistleblowing: The Whistleblowing Response Model. In P. Brough,

E. Gardiner, & K. Daniels (Eds.), *Handbook on Management and Employment Practices.* (pp. 437–458). Springer, London.

Brough, P., Raper, M., & Spedding, J. (2020). "She'll be right, mate!" Occupational stress research in Australia. In K. Sharma, C. Cooper, & D. M. Pestonjee (Eds.), *Organizational Stress Around the World: Research and Practice.* (pp. 7–22). Routledge, London.

Brough, P., Timms, C., Siu, O. L., Kalliath, T., O'Driscoll, M., Sit, C., Lo. D., & Lu, C. Q. (2013). Validation of the job demands-resources model in cross-national samples: Cross-sectional and longitudinal predictions of psychological strain and work engagement. *Human Relations, 66*(10), 1311–1335. doi: 10.1177/0018726712472915

Burgess, M. G., Brough, P., Biggs, A., & Hawkes, A. J. (2020). Why interventions fail: A systematic review of Occupational Health Psychology interventions. *International Journal of Stress Management, 27*(2), 195–207. https://doi.org/10.1037/str0000144

Chan, X. W., Shang, S., Brough, P., Wilkinson, A., & Lu, C-Q. (2022). Work, life, and the COVID-19 pandemic. *Asia Pacific Journal of Human Resources.* https://doi.org/10.1111/1744-7941.12355

Day, A. & Nielsen, K. (2017). What does our organization do to help our well-being? Creating Healthy Workplaces and Workers. In Chmiel, N., Fraccaroli, F. & Sverke, M. (Eds.), *An introduction of work and organizational psychology.* (pp. 295-314). John Wiley and Sons, Hoboken.

Deacon, R. E., & Brough, P. (2017). Veterinary nurses' psychological well-being: The impact of patient suffering and death. *Australian Journal of Psychology, 69*(2), 77–85. https://doi.org/10.1111/ajpy.12119

Di Tecco, C., Ronchetti, M., Ghelli, M., Russo, S., Persechino, B., & Iavicoli, S. (2015). Do Italian companies manage work-related stress effectively? A process evaluation in implementing the INAIL methodology. *BioMed Research International.* doi.org/10.1155/2015/197156.

Directive 1989/391 – Introductions of measures to encourage improvements in the safety and health of workers at work. https://eur-lex.europa.eu/legal-content/EN/TXT/?uri=CELEX%3A01989L0391-20081211. Reviewed 25 January, 2020.

Edwards, J. A., & Webster, S. (2012). Psychosocial risk assessment: Measurement invariance of the UK Health and Safety Executive's Management Standards Indicator Tool across public and private sector organizations. *Work & Stress, 26*(2), 130-142. https://doi.org/10.1080/02678373.2012.688554

EU-OSHA (2010) European Survey of Enterprises on New and Emerging Risks, 2010. Available at: www.esener.eu (accessed 25 April 2020).

European Commission (1989). *Council Directive of 12 June 1989 on the Introduction of Measures to Encourage Improvements in the Safety and Health of Workers at Work (89/391/EEC).* Commission of the European Communities, Luxembourg.

Framke E., & Sørensen, O. H. (2015). Implementation of a participatory organisational-level occupational health intervention – Focusing on the primary task. *International Journal of Human Factors and Ergonomics, 3*(3–4), 254–270. https://doi.org/10.1504/IJHFE.2015.072998

Gai, S., Brough, P., & Gardiner, E. (2022). Psychological adjustment and post-arrival cross-cultural training for better expatriation? A systematic review. In P. Brough, E. Gardiner, & K. Daniels. (Eds), *Handbook on Management and Employment Practices.* (pp. 827–854). Springer, London.

Heller, F., Pusic, E., Strauss, G., & Wilpert, B. (1998). *Organizational Participation: Myth and Reality.* Oxford University Press, Oxford.

Houtman, I. L. D., Eekhout, I., Venema, A., Bakhuys Roozeboom, M., & van Buuren, S. (2017). *Health and Safety Risks at the Workplace: A Joint Analysis of Three Major Surveys.* European Agency for Safety and Health at Work (EU-OSHA).

Innstrand, S. T., Christensen, M., Undebakke, K. G., & Svarva, K. (2015). The presentation and preliminary validation of KIWEST using a large sample of Norwegian university staff. *Scandinavian Journal of Public Health, 43*(8), 855–866. https://doi .org/10.1177/1403494815600562

Ipsen, C. (2019). Appointing in-house employee facilitators in organizational level interventions in SMEs – Experiences of bricoleurs. Proceeding of the Work, Stress and Health Conference, Philadelphia, 2019. https://www.apa.org/wsh/past/2019/ 2019-program.pdf. Retrieved 25 January 2020.

Ipsen, C., Poulsen, S., Gish, L., & Kirkegaard, M. L. (2020). Continuous evaluation of participants' perceptions of impact: Applying a boundary object in organisational-level interventions. *Human Factors and Ergonomics in Manufacturing & Service Industries, 30*(3), 149–164. https://doi.org/10.1002/hfm.20830

Irastorza, X., Milczarek, M., & Cockburn, W. (2016). *Second European Survey of Enterprises on New and Emerging Risks (ESENER-2): Overview Report: Managing Safety and Health at Work.* Publications Office of the European Union.

Le, H., Nielsen, K., & Noblet, A. (2021). The well-being and voice of migrant workers in participatory organizational interventions. *International Migration, 60*(3), 52–71.

Leana, C., Appelbaum, E., & Shevchuk, I. (2009). Work process and quality of care in early childhood education: The role of job crafting. *Academy of Management Journal, 52*(6), 1169–1192. https://doi.org/10.5465/amj.2009.47084651

Links, M. J., Lombard, M., Forster, B. C., Phelps, G., & Brough, P. (2021). Learning to be well in the health workplace: An integrative synthesis and model development. *Medical Education, 10*(45), 45. https://doi.org/10.15694/mep.2021.000045.1

Maitlis, S., & Christianson, M. (2014). Sensemaking in organizations: Taking stock and moving forward. *Academy of Management Annals, 8*(1), 57–125. https://doi.org/10 .5465/19416520.2014.873177

Marchington, M., & Wilkinson, A. (2005). *Human Resource Management at Work: People Management and Development.* Kogan Page, London.

Morrow, R., & Brough, P. (2019). "It's off to work we go!" Occupational stress and person–environment fit in professional mining personnel. *International Journal of Occupational Safety and Ergonomics, 25*(3), 467–475. DOI: 10.1080/10803548.2017.1396028

Nielsen, K. (2013). How can we make organizational interventions work? Employees and line managers as actively crafting interventions. *Human Relations, 66*(8), 1029–1050. https://doi.org/10.1177/0018726713477164

Nielsen, K., & Abildgaard, J. S. (2013). Organizational interventions: A research-based framework for the evaluation of both process and effects. *Work & Stress, 27*(3), 278–297. https://doi.org/10.1080/02678373.2013.812358

Nielsen, K., Abildgaard, J. S., & Daniels, K. (2014). Putting context into organizational intervention design: Using tailored questionnaires to measure initiatives for worker well-being. *Human Relations, 67*(12), 1537–1560. https://doi.org/10.1177/ 0018726714525974

Nielsen, K., Antino, M., Rodríguez-Muñoz, A., & Sanz-Vergel, A. (2021a). Is it me or us? The impact of individual and collective participation on work engagement and burnout in a cluster-randomized organisational intervention. *Work & Stress, 35*(4), 374–397. https://doi.org/10.1080/02678373.2021.1889072

Nielsen, K., & Miraglia, M. (2017). What works for whom in which circumstances? On the need to move beyond the 'what works?' question in organizational intervention research. *Human Relations, 70*(1), 40–62. DOI: 10.1177/0018726716670226

Nielsen, K., Nielsen, M. B., Ogbonnaya, C., Känsälä, M., Saari, E., & Isaksson, K. (2017). Workplace resources to improve both employee well-being and performance: A systematic review and meta-analysis. *Work & Stress, 31*(2), 101-120. https://doi.org/10.1080/02678373.2017.1304463

Nielsen, K., & Noblet, A. (2018). Introduction: Organizational interventions: Where we are, where we go from here? In K. Nielsen & A. Noblet (Eds.), *Organizational Interventions for Health and Well-Being: A Handbook for Evidence-Based Practice.* (pp. 1–23). Routledge, Abingdon.

Nielsen, K., Dawson, J., Hasson, H., & Schwarz, U. V. T. (2021b). What about me? The impact of employee change agents' person–role fit on their job satisfaction during organisational change. *Work & Stress, 35*(1), 57–73. https://doi.org/10.1080/02678373.2020.1730481

Nielsen, K., Stage, M., Abildgaard, J. S., & Brauer, C. V. (2013). Participatory intervention from an organizational perspective: Employees as active agents in creating a healthy work environment. In G. F. Bauer & G. J. J. Jenny (Eds.), *Salutogenic Organizations and Change* (pp. 327–350). Springer, Dordrecht.

Persechino, B., Valenti, A., Ronchetti, M., Rondinone, B. M., Di Tecco, C., Vitali, S., & Iavicoli, S. (2013). Work-related stress risk assessment in Italy: A methodological proposal adapted to regulatory guidelines. *Safety and Health at Work, 4*(2), 95–99. https://doi.org/10.1016/j.shaw.2013.05.002

Poulsen, S., Ipsen, C., & Gish, L. (2015). Applying the chronicle workshop as a method for evaluating participatory interventions. *International Journal Human Factors and Ergonomics, 3*(3–4), 271–290.

Raper, M., & Brough, P. (2021). Seeing into the future: The role of future-oriented coping and daily stress appraisal in relation to a future stressor. *Stress & Health, 37*(1), 186–197. https://doi.org/10.1002/smi.2984

Raper, M., Brough, P., & Biggs, A. (2020). Evidence for the impact of organizational resources versus job characteristics in assessments of occupational stress over time. *Applied Psychology: An International Review, 69*(3), 715–740. DOI: 10.1111/apps.12201

Rosskam, E. (2009). Using participatory action research methodology to improve worker health. In P. Schnall, M. Dobson, & E. Rosskam (Eds.), *Unhealthy Work: Causes, Consequences, Cures.* (pp. 211–229). Baywood Publishing Company, New York.

Searle, B., Tuckey, M., & Brough, P. (2022). Are challenges hindering us? Limitations of models that categorize work stressors. *Journal of Managerial Psychology, 37*(5), 397–403. DOI 10.1108/JMP-03-2022-0095.

Sorensen, G., Peters, S. E., Nielsen, K., Stelson, E., Wallace, L. M., Burke, L., ... & Wagner, G. R. (2021). Implementation of an organizational intervention to improve low-wage food service workers' safety, health and well-being: Findings from the Workplace Organizational Health Study. *BMC Public Health, 21*(1), 1–16. https://doi.org/10.1186/s12889-021-11937-9

Tafvelin, S., von Thiele Schwarz, U., Nielsen, K., & Hasson, H. (2019). Employees' and line managers' active involvement in participatory organizational interventions: Examining direct, reversed, and reciprocal effects on well-being. *Stress and Health, 35*(1), 69–80. https://doi.org/10.1002/smi.2841

Thompson, B. M., Brough, P., & Schmidt, H. (2006). Supervisor and subordinate work–family values: Does similarity make a difference? *International Journal of Stress Management, 13*(1), 45–63. Doi: 10.1037/1072-5245.13.1.45

Timms, C., Brough, P., Siu, O. L., O'Driscoll, M., & Kalliath, T. (2015). Cross-cultural impact of work–life balance on health and work outcomes. In L. Lu & C. L. Cooper (Eds.), *Handbook of Research on Work–Life Balance in Asia.* (pp. 295–314). Edward Elgar Publishing, Cheltenham, UK and Northampton, MA, USA.

Vander Elst, T., Baillien, E., De Cuyper, N., & De Witte, H. (2010). The role of organizational communication and participation in reducing job insecurity and its negative association with work-related well-being. *Economic and Industrial Democracy, 31*(2), 249–264. https://doi.org/10.1177/0143831X09358372

Weick, K. E. (1988). Enacted sensemaking in crisis situations. *Journal of Management Studies, 25*(4), 305–317. https://doi.org/10.1111/j.1467-6486.1988.tb00039.x

Weick, K. E. (1995). Sensemaking in organizations (Vol. 3). London: Sage.

Wilkinson, A., Gollan, P. J., Marchington, M., & Lewin, D. (Eds.). (2010). *The Oxford Handbook of Participation in Organizations.* Oxford University Press, Oxford.

World Health Organization and Burton, J. (2010). WHO Healthy Workplace Framework and Model: Background and Supporting Literature and Practices. World Health Organization. Available online at: https://apps.who.int/iris/handle/10665/113144

11. Motivating the unemployed: How motivational interviewing may help to tailor interventions to different unemployment profiles

Anja Van den Broeck & Maarten Vansteenkiste

INTRODUCTION

The International Labour Organization (2000) describes the unemployed as people of working age who do not have a paid job or are not self-employed, but are physically and psychologically available for work and are taking active steps to seek a paid job. Research and practice within the realm of unemployment is often steered towards guiding the unemployed towards registered paid employment on the labour market. Yet, this may not be so easy, as there are a number of factors that prevent the unemployed from filling open vacancies. For example, the unemployed may not have the right *abilities* or skills that match the competences needed in organizations (e.g., not all people may be able to do carpentry or be able to work full-time due to chronic illness), or they may see limited *opportunities* to find a job (e.g., they may face discrimination or the available jobs may not be within distance). However, apart from their ability and opportunity, also their motivation to work or search for a job is important if they would move from being unemployed to being employed (Appelbaum et al., 2000).

In this chapter, we argue that the individuals' experiences of being unemployed and their associated motivation to search for employment is key to alleviating the burden of unemployment. Research shows that the unemployed do not form a homogenous group, but can be categorized in different profiles as a function of the way they experience their situation. We argue that these profiles may differ in terms of the motivation to search or not to search for employment. To shed light on this issue, we adopt the perspective of Self-Determination Theory (SDT; Deci & Ryan, 2000; Vansteenkiste & Van den Broeck, 2014), which addresses both quantitative and qualitative aspects of motivation. Even when being motivated to search, not all unemployed may display those types of motivation that will lead to (high quality) reemployment. We argue that looking at the profiles of the unemployed and their (assumed) associated motivation is crucial for researchers and counsellors to consider whether and – if so – how the different types of unemployed may be success- fully guided towards paid employment. Not all unemployed may benefit from all the interventions targeted to improve their skills and/or well-being. Rather, we argue that interventions guided by motivational interviewing – a counsel- ling technique with close links to SDT – may assist to select and/or tailor the support to the needs of the different types of unemployed.

TYPOLOGY OF UNEMPLOYED INDIVIDUALS

Various classification systems have been developed to understand the diversity among the unemployed. These may be based on objective characteristics (e.g., unemployment duration) or start from a sociological or psychological perspec- tive (De Witte, 1992). Given that people's well-being, commitment to employ- ment and search behaviour are essential elements in finding a paid job (Kanfer et al., 2001; Wanberg, 2012), we focus on the psychological perspective, which includes these aspects to understand the different types of unemployed.

De Witte and his colleagues did a series of studies to understand psycholog- ical profiles of unemployed individuals based on their well-being, attitudes and behaviours. Specifically, they examined (a) the degree to which unemployed individuals *experience* unemployment negatively (e.g., feeling insecure, loss of self-worth, no longer part of society); (b) their *commitment* to employment (e.g., whether paid employment makes life meaningful and it would be better to accept any job rather than being unemployed); and (c) the degree they are *searching* for paid employment (e.g., whether one has visited a potential future employer or asked friends and family whether they knew a job opportunity). Most importantly, they investigated how these aspects combined into specific unemployment profiles. The research was done in different (economic) con- texts, yet led to remarkably similar results.

In his initial research, De Witte (1992) focused on a representative sample of long-term unemployed (more than one year) in Flanders, the Northern part of Belgium. This allowed him to examine the prevalence of different types of unemployed. De Witte and colleagues furthermore shifted the research to stud- ying (a convenience sample of) short-term unemployed individuals (less than four and a half months) around the same period (De Witte & Hooge, 1995) and about 20 years later (Cuypers & De Witte, 2021) in Flanders, and expanded this approach to two samples of long-term unemployed in South Africa. While the circumstances in Flanders changed from the 1990s to the 2020s (e.g., lower unemployment rates, higher inflation), they are considerably different from the context of the unemployed in South Africa. Compared to Western Europe, unemployment in South Africa is incredibly high. Official unemployment figures range from 30 percent to 40 percent, depending on which definition is used (Statistics South Africa, 2020). Unofficially, the numbers may even be higher as only few people have official contracts with a formal employer. The first South African sample (described in Van der Vaart et al., 2018), was dominated by Afrikaans-speaking people, who are generally not Black and may have relatively good opportunities in the labour market. The second South African sample (described in Putter et al., 2021) included Black Africans, who represent 81 percent of the labour market, but have high chances of being unemployed. The latter lived in townships, were generally lowly educated (only 38.70 percent completed secondary education) and really poor (about half of them lived in a household without any income). Given that few receive unemployment benefits, South African unemployed individuals survive based on other (limited) grants (e.g., pensions) or "getting by" by selling products (e.g., fruit, make-up) or services (e.g., dressing hair) in the informal economy. They thus experience considerable financial hardship, are strongly committed to work and look intensively for a job and report highly negative feelings (Vleugels et al., 2013).

Despite these differences, all these studies led to remarkably similar results, suggesting that the findings are generalizable and solid. In essence, four different profiles emerged across the studies. The unemployed within these profiles clearly varied in terms of their negative feelings due to their unemployment, their attitude or commitment towards paid employment and their job behaviour. They also differed somewhat in terms of demographics, which seemed to correspond to their position in the labour market. Yet, these associations were only weak, which further attests to the importance of examining the profiles of the unemployed based on their psychological rather than demographic characteristics.

First, *optimists* did not experience their unemployment situation as particularly negative. They had a neutral to moderately positive attitude towards the labour market and were intensively looking for a new job. In the 1990s sample in Flanders, this group included more young people, higher educated, and those who had been unemployed for a short while, compared to the average in the samples. In 2020, these type of unemployed were somewhat older, had children living at home and an average household wage. In Flanders, they represented 28 percent of the long-term unemployed and 29 percent in the research on short-term unemployment in 1990 and 24 percent of the group studied in 2020. In South Africa, the optimists experienced their situation as less negative, compared to two other profiles (i.e., the desperate and discouraged, described below), but experienced more negative experiences than the fourth profile (i.e., adapted) found in South Africa. They showed the lowest levels of commitment and were somewhat looking for a job in the first sample and searching the most in the second South African sample. They represented 12 percent and 35 percent of sample 1 and 2, respectively. The relatively high number of optimists in the second South African sample is potentially because of changes in the South African legislation (e.g., Employment Equity Act) which called to advantage Black South Africans on the labour market to overcome disadvantages in the past (Putter et al., 2021).

Second, the unemployed categorized as *desperate* experienced unemployment as a real burden. They were highly committed to finding employment and were relatively intensively looking for a job. While this group represented only 11 percent among the long-term unemployed in 1990 in Flanders, they made up 23 percent and 28 percent of the population of the short-term unemployed in the 1990s and 2020s, respectively. In the Flemish 1990s sample, this group was somewhat older, less educated, had a more challenging personal situation (e.g., they are single or have a non-working partner) and were unemployed somewhat longer than the average in the sample. In the 2020 sample, this group also included more singles or people living with their parents. Also, in South Africa, the desperate experienced unemployment as highly negative. They considered work highly important, and said they were more engaged in job search behaviour than the optimists. They constituted 31 percent and 19 percent of sample 1 and 2, respectively.

Third, the *discouraged* reported feeling somewhat negative about being unemployed, were also committed to finding employment, yet they were searching somewhat less actively for a new job opportunity compared to the aforementioned profiles. This profile represented 14 percent among the long-term unemployed in Flanders, but 21 percent and 23 percent of the total samples of short-term unemployed in 1990 and 2021, respectively. In South Africa, the discouraged also experienced unemployment as somewhat negative, and were somewhat committed to finding employment. They were however as engaged in job search as the South African desperate. They represented 37 percent and 38 percent of sample 1 and 2, respectively. They were unemployed slightly longer in the Flemish long-term unemployed 1990s sample. However, there were no outspoken associations with people's background variables in the other studies. In all, the discouraged seem to be very similar to the desperate unemployed.

Fourth, the *withdrawn* represent an interesting group: they did not experience unemployment as negative, were not really committed to paid employment and were (therefore) also not looking for a new job. In Flanders, they represented 30 percent of the long-term unemployed, and a comparable 28 percent and 25 percent in the samples of short-term unemployed in 1990 and 2021, respectively. This group contained slightly more female or older participants with a partner and (young) children, and a slightly higher household income. No unemployed people adopted this profile in the South African samples, which is potentially the most notable difference between the research among the long-term unemployed in Belgium versus South Africa. Again, the precarious situation of the South African unemployed may explain this, as their financial situation may prevent them from taking such a more distant orientation to the labour market.

Finally, within the sample of long-term Flemish unemployed, also an *adapted* profile emerged (De Witte, 1992). These unemployed did not feel negative about their unemployment situation, and – despite the fact that they were relatively highly committed towards paid employment – they no longer searched for a job. They represented 17 percent of the long-term unemployed as described in De Witte (1992), yet were absent among the Flemish short-term unemployed. They were somewhat older and unemployed for a longer period of time than the other groups and more frequently married and had a household with children. This profile also included relatively lowly educated or skilled people. In the South African sample, the adapted reported the lowest levels of negative experiences. They considered work to be somewhat important, yet showed the lowest engagement in job search behaviour. They constituted 20 percent and 8 percent of sample 1 and 2, respectively. In the second South African sample, which was more vulnerable, there were thus less unemployed who had adapted to their situation, potentially because the economic hardship makes it less easy for people to feel well and settle down in being unemployed.

These results indicate that the unemployed are not a homogeneous group, but differ considerably in how they experience their unemployed situation, are committed to paid employment and look for a job, and – hence – their chances of finding (re)employment. We suggest that the qualitatively different types of motivation, as outlined in SDT, may help to theoretically understand the differences among these profiles and may help practitioners to assist the unemployed in dealing with their unemployment situation. We detail this below.

SELF-DETERMINATION THEORY TO UNDERSTAND THE MOTIVATION OF THE UNEMPLOYED

Self-determination theory (SDT; Deci & Ryan, 2000; Ryan & Deci, 2017) is an encompassing theory of motivation, which focuses on the processes and conditions helping people to "function optimally", that is, to feel well, develop positive attitudes and perform the best they can (Van den Broeck et al., 2019). This theory starts off from the assumption that people have the propensity to act proactively and to steer their development towards increasing synthesis and integration, both intra- and interpersonally. Yet, this natural growth process does not take place automatically: it only unfolds when people get their basic psychological needs met. As much as we need water, food and shelter to feel physically well, according to SDT, we need the satisfaction of the basic psychological needs to function optimally from a psychological perspective (Vansteenkiste et al., 2020). Three needs are currently deemed essential, that is, the need for autonomy (i.e., experiencing a sense of psychological freedom and choice), relatedness (i.e., feeling loved and cared for, while also being able to love and care for others) and competence (i.e., to be effective and learn new things). When the environment supports the satisfaction of these psychological needs, people report being more engaged, have better mental health, are more productive and deliver more high-quality work (Van den Broeck et al., 2016). However, contexts that thwart these basic needs come with a psychological cost. In the case of need frustration, people feel pressured, rejected or like a failure, and this predicts a higher risk for ill-being, counterproductive behaviour and even psychopathology (Chen et al., 2015; Vansteenkiste & Ryan, 2013). The degree to which people have these basic needs satisfied or frustrated also associates with their motivation to engage in their activities.

In terms of motivation, SDT stipulates that people may be a-motivated, that is, lack any motivation and feel helpless or hopeless, and therefore be rather passive. In case of unemployment, this may mean that people do not send their CV to potential employers, or do so without much consideration or without expecting that such actions would lead to employment. When motivated, in contrast, people behave intentionally. Being extrinsically motivated means one does an activity for a reason that is situated outside the activity itself (Ryan & Deci, 2020). Such reasons may be integrated or "taken in" and perceived as one's own to various degrees as displayed in Figure 11.1.

First, external regulation is completely situated outside the individual. In this case people pursue an activity because they want to obtain social (e.g., recognition) or material (e.g., money) rewards from others or avoid punishments (e.g., criticism), such as when unemployed individuals seek employment merely out of financial pressure or because their spouse urges them to do so. In case of introjected regulation, people have partially taken in the external reasons for their behaviour. Their motivation does not depend on others, yet, because the regulation is only partially internalized, they still engage in the activity with a sense of inner conflict and pressure. They, for example, engage in activities to boost their self-esteem (e.g., to feel good about oneself) or experience positive (e.g., proud) or avoid other negative emotions (e.g., guilt, shame). Unemployed individuals could, for example, apply for jobs because they no longer want to feel worthless or guilty for not contributing to society. In case of external regulation and introjection, people feel pressured or controlled, either by others or themselves. Hence, these two types of motivation represent controlled types of motivation.

A-motivation	Extrinsic motivation				Intrinsic motivation
Non-regulation	**External**	**Introjected**	**Identified**	**Integrated**	**Intrinsic**
No activity, helpless or hopeless	Others administered - rewards - punishments	Self administered - proud - guilt, shame	Personal importance	Full personal endorsement, fully integrated in one's sense of self	Fun or interesting
e.g., not applying	e.g., sending out CV's not to loose unemployment benefits	e.g., applying for a job not to feel so worthless anymore	e.g., looking for a job because one wants to contribute to society	e.g., sending out your CV for a job you're passionate about	e.g., filling out talent surveys because one enjoys learning more about oneself

Controlled motivation "Has to" Not internalized, characterized by pressure	Autonomous motivation "Wants to" Internal motivation, characterized by volitional functioning

Figure 11.1   *Unemployed people's different types of motivation to search for paid employment*

The next steps in the internalization process are identification and integration, which are defined as engaging in an activity because one finds it valuable or meaningful versus an integral part of one's sense of self, respectively. A nurse may, for example, apply for a job because it is a means to develop oneself or because she sees herself as a caregiver. When people identify with the reason behind their behaviour, they engage in it out of a sense of choice self-determination. Different from intrinsically motivated activities, the behaviour is still instrumental as it is characterized by a means–end structure. Intrinsic motivation is defined as doing an activity because of its own sake. The activity is experienced as inherently enjoyable or interesting and elicits curiosity, such as when unemployed people would engage in career counselling because they are interested in getting to know themselves better. A key aspect of SDT is that identification and integration can be grouped together with intrinsic motivation as autonomous types of motivation. Abundant research shows that the different types of motivation can empirically be separated (Howard et al., 2016) and relate differently to people's well-being, attitudes and behaviours across a diversity of settings such as education (Howard et al., 2017; Vansteenkiste et al., 2005) and work (Van den Broeck et al., 2021), with more autonomous types of motivation relating to more positive outcomes.

Research also indicates that the quality of motivation matters throughout the job-seeking process: unemployed individuals who are autonomously motivated enjoy seeking further information (e.g., about potential jobs), while people who are controlled experience information seeking as stressful and feel pressured to do so. Unemployed individuals who are a-motivated only engage in information seeking half-heartedly, leading to poor information quality (Savolainen, 2008). Being autonomously motivated also helps unemployed individuals to become more employable over time (Koen et al., 2015), search more intensively for a job, dedicate themselves to fully exploring all their potential job options and be more able to self-regulate one's search process over time (e.g., in terms of goal setting, planning, monitoring and reflection; Koen et al., 2016; Vansteenkiste et al., 2004, 2005). These strategies are highly successful as they are positively linked to the number of job offers one receives (Koen et al., 2010, 2013) and the chances of becoming reemployed (Koen et al., 2016; Van Hooft et al., 2021). Autonomous motivation also helps the unemployed to procrastinate less and search less haphazardly (Van den Hee et al., 2020). Being motivated in a controlled way or being a-motivated, in contrast, associates with haphazard search behaviour over time, using trial and error and lacking any guidelines to select a particular job position to apply for, which limits one's chances of finding employment (Koen et al., 2016). In line with SDT, other research showed that other controlling aspects such as financial hardship, having only casual work or involuntarily working part-time also adversely affect job search quality, subsequent reemployment (Gerards & Welters, 2022) and the quality of reemployment (Welters et al., 2014).

Apart from helping to understand the various aspects of unemployed people's job search behaviour, SDT is also one of the few motivational theories that is being used to understand unemployed people's well-being and attitudes towards employment. Unemployed people who are autonomously motivated to search for employment report somewhat lower feelings of being worthless or meaninglessness, which are typical when being unemployed, and feel less socially isolated. They also experience better mental health. Controlled motivation to search, in contrast, is associated with more negative feelings, lower mental health and lower life satisfaction (Vansteenkiste et al., 2004, 2005). Notably, SDT-inspired research also showed that being autonomously motivated *not* to search is associated with less negative and more positive experiences, general health and life satisfaction. Controlled motivation not to search was characterized with more negative feelings (Vansteenkiste et al., 2004).

In all, these results clearly show that the quality of motivation matters: being autonomously motivated to find employment is associated with better optimal functioning among the unemployed than feeling controlled to search. However, not all unemployed individuals may hold autonomous motivation to search for employment. Moreover, some may not be motivated at all to search and/or be more motivated not to search. We advance that unemployed people's motivation to search may co-occur with the typology as detailed above. First, from all types of unemployed, optimists may have the highest chance of finding paid employment. Their profile may be high in demand, they are somewhat committed to work and invested in job searches. They – therefore – feel effective and pretty optimistic in overcoming their current situation. This aligns with research indicating that the optimists are not frustrated in their basic needs (Putter et al., 2021), and the assumption that they are autonomously motivated for searching employment. Second, the desperate experience unemployment as highly negative and are frustrated in their basic psychological needs (Putter et al., 2021). They attach high importance to finding employment and are somewhat looking for a job. The insights from the profile analyses may hint at the possibility that the desperate have controlled motivation to look for employment, either because of financial reasons (they seem to have less of a financial buffer), being pushed by others (e.g., their non-working partner or parents) or because they feel internal pressures (e.g., due to low self-esteem) to find employment. This may explain why the desperate feel they are highly invested in job searches, yet may experience more difficulties in securing a job compared to optimists: due to their motivation, their approach may be haphazard or of low quality. Third, the discouraged are committed towards employment. Yet across the different studies it may be suggested they are somewhat less invested in finding reemployment than the optimists or the desperate. However, they feel bad and are somewhat frustrated in their basic psychological needs (Putter et al., 2021), suggesting they may not have the resources to be autonomously motivated to search for employment. They may be controlled in their motivation to search or even be a-motivated. The withdrawn seem to have merely a-motivated orientation towards paid employment, given that they do not see any value in finding a job and show little interest in job searches. Similarly, we also consider the adapted to be a-motivated to (search for) paid employment but – interestingly – they are little or not negatively affected by this, as they experience low need frustration (Putter et al., 2021). We speculate that this is because they may be motivated more – perhaps also more autonomously – about other activities such as taking care of children. Future research could further investigate the proposed suggestions. If they are true, they may have vast implications for whether and – if so – how the different types of unemployed individuals can be guided towards the labour market and which interventions could be used to improve their situation.

MOTIVATIONAL INTERVIEWING BASED ON SDT TO HELP THE DIFFERENT TYPES OF UNEMPLOYED

Motivational Interviewing based on SDT as an Intervention Technique for the Unemployed

Different types of interventions exist to alleviate the burden of unemployment. Some invest in prevocational experiences (e.g., working on a farm; Ellingsen-Dalskau et al., 2016a, 2016b) as a stepping stone towards employment. Most interventions, however, focus on improving the technical skills of the unemployed (e.g., writing an appealing résumé), restoring their well-being, or both to improve the ability of unemployed people to find employment (Celume & Korda, 2022; Liu et al., 2014). Unfortunately, review papers and meta-analyses trying to establish the effectiveness of such interventions often report non-significant results (e.g., Celume & Korda, 2022; Hollederer, 2019; Hult et al., 2020; Koopman et al., 2017; Van Rijn et al., 2016) or show only low effect sizes indicating that the interventions hardly have any clinical significance. To overcome this issue, we advocate it may be useful to tailor the interventions to the needs of specific types of unemployed and their associated motivation as mentioned above. Motivational interviewing may be particularly helpful to understand how this can be achieved (Resnicow & McMaster, 2012; Vansteenkiste et al., 2012).

Motivational interviewing (MI; Miller & Rollnick, 2012a) is a way of communicating with clients or patients using a set of principles and techniques which developed from practice, but are much in line with SDT (Miller & Rollnick, 2012b; Vansteenkiste & Sheldon, 2006). For example, following SDT's premise that people are inherently growth oriented, MI starts from the perspective that people themselves may generate the motivation for change in adverse circumstances and are motivated best to change when the new behaviour is something that they want; that is, autonomously motivated, instead of something that someone else wants or something they do to obtain an external reward, that is, controlled motivation.

MI proposes a set of phases that are followed iteratively in dialogue with the client: (1) engaging in a relationship; (2) focusing on a goal; (3) evoking the willingness to change; and (4) planning the steps towards reaching the goal. First, professionals and clients build a working alliance. Then professionals aim to focus on the type of change that clients seek after. By using open questions, affirming the clients' responses, and applying accurate reflections, the professionals aim to elicit a goal among the clients that enables change. Professionals may, for example, probe whether the unemployed is ready to start searching or take steps towards reemployment by taking care of their own health. In the third stage, change is evoked by eliciting change talk from the clients and prevents them from feeling stuck. Within this phase, resistive behaviour is not seen as defensive but as a natural and useful component of the change process (Moyers & Rollnick, 2002). Feelings of ambivalence can be addressed by exploring the discrepancies between the actual and the desired behaviour (i.e., being passive while aiming for paid employment). In the final stage, the professionals guide the clients into developing a change plan and committing to it.

These different phases map onto the different stages clients may go through when aiming to change their behaviour from not even considering to change (i.e., precontemplation), over contemplation, preparation for action, and action to maintenance of the new behaviour (Prochaska & Diclemente, 1983). In each of these phases, the professional aims to support the unemployed by being need supportive. The professional may, for example, concur with the goals of the unemployed individual to satisfy the need for autonomy, try to establish a warm, caring relationship to satisfy the need for relatedness and assist the unemployed individual in making a plan to achieve his or her goals in support of the need for competence. SDT's notions of the basic psychological needs and need support are thus strong theoretical constructs that may guide the MI process and account for its effectiveness (Vansteenkiste & Sheldon, 2006). While support of all three basic psychological needs is important in each stage, during the engagement phase, professionals may pay particular attention to supporting the clients' need for relatedness. In the stage of focusing and evoking, the need for autonomy may be of primordial importance, while competence seems to be of utmost importance during the planning phase.

MI has already been proven to be effective to promote behavioural change in several healthcare contexts, such as addiction care and eating disorders (Britt et al., 2004; Frost et al., 2018; Lundahl et al., 2013; Rubak et al., 2005), and some studies indicate that it may be helpful to support the unemployed as well: it may help the unemployed to improve their mental and physical health, which is an important requisite for finding sustainable employment. For example, a health-promoting therapy endowed with MI proved to be more effective in engendering a healthy lifestyle and nutrition intake compared to the health promotion therapy without MI (Horns et al., 2012). Using MI in individual and group health promotion sessions also improved the mental health of long-term unemployed, and the MI approach seemed particularly helpful in decreasing long-term unemployed people's anxiety (Limm et al., 2015). Notably, MI seems to be particularly beneficial for people who are more vulnerable. For example, Britt et al. (2018) found that the use of MI on top of an employment program helped people who were not ready to seek employment. This effect was stronger than the effect of the employment program without MI among people who felt ready to (re-)enter the labour market. Interestingly, MI programs do not need to include regular contact between the professional and the client: already one single contact (i.e., using MI during an intake interview) can help people (i.e., homeless, unemployed substance-dependent veterans) to take significant steps in changing their lives (i.e. signing up for a program; Wain et al., 2011). Based on this evidence, we suggest that endowing unemployment programs with MI may be a fruitful avenue to guide even very vulnerable unemployed to take steps towards becoming (re-)employed.

Selecting and Tailoring Interventions to help different types of Unemployed Individuals

We argue that including MI in programs that aim to help the unemployed may help to select and tailor these approaches to the needs of the different types of unemployed based on how they experience unemployment.

- First, the *optimists* are perhaps the easiest group to guide, given that they have a strong profile on the labour market and are likely to be autonomously motivated to search for a job. Hence, optimists would likely be able to find employment by themselves, or in case they need support, we envision they themselves already formulated a clear goal to become employed and autonomously intend to change their situation. The professional counsellor using MI may thus quickly find out that optimists only need help to develop a clear change plan and/or technical advice (e.g., how to write a compelling CV, how to network) to help them turn their autonomous motivation into effective search strategies. This then will guarantee a high-quality search process, and subsequent sustainable employment. Such support would prevent the optimistic, meaning they would encounter a lot of setbacks during their search project which may otherwise turn them into discouraged unemployed individuals.
- Second, the *desperate* experience unemployment as highly negative and are frustrated in their needs. They are highly committed to find employment, yet may feel rather controlled in their job search. Professionals may help this group of unemployed first and foremost by defining a focus of the intervention. We envision that the desperate may have requested help to alleviate the burden of unemployment, and/or would need support to autonomously engage in job search. This is because, in case the desperate may feel ready to turn towards paid employment, the ways to get there may be unproductive as they hold controlled motivation and – hence – invest in the wrong behaviour. Improving the well-being of this group, relieving their need frustration and trying to develop autonomous motivation for searching may be most valuable for this group. Ideally, such help will assist them in overcoming their controlled motivation, but even when the

autonomous motivation would just be added to their existing perspective, this may result in more positive outcomes (Van den Broeck et al., 2013).

- Third, the *discouraged* may still contemplate upon the change they desire or be somewhat prepared to act, yet without engaging in job search whole-heartedly. Professionals may again focus on increasing this group's need satisfaction to alleviate the burden of unemployment, but primarily also guide them to start focusing and envision potential changes, such that they become autonomously motivated to search.

- Fourth, the Belgian research seems to suggest that the *withdrawn* are unlikely to experience need frustration, as they do not feel negative emotions about their unemployment situation, nor feel committed or engage in job search behaviour. These unemployed may thus not have any request for help, and could be situated in the precontemplation phase, being a-motivated to search for employment. Professionals may therefore have to invest in engaging with these unemployed, before taking additional steps in starting to focus on (re-)employment. Given that this group does not report well-being issues and may not even be prepared to act, we speculate that they do not benefit from programs that aim to improve their well-being or their technical job search skills directly. As they do not hold any motivation, they are unlikely to put these skills into practice. They might however benefit from prevocational training programs (e.g., Ellingsen-Dalskau et al., 2016b), that allow them to experience the need satisfying potential and the latent benefits of work. This may help them to long for engaging in paid employment and the autonomous motivation to engage in job search behaviour.

- Finally, from an outward perspective, one may argue that also the *adapted* are not in need for any additional support. Despite being committed to work, they are also not looking for paid employment. They do not feel negative about their unemployment situation and do not feel frustrated in their basic psychological needs. This group may in fact be autonomously motivated not to search for employment (Vansteenkiste et al., 2004), and fill their days with other activities that provide them satisfaction of the basic psychological needs. In case one would like to lead this group towards the labour market, first, one would need to gain greater insight into the daily activities of this group to understand their situation better. Taking an MI approach may be most beneficial to do so. Which activities help them to satisfy their needs? Why did they turn to these activities? They may be engaged in the upbringing of their (grand)children or invest in other care-taking activities or voluntary jobs, which can be highly need satisfying activities. The adapted may be guided towards the labour market in similar ways as the withdrawn. Yet, on a societal level, it could be discussed whether their alternative engagements can also be valued, and even supported financially, albeit it would not be correct to term such financial support as an "unemployment benefit", as these people are in essence not available to the labour market.

In all, we argue that the different types of unemployed may benefit from different aspects of the available interventions. MI herein proves to be of crucial importance to elicit and understand goal-directed behaviour among the different types of unemployed and help them to select these interventions that may help them to achieve the behaviour change they envision.

CONCLUSION

In conclusion, this chapter aimed to address the current and challenging situation on the labour market by suggesting that the unemployed can be better and perhaps more efficiently guided to the labour market. More specifically, we suggest to account for the heterogeneity of the unemployed and the associated quality of their motivation to engage in paid employment. Much in line with SDT, we advanced that the programs that are currently set up to help the unemployed should be selected and tailored to the needs of the different groups of unemployed using the principles of MI, for the unemployed to feel better, develop positive attitudes towards work and full-heartedly engage in job search behaviour. This may help to increase the effectiveness of these programs and to sustainably lead these unemployed to take part in the labour market, for the benefit of all stakeholders involved.

Notably, within this chapter we only assumed that unemployed people's motivation to find a job, as defined by SDT, covaried with their profile, based on their experience of unemployment, commitment to work and job search behaviour as evidenced in the work of De Witte. However, future research may examine to which degree these expectations hold, before engaging in intervention studies that examine the impact of the suggested interventions. Such studies may also take into account that people may combine different motivations (Van den Broeck et al., 2013) and, for example, study and compare unemployed holding controlled and autonomous motivation (e.g., unemployed individuals who feel pressured to earn an income ánd feel it is valuable to find a job) with those who have no motivation at all, feel only controlled (e.g., out of financial pressure), or have only autonomous motivation (e.g., like the money but do not feel pressured by it and mostly search for a job because of identified or integrated reasons).

Besides motivation, future studies also need to take into account other factors and the broader context that determines unemployed people's situation and job search. As mentioned at the beginning of this chapter, unemployed people's skills, knowledge and ability as well as opportunities matter (Appelbaum et al., 2000). Despite (the quality of) their motivation, the unemployed may lack the right abilities to find a job, either because they do not know how to look for employment or because they simply do not have the skills, knowledge or abilities that are required by employers. Or they may see few opportunities, for example, because the available jobs are in the wrong location or the unemployed do not get the opportunity to go on a job interview because they face discrimination from employers. Although being key, motivation is thus not the only factor to finding a job and the proposed interventions are not a "deus ex machina" that will help every situation. Moreover, as mentioned, even though unemployed individuals should – by definition – be available for the labour market, not all unemployed people would be open for job opportunities and being guided to the labour market may not improve their well-being as some may be autonomously motivated for other activities and have their basic needs satisfied in an alternative way (e.g., through the role of caregiver). When taking these limitations into account, we are, however, convinced that it helps to tailor any intervention to the profile of the unemployed individual and use motivational interviewing to detect what the unemployed really needs in order to consider paid employment and find a job. We even speculate that this approach may also help guide other groups (e.g., the long-term work disabled or youngsters who are not in education, employment or training) towards paid employment. We speculate that MI-endowed interventions could be of high value for them, especially when such interventions are also tailored to potential differential profiles among these groups in terms of how they experience their situation and their associated motivation and needs. However, whether and which profiles exist among such groups and how they are linked to one's autonomous or controlled motivation to engage in paid employment, also remains subject for future research.

REFERENCES

Appelbaum, E., Bailey, T., Berg, P., & Kalleberg, A. L. (2000). *Manufacturing advantage: Why high-performance work systems pay off.* Cornell University Press, Ithaca, NY.

Britt, E., Hudson, S. M., & Blampied, N. M. (2004). Motivational interviewing in health settings: A review. *Patient Education and Counseling, 53*(2), 147–155. https://doi.org/10.1016/S0738-3991(03)00141-1

Britt, E., Sawatzky, R., & Swibaker, K. (2018). Motivational interviewing to promote employment. *Journal of Employment Counseling, 55*(4), 176–189. https://doi.org/10.1002/joec.12097

Celume, M. P., & Korda, H. (2022). Three decades of interventions for the unemployed – Review of practices between 1990 and 2020 and their effects on (re)employment competencies. *Education and Training, 64*(2), 230–243. https://doi.org/10.1108/ET-02-2021-0053

Chen, B., Vansteenkiste, M., Beyers, W., Boone, L., Deci, E. L., Van der Kaap-Deeder, J., Duriez, B., Lens, W., Matos, L., Mouratidis, A., Ryan, R. M., Sheldon, K. M., Soenens, B., Van Petegem, S., & Verstuyf, J. (2015). Basic psychological need satisfaction, need frustration, and need strength across four cultures. *Motivation and Emotion, 39*(2), 216–236. https://doi.org/10.1007/s11031-014-9450-1

Cuypers, C., & De Witte, H. (2021). Replicatie van een psychosociale typologie bij Vlaamse werkzoekenden [Replication of a psychosocial typology among Flemish job seekers]. *Tijdschrift voor Arbeidsvraagstukken, 37*(4), 484–503.

De Witte, H. (1992). *Tussen optimisten en teruggetrokkenen: Een empirisch onderzoek naar het psychosociaal profiel van langdurig werklozen en deelnemers aan de Weer-Werkactie in Vlaanderen* [Between optimists and withdrawn: An empirical study of the psychosocial profile of the long-term unemployed and participants in the Weer-Werkactie in Flanders]. HIVA.

De Witte, H., & Hooge, J. (1995). Een vergelijking van typologieën van kort- en langdurig werklozen: Wetenschappelijke en beleidsmatige implicaties. In P.van der Hallen (Ed.), *De arbeidsmarktonderzoekersdag* 1995. Verslagboek (pp. 127–142). Leuven: Steunpunt Werkgelegenheid, Arbeid, Vorming.

Deci, E. L., & Ryan, R. M. (2000). The "what" and "why" of goal pursuits: Human needs and the self-determination of behavior. *Psychological Inquiry, 11*(4), 227–268. https://doi.org/10.1207/S15327965PLI1104_01

Ellingsen-Dalskau, L. H., Berget, B., Pedersen, I., Tellnes, G., Ihlebæk, C., Berget, B., Pedersen, I., & Tellnes, G. (2016a). Understanding how prevocational training on care farms can lead to functioning, motivation and well-being. *Disability and Rehabilitation, 38*(25), 2504–2513. https://doi.org/10.3109/09638288.2015.1130177

Ellingsen-Dalskau, L. H., Morken, M., Berget, B., & Pedersen, I. (2016b). Autonomy support and need satisfaction in prevocational programs on care farms: The self-determination theory perspective. *Work, 53*(1), 73–85. https://doi.org/10.3233/WOR-152217

Frost, H., Campbell, P., Maxwell, M., O'Carroll, R. E., Dombrowski, S. U., Williams, B., Cheyne, H., Coles, E., & Pollock, A. (2018). Effectiveness of motivational interviewing on adult behaviour change in health and social care settings: A systematic review of reviews. *PLoS ONE, 13*(10), e0204890. https://doi.org/10.1371/journal.pone.0204890

Gerards, R., & Welters, R. (2022). Job search in the presence of a stressor: Does financial hardship change the effectiveness of job search? *Journal of Economic Psychology, 90*(2022), 102508. https://doi.org/10.1016/j.joep.2022.102508

Hollederer, A. (2019). Health promotion and prevention among the unemployed: A systematic review. *Health Promotion International, 34*(6), 1078–1096. https://doi.org/10.1093/heapro/day069

Horns, K., Seeger, K., Heinmüller, M., Limm, H., Waldhoff, H. P., Salman, R., Gündel, H., & Angerer, P. (2012). Gesundheitskompetenztraining für Menschen in Langzeitarbeitslosigkeit Auswirkungen auf die Motivation zu einem gesünderen Lebensstil [Health literacy training for people in long-term unemployment implications for motivation towards a healthier lifestyle]. *Bundesgesundheitsbl, 55*(2012), 728–738. https://doi.org/10.1007/s00103-012-1477-4

Howard, J. L., Gagné, M., & Bureau, J. S. (2017). Testing a continuum structure of self-determined motivation: A meta-analysis. *Psychological Bulletin, 143*(12), 1346–1377. https://doi.org/10.1037/bul0000125

Howard, J. L., Gagné, M., Morin, A. J. S., & Forest, J. (2016). Using bifactor-exploratory structural equation modeling to test for a continuum structure of motivation. *Journal of Management, 44*(7), 1–27. https://doi.org/10.1177/0149206305280103

Hult, M., Lappalainen, K., Saaranen, T. K., Räsänen, K., Vanroelen, C., & Burdorf, A. (2020). Health-improving interventions for obtaining employment in unemployed job seekers. *Cochrane Database of Systematic Reviews, 2020*(1), 220–231. https://doi.org/10.1002/14651858.CD013152.pub2

International Labour Organization. (2000). 2000 Labour Overview. Computextos.

Kanfer, R., Wanberg, C. R., & Kantrowitz, T. M. (2001). Job search and employment: A personality–motivational analysis and meta-analytic review. *Journal of Applied Psychology, 86*(5), 837–855. https://doi.org/10.1037/0021-9010.86.5.837

Koen, J., Klehe, U. C., & Van Vianen, A. E. M. (2013). Employability among the long-term unemployed: A futile quest or worth the effort? *Journal of Vocational Behavior, 82*(1), 37–48. https://doi.org/10.1016/j.jvb.2012.11.001

Koen, J., Klehe, U. C., & Van Vianen, A. E. M. (2015). Employability and job search after compulsory reemployment courses: The role of choice, usefulness, and motivation. *Applied Psychology: An International Review, 64*(4), 674–700. https://doi.org/10.1111/apps.12037

Koen, J., Klehe, U. C., Van Vianen, A. E. M., Zikic, J., & Nauta, A. (2010). Job-search strategies and reemployment quality. *Journal of Vocational Behavior, 77*(1), 126–139. https://doi.org/10.1016/j.jvb.2010.02.004

Koen, J., Van Vianen, A. E. M., Van Hooft, E. A. J., & Klehe, U. C. (2016). How experienced autonomy can improve job seekers' motivation, job search, and chance of finding reemployment. *Journal of Vocational Behavior, 95–96*(2016), 31–44. https://doi.org/10.1016/j.jvb.2016.07.003

Koopman, M. Y., Pieterse, M. E., Bohlmeijer, E. T., & Drossaert, C. H. C. (2017). Mental health promoting interventions for the unemployed: A systematic review of applied techniques and effectiveness. *International Journal of Mental Health Promotion, 19*(4), 202–223. https://doi.org/10.1080/14623730.2017.1328367

Limm, H., Heinmüller, M., Gündel, H., Liel, K., Seeger, K., Salman, R., & Angerer, P. (2015). Effects of a health promotion program based on a train-the-trainer approach on quality of life and mental health of long-term unemployed persons. *BioMed Research International, 2015*, 1–10. https://doi.org/10.1155/2015/719327

Liu, S., Huang, J. L., & Wang, M. (2014). Effectiveness of job search interventions: A meta-analytic review. *Psychological Bulletin, 140*(4), 1009–1041. https://doi.org/http://dx.doi.org/10.1037/a0035923

Lundahl, B., Moleni, T., Burke, B. L., Butters, R., Tollefson, D., Butler, C., & Rollnick, S. (2013). Motivational interviewing in medical care settings: A systematic review and meta-analysis of randomized controlled trials. *Patient Education and Counseling, 93*(2), 157–168. https://doi.org/10.1016/j.pec.2013.07.012

Miller, W. R., & Rollnick, S. (2012a). *Motivational interviewing: Helping people change*. Guilford Press, New York.

Miller, W. R., & Rollnick, S. (2012b). Meeting in the middle: Motivational interviewing and self-determination theory. *International Journal of Behavioral Nutrition and Physical Activity, 9*(1), 1–2. https://doi.org/10.1186/1479-5868-9-25

Moyers, T. B., & Rollnick, S. (2002). A motivational interviewing perspective on resistance in psychotherapy. *Journal of Clinical Psychology, 58*(2), 185–193.

Prochaska, J. O., & Diclemente, C. C. (1983). Stages and processes of self-change of smoking: Toward an integrative model of change. *Journal of Consult, 51*(3), 390–395.

Putter, I., Van der Vaart, L., De Witte, H., Rothmann, S., & Van den Broeck, A. (2021). Profiling the unemployed from selected communities in South Africa based on their experiences, commitment to employment, and job search behaviour. *South African Journal of Psychology, 51*(4), 533–546. https://doi.org/10.1177/0081246320978969

Resnicow, K., & McMaster, F. (2012). Motivational interviewing: Moving from why to how with autonomy support. *International Journal of Behavioral Nutrition and Physical Activity, 9*(1), 19. https://doi.org/10.1186/1479-5868-9-19

Rubak, S., Sandbæk, A., Lauritzen, T., & Christensen, B. (2005). Motivational interviewing: A systematic review and meta-analysis. *British Journal of General Practice, 55*(513), 305–312.

Ryan, R. M., & Deci, E. L. (2017). *Self-determination theory: Basic psychological needs in motivation, development, and wellness.* Guilford Publications, New York.

Ryan, R. M., & Deci, E. L. (2020). Intrinsic and extrinsic motivation from a self-determination theory perspective: Definitions, theory, practices, and future directions. *Contemporary Educational Psychology, 61*, 101860. https://doi.org/10.1016/j.cedpsych.2020.101860

Savolainen, R. (2008). Autonomous, controlled and half-hearted. Unemployed people's motivations to seek information about jobs. *Information Research, 13*(4).

Statistics South Africa. (2020). Quarterly labour force survey: Quarter 1, 2020. http://www.statssa.gov.za/ publications/P0211/P02111stQuarter2020.pdf

Van den Broeck, A., Carpini, J. A., & Diefendorff, J. M. (2019). How much effort will I put into my work? It depends on your type of motivation. In N. Chmiel, F. Fraccaroli and M. Sverke (Eds.), *An Introduction to Work and Organizational Psychology: An International Perspective*, 3rd Edition (pp. 354–372). John Wiley & Sons, Hoboken.

Van den Broeck, A., Ferris, D. L., Chang, C. H., & Rosen, C. C. (2016). A review of self-determination theory's basic psychological needs at work. *Journal of Management, 42*(5), 1195–1229. https://doi.org/10.1177/0149206316632058

Van den Broeck, A., Howard, J. L., Van Vaerenbergh, Y., Leroy, H., & Gagné, M. (2021). Beyond intrinsic and extrinsic motivation: A meta-analysis on self-determination theory's multidimensional conceptualization of work motivation. *Organizational Psychology Review, 11*(3), 240–273. https://doi.org/10.1177/20413866211006173

Van den Broeck, A., Lens, W., De Witte, H., & Van Coillie, H. (2013). Unraveling the importance of the quantity and the quality of workers' motivation for well-being: A person-centered perspective. *Journal of Vocational Behavior, 82*(1), 69–78. https://doi.org/10.1016/j.jvb.2012.11.005

Van den Hee, S. M., Van Hooft, E. A. J., & Van Vianen, A. E. M. (2020). A temporal perspective of job search: The relation between personality attributes, motivation, job search behavior, and outcomes. *Journal of Vocational Behavior, 122*(2020), 103489. https://doi.org/10.1016/j.jvb.2020.103489

Van der Vaart, L., De Witte, H., Van den Broeck, A., & Rothmann, S. (2018). A psychosocial typology of the unemployed in South Africa. *South African Journal of Psychology, 48*(2), 179–192. https://doi.org/10.1177/0081246317721600

Van Hooft, E. A. J., Kammeyer-Mueller, J. D., Wanberg, C. R., & Kanfer, R. (2021). Job search and employment success: A quantitative review and future research agenda. *Journal of Applied Psychology, 106*(5), 674–713. https://doi.org/10.1037/apl0000675.supp

Van Rijn, R. M., Carlier, B. E., Schuring, M., & Burdorf, A. (2016). Work as treatment? The effectiveness of re-employment programmes for unemployed persons with severe mental health problems on health and quality of life: A systematic review and meta-analysis. *Occupational and Environmental Medicine, 73*(4), 275–279. https://doi.org/10.1136/oemed-2015-103121

Vansteenkiste, M., & Ryan, R. M. (2013). On psychological growth and vulnerability: Basic psychological need satisfaction and need frustration as a unifying principle. *Journal of Psychotherapy Integration, 23*(3), 263–280. https://doi.org/10.1037/a0032359

Vansteenkiste, M., & Sheldon, K. M. (2006). There's nothing more practical than a good theory: Integrating motivational interviewing and self-determination theory. *British Journal of Clinical Psychologyy, 45*(1), 63–82. https://doi.org/10.1348/014466505X34192

Vansteenkiste, M., & Van den Broeck, A. (2014). Understanding the motivational dynamics among unemployed individuals: Refreshing insights from the self-determination theory perspective. In U-E. Klehe & E. A. J. Van Hooft (Eds.), *The Oxford Handbook of Job Loss and Job Search*, pp. 159–180. Oxford Academic, New York. https://doi.org/10.1093/oxfordhb/9780199764921.013.005

Vansteenkiste, M., Lens, W., De Witte, S., De Witte, H., & Deci, E. L. (2004). The "why" and "why not" of job search behaviour: Their relation to searching, unemployment experience, and well-being. *European Journal of Social Psychology, 34*(3), 345–363. https://doi.org/10.1002/ejsp.202

Vansteenkiste, M., Lens, W., De Witte, H., & Feather, N. T. (2005). Understanding unemployed people's job search behaviour, unemployment experience and well-being: A comparison of expectancy-value theory and self-determination theory. *The British Journal of Social Psychology/The British Psychological Society, 44*(2), 268–287. https://doi.org/10.1348/014466604X17641

Vansteenkiste, M., Ryan, R. M., & Soenens, B. (2020). Basic psychological need theory: Advancements, critical themes, and future directions. *Motivation and Emotion, 44*(1), 1–31. https://doi.org/10.1007/s11031-019-09818-1

Vansteenkiste, M., Williams, G. C., & Resnicow, K. (2012). Toward systematic integration between self-determination theory and motivational interviewing as examples of top-down and bottom-up intervention development: Autonomy or volition as a fundamental theoretical principle. *International Journal of Behavioral Nutrition and Physical Activity, 9*(1), 1–11.

Vleugels, W., Rothmann, S., Griep, Y., & De Witte, H. (2013). Does financial hardship explain differences between Belgian and South African unemployed regarding experiences of unemployment, employment commitment and job search behavior? *Psychologica Belgica, 53*(2), 75–95.

Wain, R. M., Wilbourne, P. L., Harris, K. W., Pierson, H., Teleki, J., Burling, T. A., & Lovett, S. (2011). Motivational interview improves treatment entry in homeless veterans. *Drug and Alcohol Dependence, 115*(1–2), 113–119. https://doi.org/10.1016/j.drugalcdep.2010.11.006

Wanberg, C. R. (2012). The individual experience of unemployment. *Annual Review of Psychology, 63*(1), 369–396. https://doi.org/10.1146/annurev-psych-120710-100500

Welters, R., Mitchell, W., & Muysken, J. (2014). Self determination theory and employed job search. *Journal of Economic Psychology, 44*(2014), 34–44. https://doi.org/10.1016/j.joep.2014.06.002

PART V

METHODS MATTER!

12. Methodological challenges for studying trends in perceived immigrant threat

Jaak Billiet & Bart Meuleman

It is true that each of the steps in a survey introduces the possibility of one or more artifacts, but these same dangers allow opportunities for deeper understanding of both responses and respondents.

(Schuman, H., 1982, p. 21)

INTRODUCTION

The work of Hans De Witte has contributed significantly to our insights into ethnic threat perceptions, anti-immigrant sentiments and radical right-wing voting, and more specifically how labor market positions contribute to prejudiced attitudes (e.g., Billiet & De Witte, 1995, 2008; Billiet et al., 2014; De Witte & Meuleman, 2007; Duriez et al., 2007). For scholars studying complex and abstract concepts, such as attitudes or beliefs, theoretical and measurement validity are an issue of continuous concern. In this contribution, we illustrate the importance of measurement operations by focusing on the evolution of ethnic threat perceptions in Flanders. Previous research has studied how ethnic threat perceptions – as measured by the ISPO Belgian National Election Study (BNES) – have evolved between 1991 and 2014 (Billiet et al., 2017). Furthermore, in Flanders these ethnic threat perceptions were found to show a strong, positive relationship to Flemish sub-national identities (Billiet et al., 2021). In this chapter, we add the 2020 round of BNES to investigate evolutions in perceived ethnic threat from 1991 to 2020. Simultaneously, we address important methodological challenges for studying time trends. What are important threats for making comparisons over time, and how can they be addressed?

We start by describing the data used and discuss several serious potential pitfalls that face survey researchers attempting to make over-time comparisons based on repeated cross-sectional data. Notably, we emphasize the importance of having a measurement instrument that performs equivalently over time.

Furthermore, we argue that Multiple Group Structural Equation Modeling (MGSEM) is a useful tool to test measurement equivalence and to take acquiescence response bias into account. Subsequently, we present the results of our analysis into the evolution of perceived ethnic threat and reflect on the possible explanations for the observed trend.

BNES: DATA, MEASUREMENTS, METHODOLOGICAL CHALLENGES

Description of the Datasets and Indicators

The samples of the BNES organized by ISPO[1] are purposefully designed to study the over-time evolution of perceived ethnic threat (and sub-national identity) in Flanders. ISPO started this post-elector data collection in the 1990s with a three-wave panel survey at the time of the general elections of 1991, 1995, and 1999. Additional rounds of BNES were collected after the general elections of 2003, 2007, 2010, and 2014. A data collection in 2020 completes the available time series of this study.[2] These data collections use a repeated cross-sectional design (meaning that every time, different respondents are interviewed). To avoid the statistical complexities associated with panel data (containing the same respondents), this study only analyzes the 1995 data from the panel (and discards the 1991 and 1999 measurements). For reasons of availability of indicators that are also included in the more recent surveys (2003 to 2020), the survey of 1995 is selected as year zero in this comparative study.

Measurement of perceived ethnic threat. A preliminary version of the items intended to measure perceived ethnic threat was developed in the context of a research project on opinions of Belgians towards migrants (Billiet et al., 1990). This project was commissioned by the Minister and State Secretary of Science Policy, and was a direct result of the sudden increase in the number of votes for the extreme right-wing party "Vlaams Blok" in the municipal elections of 1988.[3] As a member of the steering committee of this project, Hans De Witte suggested contacting the researchers who participated in the SOCON-project, that is a large project on socio-cultural developments in the Netherlands (Eisinga & Scheepers, 1989; Felling et al., 1986; Scheepers et al., 1989). Because of differences in substantive emphasis between the projects – the SOCON study mainly emphasized stereotypes about immigrants, whereas the ISPO project focused on feelings of being threatened by immigrants – the overlap in survey items between both studies was limited. Nevertheless, the cooperation between the Dutch and Flemish researchers resulted in 1990–1991 in a common follow-up survey on ethnocentrism (Billiet et al., 1996, p. 404). The focus on perceived ethnic threat can also be found in the *European Values*

Study that contains six items referring to threat perceptions concerning jobs, cultural life, crime, welfare, number, manners and customs (Billiet, 2011, p. 219). Also in the core questionnaire of the *European Social Survey*, similar measurements of ethnic threat perceptions are included (Meuleman et al., 2009, 2018).

From 1995 onwards, the ISPO surveys measured perceived ethnic threat using a multi-item instrument. Using an identical five-point Likert scale respondents were asked whether they agreed or disagreed with a series of statements referring to the perceived impact the presence of immigrants has on economy and cultural life (see Table 12.1 for exact question wordings). Four of these items are strictly identically worded across the time series and hence optimally usable for over-time comparisons (Billiet et al., 2017).[4] A fifth item referring to the contribution of immigrants to society was formulated identically in the surveys up to 2007 (*"immigrants contribute to our society"*), but the wording in 2014 changed since a condition (*"immigrants who work here"*) and a specification of the subject made the statement more specific (*"contribute to the welfare of our country"* vs. *"contribute to affordable pensions"*). In the 2020 survey the wording of this item was restored to its original wording. This change in question wording deserves special attention from the viewpoint of measurement invariance (see below).

Measurement of (sub)national identity. This concept is operationalized with four indicators. The first indicator is a four-point scale based on two-choice questions about the first and second geo-political (subjective) identity preferred by the respondent: Flemish (score 3), Belgian (score 0), and intermediate positions. The second indicator is the so-called *Linz-Moreno question* about exclusive or dual identity, where low values express exclusive identification with Belgium and high values express exclusive identification with Flanders. The next indicator is an 11-point scale with scores depending on the degree to which the respondent endorses that the federal level (Belgian state) should decide everything (lower scores), or the degree to which the respondent endorses the opposite view, that Flanders/Wallonia should decide (higher scores). The fourth and last indicator is measured by five ordered categories where respondents had to mark their preference with regard to Belgian constitutional state structure ranging from "the Unitarian Belgian state must be restored" (score 0), to "splitting up Belgium into two separate states" (score 4). The response scales are shown in Table 12.1. There one can find out that this fourth indicator varies slightly between the rounds of data collection and requires specific attention regarding comparability.

The focus of this study is on perceived ethnic threat. The interrelated (sub) national identity variable is also included in the tested measurement models since tests of measurement quality are more stringent in a model that includes two latent variables instead of one.

Table 12.1   *Items for measuring perceived ethnic threat and (sub) national identity in the six BNES (with their abbreviated labels in brackets)*

Perceived ethnic threat	
Five-point response scale of each item: 0 = completely disagree to 4 = completely agree	
Item 1	In general, immigrants cannot be trusted (No_Trust)
Item 2	Guest workers come here to take advantage of our social security system (Exploit_Soc_Sec)
Item 3	Immigrants are a threat to our culture and customs (Cul_Threat)
Item 4	The presence of different cultures enriches our society (Enrich)
Item 5	Immigrants contribute to the country's welfare (Contribute)
Item 5a (2003, 2010)	Immigrants contribute to our welfare (Contribute)
Item 5b (2014 only)	Immigrants who work here contribute to affordable pensions (Contribute)
Item 5c (2020)	Immigrants contribute to the welfare of our country (Contribute)
(Sub)national identity	
A set of four different indicators	
Indicator 1	Which group do you consider yourself to be a member of: in first place, and in second place? (Response card with eight (+ other) entities listed) Transformed into a four-point scale: 0 = first identification with Belgium; 3 = first identification with Flanders. The second choice was taken into account for ranks 1 and 2 (VW_ID).
Indicator 2 (Linz-Moreno question)	Considering oneself as a Fleming/Belgian (five-point scale: 0 = exclusively Belgian; 1 = more Belgian than Fleming; 2 = as much Belgian as Fleming; 3 = more Fleming than Belgian; 4 = exclusively Fleming). Order was reversed in the questionnaire. (Exclu_v)
Indicator 3	The preferred form of administrative state for the country is still being discussed. Some think that "Flanders must be able to decide about everything itself". Others think that "Belgium must be able to decide about everything". Where would you place yourself? 11-point scale (0 = Belgium should make decisions; 10 = Flanders should make decisions). Order was reversed in the questionnaire. (Decide)
Indicator 4 (varies per survey year) 1995	In your opinion, how far should Flanders/Wallonia evolve in self-determination? "Independence", "merger with another country", "independent part of Belgium"? Flanders: "Strive for the independence of Flanders"; Wallonia: "Stop the division of Belgium" (five-point Likert item, scale reversed in Flanders), plus follow-up questions: "return to a unitary Belgium?" (Yes/No) (Indepnt)

Perceived ethnic threat	
Five-point response scale of each item: 0 = completely disagree to 4 = completely agree	
2003[5]	(0) Restoration of a unitary Belgian state; (1) A federal state, but more power for the central authorities; (2) A federal state, but more power for the communities and regions; (3) Keep the present situation. The latter was last on the response card, but in the analysis it is considered as the middle category.
2007 and 2014	(0) Restoration of a unitary Belgian state; (1) A federal state should stay, but with more power for the central government than is now the case; (2) The present situation should be kept; (3) The federal state should stay, but with more power for the communities and regions than is now the case; (4) Belgium should be split. (In the analysis, the scale of this item ranged from 0 to 4)

Methodological Challenge 1: Non-response, Representativeness, and Comparability

In all ISPO surveys, participants were selected by means of regionally stratified, two-step, random samples of the 18-to-85-year-old population of Belgian citizens living in Flanders (for more details, see Swyngedouw et al., 2009). These are randomly drawn from the National Population Register using a two-step procedure with equal selection probabilities of the secondary sampling units. The realized sample sizes of the surveys vary between 1,778 (in 1995) and 685 (in 2010). Net response rates for the Flemish samples are about 64 percent in the surveys of 1995, 2003 and 2007. The net response rate takes only usable addresses into account and therefore excludes respondents who were deceased, did not have sufficient knowledge of the language, were ill or disabled, were not allowed to vote, had moved, did not have a traceable address, or had a non-existent address (Swyngedouw et al., 2009, p. 19). However, response rates dropped substantially after the 2010 general elections, to 48 percent in 2014 and 39 percent in 2020. This over-time decline in response rates is not just a *"fait divers"* but goes to the heart of our first methodological challenge for estimating changes over time, namely representativeness according to relevant variables in view of the comparability of the samples (Bethlehem et al., 2008).

Research into non-response in the *European Social Survey* (where refusal conversion data was available) revealed that the unwillingness to participate in surveys correlates with the attitude towards immigrants. Cooperative respondents are more likely to voice positive attitudes towards immigrants than reluctant respondents (Billiet et al., 2007, p. 152). In other words, the estimated over-time changes for this measured concept might be biased by the changing willingness to participate in surveys. Since the focus of this study is the estimation of comparable population statistics over time, we will not only include important composition variables as age and education in the measurement models but also check the outcomes of unweighted samples with samples weighted by age category, education level, and (reported) voting behavior. These are three important predictors of perceived ethnic threat (Billiet & Loosveldt, 1998) and – possibly to a lesser degree – sub-national identity. These covariates included in the post-stratification weighting adjustments may help to mitigate the non-response bias (Little & Vartivarian, 2005).

Methodological Challenge 2: Measurement Invariance

Before valid comparisons can be made across time, it is necessary to establish whether the measurement instruments operate in a similar way across time. Even if exactly the same indicators are used, it is still not guaranteed that the way in which respondents interpret particular question wordings does not change across time. In the case where certain item wordings have changed, there is obviously even more need for a thorough assessment of comparability. The notion of measurement invariance testing (Billiet, 2003; Davidov et al., 2014) provides a framework to do exactly that. Measurement invariance can be tested by formulating measurement models for the various time points – for example in a multigroup structural equation model (MGSEM) – and comparing certain measurement parameters across time (Poznyak et al., 2014), depending on the purpose of the study. This study focuses on trends, which implies that changes in latent means over time are analyzed. The conditions that enable the comparison of means scores are much stricter than in the study of correlations. Comparing latent means assumes that a higher level of invariance is obtained, namely scalar invariance. An adequate measurement model for comparison of latent means requires that not only are the estimated loadings of the indicators constrained to be invariant in the over-time samples but also the estimated item intercepts (Davidov et al., 2018, p. 158). Concretely, our test will start with a model in which both the loadings and intercepts of all corresponding indicators are set invariant over the years. Then the modification indices are checked step-by-step to find out what parameters should be freed.

In practice, measurement equivalence tests often conclude that the invariance assumptions for at least some items are violated. In our strategy, non-equivalence is not a situation that should be avoided at all costs but instead offers an opportunity to obtain more, and potentially better, insights into substantial over-time changes. This basic philosophy of our methodology is in line with other approaches that try to find out how sensitive the latent means of the measured concepts are to modifications in the model parameters (Meuleman, 2012; Oberski, 2018). A careful inspection of the modification indices that provide information about eventual local indications of non-invariance is combined with thorough knowledge, and experience, with question wording effects in surveys (see Billiet & Matsuo, 2012). For example, in some cases, high modification indices were observed in slope parameters and residual co-variances that on theoretical grounds were expected to be zero. However, experience with question wording effects enabled us to understand why the modification indices were high. This approach is highly informative, not only with regard to statistical invariance, but particularly with regard to empirical insights into the substantive research questions (Billiet et al., 2021, p. 6).

Methodological Challenge 3: Systematic Response Error

Standard latent variable models are well suited to take random measurement errors into account. Survey responses, however, are not only contaminated by random measurement errors, but can also be affected by systematic response biases. The agree–disagree scales the BNES uses to measure perceived ethnic threat, for example, are typically prone to acquiescence bias – that is the tendency of some respondents to agree with all statements, irrespective of the specific contents. When item batteries are balanced – that is, roughly half of the items are positively worded while the other half are negatively worded – the acquiescence response style (ARS) can be controlled for by formulating an additional latent variable that loads equally strong on all items. In previous studies we found considerable evidence that the inclusion of acquiescence facilitates the acceptance of theoretically expected measurement models of higher measurement quality (Billiet & McClendon, 2000). BNES's measure of perceived threat is balanced indeed, making it possible to model ARS in the structural equation models.

In sum, previous sections show that several pitfalls accompany all steps in comparative survey research: the samples may not be comparable with respect to composition due to differences in the respondents' readiness to cooperate; the variation in response rates may disturb the view on real differences; different modes of data collection may affect the responses; differences in question wordings may coincide with real changes in measured opinions and attitudes; systematic response biases might affect the observed responses. It is not always possible to avoid all pitfalls, but it is a requirement to take them all as much as possible into account during the analysis and when interpreting the results.

RESULTS: ESTIMATING THE OVER-TIME CHANGES IN PERCEIVED ETHNIC THREAT

To analyze the trend in perceived ethnic threat while taking the above-mentioned methodological challenges into account as much as possible, we use a MGSEM approach. Every BNES round is considered as a separate group for which a measurement model is estimated containing three latent variables, namely perceived ethnic threat, (sub)national identity and an ARS (see Figure 12.1 for a graphical representation). The parameters of prime interest in these models are latent means of the substantive latent variables (perceived ethnic threat, (sub)national identity).[6] In order to determine these parameters, a reference time point has to be chosen for which the latent means are fixed to zero (in our case: 1995). The means at the other time points can then be interpreted as the change relative to the reference group. This allows us to compare the trend of each, for example how strong the upward or downward trend in each year is. Before latent means can be compared across time, however, scalar invariance needs to be tested.

We include age and education as control variables that are related to perceived ethnic threat, (and possibly to (sub)national identity) to prevent conclusions about latent mean changes being driven by sample composition effects, and not real change in the attitudes studied. Furthermore, to correct for non-response bias we utilize post-stratification weights for age, gender, education, and voting behavior. The later variable is also clearly related to both outcome variable(s). The analysis of the weighted sample has the same function as the control variables in the measurement model: to refine our estimates of changes in the two latent attitudinal outcome variables. We should, however, realize these post-stratification weights do not rule out the presence of non-response bias. Strong *over-time differences in non-response rates* may still lead to differential sample composition and bias the trend estimates (Stoop et al., 2010). Weighting the samples and comparing weighted with unweighted samples can give an impression of the direction of non-response effects but is still not able to fully guarantee representativeness.

Testing for Scalar Invariance across Time while Controlling for ARS

Let us start with the study of the trend in a measurement model wherein a factor capturing an acquiescent response style is included. Table 12.2 shows the stepwise selection of the measurement models with different cross-group equality constraints. The starting model (Model 1_A) is not a classic null model but a model in which all slope (λ_y) parameters and intercept (τ_y) parameters are equal across groups (full scalar equivalence). Judging by various fit indices, this model has a poor fit.

There is a significant improvement over the starting model if the intercept parameter of the ninth indicator ("state reform") in the second group (2003) is freely estimated (specified as "not invariant") – see Model 1_B. The loss of only one degree of freedom *(df)* realizes a drop in the Chi-square value of 1,092.3 units. The deviation in 2003 for this intercept can be understood

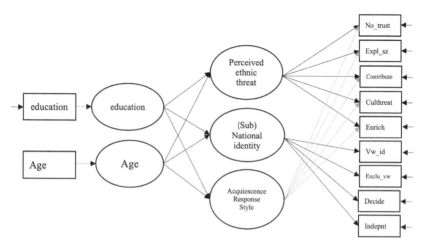

Figure 12.1   Graphical representation of SEM explaining perceived ethnic threat and (sub)national identity

as a result of the fact that the answer scale in 2003 used a slightly different wording for this item. After this model re-specification, model fit has increased substantially, but the RMSEA value is still higher than the cut-off value 0.05 (West et al., 2012). According to the modification indices, however, the model can be further improved by relaxing the factor loading as well as the intercept for the "contribute" item in the 2014 model. Freeing these two parameters reduces the Chi-square value with more than 200 units for two degrees of freedom (which is a strongly significant improvement) and the resulting Model 1_D has an acceptable fit. These model changes reflect the differences in question wording for that item in 2014. Between 1995 and 2010, and in 2020, between 38 percent and 19 percent of the respondents endorsed the "contribute" item number five. In 2014, the percentages agreement was as high as 63 percent because of the change in question wording. Clearly, the invariance tests can pick up this differential functioning of the 2014 item.

Latent Mean Comparisons for Perceived Ethnic Threat in the Presence of Partial Scalar Invariance

The invariance tests have shown that while most items are comparable, the "contribute" item five of perceived ethnic threat functioned differently in 2014 (because of changes in the wording). Obviously, a comparison of this item at face value could bias an over-time comparison. Yet, the latent variable approach offers the opportunity to account for deviations in measurement

Table 12.2   *Test of the proposed measurement model for perceived ethnic threat and (sub)national identity measured in a model with ARS factor*

Model	Chi²	df	RMSEA	CFI	SRMR
1_A	2,359.79	286	0.081	0.900	0.046
1_B	1,267.49	285	0.056	0.952	0.044
1_C	1,248.34	284	0.055	0.953	0.044
1_D	1,031.69	283	0.049	0.964	0.045

parameters for a limited number of items and still make valid latent mean comparisons under the condition of partial scalar invariance. Figure 12.2 displays the latent means for perceived ethnic threat, (sub)national identity as well as ARS across the time series (based on the partially scalar invariant Model 1_D).

Note that 1995 is chosen as a reference point, implying that the latent means in this year are fixed at zero. The latent variable measuring Flemish (sub) national identity as well as acquiescence are quite stable over time, as the latent mean estimates do not deviate strongly from zero. Perceptions of ethnic threat, however, appear to decrease substantially after 2010: in 2014 and 2020, the latent mean estimate for perceived ethnic threat equals –0.17 and –0.33 respectively, which is significantly lower than in reference year 1995.

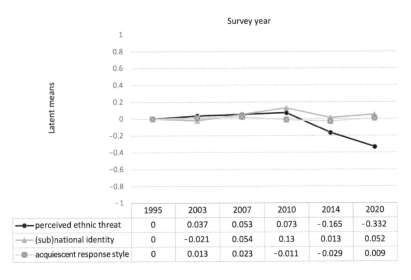

Figure 12.2   *Evolution of latent means of perceived ethnic threat, (sub) national identity and ARS*

Table 12.3   *Test of the proposed measurement model for perceived ethnic threat and (sub)national identity without ARS factored in*

Model	Chi²	Df	RMSEA	CFI	SRMR
2_A	1,922.27	246	0.078	0.911	0.054
2_B	882.67	245	0.048	0.966	0.052

Note: Perceived ethnic threat and (sub)national identity were measured with four items each.

Is there an Impact of Changes in Question Wording?

Can we really conclude that perceived ethnic threat decreased substantially in the election surveys after 2010? Remember that the wording of the "contribute" indicator was changed considerably in 2014 (and has been restored in the survey related to the 2019 elections). Is the partial scalar equivalence model able to deliver an unbiased estimate, taking the differences in wording into account? To shed more light on this issue, we decided to exclude the "contribute" item from the measurement of perceived ethnic threat and see whether this impacts the estimation over-time trend of perceived ethnic threat in the 1995–2020 period. This implies that the measurement of perceived ethnic threat uses four indicators only – three negatively and once positively worded. As a consequence of this imbalance between positively and negatively worded items, it is no longer possible to estimate the ARS factor.

Table 12.3 shows the fit indices of the selected model in the situation of four perceived ethnic threat indicators. The first suggested parameter change relative to the starting model is the same as in the model with five indicators: in 2003, the "state reform" indicator of (sub)national identity again functions differently (because of the differences in the formulation of answer categories). Figure 12.3 shows the trend of the latent means of perceived ethnic threat and (sub)national identity as estimated under Model 2_B. The observed trend in latent means is very similar to what we observed before: while Flemish identification is quite stable, we notice a marked decrease in perceived ethnic threat after 2010. In other words, a drop in perceived ethnic threat after 2010 cannot be attributed to the change in question wording, and the partial scalar invariance model is able to take the differential functioning of the item into account.

The Effect of Non-response on the Estimates of Perceived Ethnic Threat

Can we now conclude that the less negative attitude estimated in the election surveys in Flanders in both 2014 and 2020 is real, or could it still be a methodological artifact driven by other sources of bias? A next potential source of underestimation of perceived ethnic threat is the increase of non-response in the surveys after 2010. Is it possible to estimate the effect of non-cooperation

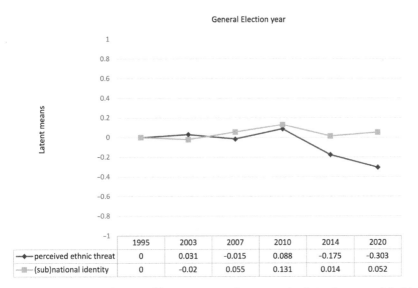

General Election year	1995	2003	2007	2010	2014	2020
perceived ethnic threat	0	0.031	-0.015	0.088	-0.175	-0.303
(sub)national identity	0	-0.02	0.055	0.131	0.014	0.052

*Figure 12.3   Evolution of latent means of perceived ethnic threat and (sub)
national identity - without the "contribute" indicator*

on the estimates of perceived ethnic threat and (sub)national identity? Unfortunately, the answer to that question is negative because we have no relevant information about the non-respondents. In contrast to ESS there is no "refusal conversion" data available in ISPO data. Information at the individual level of the non-respondents makes it possible to measure in a reasonable reliable way the effect of voluntary dropout of sampled potential respondents (Billiet et al., 2007; Matsuo et al., 2009). Are we then completely blind to non-participation effects? No, there are some weaker methods to obtain a view on the direction of non-response bias without, however, being able to correct it. One way to obtain some insight into the effect of non-response on the estimates of the trend of perceived ethnic threat is weighting the sample for known distributions of population characteristics that covary substantially with non-response, and perceived ethnic threat and (eventually) (sub)national identity (Little & Vartivarian, 2005). Available candidates are education level, age category, and the (reported) voting behavior in each of the general elections in Flanders in the years in the 1995–2019 period. The latter is promising since some electorates characterized by larger non-response differ strongly on attitudes as perceived ethnic threat of (sub)national identity.

Figure 12.4 compares observed scale means for perceived ethnic threat, unweighted vs. weighted for education (level) by age (category) distribution, and by voting behavior.[7] The estimates of perceived ethnic threat are, as expected, somewhat higher in the weighted samples than in the unweighted, but the effect of weighing on estimates of the observed means is very small. It is only significant in the samples of 2003 and 2007.[8] Most importantly for our argumentation is that the downward trend in perceived ethnic threat after 2010 remains present, even after applying post-stratification weights.

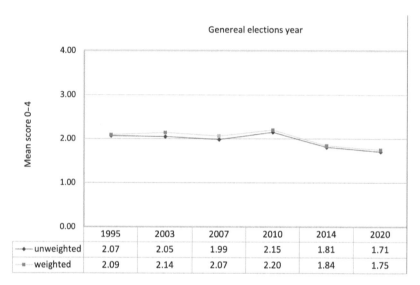

Figure 12.4   *Evolution of observed scale means of perceived ethnic threat*

Composition Effects: The Effect of an Increase of the Share of Respondents with a Migration Background

So far, we rejected the hypotheses that over-time changes in question wording and increasing non-response rates account for the observed decline in negative attitudes towards immigrants after 2010. In order to check whether over-time changes in perceived ethnic threat might be attributed to (natural) changes in the population composition (and samples) we designed hypothetical over-time data in which samples are weighted according to the distribution of education by age and voting behavior in one general election year (2010). This is the year in which the highest mean score of perceived ethnic threat was observed. All six over-time samples now have an identical distribution on education by age and voting behavior. The trend of perceived ethnic threat in this artificial population enables us to find out how far the decline in perceived ethnic threat was due to the changes in these composition effects since these are now neutralized. It was found that the decline is barely affected by the sample composition. The decline in perceived ethnic threat is in the hypothetical situation in which the composition effects are neutralized even somewhat larger than before where changes in sample composition played a role.

The question now raises whether the three analyzed composition variables are sufficiently correlated with perceived ethnic threat to find an effect on the decline after 2010. It is possible that we miss a more relevant composition variable which is subjected to change over time. In the BNES surveys all selected sample units are Belgian nationals at the time of sample selection, but the samples may differ according to the migration background of these sampled Belgians. An imperfect but useful measure of migration background is citizenship of both father and mother at time of birth of the sampled units. In the 2010 sample, 93 percent of respondents have parents who both have Belgian nationality. This portion of respondents from Belgian origin decreased to 90 percent in 2014. Although perceptions of ethnic threat are also prevalent among citizens with a migration background (Meeusen et al., 2019), it is reasonable to assume that migration background is related to perceived ethnic threat. To find out whether the drop in perceived ethnic threat over time (2014 vs. 2010) might be affected by migration background, we compare the complete sample with the subsample of respondents born from two Belgian parents. We expect that the decline after 2010 in positive attitudes towards immigrants is still observed but is smaller among this group of respondents of Belgian origin than among the complete sample of all respondents. We look at the means of composite scores of the three negatively worded indicators (without the "contribute" and "enrichment" items). In the sample of all respondents, the mean composite score was 2.092 (SD= 0.852) in 2010 and decreased to 1.812 (SD = 0.838) in 2014. The decline among the respondents of Belgian origin is about of the same order: 2.117 in 2010 (SD = 0.843) to 1.839 (SD = 0.831). The decline in both samples is about the same, 0.280 units. One cannot explain the decline in perceived ethnic threat by an increase of the share of respondents with a background in migration.

A Convincing External Argument: The Trend in Perceived Ethnic Threat in the Social Cultural Trends Surveys

So far, our attempt to explain the downward trend in perceived ethnic threat after 2010 as a methodological artifact has failed. As a final argument, we can resort to external data sources to investigate to what extent the decrease in threat perceptions is replicated in other studies. The survey on Social Cultural Trends in Flanders (SCV) is an excellent source, as it offers a series of independent samples from a more or less comparable population (Barbier et al. 2017, pp. 219–222). Importantly, these surveys follow very similar procedures as the BNES regarding data collection and sampling (with even slightly higher response rates). These surveys furthermore contain the same four perceived ethnic threat items as the BNES. An identical decline of perceived ethnic threat is observed as in the ISPO surveys, as Figure 12.5 shows. Concretely, we can see that the downward trend started after 2011. Clearly, the downward trend in perceived ethnic threat is not a methodological artifact that specifically plagues BNES but can be observed in other data sources as well.

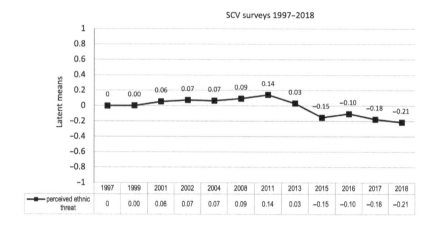

Figure 12.5   *Evolution of latent means of perceived ethnic threat - SCV surveys*

CONCLUSIONS

Despite several methodological challenges, it seems legitimate to conclude that perceptions of ethnic threat have decreased somewhat rather than increased over the past 25 years. Even when a series of possible methodological artifacts – such as changes in population composition, question wording or non-response bias – are taken into account, a marked drop in perceived ethnic threat remains present in the BNES data as well as in another data source.

On the one hand, this finding might come across as counterintuitive. Recent electoral successes of the extreme right-wing party Vlaams Belang, for example, seem to suggest that anti-immigrant sentiments are becoming more widespread. However, public opinions cannot be inferred in a straightforward manner from election results. Voters might have numerous reasons to vote for Vlaams Belang (including protest voting, Flemish nationalist motives or welfare populist arguments). Furthermore, the changed role of social media in the political landscape – a strategy that Vlaams Belang has developed strongly – can play a role in their electoral success. Yet, on the other hand, the increased acceptance of ethnic minority groups in society can be easily understood in terms of contact theory. As a result of increased diversity of society, day-to-day encounters with ethnic minority group members are a daily reality for most Flemish. Most often, these contacts take place in a positive and cooperative setting, thereby undercutting the breeding ground for prejudices and negative sentiments. The (slight) decrease in perceived threat resonates with findings from cross-national research on ethnic threat perceptions. After a steep rise of anti-immigrant sentiments in the 1990s (Semyonov et al., 2006), perceived ethnic threat was found to be relatively stable since the early 2000s in data from the European Social Survey. Although the Great Recession induced a small increase in economic threat perceptions (but not in cultural threat), this increase was very short-lived (Meuleman et al., 2009). Furthermore, notwithstanding the increased migration movements, attitudes towards asylum seekers have become slightly more positive between 2002 and 2016 in various European countries, including Belgium (Van Hootegem et al., 2020).

Reaching beyond this substantive finding, this chapter has emphasized that comparative research must contend with challenging methodological issues. Valid conclusions about over-time evaluations (or cross-national differences) presuppose not only that sample compositions and missingness mechanisms are similar, but also that measurement operations are similar. Latent variable modeling is a versatile framework to tackle these methodological challenges. This chapter has illustrated how multigroup structural equation modeling can take differential item functioning into account for a limited number of items and is able to correct for acquiescence bias when balanced scales are present. Furthermore, using post-stratification weights and the inclusion of control variables, attempts can be made to make samples as comparable as possible. Yet, even in the present careful research design and rigorous statistical modeling, researchers have to keep an eye on the many pitfalls that can distort substantive findings.

NOTES

1.   ISPO: Interuniversity Institute of Political and Social Opinion research.
2.   For reasons of Corona, the vast majority of the sample related to the 2019 elections was realized in 2020. Therefore, we refer further in this study to 2020.
3.   The number of seats obtained by "Vlaams Belang" increased from two in 1982 to 23 in 1988 (Ackaert, 1989, p. 366). The increase in Antwerp became a concern among politicians.
4.   Perceived ethnic threat is also regularly measured by the annual survey "Socio-Cultural Trends in Flanders" (SCV) that was organized by Statistics Flanders between 1996 and 2018.

5.   It should be noted that the wording was adapted to the actual position of state reform at the time of the survey.
6.   An alternative procedure would be to analyze the mean score of the indicators that are used to measure each of the two concepts. The mean score of perceived ethnic threat ranges in each survey year from not feeling threatened (0.0) by the presence of immigrants to strongly feeling threatened (4.0). The mean score of indicators of (sub)national identity varies between a low sub-national consciousness (score 0.0) and a strong sub-national consciousness (maximum score 7.6). It is, however, difficult to compare these scores since the response scales of the indicators are very different in the two sets of indicators. One may standardize the scores by transforming both in an identical range, let us say from zero to five, or from zero to ten. However, this does not solve the problem of comparability.
7.   Contrary to the joint distribution of education and age, the three-way joint distribution of age, education and voting behavior in the population is unknown. Therefore, we assume that voting behavior is independent from the age * education distribution in the computation of the weights.
8.   These small differences seem somewhat surprising since there are substantially more extreme right-wing voters in the weighted than in the unweighted samples. It shows that weighting might not be an optimal way to correct for non-response because of the complex relation between PET, reported vote, and the weights based on education by age, and party strength in the population statistics.

REFERENCES

Ackaert, J. (1989). De gemeenteraadsverkiezingen van 9 oktober 1988. *Res Publica. 1989*(2), 259–384.

Barbier, S., Loosveldt, G., & Carton, A. (2017). Het surveyklimaat in Vlaanderen: Een analyse op basis van de SCV-surveys? In A. Carton, J. Pickery, & D. Verlet (Eds.), *De survey "sociaal-culturele verschuivingen in Vlaanderen"* (pp. 195–222). Studiedienst van de Vlaamse Regering.

Bethlehem, J., Cobben, F., & Schouten, B. (2008). Indicators for the representativeness of survey response. *Proceedings of Statistics Canada Symposium, 2008*, 522–531.

Billiet, J. (2003). Cross-cultural equivalence with structural equation modeling. In J. Harkness, F. Van de Vijver, & P. Mohler (Eds.), *Cross-Cultural Survey Methods* (pp. 247–265). New York: Wiley.

Billiet, J. (2011). Godsdienstige betrokkenheid en de houding tegenover het vreemde: Een verdwijnend verband. In K. Abts, K. Dobbelaere, & L. Voyé (Eds.), *Nieuwe tijden nieuwe mensen* (pp. 215–243). Lannoo: Tielt.

Billiet, J., Abts, K., Galle, J., Meuleman, B., & Swyngedouw, M. (2017). Vijfentwintig jaar onderzoek naar de houding tegenover migranten in België. Verandering en stabiliteit in de periode 1991–2014. *Sociologos, 38*(1–2), 3–19.

Billiet, J., Carton, A., & Huys, R. (1990). *Onbekend of onbemind? Een sociologisch onderzoek naar de houding van de Belgen tegenover migranten*. KU Leuven. Sociologisch onderzoeksinstituut; Leuven.

Billiet, J., & De Witte, H. (1995). Attitudinal dispositions to vote for a "new" extreme right-wing party: The case of "Vlaams Blok". *European Journal of Political Research, 27*(2), 181–202.

Billiet, J., & De Witte, H. (2008). Everyday racism as predictor of political racism in Flemish Belgium. *Journal of Social Issues, 64*(2), 253–267. https://doi.org/10.1111/j.1475-6765.1995.tb00635.x

Billiet, J., Eisinga, R., & Scheepers, P. (1996). Ethnocentrism in the low countries: A comparative perspective. *New Community, 22*(3), 401–416. https://doi.org/10.1080/1369183X.1996.9976547

Billiet, J., & Loosveldt, G. (1998). De houding tegenover migranten en het stemgedrag in Vlaanderen. Evolutie tussen 1989 en 1995 en een verklaringsmodel. In M. Swyngedouw, J. Billiet, A. Carton, & R. Beerten (Eds.), *De (on)redelijke kiezer. Onderzoek naar de politieke opvattingen van Vlamingen: verkiezingen van 21 mei 1995* (pp. 95–118). Leuven: Acco.

Billiet, J., & Matsuo, H. (2012). Non-response and measurement error. In L. Gideon (Ed.), *Handbook of Survey Methodology for the Social Sciences* (pp. 149–178). New York: Springer.

Billiet, J., & McClendon, M. J. (2000). Modeling acquiescence in measurement models for two balanced sets of items. *Structural Equation Modeling, 7*(4), 608–628. https://doi.org/10.1207/S15328007SEM0704_5

Billiet, J., Meeusen, C., & Abts, K. (2021). The relationship between (sub)national identity, citizenship conceptions, and perceived ethnic threat in Flanders and Wallonia for the period 1995–2020: A measurement invariance testing strategy. *Frontiers in Political Science-Methods and Measurement*, 676551. DOI: 10.3389/fpos.2021.676551

Billiet, J., Meuleman, B., & De Witte, H. (2014). The relationship between ethnic threat and economic insecurity in times of economic crisis: Analysis of European Social Survey data. *Migration Studies, 2*(2), 135–161. https://doi.org/10.1093/migration/mnu023

Billiet, J., Philippens, M., Fitzgerald, R., & Stoop, I. (2007). Estimation of non-response bias in the European Social Survey: Using information from reluctant respondents. *Journal of Official Statistics, 23*(2), 135–162.

Davidov, E., Datler, G., Schmidt, P., & Schwartz, S. H. (2018). Testing the invariance of values in the Benelux countries with the European Social Survey: Accounting for ordinality. In E. Davidov, P. Schmidt, J. Billiet, & B. Meuleman (Eds.), *Cross-Cultural Analysis: Methods and Applications* (pp. 157–180). New York and Abingdon: Routledge.

Davidov, E., Meuleman, B., Cieciuch, J., Schmidt, P., & Billiet, J. (2014). Measurement equivalence in cross-national research. *Annual Review of Sociology, 40*(1), 55–75. https://doi.org/10.1146/annurev-soc-071913-043137

De Witte, H., & Meuleman, B. (2007). Job insecurity and voting for an extreme right-wing party. In G. Loosveldt, M. Swyngedouw, & B. Cambré (Eds.), *Measuring Meaningful Data in Social Research* (pp. 93–112). Leuven: Acco.

Duriez, B., Vansteenkiste, M., Soenens, B., & De Witte, H. (2007). The social costs of extrinsic relative to intrinsic goal pursuits: Their relation with social dominance and racial and ethnic prejudice. *Journal of Personality, 75*(4), 757–782. https://doi.org/10.1111/j.1467-6494.2007.00456.x

Eisinga, R. N., & Scheepers, P. (1989). Etnocentrisme in Nederland, Nijmegen. Instituut voor Toegepaste Sociale Wetenschappen.

Felling, A., Peters, J., & Scheepers, P. (1986). *Theoretische modellen ter verklaring van etnocentrisme*. Nijmegen: ITS.

Little, J. R., & Vartivarian, S. (2005). Does weighting for non-response increase the variance of survey means? *Statistics Canada, 31*(2), 161–168.

Matsuo, H., Billiet, J., & Loosveldt, G. (2009). Measurement and correction of non-response bias based on non-response surveys in Belgium, Norway, Poland and Switzerland: European Social Survey – round 3 (2006–2007). Leuven: Centrum voor Sociologisch Onderzoek (CeSO).

Meeusen, C., Abts, K., & Meuleman, B. (2019). Between solidarity and competitive threat? The ambivalence of anti-immigrant attitudes among ethnic minorities. *International Journal of Intercultural Relations, 71*, 1–13. https://doi.org/10.1016/j.ijintrel.2019.04.002

Meuleman, B. (2012). When are item intercept differences substantively relevant in measurement invariance testing? In S. Salzborn, E. Davidov, & J. Reinecke (Eds.), *Methods, Theories, and Empirical Applications in the Social Sciences* (pp. 97–104). Wiesbaden: Springer VS. ISBN: 978-3-531-17130-2.

Meuleman, B., Davidov, E., & Billiet, J. (2009). Changing attitudes toward immigration in Europe, 2002–2007: A dynamic group conflict theory approach. *Social Science Research, 38*(2), 352–365.

Meuleman, B., Davidov, E., & Billiet, J. (2018). Modeling multiple-country repeated cross-sections: A societal growth curve model for studying the effect of the economic crisis on perceived ethnic threat. *Methods, Data, Analyses: A Journal for Quantitative Methods and Survey Methodology (MDA), 12*(2), 185–209. https://doi.org/10.12758/mda.2017.10

Oberski, D. L. (2018). Sensitivity analysis. In E. Davidov, P. Schmidt, J. Billiet, & B. Meuleman (Eds.), *Cross-Cultural Analysis: Methods and Applications* (pp. 593–614). New York: Routledge.

Poznyak, D., Meuleman, B., Abts, K., & Bishop, F. D. (2014). Trust in American government: Longitudinal measurement equivalence in the ANES, 1964–2008. *Social Indicators Research, 118*, 741–758. https://doi.org/10.1007/s11205-013-0441-5.

Scheepers, P., Felling, A., & Peters, J. (1989). Etnocentrimse in Nederland: Theoretische bijdragen empiricsch getoetst. *Sociologische Gids, 36*(1), 31–47.

Schuman, H. (1982). Artifacts are in the mind of the beholder. *The American Sociologist, 17*, 21–28.

Semyonov, M., Raijman, R., & Gorodzeisky, A. (2006). The rise of anti-foreigner sentiment in European societies, 1988–2000. *American Sociological Review, 71*(3), 426–449. https://doi.org/10.1177/0003122406071003

Stoop, I., Billiet, J., Koch, A., & Fitzgerald, R. (2010). *Improving Survey Response. Lessons Learned from the European Social Survey.* Chichester: John Wiley & Sons Ltd.

Swyngedouw, M., Rink, N., Abts, K., Poznyak, D., Frognier, A. P., & Baudewyns, P. (2009). *2007 General Election Study Belgium: Codebook: Questions and Frequency Tables.* Leuven: ISPO/UCL: PIOP.

Van Hootegem, A., Meuleman, B., & Abts, K. (2020). Attitudes toward asylum policy in a divided Europe: Diverging contexts, diverging attitudes? *Frontiers in Sociology, 5*, 35. https://doi.org/10.3389/fsoc.2020.00035

West, S. G., Taylor, A. B., & Wu, W. (2012). Model fit and model selection in structural equation modeling. In R. H. Hoyle (Ed.), *Handbook of Structural Equation Modeling* (pp. 209–231). New York: Guilford Press.

APPENDIX

Table 12A.1   Overview of the standardized parameter estimates of Model1_D

	1995			2003			2007	
E_THREAT	SUB_ NAT	AR_ STYLE	E_THREAT	SUB_ NAT	AR_ STYLE	E_THREAT	SUB_ NAT	AR_ STYLE
no_trust	0.764	0.230	no_trust	0.773	0.149	no_trust	0.782	0.144
expl_sz	0.825	0.230	expl_sz	0.836	0.149	expl_sz	0.845	0.144
contribu	0.728	0.230	contribu	0.737	0.149	contribu	0.745	0.144
cuthreat	0.780	0.230	cuthreat	0.790	0.149	cuthreat	0.799	0.144
enrich	0.702	0.230	enrich	0.711	0.149	enrich	0.718	0.144
vw_id	–	0.775	vw_id	–	0.684	vw_id	–	0.719
exclu_vw	–	0.783	exclu_vw	–	0.691	exclu_vw	–	0.727
decide	–	0.834	decide	–	0.736	decide	–	0.774
indepnt	–	0.687	indepnt	–	0.606	indepnt	–	0.637

	2010			2014			2020	
E_THREAT	SUB_ NAT	AR_ STYLE	E_THREAT	SUB_ NAT	AR_ STYLE	E_THREAT	SUB_ NAT	AR_ STYLE
no_trust	0.800	0.177	no_trust	0.767	0.260	no_trust	0.806	0.273
expl_sz	0.864	0.177	expl_sz	0.825	0.260	expl_sz	0.870	0.273
contribu	0.762	0.177	contribu	0.397	0.260	contribu	0.768	0.273
cuthreat	0.817	0.177	cuthreat	0.784	0.260	cuthreat	0.822	0.273
enrich	0.735	0.177	enrich	0.713	0.260	enrich	0.740	0.273
vw_id	–	0.698	vw_id	–	0.707	vw_id	–	0.766
exclu_vw	–	0.705	exclu_vw	–	0.714	exclu_vw	–	0.774
decide	–	0.751	decide	–	0.760	decide	–	0.824
indepnt	–	0.618	indepnt	–	0.626	indepnt	–	0.679

13. What's in a name! The thin line between being bullied and lacking social support: Are both 'just' the same?

Elfi Baillien & Guy Notelaers

Over the last decades, the issue of workplace bullying has gained immense scholarly interest (Einarsen et al., 2020). Scientists have explored its prevalence, outcomes, and antecedents. The latter drawing from insights on evidence of a plethora of negative effects from bullying; with the grander aspiration to identify important leads for prevention. Regarding the latter, studies established the important role of job characteristics, and particularly the presence of *demands*, for those being exposed to workplace bullying (Salin & Hoel, 2020). Alternatively, these studies also found that job characteristics signalling *resources* can prevent bullying (Balducci et al., 2021). Against this backdrop, scholars were successful in using well-known job stress models to explain why workplace bullying arises from these job characteristics. While this research has shed light on job characteristics moulding a suitable situation for employees becoming targeted with negative acts – inspiring for bullying prevention – they have also fuelled considerable debate on the status of one notable resource that is part of many of these job stress models. On the one hand, some scholars have explicitly questioned the validity of investigating 'social support' as a potential antecedent (De Witte, 2015 – see also Baillien et al., 2011a), as if it were separate from bullying. Instead, they argue that the concept of social support is tautological to that of workplace bullying. Or, in other words, being exposed to workplace bullying and having no or low social support would be... the same. This is because bullying implies that an employee is repeatedly targeted with negative social behaviours enacted by (one or more) other organizational members (Einarsen, 2000), hence social support from colleagues or the supervisor is obviously lacking – they are bullying or allowing the bullying to happen (i.e., 'bystanders'; Ng et al., 2022). On the other hand, from the perspective of bullying research and, relatedly, workplace peace-making, social support – or the lack thereof – is by content and experience different from bullying. In this chapter, we aim to settle this debate in view of understanding whether (and how) initiatives related to social support could in fact be of significance for workplace bullying prevention. We empirically explore whether or not social support is inherently intertwined with the bullying process (and, thus, the same), or, in fact, can be regarded as a distinct phenomenon (and, thus, different). And if they are conceptually different, what does this tell us in terms of potential actions?

REASONS FOR WORKPLACE BULLYING: JOB CHARACTERISTICS

Workplace bullying is well known from cases in popular media as well as from contemporary research in the fields of psychology and management. It entails a form of interpersonal workplace mistreatment typically manifested in negative social behaviour of a personal (e.g., gossiping) or work-related (e.g., withholding information) nature. When being persistently (e.g., minimum six months) and repeatedly (e.g., at least weekly) exposed to such behaviours, they become a serious source of stress (i.e., social stressor; Zapf, 1999). In this respect, a plethora of studies have found that targets of bullying worry more, have a higher recovery need, a lower quality of sleep (Notelaers et al., 2006), and have more suicidal thoughts (Nielsen et al., 2015). They have an elevated risk of burnout (Balducci et al., 2011), and show lower job commitment (as a component of engagement) after six months, and lower job satisfaction after one year (Baillien et al., 2011b).

Given these significant consequences for employees who experience workplace bullying combined with legal codification in many European countries as well as globally (e.g., Belgian Wellbeing Codex – KB2014 on the prevention of psychosocial risks), scholars have dug into its causes aiming to detect valuable leads for bullying prevention in practice. Their studies soon established a significant role for the work environment, particularly when being poorly organized and fuelling stress and conflicts (work environment hypothesis; Leymann & Gustafsson, 1996). A systematic review specifically on *job demands* – aspects of the job taxing the employee's ability or energy for meeting them (Abramis, 1994) – could identify role conflict, workload, role ambiguity, job insecurity, and cognitive load as the most significant antecedents of bullying (Van den Brande et al., 2016). Alternatively, scholars have also linked workplace bullying to job characteristics that, instead of demands, energize the employees and support them in achieving their work goals: they found that the presence of such *resources* (Bakker & Demerouti, 2007) prevents bullying (e.g., decision authority; see Balducci et al., 2011). In all, these job characteristics play their part in bullying by creating (or not) easy targets experiencing difficulties in defending themselves against negative acts (see Three Way Model; Baillien et al., 2009).

Interestingly, these findings on bullying antecedents have fuelled a line of research in which scholars looked at whether established job stress models could make sense of exactly how the job characteristics relate to bullying: and they very much did. Job factors could successfully be linked to bullying using the lenses of, for example, the Michigan model (Notelaers et al., 2010), the Job Demand–Control Model (Baillien et al., 2011a; Notelaers et al., 2013), the Job Demands–Resources Model (Baillien et al., 2011b), the Effort-Reward Imbalance Model (Notelaers et al., 2019a), and Warr's Vitamin Model (Notelaers et al., 2010). Especially the Job Demand-Control and Job Demands-Resources Model have inspired many cross-sectional and longitudinal studies in the bullying field, with scholars increasingly adhering to social support – from colleagues and supervisors – as a significant (lacking) resource in a bullying situation (Branch et al., 2021).

SOCIAL SUPPORT 'AND' OR 'IN' BULLYING?

While many researchers grasp at social support as a job factor crucial in explaining why workplace bullying can happen, there are some notable sceptical voices in the research arena. These voices question whether looking at social support as a potential antecedent of bullying is a valid research practice (e.g., De Witte, 2015 – see also Baillien et al., 2011a). They build their arguments on the conceptual definition of social support. Generally, social support entails '*an exchange of resources between two individuals perceived by the provider or the recipient to be intended to enhance the well-being of the recipient*' (Shumaker & Brownell, 1984, p. 11). In research on job characteristics specifically, scholars have further explained the energizing effects of social support along the lines of (a) being useful or instrumental in getting the job done; and (b) being helpful in regulating feelings or emotions the employee is currently dealing with (Warr, 1994). Regarding (a), an employee receives tangible help when at work, for example in dealing with a high workload or in resolving work-related questions. Regarding (b), an employee receives comfort and compassion from colleagues and the supervisor, for example by listening to problems and recognizing the frustration experienced because of them. Mirroring this to workplace bullying, there could then be an obvious similarity with the work-related (instrumental) and personal (emotional) nature of the bullying acts. Even more so, while social support leads to positive outcomes such as organizational commitment, job satisfaction, and decreased turnover, a lack of support – possibly manifested in bullying – triggers a range of stress responses (Uchino et al., 2012). As such, it could be very well that experiencing a lack of social support and being targeted with workplace bullying are hardly different. This ties in with results from latent class analyses across different samples and countries that social isolation is characteristic for both occasionally bullied and targets of bullying (Leon-Perez et al., 2014; Notelaers et al., 2011; Notelaers et al., 2019b). In other words, (lacking) social support is located 'in' the experience of bullying and can, therefore, not be seen as an antecedent.

However, when arguing from the perspective of other workplace bullying researchers and, more broadly, from insights on workplace peace-making, the idea that lacking social support and bullying are 'the same' can be strongly contested. In other words, experiencing low or no social support is conceptually distinct from exposure to workplace bullying. It is therefore correct and meaningful to study support as a bullying antecedent, as this could serve to provide valuable pathways for prevention. From the research stream on workplace bullying, being a target includes more than 'just' the lack of something that is positive for or needed by the employee. The definition of workplace bullying explicitly entails repeated exposure to *negative* social behaviours. When looking at the negative social behaviour part of bullying – for example as part of measurements such as the Leymann Inventory of Psychosocial Terror (LIPT; Leymann & Gustafsson, 1996) or the highly established Short Negative Acts Questionnaire (S-NAQ; Notelaers et al., 2019b) – we see that acts such as 'withholding necessary information for your work' and 'silence as a response to your questions' are complemented with acts in which a target is confronted with the obvious presence of negative behaviours (e.g., 'repeated offensive remarks' or 'devaluating your work'). More in-depth analyses of the existing measurement scales underscored that bullied employees distinguish themselves from those experiencing work-related critique or incivility through – even on top of the work-related and person-related negative social acts – also tending to be actively socially isolated by others (Notelaers et al., 2013; Notelaers et al., 2019b). Therefore, bullying is more enriched in negative actions than the mere lack of (or low) social support. Because of this, bullying would be experienced inherently differently – and more negatively – by employees in terms of its stress and motivational outcomes. Moreover, even when being bullied, the social context in mind when it comes to experiencing and evaluating social support is likely to be (much) larger than 'just' the actors involved in the bullying incidents. Consequently, it may be so that an employee *does* receive instrumental or emotional support in the job… except just not from the bully or bullies. As such, while a measure on bullying specifically taps the negative behaviours enacted by a subgroup, the experience of social support from the larger group would be reflected in the employees' reports about the availability of social support. Next, while research on abusive supervision has highlighted that bosses could be a potential bully (Tepper et al., 2017), most bullying situations are from a horizontal, peer-to-peer nature (Escartín et al., 2013). This means it is not necessarily so that being bullied implies that an employee is not experiencing social support from the supervisor, perhaps just on a different aspect of the job. And even if the supervisor was the bully, it is not always so that the targeted employee is not receiving support from co-workers. Similarly, the context in which bullying happens is rarely limited to target and perpetrator only. In this respect, scholars have looked at witnesses – 'bystanders' – of the negative social behaviours (Ng et al., 2022). Their studies revealed that these are not always actively interfering in the bullying incidents (supporters; Pouwelse et al., 2021), yet may help the targets by signalling the events to a person in charge or by lending an ear (sympathizers; Pouwelse et al., 2021). So, in other words, while colleagues may not openly go against a perpetrator of bullying, a target could still experience support. These latter empirical observations largely align with research on peace-making, being voluntarily helping behaviour in interpersonal conflict – enacted by a colleague without formal authority over the conflicting parties who acts impartial to constructively solve the situation (Zhang et al., 2018). These studies too have detected individual differences in the extent to which employees engage in peace-making behaviours (Zhang et al., 2020).

Taken together, while there are convincing reasons to assume that social support is tautological to workplace bullying, others position themselves around the idea that they are different concepts. Time to reveal the empirical truth.

CLARIFYING THE AMBIGUITY: EMPIRICAL DATA AND – OF COURSE – STATISTICS

The current debate is settled based upon a re-analysis of data on workplace bullying published earlier. The sample is a convenience sample: it consists of 6,175 employees from 19 highly heterogeneous working organizations (for more details, see Notelaers et al., 2019b). The central concepts are:

- *Perceived social support of colleagues and the supervisor* was measured with four items – addressed as 'never', 'sometimes', 'often', and 'always' – of the SIMPH (Notelaers et al., 2007). These items were: 'Can you count on your colleagues when you come across difficulties in your work?' (rc1); 'If necessary, can you ask your colleagues for help?' (rc2); 'Can you count on your supervisor when you have problems in your work?' (rl1); and 'If necessary, can you ask your direct boss for help?' (rl2).
- *Workplace bullying* was tapped with six items – two items for each type of negative act – selected from the S-NAQ (Notelaers et al., 2019b). These items had the highest factor loadings in an earlier confirmatory latent class factor analysis (Notelaers & Einarsen, 2008). Example items (pow) are: 'Repeated reminders about your mistakes' (work-related act); 'Repeated reminders about your blunders' (person-oriented act); or 'Social exclusion

from co-workers or work group activities' (act of social isolation). Using the response categories of 'never', 'now and then', 'once a month', and 'once a week or more often', respondents indicated how often they had been subjected to these behaviours during the last six months.

Our research question is addressed by contrasting a Latent Class Cluster model with Latent Class Factor Models; that is, Confirmatory Factor Models (CFA) and Exploratory Factor Models (EFA).

'AND THE WINNER IS…': RESULTS

First, our analyses point at a structure in which three factors (i.e., social support of colleagues, social support of the supervisor, and workplace bullying) each have five clusters. As shown by BIC, AIC and AIC3 (see Table 13.1), the factor models fit our data better than the cluster models. Within these factor models, the BIC for the EFA's is lower and thus better than the one for the CFA's. Finally, the EFA model in which each of the three latent class factors have five clusters fits our data best (i.e., lowest AIC and AIC3). The total proportion of residuals explained by this model is at least 99 percent. All cross-loadings are smaller than 0.05.

Table 13.1   Summary of the LLC, CFA, and EFA

		BIC(LL)	AIC(LL)	AIC3(LL)	Npar	L²	Class.Err.	Entropy R²
LCC	1-Cluster	106,256	106,055	106,085	30	31,651	0	1
	2-Cluster	98,399	98,125	98,166	41	23,699	0.07	0.74
	3-Cluster	95,763	95,415	95,467	52	20,967	0.08	0.79
	4-Cluster	94,263	93,843	93,906	63	19,373	0.11	0.77
	5-Cluster	93,020	92,526	92,600	74	18,034	0.12	0.79
	6-Cluster	91,876	91,309	91,394	85	16,794	0.12	0.80
CFA	3F(3,3,3)	88,227	87,900	87,949	49	13,458	0.07	0.83
	3F(4,4,4)	86,987	86,640	86,692	52	12,192	0.09	0.81
	3F(5,5,5)	86,909	86,542	86,597	55	12,088	0.12	0.75
	3F(6,6,6)	86,643	86,122	86,200	78	11,622	0.22	0.68
EFA	3F(4,4,4)	86,694	86,213	86,285	72	11,725	0.06	0.84
	3F(5,5,5)	86,618	86,117	86,192	75	11,623	0.15	0.75
	3F(5,5,6)	86,659	86,151	86,227	76	11,655	0.20	0.48
	3F(5,5,4)	86,613	86,119	86,193	74	11,627	0.15	0.75
	3F(5,4,4)	86,630	86,143	86,216	73	11,653	0.22	0.48

Second, our results give a first indication that social support should not indubitably be located 'in' bullying when looking at the cluster patterns of all factors as compared to each other. Looking at both social support factors, the classes can be easily labelled since the conditional average matched the response category. Regarding supervisory support (see Figure 13.1), 24 percent of the respondents experienced this on average 'always (4)', 40 percent 'often (3)', and 31 percent 'occasionally (2)'. Only 5 percent 'never (1)' received support from their supervisor. Strikingly, the levels of social support from the supervisor do not vary much across the items measuring social support from colleagues and vary hardly with respect to the bullying items. The latent classes for the social support from colleagues (see Figure 13.2) have a rather similar meaning and prevalence. About 25 percent experienced on average 'always (4)' social support from colleagues, 47 percent 'often (3)', and 26 percent 'occasionally (2)'. Only 2 percent 'never (1)' received support from their colleagues. Again, the levels of social support do not vary much across the items measuring social support from the supervisor and varied hardly in the bullying items.

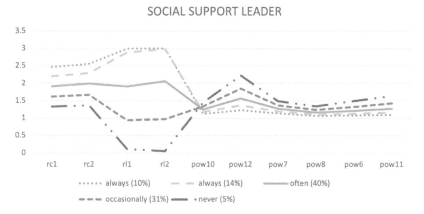

Figure 13.1   Visualization of the several classes on social support of the leader (lr) and their item responses on the studies measurement

Regarding workplace bullying (see Figure 13.3), 48 percent was 'never' subjected to the negative acts during the last six months, 13 percent reported only 'limited' exposure to the two first items referring to work-related negative acts. The next latent class houses 33 percent whose, except for pow12, average response was between 'never (1)' and 'occasionally (2)'. They were 'rarely' confronted with bullying acts. The fourth class (6 percent) shows an average

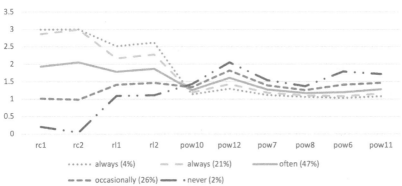

*Figure 13.2   Visualization of the several classes on social support of
the colleagues (rc) and their item responses on the studies
measurements*

response between 'occasionally (2)' and 'monthly (3)' and were 'occasionally'
bullied. Finally, about 0.6 percent were 'targets': their conditional average
varied between 'monthly (3)' and 'weekly (4)'. Interestingly, the classes
of bullying indicate hardly any variation across the items measuring social
support.

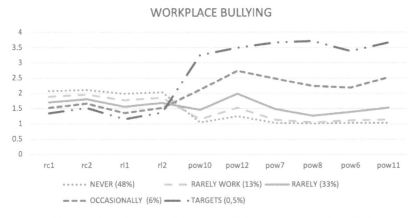

*Figure 13.3   Visualization of the several classes on workplace bullying
(pow) and their item responses on the studies measurements*

In summary, when looking at these figures and the distinct latent classes, we see that each factor yields five classes (notably with classes five and four in social support both aligning with 'always' experiencing social support). However, we cannot detect a clear pattern of experiencing social support in different exposure classes of bullying. And alternatively, there is no clear pattern of experiencing negative acts in the different classes of both social support of the supervisor and of colleagues. Thus, there seems to be a difference between the experience of support and that of bullying.

Finally, we focus in more detail on those being occasionally bullied or being a target of bullying. For these levels (classes) of exposure to workplace bullying acts, we specifically inspect the number of respondents that report certain levels of social support both from the supervisor and colleagues. Table 13.2 summarizes our findings: on the left it depicts the class of exposure to workplace bullying we are specifically looking at (i.e., occasionally bullied and targets). The top of the table represents the different classes of social support of the supervisor (i.e., always, often, sometimes, never – note that we merged the two initial classes referring to 'always' exposure clusters based on the earlier findings in Figure 13.1). This is combined with the different classes of social support of colleagues (in line with social support from the supervisor) reported for each of the classes of social support of the supervisor. Table 13.2 also represents the total number over the classes.

From these results, we see that the bullied are not necessarily deprived of social support. Only seven out of 26 targets and only 31 out of 283 occasionally bullied reported they had no support at all. Alternatively, five out of 26 targets and 98 out of 283 occasionally bullied were experiencing social support 'often' and nearly 'always'. Again, these results indicate that, when looking at empirical data, it is not so that lacking social support is by definition part of bullying. Employees exposed to bullying behaviours may still receive support from their supervisor and/or colleagues.

Table 13.2   Three-way contingency table (N)

			SSL				Total
			always	often	sometimes	never	
Occasionally bullied	SSC	always	18	9	8	1	36
		often	20	51	38	6	115
		sometimes	8	30	64	16	118
		never	2	1	3	8	14
	Total		48	91	113	31	283

			SSL				Total
			always	often	sometimes	never	
Target of bullying	SSC	always	1	0	1	0	2
		often	0	4	1	1	6
		sometimes	1	2	9	3	15
		never	0	0	0	3	3
	Total		2	6	11	7	26

WHAT ARE WE TAKING HOME FROM THIS AS SCIENTISTS?

While conceptually workplace bullying and social support seem to be on the same boat, our analyses indicate that considering social support as a job characteristic – more specifically, a resource – that could impact bullying is a valid research practice. With this we have furthered the research stream and settled an important debate on whether or not lacking social support and experiencing bullying are somewhat tautological. And look at that, they are not. Time to open the next black box in our scientific knowledge: when exactly in the dynamic developmental process of workplace bullying does social support play a role and how?

In all, workplace bullying is a gradually escalating process that unfolds over time (Einarsen, 2000). In the first phase, the negative acts are low in intensity, mostly indirect, and highly ambiguous in meaning; leading a target to typically not go against them (Björkqvist, 1994). Interestingly, our findings from Figure 13.3 indicate that for most, in this first phase, social support is still there. Accordingly, we could ask ourselves whether employees who are not experiencing high levels of support should invest in crafting their social resources so as to prevent a further escalation towards higher exposure levels to workplace bullying acts. In this respect, a recent diary study underscored the benefits of social resources by detecting a moderating effect of emotional support on the relationship between direct negative acts and needs frustration (Trépanier et al., 2022). However, these researchers could not replicate the same for indirect negative acts. This could perhaps be so because, in this situation, employees are not very likely to craft their social resources and call on their support. In a similar vein, both cross-sectional and experimental vignettes studies found that the lower the intensity and the higher the ambiguity attributed to negative social acts, the more recipients resort to minimizing the situation instead of seeking support (Meral et al., 2022).

Can this be a catch-22? Because, if the negative connotation of a situation is not entirely clear *yet* for employees in the first phase of experiencing negative social acts, they might feel little need for workplace peace-making behaviours from others (we do not want to be a 'nag', right) and there could perhaps be hardly any engaged basis for conflict mediation as a tool for bullying prevention. Should we then just… give up on such prevention from a social resource perspective? Luckily, the research stream on psychosocial safety climate and bullying could be highly inspiring here. Their results have underscored its important role in providing employees with the necessary resources – including active leadership – that decrease exposure to bullying behaviours (Plimmer et al., 2022). In other words, investing in a psychological safety climate could make the early stage of experiencing negative social acts more tangible for nipping the bud.

In the following phases of the bullying process the nature of the social acts becomes clearer. However, when evolving through these latter phases the recipient of the negative acts enters a resources loss spiral with social (and personal) resources diminishing to a point in which the employee is not able to defend him or herself against the acts. Finally, this target is either passively or actively expelled from the workplace (Leymann & Gustafsson, 1996). In the second phase in which the negative characteristics of the acts are becoming less ambiguous for the recipient, again, we could adhere to the importance of social support in the further escalation of the bullying. Table 13.2 shows that the majority of the occasionally bullied are often or always experiencing support from both colleagues and supervisors. In fact, only 15 percent of these employees had no support. However, given the nature of bullying, one should be cautious in expecting occasionally bullied and especially targets to resort to crafting more social resources. This is because crafting social resources also consumes energy and personal resources (Kerksieck et al., 2019), which is exactly what is at the same time also affected by the bullying behaviours. In other words, the target may find it rather taxing to seek support due to the energy draining process that the bullying itself – as a social stressor (Zapf, 1999) – sets in motion. Therefore, especially in phases where the negative connotation of the behaviour is less ambiguous, but the employee has not entered the most escalated phases yet, the recipient could benefit from workplace peace-making or mediation. In both situations, an external party to the conflict initiates a problem-solving process that can contribute to tempering a further escalation in the bullying process and restore to lower conflict levels. In this respect, earlier research has clearly underscored the benefit of a problem-solving conflict management style in decreasing later exposure in bullying (Baillien et al., 2014).

With a cross-sectional design one clearly cannot uncover our further ideas on how social support, both in kind and extent, contributes to how the bullying process unfolds and what measures would be most suitable when. Therefore, we look forward to more longitudinal and dynamic research designs able to unravel how social support and negative behaviours are intertwined.

ANY NUTS FOR PRACTITIONERS WHO WANT TO DO SOMETHING 'NOW'?

What can we give away to practice that obviously cannot just wait for scientists to dig into yet to be collected longitudinal and dynamic data? Given that we have now found evidence for 'bullying *and* (no/low) social support', practitioners can be more confident in looking at a lack of social support as a driver of bullying cases. And, to the presence of social support as a preventive measure. In terms of primary prevention – intervening before bullying arises (cfr. Cooper et al., 2001) – they should be aware of ensuring sufficient levels of social support in the work design. For example, when selecting (and promoting) supervisors, HR recruiters could opt for candidates scoring high on supportive behaviours towards their staff. Especially when these leaders adopt an authentic leadership style, their supportive behaviours are likely to trickle down to the subordinates (Avolio et al., 2004) and contribute to more social support amongst colleagues as well. Alternatively, social support is fuelled by shared goals in a common social identity (Avanzi et al., 2015); work teams could therefore, in terms of elevated levels of social support, benefit from clear arrangements regarding the collective output and the members' roles in reaching them, and in – to the least – task cohesion (Eys & Carron, 2001) between the group members. In terms of secondary prevention – intervening in the evolution of bullying to more severe phases of the process (cfr. Cooper et al., 2001) – social support could be inserted externally through conflict mediation (Fox & Stallworth, 2009), which is so when employees and work groups can adhere to an occupational health and safety advisor, a person of confidence, HRM, or a specialized mediator. Or it can be installed internally through peace-making initiatives (Zhang et al., 2020). Such peace-making could, for example, be settlement-oriented, focused on getting the bullying situation solved. This approach entails active shaping of solutions, giving proposals, and – if needed – pressure tactics: as such, a clear and good organizational policy setting the guidelines for such settlements is highly important (Baillien et al., 2009). Such peace-making could also be emotion-oriented, for example by aiming to transform the bullying conflict through eliciting communication about emotions. This, moreover, ties in with the highly contemporary practice in organizations of bystander training for a range of negative behaviours at work, including bullying. In all, such trainings build on the idea that if co-workers are better aware of how situations such as bullying manifest themselves (i.e., identify them) and are given specific guidance in how they could intervene when observing potential bullying (i.e., leads for responses), they themselves could be key in prevention (Lassiter et al., 2021). However, given the importance of sensemaking in the bullying process, such trainings should – instead of drawing the attention to 'when behaviour is wrong' – better invest in strengthening the employees' ability to positively mould the meaning that a recipient might give to a certain event. Especially in the early and ambiguous phases of bullying, or even before, employees could support one another in by actively attaching fewer negative emotions or less significance to an event (e.g., 'oh, don't mind his manners, he is being clumsy again'). In all, successful bullying prevention builds on a context of a psychologically safe climate in organizations, departments, or teams (Hall et al., 2010). Such a climate builds on management commitment, managerial prioritizing, organizational communication, and employee participation in psychosocial well-being. How psychologically safe a certain climate is, can be plotted using PSC-12 (Hall et al., 2010).

REFERENCES

Abramis, D. J. (1994). Relationship of job stressors to job performance: Linear or an inverted-U? *Psychological Reports, 75,* 547–558. https://doi.org/10.2466/pr0.1994.75.1.5

Avanzi, L., Schuh, S. C., Fraccaroli, F., & Van Dick, R. (2015). Why does organizational identification relate to reduced employee burnout? The mediating influence of social support and collective efficacy. *Work & Stress, 29,* 1–10. https://doi.org/10.1080/02678373.2015.1004225

Avolio, B. J., Gardner, W. L., Walumbwa, F. O., Luthans, F., & May, D. R. (2004). Unlocking the mask: A look at the process by which authentic leaders impact follower attitudes and behaviors. *The Leadership Quarterly, 15,* 801–823. https://doi.org/10.1016/j.leaqua.2004.09.003

Baillien, E., Bollen, K., Euwema, M., & De Witte, H. (2014). Conflicts and conflict management styles as precursors of workplace bullying: A two-wave longitudinal study. *European Journal of Work and Organizational Psychology, 23,* 511–524. https://doi.org/10.1080/1359432X.2012.752899

Baillien, E., De Cuyper, N., & De Witte, H. (2011a). Job autonomy and workload as antecedents of workplace bullying: A two-wave test of Karasek's Job Demand Control Model for targets and perpetrators. *Journal of Occupational and Organizational Psychology, 84,* 191–208. https://doi.org/10.1348/096317910X508371

Baillien, E., Neyens, I., De Witte, H., & De Cuyper, N. (2009). A qualitative study on the development of workplace bullying: Towards a Three-Way model. *Journal of Community & Applied Social Psychology, 19,* 1–16. https://doi.org/10.1002/casp.977

Baillien, E., Rodriguez-Muñoz, A., Van den Broeck, A., & De Witte, H. (2011b). Do demands and resources affect target's and perpetrators' reports of workplace bullying? A two-wave cross-lagged study. *Work & Stress, 25,* 128–146. https://doi.org/10.1080/02678373.2011.591600

Bakker, A. B., & Demerouti, E. (2007). The job demands-resources model: State of the art. *Journal of Managerial Psychology, 22,* 309–328. https://doi.org/10.1108/02683940710733115

Balducci, C., Conway, P. M., & Van Heugten, K. (2021). The contribution of organizational factors to workplace bullying, emotional abuse, and harassment. In P. D'Cruz, E. Noronha, E. Baillien, B. Catley, K. Harlos, A. Høgh, & E. G. Mikkelsen (Eds.), *Pathways of Job-Related Negative Behaviour – Handbooks of Workplace Bullying, Emotional Abuse and Harassment* (pp. 3–28). Singapore: Springer.

Balducci, C., Fraccaroli, F., & Schaufeli, W. B. (2011). Workplace bullying and its relation with work characteristics, personality, and post-traumatic stress symptoms: An integrated model. *Anxiety, Stress & Coping, 24*, 499–513. https://doi.org/10.1080/10615806.2011.555533

Björkqvist, K. (1994). Sex differences in physical, verbal, and indirect aggression: A review of recent research. *Sex Roles, 30*, 177–188. DOI: 10.1007/BF01420988

Branch, S., Shallcross, L., Barker, M., Ramsay, S., & Murray, J. P. (2021). Theoretical frameworks that have explained workplace bullying: Retracing contributions across the decades. In P. D'Cruz, E. Noronha, C. Caponecchia, J. Escartín, D. Salin, & M. R. Tuckey (Eds.), *Concepts, Approaches and Methods – Handbooks of Workplace Bullying, Emotional Abuse and Harassment* (pp. 87–130). Singapore: Springer.

Cooper, C. L., Dewe, P. J., & O'Driscoll, M. P. (2001). *Organizational Stress: A Review and Critique of Theory, Research, and Applications.* London: Sage Publications.

De Witte, H. (2015). *Social Support and Bullying are Tapping into the Same Thing.* Personal conversation, 13 January.

Einarsen, S. V. (2000). Harassment and bullying at work: A review of the Scandinavian approach. *Aggression and Violent Behavior, 5*, 379–401. https://doi.org/10.1016/S1359-1789(98)00043-3

Einarsen, S. V., Hoel, H., Zapf, D., & Cooper, C. L. (Eds.). (2020). *Bullying and Harassment in the Workplace: Theory, Research, and Practice.* London: CRC Press.

Escartín, J., Ullrich, J., Zapf, D., Schlüter, E., & Van Dick, R. (2013). Individual-and group-level effects of social identification on workplace bullying. *European Journal of Work and Organizational Psychology, 22*, 182–193. https://doi.org/10.1080/1359432X.2011.647407

Eys, M. A., & Carron, A. V. (2001). Role ambiguity, task cohesion, and task self-efficacy. *Small Group Research, 32*, 356–373. https://doi.org/10.1177/104649640103200305

Fox, S., & Stallworth, L. E. (2009). Building a framework for two internal organizational approaches to resolving and preventing workplace bullying: Alternative dispute resolution and training. *Consulting Psychology Journal: Practice and Research, 61*, 220–241. https://doi.org/10.1037/a0016637

Hall, G. B., Dollard, M. F., & Coward, J. (2010). Psychosocial safety climate: Development of the PSC-12. *International Journal of Stress Management, 17*, 353–383. https://doi.org/10.1037/a0021320

Kerksieck, P., Bauer, G. F., & Brauchli, R. (2019). Personal and social resources at work: Reciprocal relations between crafting for social job resources, social support at work and psychological capital. *Frontiers in Psychology, 10*, 2632. https://doi.org/10.3389/fpsyg.2019.02632

Lassiter, B. J., Bostain, N. S., & Lentz, C. (2021). Best practices for early bystander intervention training on workplace intimate partner violence and workplace bullying. *Journal of Interpersonal Violence, 36*, 5813–5837. https://doi.org/10.1177/0886260518807907

Leon-Perez, J. M., Notelaers, G., Arenas, A., Munduate, L., & Medina, F. J. (2014). Identifying victims of workplace bullying by integrating traditional estimation approaches into a latent class cluster model. *Journal of Interpersonal Violence, 29,* 1155–1177. https://doi.org/10.1177/0886260513506280

Leymann, H., & Gustafsson, A. (1996). Mobbing at work and the development of post-traumatic stress disorders. *European Journal of Work and Organizational Psychology, 5,* 251–275. https://doi.org/10.1080/13594329608414858

Meral, E. O., Vranjes, I., van Osch, Y., Ren, D., Van Dijk, E., & Van Beest, I. (2022). Intensity, intent, and ambiguity: Appraisals of workplace ostracism and coping responses. *Aggressive Behavior.* Advance online publication. https://doi.org/10.1002/ab.22060

Ng, K., Niven, K., & Notelaers, G. (2022). Does bystander behavior make a difference? How passive and active bystanders in the group moderate the effects of bullying exposure. *Journal of Occupational Health Psychology, 27,* 119–135. DOI: 10.1037/ocp0000296

Nielsen, M. B., Tangen, T., Idsoe, T., Matthiesen, S. B., & Magerøy, N. (2015). Post-traumatic stress disorder as a consequence of bullying at work and at school. A literature review and meta-analysis. *Aggression and Violent Behavior, 21,* 17–24. https://doi.org/10.1016/j.avb.2015.01.001

Notelaers, G., & Einarsen, S. (2008). *The Construction and Calidation of the Short–Negative Acts Questionnaire.* Paper presented at 6th International Conference on Workplace Bullying. 4–6 June. Montreal, Canada.

Notelaers, G., Baillien, E., De Witte, H., Einarsen, S., & Vermunt, J. K. (2013). Testing the strain hypothesis of the Demand Control Model to explain severe bullying at work. *Economic and Industrial Democracy, 34,* 69–87. https://doi.org/10.1177/0143831X1243874

Notelaers, G., De Witte, H., & Einarsen, S. (2010). A job characteristics approach to explain workplace bullying. *European Journal of Work and Organizational Psychology, 19,* 487–504. https://doi.org/10.1080/13594320903007620

Notelaers, G., De Witte, H., Van Veldhoven, M., & Vermunt, J. K. (2007). Construction and validation of the Short Inventory to Monitor Psychosocial Hazards. *Médecine du Travail & Ergonomie, 44,* 11–17.

Notelaers, G., Einarsen, S., De Witte, H., & Vermunt, J. K. (2006). Measuring exposure to bullying at work: The validity and advantages of the latent class cluster approach. *Work & Stress, 20,* 289–302. https://doi.org/10.1080/02678370601071594

Notelaers, G., Tornroos, M., & Salin, D. (2019a). Effort–Reward Imbalance: A risk factor for exposure to workplace bullying. *Frontiers in Psychology, 10.* https://doi.org/10.3389/fpsyg.2019.00386

Notelaers, G., Van der Heijden, B., Hoel, H., & Einarsen, S. (2019b). Measuring bullying at work with the short–negative acts questionnaire: Identification of targets and criterion validity. *Work & Stress, 33,* 58–75. https://doi.org/10.1080/02678373.2018.1457736

Notelaers, G., Vermunt, J. K., Baillien, E., Einarsen, S., & De Witte, H. (2011). Exploring risk groups workplace bullying with categorical data. *Industrial Health, 49,* 73–88. DOI: 10.2486/indhealth.ms1155

Plimmer, G., Nguyen, D., Teo, S., & Tuckey, M. R. (2022). Workplace bullying as an organisational issue: Aligning climate and leadership. *Work & Stress, 36,* 202–227. https://doi.org/10.1080/02678373.2021.1969479

Pouwelse, M., Mulder, R., & Mikkelsen, E. G. (2021). The role of bystanders in workplace bullying: An overview of theories and empirical research. In P. D'Cruz, E. Noronha, E. Baillien, B. Catley, K. Harlos, A. Høgh, & E. G. Mikkelsen (Eds.),

Pathways of Job-Related Negative Behaviour – Handbooks of Workplace Bullying, Emotional Abuse and Harassment (pp. 385–422). Singapore: Springer.

Salin, D., & Hoel, H. (2020). Organizational risk factors of workplace bullying. In S. V. Einarsen, H. Hoel, D. Zapf, & C. L. Cooper (Eds.), *Bullying and Harassment in the Workplace* (pp. 305–329). London: CRC Press.

Shumaker, S. A., & Brownell, A. (1984). Toward a theory of social support: Closing conceptual gaps. *Journal of Social Issues, 40*, 11–36. https://doi.org/10.1111/j.1540-4560.1984.tb01105.x

Tepper, B. J., Simon, L., & Park, H. M. (2017). Abusive supervision. *Annual Review of Organizational Psychology and Organizational Behavior, 4*, 123–152. https://doi.org/10.1146/annurev-orgpsych-041015-062539

Trépanier, S.-G., Peterson, C., Ménard, J., & Notelaers, G. (2022). When does exposure to daily negative acts frustrate employees' psychological needs? A within-person approach. *Journal of Occupational Health Psychology*. Advance online publication. https://doi.org/10.1037/ocp0000338

Uchino, B. N., Bowen, K., Carlisle, M., & Birmingham, W. (2012). Psychological pathways linking social support to health outcomes: A visit with the 'ghosts' of research past, present, and future. *Social Science & Medicine, 74*, 949–957. https://doi.org/10.1016/j.socscimed.2011.11.023

Van den Brande, W., Baillien, E., De Witte, H., Vander Elst, T., & Godderis, L. (2016). The role of work stressors, coping strategies and coping resources in the process of workplace bullying: A systematic review and development of a comprehensive model. *Aggression and Violent Behavior, 29*, 61–71. https://doi.org/10.1016/j.avb.2016.06.004

Warr, P. (1994). A conceptual framework for the study of work and mental health. *Work & Stress, 8*, 84–97. https://doi.org/10.1080/02678379408259982

Zapf, D. (1999). Organisational, work group related and personal causes of mobbing/bullying at work. *International Journal of Manpower, 20*, 70–85. https://doi.org/10.1108/01437729910268669

Zhang, X., Bollen, K., & Euwema, M. (2020). Peacemaking at work and at home. *International Journal of Conflict Management, 31*, 801–820. https://doi.org/10.1108/IJCMA-10-2019-0186

Zhang, X., Bollen, K., Pei, R., & Euwema, M. C. (2018). Peacemaking at the workplace: A systematic review. *Negotiation and Conflict Management Research, 11*, 204–224. https://doi.org/10.1111/ncmr.12128

Index